Service to Country

The BCSIA Studies in International Security book series is edited at the Belfer Center for Science and International Affairs (BCSIA) at Harvard University's John F. Kennedy School of Government and is published by The MIT Press. The series publishes books on contemporary issues in international security policy, as well as their conceptual and historical foundations. Topics of particular interest to the series include the spread of weapons of mass destruction, internal conflict, the international effects of democracy and democratization, and U.S. defense policy.

A complete list of BCSIA Studies appears at the back of this volume.

Service to Country

Personnel Policy and the Transformation of Western Militaries

Curtis L. Gilroy and Cindy Williams, editors

BCSIA Studies in International Security

The MIT Press
Cambridge, Massachusetts
London, England

Library of Congress Cataloging-in-Publication Data

Service to country : personnel policy and the transformation of Western militaries /
Curtis L. Gilroy and Cindy Williams, editors.
    p. cm. — (BCSIA studies in international security)
  ISBN: 978-0-262-07276-2 (hardcover: alk. paper)—978-0-262-57235-4 (pbk.: alk. paper)
  1. Military administration. 2. Armed Forces—Personnel management. I. Gilroy,
Curtis L. II. Williams, Cindy.

UB146.S37 2006
355.3'30068—dc22   2006049441

Printed in the United States of America

Cover photos courtesy of NATO and U.S. Department of Defense.
Edited and typeset by Teresa J. Lawson Editorial Consulting
Port Townsend, Washington

To those who serve

Contents

Preface and Acknowledgments

This volume grew out of a symposium held June 13–15, 2004, in Brussels, Belgium, sponsored jointly by The Honorable David S.C. Chu, U.S. Under Secretary of Defense for Personnel and Readiness, and The Honorable R. Nicholas Burns, U.S. Permanent Representative to the North Atlantic Treaty Organization. The symposium, *Building Military Capability: The Transformation of Personnel Policies,* provided a forum for discussion of important personnel issues facing the NATO alliance today and in the future.

The symposium examined an array of topics that relate to building and sustaining armed forces, whether they be all-volunteer militaries or mixed forces consisting of both volunteers and conscripts. Topics included the costs of a volunteer force, the challenges in transitioning to a volunteer military, demographic and social constraints on filling the ranks, and the future role of reserve forces. The subjects were approached from multiple viewpoints, as the speakers and moderators represented diverse disciplines and came from a variety of institutions, including defense departments and governments, academia, and research organizations.

In bringing together experts from across Europe and North America, we were struck by the breadth and depth of interest in the transformation of military personnel policies throughout the NATO alliance. The meeting drew delegations from all of NATO's member nations and from several members of NATO's Partnership for Peace. We were pleased with the participation of senior European defense leaders, including General Sir Rupert Smith and General Klaus Naumann.

Many individuals contributed to the success of the symposium, and the authors of this volume are most grateful to them. Mr. William Carr, U.S. Acting Deputy Under Secretary of Defense for Military Personnel Policy, and Mr. Clarence Juhl, Deputy Defense Advisor in the U.S. Mission to NATO, provided invaluable support and counsel in making the symposium a success. Special thanks are extended to Lieutenant Colonel Heidi Schwenn of Dr. Curtis Gilroy's staff in the U.S. Office of the Secretary of Defense and to Lieutenant Colonel John Garey of the U.S. Mission to NATO.

Thoughtful reviews of the chapters of this book were provided by Beth Asch, Ilana Bet-El, Christopher Dandeker, Martha Farnsworth-Riche, Anita Hattiangadi, James Hosek, Chris Madsen, Aline Quester, Gerrard Quille, and Zachary Selden. The authors wish to thank Sean Lynn-Jones for his thoughtful comments on the manuscript. We also thank the many experts and practitioners who gave of their time to provide perspectives, including William Drozdiak, Etienne de Durand, Helga Haftendorn, Corinna Horst, Catherine Kelleher, Ulrich vom Hagen, Hilmar Linnenkamp, Simon Lunn, Marina Nuciari, Ralph Thiele, and Jörn Thiessen.

Strategic Analysis, Inc. provided outstanding support in both preparation for and conduct of the symposium and with the publication of this volume. Jesse Durham Strauss and Melissa Trapani served as coordinators of the symposium. Barbara Bicksler made vital and much appreciated contributions to the planning of the symposium and to the organization and preparation of this volume. Greg Byerly did an excellent job in preparing the book's tables and figures for publication, as did Amy Cauffman in preparing photos for the book cover.

We wish to thank the German Marshall Fund of the United States for hosting Dr. Cindy Williams at its Transatlantic Center in Brussels, Belgium, from September 2002 until July 2003, and for sponsoring and hosting a transatlantic roundtable in September 2003 that informed our thinking and brought together some of the contributors to this edited volume. Dr. Williams is also grateful to the Smith Richardson Foundation for its support of her work on the project, and to the Proteus Fund and the Ford Foundation for their support of related work.

Special thanks are due to our consulting editor, Teresa Lawson, for helping us to say what we meant to say and turning a collection of articles into a book, and to Lisa Nolan for her many contributions to the quality and readability of the volume. Pat Zerfoss did outstanding work supporting the editing and typesetting of this manuscript. Harlene Miller of the Security Studies Program at MIT helped to keep us organized and contributed in numerous other ways. Thanks also to Pierce Butler for excellent work on the book's index.

The challenge in preparing a list of acknowledgements for a book to which so many people contributed in so many ways is that, inevitably, important contributions will be left out. Please accept our apologies for any inadvertent oversight.

Chapter 1

Introduction

Cindy Williams

The past two decades have brought dramatic changes in the political and security landscapes of Europe and North America. At the same time, technological advances have opened the door to new possibilities and fresh challenges for the way militaries operate. On both sides of the Atlantic, nations are adapting their armed forces to the new realities and transforming their military capabilities to take advantage of emerging technologies and to measure up to the challenges of the future. Developments at the national level are accompanied by sea changes in the military arrangements and capabilities of the NATO alliance and the European Union (EU).

Discussions of military capabilities often emphasize the size of forces or the machines of warfare. It is easy to lose sight of the fact that individual servicemembers are just as crucial to military innovation and change and to the success of any military operation. The ability of European and North American militaries—whether in a national, NATO, or

The author is grateful to the German Marshall Fund of the United States for hosting her at its Transatlantic Center in Brussels, Belgium during the 2002–2003 academic year, and for sponsoring and hosting the September 2003 Transatlantic Roundtable on military personnel policies in NATO countries, which provided much of the background information for this chapter. She also wishes to thank the Smith Richardson Foundation for the generous support of her work on U.S. military pay and personnel policy and the Ford Foundation and the Proteus Fund for their support of related work.

EU context, or in an international "coalition of the willing"—to meet the expectations of the ongoing military transformations, to deliver promised capabilities and politically useful forces, and to operate effectively in the missions of the future will depend greatly on the quality, characteristics, and numbers of men and women who serve their countries in uniform.[1]

In many countries of the world, national laws make a period of military service compulsory for young men.[2] Even in those countries, however, the core of the armed forces is typically staffed by long-serving professional volunteers. Whether in all-volunteer militaries or in conscript militaries with a professional core, the people who volunteer to join or stay in the armed forces do so for a variety of both intangible factors, such as patriotism or the pride of being part of a respected institution, and tangible rewards, such as good pay, benefits, and opportunities for training.

Whatever the mix of individuals' reasons, a military's personnel policies, including those related to pay and benefits, are crucial to its success in bringing in and retaining the capable and dedicated men and women it needs. Such policies comprise an incentive structure meant to attract people to join the force, encourage those with the right skills to stay in, motivate them to work hard and do their jobs well, and influence those whose skills are no longer needed to leave. As such, personnel policies are crucial to achieving the transformations underway in the militaries of Europe and North America.

Since the end of the Cold War, the nations of Europe and North America have intensified efforts to reform their military personnel policies. For several European countries, the most significant of those reforms surround their decisions to abolish conscription in favor of all-volunteer professional forces. Even those European countries that retain conscription are generally increasing the proportion of volunteers in

---

1. By military transformation, I mean fundamental change in the way militaries operate. Transformation can require broad changes in military organizational structure, personnel policies, training, operating concepts, and doctrine, as well as the new equipment that is frequently the focus of transformation discussions.

2. In Israel, service is also compulsory for young women. In some other countries, including Angola, Chile, and Libya, women are liable for military service, but are typically not drafted in large numbers.

their forces, expanding the role of career non-commissioned officers, and shortening the initial period of compulsory service. Other reforms include changes in pay, new pension arrangements, altered policies to make military life more attractive to the families of servicemembers, new policies toward women in the military, and changes in policies related to reserve forces.

The policies that surround military personnel in Europe and North America are as diverse as the nations and militaries themselves. Some are rooted in a shared European military tradition, but choices about military personnel policies are ultimately national choices. States settle on such policies based upon their perceived security interests and their alliance commitments, as well as internal political, economic, demographic, budgetary, and social considerations. Thus states differ, both in broad principles such as compulsory versus voluntary service, and in the finer details such as linkages between military and public service pay or the factors to be considered in promotion decisions.

European integration and shared challenges are beginning to narrow some of those differences, as Jolyon Howorth discusses in Chapter 2. For example, the European Court of Justice held in January 2000 that national restrictions preventing women from bearing arms for the nation were contrary to the European Union's principle of equal treatment for men and women in the workplace.[3] As a result, all of the member states of NATO and the EU now permit women to serve in an increasing variety of capacities. Europe's militaries may, in the future, also be deemed subject to other European labor laws, including policies related to working hours and workplace safety.[4]

In addition, globalization and combined operations may trigger convergence. Soldiers and sailors share information about pay and other conditions of service over the Internet. Military people serving together in international peacekeeping operations also share such information,

---

3. European Court of Justice, Decision in Case C-285/98, *Tanja Kreil v Bundesrepublik Deutschland*, January 11, 2000.
4. Euromil, an umbrella organization for associations representing people in Europe's militaries, which had a hand in bringing the case for women to the European Court, is working to bring other personnel policies before national and European courts. See <www.euromil.org>.

and they express concern at home if they think their pay does not measure up.[5]

Nations that face shared challenges and that expect their militaries to
interoperate have much to learn from each other's experiences in bringing the right people into their militaries, motivating them, and keeping
them for an appropriate period of time. A shared understanding of the
benefits and pitfalls of various personnel policies, reform efforts, implementation schemes, and transition patterns could reduce military
costs and improve prospects for effective combined military operations.
Nations can adopt practices that others have found beneficial, avoid
those that are likely to fail, and inform their decisions about how to implement change. In addition, the eventual adoption of some shared
practices may produce militaries that are more similar to one another.
Moreover, to the extent that such similarity breeds mutual understanding and respect, shared practices might facilitate cooperation in the field.

For these reasons, this book explores the current transformation of
military personnel policies in Europe and North America. It looks at
causes as well as potential costs and benefits of personnel policy transformation. Contributors to the volume come from across Europe and
North America and from diverse backgrounds. They include experts
from militaries, governments, universities, and think tanks; practitioners
and scholars; and experts in economics, political science, demographics,
and other fields.

This chapter sets the stage for the ones that follow by reviewing
briefly the broad changes at work on both sides of the Atlantic that will
affect militaries' future needs for people, the availability of people to

---

5. For example, in 2001, a Pay Review Body, faced with numerous complaints from British soldiers that their pay was lower than military pay in
other countries, found it necessary to undertake a comparative analysis of
pay structures and levels across countries. The Rt. Hon. Baroness Dean of
Thornton-le-Fylde (Chairman), "Armed Forces Pay Review Body Thirty-First
Report" (Norwich, UK: The Stationery Office (TSO), 2002), pp. 2–3. The
analysis noted that any comparison of pay and benefits across countries is
made difficult by the fact that compensation structures vary widely; for example, one country might provide lower basic pay than another but larger
allowances or special pays, or more in kind but less in cash. The study
found, however, that overall UK military compensation is generally competitive with or better than compensation in the other countries examined.

serve, and policies related to people. It begins with a brief review of the factors that are reshaping militaries' personnel needs—that is, the demand side of each nation's contest for military people. It continues with a look at factors affecting the supply side: the pool of people who might be available to serve in their nations' militaries in the future. The chapter then highlights some major developments, both recent and proposed, in personnel policies across Europe and North America. The chapter ends with a short tour of the book and its scope.

The Future Demand for Military People

The disintegration of the Soviet Union and the end of the Cold War brought dramatic changes in the political and security environments of Europe and North America. Experiences since then, including wars, acts of terrorism, state collapse, and large-scale population migration, have utterly altered perceptions of security and defense. At the same time, technological advances are changing the way militaries operate.

On both sides of the Atlantic, nations have reassessed their strategic environments, revamped foreign policies, articulated new security strategies, and begun the work of adapting their militaries to meet new challenges and exploit emerging technologies. Responding to the changed environment, most of the countries of Europe and North America have substantially reduced the number of people serving in uniform (see Figure 1.1). They have also embraced ambitious plans to transform their military structures and equipment. Those changes have profound implications for the number and types of people their militaries will require in the future.

The military arrangements in NATO and the EU have also changed. NATO has reinvented itself, with ten new member states, new partnerships, altered missions and an outlook that extends beyond Europe, nascent new military capabilities and command structures, and ambitious plans for future forces and equipment. The European Union is working toward a Common Foreign and Security Policy (CFSP) and a European Security and Defense Policy (ESDP), including the capability to call upon and lead military forces independent of NATO. The EU has put forward a shared security strategy and established a common defense procurement agency, and military forces under EU auspices are undertaking combined operations in the Balkans.

Figure 1.1. Active-Duty Troops of Selected NATO Countries, 1985 and 2003

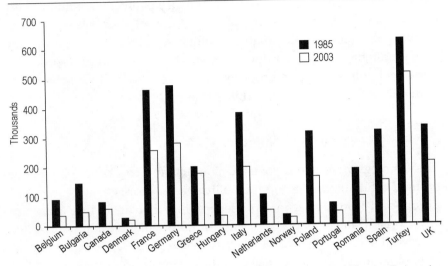

Source: International Institute for Strategic Studies (IISS), *The Military Balance 2003–04* (London: Taylor and Francis, 2004); IISS, *The Military Balance 2004–05* (London: Routledge, 2005). Note: The figure excludes Iceland, Luxembourg, and the countries that did not exist as individual states in 1985: the Czech Republic, the Slovak Republic, Slovenia, Latvia, Lithuania, and Estonia. For reasons of scale, it also excludes the United States.

NEW THREATS AND RISKS

European and American perceptions of threats and risks to national security have changed significantly since the end of the Cold War.[6] The

6.   Since the end of the Cold War, the United States, Canada, and most European countries have published successive white papers or strategy documents that point to a changed strategic environment and spell out their leaders' current understanding of the most important threats to national security. In Europe, France was perhaps the first to articulate the importance of strategic reform. The 1994 White Book, "Livre Blanc sur la Defense 1994" (Paris: La Documentation Française, 1994), identified an array of threats and recommended a strategy based on international engagement and crisis management. Reflecting concerns that French forces were still badly in need of reshaping for the post–Cold War environment, in 1996 the strategic reform committee (*Communauté Stratégique*) established by President Jacques Chirac recommended major changes, including the shift to an all-professional force. For an account of French strategic assessments and policy changes, see George A. Bloch, "French Military Reform: Lessons for America's Army?" in

United States continues to regard competition among the great powers as a possible future risk, but its published strategy documents emphasize the growing importance of other threats.[7] For nations on both sides of the Atlantic, the specter of large-scale war in Europe has been replaced by terrorism, the proliferation of chemical, biological, and nuclear weapons, cyber attacks, regional conflicts, and state failure as the most likely threats to security. In addition, European countries typically see ethnic conflict, uncontrolled migration, threats to energy resources, environmental threats, and organized crime as posing substantial risks. Some of Europe's nations also still face threats from longstanding territorial or ethnic disputes.

At the alliance level, NATO's perception of risks and dangers has also undergone a dramatic shift. During the decade after the fall of the Berlin Wall in 1989, the alliance's traditional focus on the Soviet threat to the territorial integrity of the nations of Western Europe was replaced by concern over regional crises on Europe's periphery, potential spillover from ethnic and religious rivalries and territorial disputes, the proliferation of nuclear, chemical, biological, and other weapons, disruption of information systems and the flow of resources, organized crime, and uncontrolled migration of refugees.[8]

Parameters, Summer 2000, pp. 33–45. Recent British strategy documents include "Delivering Security in a Changing World: Defence White Paper 2003" (December 2003); and "Delivering Security in a Changing World: Future Capabilities" (July 2004). Also see, for example, Republic of Slovenia Ministry of Defense, "Strategic Defence Review" (May 2004); and Netherlands Ministry of Defense, "Defence White Paper 2000."

7.   In the United States, the White House articulates the national security strategy in an overarching strategy document. The most recent is President George W. Bush, "The National Security Strategy of the United States" (Washington, D.C.: The White House, March 2006). That document makes less of the threat of great-power competition than of terrorism, state failure, and the spread of weapons of mass destruction. The Defense Department's *Report of the Quadrennial Defense Review* says that traditional threats have waned in importance, while nontraditional threats have grown in salience, including conflicts against non-state enemies, terrorist attacks using weapons of mass destruction, and "disruptive" threats based on technological breakthroughs. Donald H. Rumsfeld, *Report of the Quadrennial Defense Review* (Washington, D.C.: Department of Defense, February 2006).

8.   NATO, "The Alliance's Strategic Concept," Press Release NAC-S(99)65, April 24, 1999, <www.nato.int/docu/pr/1999/p99-065e.htm>.

The EU published its first "European Security Strategy" document in 2003.[9] Asserting that "large-scale aggression against any Member State is now improbable," the document cites, as the critical threats to European security, terrorism, the proliferation of missile technology and of biological, chemical, nuclear, or radiological weapons, regional conflicts (including those as far away as Kashmir and the Korean Peninsula), state failure, and organized crime.[10]

Not every threat that is viewed as important to the nations of North America and Europe requires a military solution. The security strategies published on both sides of the Atlantic call for using every instrument of power—political and diplomatic means, law enforcement and domestic security measures, intelligence resources, and economic and financial measures, as well as military efforts—to deal with the new threats.

Nevertheless, such radically altered threats still have important effects on the personnel needs of militaries. For example, countering international terrorism and halting the spread of weapons of mass destruction may require more people who have special-operations experience and more intelligence specialists with a broader range of area expertise and language skills. Dealing with cyber threats requires highly trained information-technology specialists. Such effects are compounded by the rapidly changing security objectives and missions of military forces on both sides of the Atlantic.

CHANGED MILITARY OBJECTIVES AND MISSIONS

To meet the new threats, the nations of North America and Europe have embraced new military objectives and undertaken missions that are vastly different from those of the Cold War. The changes in intended missions will have important impacts on the numbers and types of people needed by the militaries of the future.

The most significant change in military missions during recent decades may be the post–Cold War growth of multi-national crisis man-

---

9. Javier Solana, Secretary-General of the Council of the European Union and High Representative for the Common Foreign and Security Policy, "A Secure Europe in a Better World: European Security Strategy," Brussels, December 12, 2003.
10. Ibid.

agement, peacekeeping, and stability operations. Although for decades militaries from both sides of the Atlantic have participated in multinational peace operations, often under UN auspices, during the 1990s such operations expanded in size, scope, and intensity with interventions in Somalia and the Balkans (see Table 1.1).

During the mid-1990s, NATO members argued over whether the alliance should become involved in operations outside the borders of its member states. The missions in the Balkans and Afghanistan set precedents, however, and NATO now formally recognizes an alliance role in crisis management, peace operations, and stability operations outside of its traditional boundaries.[11] Increasingly, NATO and the EU hold leadership roles in such operations.

Crisis management and stability operations can affect the numbers and characteristics of military personnel needed in the militaries of the nations that participate. For example, even before the Iraq War, U.S. military leaders complained about the strain imposed on personnel by frequent deployments to peacekeeping operations around the globe. Since the beginning of that war in 2003, the U.S. Army has added some 17,000 active-duty troops above previously authorized levels, and hundreds of thousands of Guard and Reserve members have been mobilized. Nevertheless, many observers argue that U.S. ground forces are still too small to sustain the operation beyond 2007.

For some European countries that retain compulsory service, the personnel strain that comes with peacekeeping and peacemaking operations and other expeditionary military interventions is compounded by national laws that prohibit the deployment of conscripts to missions outside national borders.[12] U.S. and NATO leaders argue that professional forces are thus better suited to such missions than conscripts.[13]

---

11. "Prague Summit Declaration issued by the Heads of State and Government participating in the Meeting of the North Atlantic Council on 21 November 2002," NATO Press Release (2002) 127, November 21, 2002, <www.nato.int/docu/pr/2002/p02-127e.htm>.

12. For example, France's limited contribution to the 1991 Persian Gulf War is often blamed on its legal prohibition against the deployment abroad of conscripts. From its 289,000 active-duty troops, France was able to put together an expeditionary force of only 15,000. See Bloch, "French Military Reform," p. 34.

13. "No, We Ain't Dead Yet," interview with NATO Secretary-General

Table 1.1. Personnel Contributions to Major Multi-national Peace Operations, by Selected NATO Countries and Selected Years

	1995	1999	2000	2001	2002	2003
United States	2,449	11,948	11,138	9,567	5,312	4,569
Italy	78	8,547	8,504	7,954	6,295	4,391
Germany	29	7,636	8,124	7,494	6,841	4,337
France	494	8,218	8,577	8,546	6,624	4,176
United Kingdom	437	7,390	5,430	5,317	3,554	2,083
Spain	22	2,454	2,725	2,716	2,180	1,753
Poland	n.a.	1,268	2,168	1,884	1,575	1,478
Canada	956	3,394	2,006	1,784	1,457	1,444
Netherlands	230	2,639	1,569	1,478	1,348	1,238
Turkey	17	1,671	2,361	2,144	2,731	937
Portugal	274	1,357	1,674	1,528	1,048	833
Greece	12	1,436	2,043	2,175	1,382	705
Hungary	n.a.	386	641	632	668	691
Norway	995	1,338	1,244	1,236	994	469
Denmark	273	551	1,288	969	869	440
Czech Republic	n.a.	519	831	231	604	427
Belgium	682	331	1,101	1,039	646	237
Luxembourg	0	0	26	23	25	23

Note: 1995 data reflect forces contributed to UN operations only. Data not provided for Czech Republic, Hungary, and Poland prior to their admission to NATO in 1999. The table excludes Iceland, which has no armed forces, and the seven newest member states of NATO, for which data were not available. Yearly data are rounded.

Source: U.S. Secretary of Defense Donald Rumsfeld, *2004 Statistical Compendium on Allied Contributions to the Common Defense* (Washington, D.C.: U.S. DoD, 2004), Table D-7.

George Robertson, *Newsweek*, May 20, 2002; NATO Secretary-General George Robertson, "The Role of NATO in the Twenty-First Century," speech at the *"Welt am Sonntag* Forum," November 3, 2003 <www.nato.int/docu/speech /2003/s031103a.htm>; R. Nicholas Burns, U.S. Ambassador to NATO, "Launching NATO's Transformation at Prague," Manfred Woerner Memorial Lecture at Konrad-Adenauer Stiftung, Berlin, October 30, 2002, <nato.usmission.gov/ambassador/2002/s021030a.htm>.

Peacekeeping and stability operations can create demands for more military people who are skilled in diplomacy, intelligence, civil affairs, and policing. In addition, multi-national expeditionary missions require language translators and foreign-area specialists as well as a high proportion of officers (and also some enlisted members) who are skilled in the language of multi-national operations, typically English.

The United States, NATO, and the EU are unequivocal in the view that military force has a role in countering the threat of terrorism.[14] After September 11, 2001, the role of the U.S. military in homeland security expanded significantly. For U.S. forces, preventive war, counterinsurgency, urban warfare, and operations aimed at regime change have grown in importance.[15] Such missions are likely to become more salient for Canada and Europe as well, if only because they are drawn in as partners to, or in the aftermath of, U.S. operations. New missions will affect future demands for military people.

FORCE REDUCTIONS

Most of the nations of Europe and North America downsized their militaries soon after the Cold War ended. Some nations cut the numbers further in response to budgetary pressures or as part of military reform. The reductions are deeply intertwined with the altered perceptions of threats and risks and the new missions discussed above. They also reflect the notion that modern information technologies can serve as "force multipliers," making it possible for a military to become more effective even as it reduces in size.

Smaller forces mean that militaries must pay closer attention to the distribution of skills and abilities among their people. When forces are large, wasting talent may not matter much; when they are small, the

---

14. The European response to terrorism took on a new urgency immediately following the brutal attacks in Madrid on March 11, 2004. See European Council, "Declaration on Combating Terrorism" (Brussels, March 25, 2004); and "EU Plan of Action on Combating Terrorism—Update" (Brussels, December 14, 2004), both at <ue.eu.int/showPage.asp?id=631&lang=en&mode=g>. In addition, see Solana, "A Secure Europe in a Better World"; and North Atlantic Council, "Prague Summit Declaration" (2002) <www.nato.int/docu/pr/2002/p02-127e.htm>.
15. Rumsfeld, *Report of the Quadrennial Defense Review* (2006).

ability of every person to contribute effectively counts more. For some countries, the post–Cold War drawdowns left militaries with inappropriate distributions of uniformed people across ranks, experience levels, and occupations. The United States managed its downsizing—from about 2.1 million active-duty troops in 1989 to about 1.4 million in 2002—through a combination of attrition, lowered recruitment, and financial incentives to leave.[16] Imbalances across occupations remain, however, with too few people in some occupations and too many in others.[17] In its drawdown, France used similar tools, and also offered substantial cash payments to encourage older officers to leave the force. The result was a relatively balanced distribution of people across ranks and experience levels.[18]

Most countries handled their drawdowns more passively, largely relying on attrition and reduced intake. The resulting forces have more older servicemembers than are needed for current operations and too few younger ones coming up the ranks. In Canada, for example, the age cohort of 24 to 29-year-olds is badly underpopulated.[19] Thirty-year-old privates are not uncommon.[20] Belgium even has some forty-seven-year-old corporals.[21] Romania faces a serious problem of "colonelization"—too many people at the highest ranks. Yet shedding older or higher-ranking members risks leaving too few experienced people to train in-

---

16. The U.S. military's authorized active-duty end strength for 2005 was about 1.42 million troops. In February 2006, both the Navy and the Air Force announced plans to reduce troop levels during the coming years.

17. Congressional Budget Office (CBO), *Budget Options* (Washington, D.C.: CBO, February 2005), p. 43.

18. Cindy Williams, "From Conscripts to Volunteers: NATO's Transitions to All-Volunteer Forces," *Naval War College Review*, Vol. 58, No. 1 (Winter 2005).

19. Report of the Auditor General of Canada to the House of Commons, April 2002, Chapter 5, "National Defence—Recruitment and Retention of Military Personnel."

20. In 1996, fewer than one-third of the members of Canada's military were under 30 years of age, compared with nearly 60 percent in 1986. Susan Truscott and Kate Dupre, Directorate of Human Resource Research and Analysis, Department of National Defence, Canada, "Organizational, Social and Demographic Change in the Canadian Forces," Paper AB-37, 1998 Conference of the International Military Testing Association.

21. Philip Shishkin, "How Europe's Armies Let Their Guard Down," *The Wall Street Journal*, February 13, 2003.

coming cohorts. Canada's Auditor General estimates that it could take thirty years for the Canadian forces to regain the right numbers of people with the right skills and experience to match needs.[22] Such imbalances will affect personnel requirements for years to come.

EMERGING TECHNOLOGIES AND MILITARY TRANSFORMATION

Leaders on both sides of the Atlantic hope to transform their military capabilities to handle the missions and objectives of the future. The desire for personnel transformation reflects a shared concern that forces today are still better suited to Cold War missions than to new missions, and a shared belief that creativity and innovation should be brought to bear to improve every aspect of military capability. It also reflects the belief that modern technologies, particularly information systems, offer new ways to address military problems and can thus reduce the number of people the armed forces need. In strategy documents and other writings, the nations of North America and Europe have declared their commitment to fundamental alterations in the way military operations are conducted, the structure of military forces, and the equipment they use.[23]

NATO leaders agreed at the alliance's 2002 summit meeting in Prague to work to transform capabilities. The military command structure is being streamlined, the allies have committed to improve capital stock, and the alliance has fielded a nascent version of the desired rapidly de-

---

22. Report of the Auditor General of Canada, "National Defence—Recruitment and Retention of Military Personnel," p. 12.

23. See Rumsfeld, *Report of the Quadrennial Defense Review* (2001). There are important differences between European and U.S. views of military transformation. Not surprisingly, given its technological and military advantages, the U.S. military tends to favor precision weapons, space technologies, and stealth as key ingredients; European discussions typically focus more on military doctrine, leadership, and culture. For a discussion of current U.S. military advantages and their limits in determining military outcomes, see Barry R. Posen, "Command of the Commons: The Military Foundation of U.S. Hegemony," *International Security*, Vol. 28, No. 1 (Summer 2003), pp. 5–46. For a comparison of U.S. and European images of transformation, see General Harald Kujat, "The Transformation of NATO's Military Forces and its Link with U.S. Transformation," speech at SACLANT's "OPEN ROAD," Norfolk, Virginia, January 21, 2003, <www.nato.int/ims/2003/s030121e.htm>.

ployable, sustainable, and technologically advanced NATO Response Force.[24]

The results of such military transformation will have important consequences for military personnel needs. For example, a fundamental tenet of transformation on both sides of the Atlantic is that in the future, military units at all echelons will be equipped with networked information systems and will have to make rapid decisions formerly made at higher levels of command. Thus, lower-ranking officers and even enlisted personnel must have training to help them exercise judgment well beyond today's requirements in most militaries. They will also require greater expertise with information technologies.[25]

Achieving these visions of transformation demands changes in military culture and long-term focus and engagement by strong leaders.[26] Experienced, technically savvy people will be required to maintain high-technology equipment, manage computer networks, and troubleshoot command and control systems. Realizing transformational capabilities that combine technological innovations with new military doctrine and new ways of fighting will require experimentation, analysis, development, and procurement by teams of experts who are technically savvy, well versed in the conduct of military operations, and highly creative, innovative, and adaptive.[27]

The Supply of People for Tomorrow's Militaries

Regardless of the number and types of people a military needs, its success in getting and keeping them depends upon demographic factors, public attitudes toward the armed forces and military service, national policies related to military service, societal factors, and economic and

24. North Atlantic Council, "Prague Summit Declaration," (2002) <www.nato.int/docu/pr/2002/p02-127e.htm>; NATO Update, "Response Force Ready for Missions," October 13, 2004, <www.nato.int/docu/update /2004/10-october/e1013a.htm>.

25. Owen R. Cote, Jr., "The Personnel Needs of the Future Force," in Cindy Williams, ed., *Filling the Ranks: Transforming the U.S. Military Personnel System* (Cambridge, Mass.: The MIT Press, 2004), pp. 55–68.

26. Kujat, "The Transformation of NATO's Military Forces and its Link with U.S. Transformation."

27. Cote, "The Personnel Needs of the Future Force."

labor conditions. Flux along all of these dimensions is already having an effect on the militaries of Europe and North America, and these fluctuations will continue to affect the supply of military people in the future.

THE LOOMING DEMOGRAPHIC CRISIS

In the United States and Canada, average birth rates are lower today than in the past, but the number of young people eligible for military service is still growing, fueled largely by immigration and higher birth rates among immigrant families. As Rickard Sandell discusses in Chapter 3, however, the number of people between the ages of 15 and 29—the population slice that includes the usual armed-forces entry cohort—will fall markedly throughout the next four decades in most of Europe. That demographic reality will greatly limit the future pool of young people from whom militaries must draw their members and, at the same time, will toughen the competition with nonmilitary employers for workers.

CHANGING PUBLIC ATTITUDES

Public attitudes toward the armed forces and military service also play a role. In the United States, as Bernard Rostker and Curtis Gilroy note in Chapter 9, the all-volunteer force was launched against a backdrop of public disapproval of the military; recruiting enough troops with the personal attributes desired was, at first, a challenge. Today, the U.S. military as an institution enjoys high levels of public support and confidence. Nevertheless, young people's inclination to serve declined during the 1990s.[28] Moreover, casualties and public uneasiness over operations in Iraq have reportedly eroded the inclination of parents to encourage their sons and daughters to consider serving, as well as the desire of young people to serve.[29]

In Canada and much of Europe, public attitudes toward the armed forces are generally positive, but high regard for the armed forces does

---

28. U.S. Office of the Assistant Secretary of Defense (Force Management and Policy), *Population Representation in the Military Services Fiscal Year 1999*, November 2000, Chapter 2. Propensity to join the military dropped sharply for young men after 1991; it recovered somewhat, but not to 1991 levels, by 1999.
29. Dave Moniz, "Army Misses Recruiting Goal," *USA Today*, March 3, 2005, p. 9.

not always result in higher numbers of young men and women willing to serve. In Germany, for example, public trust in the military is strong, yet rising numbers of young men claim conscientious-objector status to avoid military duty.[30]

In the Baltic states, as Vaidotas Urbelis describes in Chapter 4, the prospect of NATO membership, military reform, and increased military budgets enhanced public support for the military. There, the armed forces now enjoy high levels of popular prestige and trust, and the military profession is increasingly seen as desirable. Militaries on both sides of the Atlantic, however, need to sustain public support to be effective in bringing in, motivating, and keeping the people they need in the future.

In some European nations, reserve forces with broad citizen participation help to sustain strong public support of the armed forces.[31] Hannu Herranen in Chapter 7, Chris Donnelly in Chapter 16, and Peter Švec in Chapter 18 discuss linkages between reserves and public support. Even in the United States, where the reserve is smaller than the active force, leaders believe that coupling reserve structures and missions to the active force can help sustain public support for the military overall and bolster national will during wars, as John Winkler, Robert St. Onge, Jr., Karen McKenney, and Jennifer Buck point out in Chapter 17.

NATIONAL POLICIES AND EUROPEAN LEGAL FRAMEWORKS

National policies and laws, especially those related to conscription, can have a significant impact on the supply of people for the armed forces. The United States, Canada, the United Kingdom, and Luxembourg have had all-volunteer militaries for decades. In contrast, throughout the Cold War, the constitutions of most European nations required virtually all young men to serve their countries. Since the Cold War ended, however, twelve of NATO's twenty-six member states have suspended compulsory service or announced plans to phase it out (see Table 1.2).

---

30. Bernhard Fleckenstein, "Germany: Forerunner of a Postnational Military?" in Charles C. Moskos, John Allen Williams, and David R. Segal, eds., *The Postmodern Military* (New York: Oxford University Press, 2000), pp. 88–89.

31. Christopher Jehn and Zachary Selden, "The End of Conscription in Europe?" *Contemporary Economic Policy*, Vol. 20, No. 2 (April 2002), pp. 93–100.

While compulsory service can bring people into a military, it cannot make them stay: the term of conscription in most European countries is now just a year or less. Thus, even countries with compulsory service must find ways to attract enough of the right people to take up a full military career or at least volunteer to stay in the military longer. Some experts argue that conscription bolsters volunteerism for longer terms of service by giving individuals a taste of military life.[32]

In countries with compulsory service, supply can be limited by laws that permit youth to opt out of the military. In Europe, countries with compulsory service typically provide a legal out, allowing young men to work in alternative nonmilitary roles, usually by claiming status as conscientious objectors to war or military service.[33] Across the continent, the pool of young men available to the armed forces shrank after the Cold War ended, as increasing numbers opted for alternative service.[34] For example, Germany's *Zivildienst* (alternative community ser-

---

32. For example, the German Ministry of Defense says that about one-half of the *Bundeswehr's* future leaders begin as conscripts. See "Why do we need conscription?" in "The History of Compulsory Military Service," website of the German Defense Ministry, <eng.bmvg.de/bundeswehr/wehrpflicht /grundlagen/wehrdienst_geschichte_01.php>.

33. In European countries, the right to perform alternative service is generally limited to conscientious objectors. See Dick Marty, Rapporteur, Report of the Committee on Legal Affairs and Human Rights, "Exercise of the right of conscientious objection to military service in Council of Europe member states," European Council Doc. 8809, revised May 4, 2001. The Council of Europe has recognized a right of conscientious objection since 1967, although the national laws of some of its member states do not codify any such right. The Assembly of the European Committee of Ministers recommended strengthening the right even in member countries whose laws already recognize a right of conscientious objection; see Council of Europe Recommendation 1518, "Text adopted by the Standing Committee, acting on behalf of the Assembly," May 23, 2001.

34. Levels of conscientious objection and other draft avoidance means were increased by a variety of factors, including policy changes that made it easier for young men to claim conscientious-objector status, a weakening of the social stigma associated with not serving in the military, and reduced public support for conscription. Military downsizing also played a role: as militaries shrank, fewer people were called up for military service each year, and the requirement to serve appeared increasingly unfair to those who were called up. See Jehn and Selden, "The End of Conscription in Europe?"; Wil-

Table 1.2. Conscription Policies in NATO Countries

Countries with Long-term All-volunteer Forces No conscripts				Countries that Stopped Conscription after Cold War Ended No conscripts			
Country	Status of Conscription	Number in Active Forces	Number in Reserves	Country	Status of Conscription	Number in Active Forces	Number in Reserves
Canada	No peacetime conscription	62,000	36,900	Belgium	Ended 1994	36,900	18,650
Luxembourg	Ended 1967	900	0	Czech Republic	Ended 2005	22,272	n.a.
United Kingdom	Ended 1963	205,890	272,550	France	Ended 2001	254,895	21,650
United States	Ended 1973	1,389,400	1,113,400	Hungary	Ended 2004	32,300	44,000
				Italy	Ended 2005	191,875	56,500
Notes: Except for dates in "Conscription" column, figures are as of 2005. Most countries that have ended conscription have in actuality suspended it; that is, they retain the option of restoring it if necessary. Iceland is not included because it has no armed forces. a. Slovak Republic retains the authority to conscript for three months to fill any gaps in military specialties.				Nether-lands	Ended 1996	53,130	54,400
				Portugal	Ended 2003	44,900	210,930
				Slovak Republic	Ended 2006 [a]	20,195	n.a.
				Slovenia	Ended 2004	6,550	20,000
				Spain	Ended 2001	147,255	49,067

vice), once a small group, now draws in more young men each year than the military brings in as conscripts.[35] In Spain, some 75 percent of eligible men claimed conscientious-objector status by the time conscription ended in 2001.[36]

Supply may also be limited because young men simply fail to report for service, a situation common in the Baltic states and Russia during the 1990s.[37] Whether through legal means or just not showing up, draft

---

liams, "From Conscripts to Volunteers"; Cindy Williams, "Draft Lessons from Europe," *Washington Post*, October 5, 2004, p. A25.

35. See the chapter by Gerhard Kümmel in this book.

36. David R. Sands, "Even Military Experts Consider Draft Antiquated," *Insight on the News*, February 12, 2001.

37. In Latvia, Lithuania, Moldova, Russia, and Ukraine, an average of only 10 to 20 percent of those subject to conscription actually enlisted for service as of 2001; see Marty, "Exercise of the right of conscientious objection to military service in Council of Europe member states." See also Mel Huang, "So Far So Smooth: Interview with Brigadier General Jonas A. Kronkaitis," *Central Europe Review*, Vol. 2, No. 27 (July 10, 2000).

Table 1.2 (continued)

Country	Status of Conscription	Term of Conscription	Number of Conscripts (conscript % of forces)	Number in Active Forces	Number in Reserves
Countries That Retain Conscription as of July 2006					
Bulgaria	Plans to keep	9 months	45,000 (88%)	51,000	303,000
Denmark	Plans to keep	4 months	7,000 (33%)	21,180	129,700
Estonia	Plans to keep; AVF under consideration	8 months [b]	1,552 (31%)	4,934	24,000
Germany	Plans to keep; increasing volunteers	9 months	63,600 (25%) [c]	254,400	334,000
Greece	Plans to keep	12–15 months	89,800+ (55%+)	163,850	325,000
Lithuania	Plans to keep; AVF under consideration	12 months	3,981 (29%)	13,510	6,700
Norway	Plans to keep	12 months [d]	15,200 (59%)	25,800	219,000
Poland	Plans to keep	9 months	48,900+ (35%+)	141,500	234,000
Turkey	Plans to keep	15 months	391,000 (76%)	514,850	378,700
Countries That Plan to End Conscription Later					
Latvia	Phase out by end of 2006	12 months	1,007 (19%)	5,238	11,204
Romania	Phase out by 2007	6–12 months	22,300 (23%)	97,200	104,000

Notes (continued):

b. Estonia's conscription term is 11 months for officers and some specialists.

c. In Germany, the number of conscripts includes some 25,400 servicemembers who have voluntarily extended their periods of conscription to a total of up to 23 months.

d. Norway's 12-month conscription term may also include refresher periods; for some, possibility of 6 months with follow-on service in Home Guard.

Sources: International Institute for Strategic Studies (IISS), *Military Balance 2005–2006* (London: Routledge /IISS, 2005); NATO Parliamentary Assembly, "25–28 March 2003—Visit to Latvia and Estonia," <www.nato-pa.int>; NATO Parliamentary Assembly, "16–19 June 2003—Visit to Poland and Lithuania by the Defence and Security Sub-Committee on Future Security and Defence Capabilities," <www.nato-pa.int>; NATO Parliamentary Assembly, "Invited NATO Members' Progress on Military Reforms, 2003 Annual Session," 146 DSCFC 03 E, <www.nato-pa.int>; and authors of this book.

avoidance can cut deeply into the number of people available to a military that relies upon conscription.

On the other hand, European integration and new legal frameworks are expanding the pool of people available for military service. The January 2000 decision of the European Court of Justice on women in the armed forces opened a pool of talent that previously was largely untapped in most European countries.

SOCIETAL FACTORS

A variety of societal factors can also affect supply. For example, service by women has the theoretical potential to double the cohort of young people eligible for military duty. Immigrants and foreigners can be another source of military people, as can populations previously excluded from military service such as, in some countries, gays and lesbians. The United States, the UK, and Canada have met with substantial success in integrating women into their armed forces. Canada welcomes openly gay men and women into its armed forces and is proud of its military's record of diversity.

It would be easy to conclude that because some countries have met with success in tapping into nontraditional populations, others can and should follow suit. Social and cultural differences among countries may make it difficult to duplicate one country's success in another setting, however. For example, the role of women in society is often deeply ingrained in a country's social culture. In addition, varying cultural values and traditions among countries may shape different attitudes toward women in the workplace, women in uniform, or women in fighting roles. For those reasons, the receptiveness of individuals, leaders, and institutions to increasing the numbers and changing the roles of women in the armed forces may differ from one country to another, as may their willingness or ability to make the efforts and adjustments necessary to make those changes successful.[38] As a result, even though all the countries of NATO are now bringing women into their militaries, the relatively quick and successful integration of women into the U.S., UK, and Canadian militaries may not necessarily be duplicated in all of Europe's militaries.

---

38. I am grateful to Marina Nuciari for insights into the role of cultural differences in this regard. For analysis of how a country's culture may affect women's participation in the military, see Mady W. Segal, "Women's Military Roles Cross-Nationally: Past, Present, and Future," *Gender and Society*, Vol. 9, No. 6 (December 1995), pp. 757–75; Darlene Iskra, Stephen Trainor, Marcia Leithauser, and Mady W. Segal, "Women's Participation in Armed Forces Cross-Nationally: Expanding Segal's Model," *Current Sociology*, Vol. 50, No. 5 (September 2002), pp. 771–797; Gerhard Kümmel, "When Boy Meets Girl: The 'Feminization' of the Military. An Introduction Also to be Read as a Postscript," *Current Sociology*, Vol. 50, No. 5 (September 2002), pp. 615–639; Christopher Dandeker and Mady W. Segal, "Gender Integration in Armed Forces: Recent Policy Developments in the United Kingdom," *Armed Forces and Society*, Vol. 23 (Fall 1996), pp. 29–47.

ECONOMIC AND LABOR CONDITIONS

Economic and labor conditions have important implications for the supply of people to serve in the military. All-volunteer militaries compete directly with other public employers and the private sector for talented people. As a result, volunteer militaries find it harder to recruit and retain the right people in economic good times than during downturns. Even militaries with compulsory service can find themselves competing when good jobs open up in the private sector. John Warner and Sebastian Negrusa detail the economics of supply and demand in Chapter 5. Other chapters describe measures undertaken to improve supply in the face of stiff economic competition from the private sector in the United States (Chapter 9 by Bernard Rostker and Curtis Gilroy and Chapter 10 by Deborah Clay-Mendez); the UK (Chapter 11 by Keith Hartley); France (Chapter 12 by Sylvain Daffix, Vincent Medina, and Cyr-Denis Nidier); Spain (Chapter 13 by Juan Lopez Diaz); Romania (Chapter 14 by Mihaela Matei); and Italy (Chapter 15 by Domenico Villani).

The Transformation of Personnel Policies

Across Europe and North America, nations are planning to transform military personnel policies, aiming to build future capabilities consistent with new strategic environments and with the demographic and societal realities of the future. For many nations, a key reform is to cease conscription and dramatically reduce the number of people in uniform. Other important reforms include expanding recruitment capacity, improving working conditions, revamping career paths, overhauling military pay schemes and increasing military pay, modernizing pension models, enhancing the post-service prospects for those who serve, and improving quality of life for military members and their families.

The capacity of militaries to get and keep the people they need, deliver the capabilities required for the missions of the future, and contribute successfully to multi-national operations will depend greatly on their success in carrying through such reforms. Fostering a shared understanding of these reforms is the central purpose of this book, and later chapters offer detailed discussions of the changes. The next sections of this chapter highlight key areas of reform.[39]

DOWNSIZING AND TURNING TO ALL-VOLUNTEER FORCES

Most of the nations of Europe and North America reduced their forces substantially after the Cold War ended. Several have shifted from conscript systems to all-volunteer forces, and two more plan to do so within the next few years.

National decisions to suspend conscription are motivated by a variety of factors, including the unavailability of conscripts for the foreign missions that are an increasing feature of the changed geopolitical environment, economic and budgetary pressures, domestic politics, and the preferences expressed by NATO's leaders and advisers.[40] Many experts believe that smaller forces with a high proportion of volunteers are better suited to transformation. One reason is that by saving money on personnel, the "small but solid" model can free up funds to invest in modern equipment.[41] Indeed, the militaries of continental Europe

---

39. The section draws heavily on insights gathered from participants at the September 2003 Transatlantic Roundtable in Brussels, including several authors of this book as well as William Carr, Lindsay Cohn, Andrew Dorman, Teodora Fuior, Gina Grosso, Ulrich vom Hagen, John Hoag, Corinna Horst, Karel Hotovy, Reiner Huber, Jaroslav Kuča, George-Cristian Maior, Andreas Prüfert, Arne Røksund, Maurizio Scardino, Horst Schmalfeld, and Carlo Wouters.

40. For more detailed accounts of the factors affecting decisions to halt conscription, see Jehn and Selden, "The End of Conscription in Europe?"; and Williams, "From Conscripts to Volunteers."

41. For the view that use of conscripts diverts funds from modernizing military equipment and thus contributes to the capabilities gap between the United States and Europe, see Richard L. Russell, "NATO's European Members: Partners or Dependents?" *Naval War College Review,* Vol. 56, No. 1 (Winter 2003), pp. 30–40; David S. Yost, "The NATO Capabilities Gap and the European Union," *Survival,* Vol. 42, No. 4 (Winter 2000–01), pp. 100–101; Elinor Sloan, "Military Matters: Speeding Deployment," *NATO Review,* Vol. 49, No. 1 (Spring 2001), pp. 30–33; Shishkin, "How Europe's Armies Let Their Guard Down." Nicholas Burns, the former U.S. Ambassador to NATO, has argued that "even without spending more money, many allies could use their existing defense Euros more wisely by providing professional military units ... rather than retaining static conscript forces." Burns, "Launching NATO's Transformation at Prague." The report of the Weizsäcker Commission to the German federal government,

(which, with the exception of that of Luxembourg, continued to rely heavily on conscripts at least until the mid-1990s) generally devote larger shares of their military budgets to military people than do the United States or the United Kingdom, two countries with long-standing all-volunteer forces (see Figure 1.2). For this and other reasons, they typically have less money than the latter to spend per troop on modernizing their equipment (as Figure 1.2 shows).[42]

With the short terms of conscription common in Europe today, volunteers may be better suited to transformation than conscripts for another reason: they remain in service long enough to be trained effectively to operate and maintain the high-technology equipment of the future. The lower turnover rates in all-volunteer forces can also lead to reductions in training infrastructure and lower training costs, leaving more funds free to modernize equipment.

On the other hand, all-volunteer forces are not suited to every national circumstance. For example, if such large forces are needed for territorial defense or other purposes that a significant fraction of the youth population must be called to service each year, then conscription may be the best solution, for reasons explained in Chapter 5 by John Warner and Sebastian Negrusa. Such is the case in Finland, as Hannu Herranen points out in Chapter 7. In addition, some countries find that conscription is fundamentally important to preserving the character of their military reserves, or to maintaining important linkages between their armed forces and their society, as Bertel Heurlin, Hannu Herranen, Gerhard Kümmel, and Chris Donnelly discuss in chapters 6, 7, 8, and 16 respectively.

EXPANDING RECRUITMENT CAPACITY

Most militaries are working to boost recruitment capacity through professional recruiting teams, mass-media advertising, and other measures. In addition, nations are seeking to expand the pool of prospective volunteers by opening more jobs to and recruiting more vigorously among

---

"Common Security and the Future of the Bundeswehr," May 23, 2000, provides explicit estimates of personnel and infrastructure savings that would accrue from reducing the number of conscripts in the German forces.
42. The first decade of an AVF can be difficult. As Figure 1.2 reveals, militaries in that transition period may be the hardest-hit in terms of a shortage of funds for modernization.

Figure 1.2. Share of Military Budget Devoted to Equipment Modernization, and Equipment Modernization Spending per Active-Duty Troop, Selected Countries, 2002

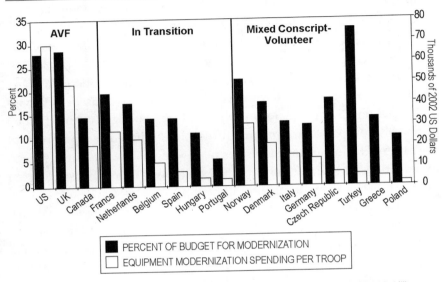

Source: Based on data from U.S. DoD, *Allied Contributions to the Common Defense*, July 2003; IISS, *Military Balance*, 2003–04. Countries are those for which data are readily available through the DoD report: NATO member states, with the exception of Iceland and the newest members of NATO. Luxembourg is also excluded due to the small size of its military.

Equipment modernization spending per troop shown in thousands of 2002 U.S. dollars.

women, immigrants, and other populations that have been under-represented.

For example, in the German Federal Armed Forces, which just a few years ago permitted women only in the music corps and the medical profession, all jobs are now open to women. Between 2001 and 2004, the fraction of women in the armed forces climbed dramatically in several NATO countries, including Canada (from 11.9 percent to 16.9 percent), the Czech Republic (from 3.7 percent to 12.2 percent), Turkey (from 0.1 percent to 4.0 percent), and Greece (from 3.8 percent to 16 percent).[43]

43. For country-by-country discussions of the changing roles and numbers of women in NATO's forces, see NATO Committee on Women in the NATO Forces, *Year-In-Review 2004*, <www.nato.int/ims/2004/win/03-index.htm>. For a summary table depicting the representation of women in NATO's forces between 2001 and 2004, see the website of the Committee at

The Royal Netherlands forces are looking for ways to tap into the potential of the country's ethnic minority population more effectively.[44] The United States is expediting the process of obtaining citizenship for legally resident noncitizens who serve in the military.[45]

Some countries are also beginning to recruit young people from foreign countries as a way to widen the pool of potential enlistees. Spain has increased the proportion of immigrants permitted in its armed forces and is actively recruiting young people of Spanish heritage from South America and Equatorial Guinea.[46] The British military holds regular recruiting drives in Fiji, a former colony that has been independent since 1970.[47] However, if recruits from nontraditional populations have negative perceptions of the military, or find that their integration into the armed forces does not go well, those potential pools may become more difficult to tap. Moreover, recruitment of foreigners can raise concerns about the extent to which a military reflects the society it represents, and may lead to worries about loyalty and the protection of national secrets.

Despite the potential drawbacks, such efforts may prove crucial to the future military capability of all-volunteer forces. With daunting demographic challenges on the horizon, they may be equally important even for militaries that retain conscription.

IMPROVING WORKING CONDITIONS

Another crucial class of reforms is aimed at improving working conditions for the people who serve, both by eliminating military traditions and regulations that annoy servicemembers but do not contribute to military effectiveness, and by improving infrastructure and equipment. For example, the U.S. Navy has sharply reduced the practice of sending sailors on tours of duty to which they object, by setting up an on-line

---

<www.nato.int/issues/women_nato/index.html>.

44. Ministry of Defense of the Netherlands, "Summary of the Defence White Paper 2000," July 17, 2001, p. 13.

45. James C. McKinley, Jr., "Mexican Pride and Death in U.S. Service," *New York Times*, March 22, 2005.

46. See the chapter by Juan Lopez Diaz in this book. See also "Spain's army fills gaps from abroad," *BBC News*, June 19, 2001, <news.bbc.co.uk/2 /hi/Europe/1397221.stm>.

47. Catherine Miller, "The death of conscription," *BBC News Online*, June 29, 2001, <news.bbc.co.uk/2/hi/europe/1414033.stm>.

auction that directs bonuses to people who volunteer for unpopular tours.[48] The Belgian military is reviewing staff regulations to identify more flexible procedures. Spain's Ministry of Defense has established a telephone hotline for soldier complaints. The German Federal Armed Forces have undertaken a study to determine whether rules limiting the wearing of jewelry should be relaxed, a step that is symbolic of a military lifestyle more attractive to today's potential volunteers.[49]

The countries of the former Warsaw Pact and Soviet Union are spending substantial sums to improve military infrastructure and equipment, in part to establish better working conditions for the troops. For example, the Czech Republic is investing in infrastructure at its military garrisons.[50] Improved working conditions can go a long way toward increasing future military capability by boosting the number of recruits and the willingness of members to remain in service.

REVAMPING CAREER PATHS

Militaries are working to create new corps of non-commissioned officers (NCOs) and give them good prospects for a career in the military, especially in the countries of the former Eastern Bloc, where a decade ago the armed forces were made up almost exclusively of officers and junior-ranking conscripts. Romania, the Czech Republic, and the Slovak Republic are investing substantial sums in technical-skills training and leadership development for the new NCO corps. In addition, the new member states plan to develop more transparent and merit-based promotion systems.

In recent years, Canada has altered its military entry and exit policies to ameliorate the staffing imbalances that developed during the downsizing of the 1990s. A new lateral-entry policy allows the services to make short-term contracts with individuals who have already acquired useful experience from the private sector. To retain the senior military people who are needed to train and mentor the next generation, it raised the compulsory retirement age from 55 to 60. In addition, the Canadian

---

48. George Cahlink, "Fewer Hands on Deck," *Government Executive Magazine*, June 1, 2004.
49. Williams, "From Conscripts to Volunteers." As of early 2006, changes in the jewelry rules are still pending.
50. Ibid.

forces now offer more variety in the duration of a volunteer's commitment to the military, depending upon occupation and the anticipated needs of the military.[51]

France has opened new positions for specialists with expertise that its military needs; they will be allowed to rise in rank and pay without taking up the duties of command. Romania is working to attract more officers with civilian academic credentials. Such initiatives are crucial to the technologically capable militaries at the heart of transformation.

OVERHAULING MILITARY PAY SCHEMES AND INCREASING MILITARY PAY

Countries on both sides of the Atlantic are seeking ways to make military pay more attractive in the competition for talent. Some European countries have raised military pay. Such increases constitute an important step.

In some European countries, military pay is tied directly to the pay of other public-sector workers (see Table 1.3). The United States and the UK each has some form of explicit linkage between military pay and pay in the private sector. Over time, the nations of continental Europe may find it necessary to follow their model and develop explicit links to private-sector pay.

Making pay competitive can also require a pay model that allows for greater flexibility across occupations and duties. Many countries use bonuses to put more pay in the hands of people in hard-to-fill military specialties or with dangerous or especially stressful duties. Canada builds such flexibility directly into its pay table. The pay of a noncommissioned member depends not only on a person's rank and time in that rank but also on his or her trade group; individuals in trades that command higher pay in the private sector get paid more in the military too.[52] The flexibility to pay military specialists more for jobs that are highly rewarded in the private sector may be crucial to realizing transformation centered around high-technology equipment and information systems.

---

51. Department of National Defence, Canada, Backgrounder, "Recommended Changes to Canadian Forces Terms of Service," BG-01.016, June 27, 2001, <www.dnd.ca/eng/archive/june01/27terms_b_e.htm>.

52. Department of National Defence, Canada, Directorate of Pay Policy and Development, "Regular Force Non-Commissioned Members (NCM) Rates," February 18, 2005, <www.forces.gc.ca/dgcb/dppd/pay/engraph/NCMRegFPayRate_e.asp?sidesection=3&sidecat=28>.

Table 1.3. Characteristics of Cash Pay in Selected Militaries

	Link to Other Public Employees' Pay	Link to Private-sector Pay	Variation by Occupation or Duty
Belgium	No automatic link, but General Staff works to keep pay comparable by education level to pay in public sector	Indirect [a]	Differential pay for pilots, medical, civil engineers, graduates of staff colleges; skills-based special pays for, e.g., pilots, divers, paratroopers; special pays for deployment to operations abroad
Canada	Not officially tied, but tracks salaries in federal civil service	No systematic tie [b]	Enlisted pay varies according to trade group; special pays for combat, deployment to theater, living abroad or in the Far North
Czech Republic	Yes, explicit link	No	Bonuses for hazardous positions, missions abroad
France	Yes, explicit link	No	Special pays, bonuses for some specialists such as pilots and submariners; for living in Paris or abroad; for being deployed to interventions
Germany	Yes, explicit link	No	Bonuses in specified occupations; daily bonus for service abroad
Italy	Pay is set separately for defense and security-sector employees	No	Operational allowance depending on grade and assignment: people in deployable units earn up to 50% more than in administrative units; elite units (e.g., airborne) up to 80% more
Norway	Pay is negotiated for public sector as a whole, military included	No	Special pay for some occupations, e.g., aviation
Romania	Yes, explicit link	No	Special pays for merit, based upon recommendation of supervisor
Slovak Republic	No explicit link	No	Bonuses for hazardous conditions (1% to 6%)
Spain	No explicit tie, but pay is comparable with that of other public-sector employees	No	Special pays for, e.g., parachute, marine, pilot, submarine, and for units with expeditionary capacity
United Kingdom	No explicit link	Explicit link [c]	Extra pay for some skills, such as pilots and submariners
United States	Annual pay raise often linked by law to raise for federal civilian workers or to wage growth of civilians in private sector	Explicit link [d]	Numerous special pays and bonuses for term of service, duty location, deployments, and occupation

SOURCE: Table adapted from Williams, "From Conscripts to Volunteers."

NOTES: a. In Belgium, link is indirect, through public-sector link, as public-sector pay is tied to average pay rates in private sector.

b. In Canada, no systematic tie, but salaries and bonuses in some trades have been boosted to be competitive with private sector.

c. In the UK, an independent armed forces pay review body monitors pay in "equivalent" private-sector professions to benchmark its pay recommendations; adds an "X-factor" to help offset the difficulties of military life.

d. In the United States, a 2000 law required military pay raises in 2001 to 2006 to exceed average wage rise in private sector. Earlier law called for raise somewhat lower than in private sector; such standing law can be ignored, however, as pay raises are typically granted through new defense legislation each year.

MODERNIZING PENSION MODELS

The nature of the military pension scheme can have a profound effect on members' decisions about how long to remain in the military, and thus affects the size and shape of every military force. For example, the U.S. military retirement system offers an immediate pension and a generous health-care benefit to members who serve in uniform for twenty years or more, but provides no pension for those who stay in the military for fewer than twenty years. Unlike the retirement schemes typical of the U.S. private sector today, the system is not portable, that is, the servicemember does not receive a government contribution toward future retirement that could be carried forward to another employer when he or she leaves military service. The system encourages members who stay for at least eight or ten years to remain for a total of twenty, but to depart shortly after.

Because the U.S. rules for military retirement do not vary based upon a member's military occupation, they encourage many people to stay in the armed forces for longer than they are needed, but induce many others to leave well before their expertise loses its value. Partly as a result, the U.S. military is imbalanced across occupations, with too many people in some jobs and too few in others.[53] Some experts believe that fundamental changes in the military retirement system will be necessary for the United States to achieve transformation.[54]

Canada and Italy reformed their military pension schemes during the 1990s. Their schemes are more portable than those of most militaries and may provide useful tools for shaping forces. Modern pension models could prove key to the flexible force management capability that future leaders will need in order to correct the current staffing imbalances in their militaries and ready them for transformation.

IMPROVING POST-SERVICE CAREER PROSPECTS

In countries with all-volunteer forces, the prospect of a better economic future in the outside world following a few years in the military can be

---

53. CBO, *Budget Options* (February 2005), p. 43.
54. Donald J. Cymrot and Michael L. Hansen, "Overhauling Enlisted Careers and Compensation," in Williams, *Filling the Ranks*, pp. 119–143; and Bernard Rostker, "Changing the Officer Personnel System," ibid., pp. 145–166.

a strong incentive for people to serve. The United States emphasizes training in skills valued in the civilian job market, together with money for college, as a way to attract people into the services. Some countries provide transition assistance and training as members depart service, coupled with guarantees of public-sector jobs afterwards.

For example, Germany provides its twelve-year enlisted volunteers with a full year of training at the end of service, followed by a full year of government pay in a transitional job in the private sector. Spain now offers its volunteers two to ten months of training in an occupational specialty at the beginning of their careers and additional training for their return to the private sector. In addition, Spain's volunteers now have the opportunity to receive credentials as "military technicians" that are intended to help soldiers and sailors as they return to civilian life. The Netherlands also plans to invest in training courses to help servicemembers make the transition to civilian employment. Romania is establishing a career assistance program for those who have served in the volunteer military. The Italian Ministry of Defense pays for six months of training as volunteer members depart service.[55]

In some countries, a crucial reform has been to reserve a substantial share of public-sector jobs for military volunteers. Italy now requires its national police officers to volunteer first for a year in the military, and all of Italy's four-year enlisted volunteers are assured of a career in the police forces or the armed forces.[56] Spain reserves 50 percent of Civil Guard posts for veterans, and the Spanish Ministry of Defense is negotiating agreements with other ministries to reserve jobs for separating soldiers and sailors.[57] In other European countries, ministries of defense are making arrangements with employer associations, labor associations, and other public agencies to assist former servicemembers with placement.[58]

---

55. Williams, "From Conscripts to Volunteers."
56. See chapter by Domenico Villani in this book.
57. See chapter by Juan Lopez Diaz in this book.
58. Williams, "From Conscripts to Volunteers."

IMPROVING QUALITY OF LIFE

Several countries are improving family benefits and other quality-of-life measures to make military life more attractive for volunteers. For example, France has expanded family assistance programs such as help with searching for children's schools; it is also building new family housing. Romania is building new housing, while the Czech Republic is working to improve family support. Germany and Belgium are opening child-care centers for military families, and the Netherlands is considering such a step. Several countries are working to minimize family separations. Such noncash compensation can provide important extra leverage in attracting and keeping volunteers, but it also has its drawbacks, as Deborah Clay-Mendez points out in Chapter 10.

Organization of the Book

The book is organized into four parts. Following this introductory chapter, Part I looks at the changing environment related to the supply and demand of people for military forces of the future. Political scientist Jolyon Howorth of the University of Bath in the UK and Yale University in the United States discusses the demand side, exploring how new technologies and altered geopolitical and security landscapes in Europe and North America affect needs for military people. Rickard Sandell of Spain's Royal Institute Elcano details the looming demographic crisis in Europe and what it portends for military recruiting in the coming decades. Vaidotas Urbelis of the Institute of International Relations and Political Science at Vilnius University in Lithuania explores the new geopolitical environment in the Baltic States and the consequences of NATO membership for public perceptions of the military and military service in those states.

Part II offers four perspectives on the choice of a personnel model. John Warner of Clemson University in the United States and Sebastian Negrusa, a doctoral candidate at Clemson University, make the economic case for all-volunteer forces using examples from the United States and Romania. Bertel Heurlin of the Danish Institute for Military Studies at the Royal Danish Defense College argues that Denmark's new strategic environment is best served by a mixed model, based on a professional core supplemented by conscripts who train for a few months and are available for homeland security duties, but who do not serve in military operations abroad. Hannu Herranen of the Finnish Defense Forces argues for a different mixed model, one in which conscription feeds both a professional core and the reserve that is the heart of Finland's military. Gerhard Kümmel of the Bundeswehr Institute of Social Research explains the German decision to retain a mixed model in which compulsory national service sustains a pool of recruits for the volunteer and professional forces.

Part III explores the transitions of six countries from a mixed conscript-volunteer model to an all-volunteer model. The first chapter in this part, by Bernard Rostker of the RAND Corporation in the United States and Curtis Gilroy of the U.S. Office of the Secretary of Defense, reviews the U.S. shift during the 1970s from a conscript-based force to an all-volunteer force. The chapter by Deborah Clay-Mendez, recently of the U.S. Congressional Budget Office, offers lessons based on thirty years of U.S. experience in managing the balance between cash and in-kind compensation. Keith Hartley of the University of York in the UK describes the UK's transition to an all-volunteer force during the 1960s and 1970s, and reviews the current state of the UK's AVF. Four chapters review the experiences of France, Spain, Romania, and Italy with transformation to an all-volunteer model. These chapters are by Sylvain Daffix, Vincent Medina, and Cyr-Denis Nidier of the Economic Observatory of Defense in the French Ministry of Defense; Juan Lopez Diaz of Spain's Ministry of Defense; Mihaela Matei of the Ministry of National Defense in Romania; and Domenico Villani of the Italian Defense General Staff.

Finally, Part IV looks at the transformation of personnel policies related to reserve forces. Chris Donnelly, formerly the Special Advisor to the Secretary-General of NATO for Central and Eastern European Affairs and now at the Defence Academy of the UK, looks at the implications of the new European security context for reserve forces. John D. Winkler, Karen McKenney, and Jennifer Buck of the U.S. Office of the Secretary of Defense and Robert St. Onge, Jr., of MPRI, a defense consulting firm, outline the ongoing U.S. transformation of reserve forces. A chapter by Peter Švec, formerly of the Ministry of Defense of the Slovak Republic, looks at the choices for small countries about reserve forces.

The book ends with a brief concluding chapter by Curtis Gilroy and Cindy Williams that draws on the rest of the book for insights and lessons from the personnel policy transformations that have already been undertaken or that are underway in Europe and North America.

Looking Ahead

Sound personnel policies are now crucial to tomorrow's militaries. For Western nations, recent dramatic alterations in concepts of security, threats and interests, and military missions, as well as emerging technologies, especially information technologies, have prompted nations and institutions to contemplate transforming their military capabilities.

Such changes have profound implications for the numbers and characteristics of the people who will be needed in militaries on both sides of the Atlantic during the coming decades. Important demographic and societal changes also portend shifts in the populations available and ready to serve. To deal with those new realities and enable transformation in other dimensions of military capability, the nations of North America and Europe have committed to transform a wide range of policies, structures, and institutions related to military personnel.

The contributors to this volume offer numerous ideas and lessons from the transformations in a number of countries. Among the most important lessons, we find that:

- the transformation of personnel policies is vital to the fundamental overhaul of military affairs;

- an all-volunteer force (AVF) model can offer important economic advantages for nations seeking to transform their military capabilities to deal with new threats and missions while capitalizing on modern technologies;

- AVFs are not well suited to every set of circumstances, and a mixed model that includes both conscripts and volunteers is still a sound choice for some countries;

- the transition to an AVF can be challenging and may be more costly than anticipated;

- to be successful in attracting, retaining, and motivating qualified people, and getting the right people into the right jobs, all-volunteer forces must be competitive employers and effective human resource managers;

- the nations of Europe and North America face important decisions and challenges as they transform reserve forces to complement shrinking active-duty forces and meet the security needs of the future;

- countries in Europe and North America are developing creative solutions to the challenges of filling their ranks with the right people.

Policies that work well in one country may not translate directly to other countries for a variety of reasons, including cultural differences or historical precedent. Nevertheless, the contributors to this book believe that countries and militaries have much to learn from each other's experiences with military personnel policies. We hope this volume will be a vehicle for such learning.

Part I
The Changing Environment

Chapter 2

The Transformation of European Military Capability, 1989–2005

Jolyon Howorth

Since the end of the Cold War, European nations have been compelled to transform their militaries. The type of forces required for the territorial defense objectives of the Cold War proved inappropriate to the new crisis-management and peacekeeping missions of the post–Cold War world. This chapter reviews the issues raised by this transformation, first presenting background on the changes of the post–Cold War world, then the steps that Europe has taken to address the challenges thus presented: the formation of the European Security and Defense Identity (ESDI) and then the European Security and Defense Policy (ESDP), establishment of specific goals with the "Headline Goal 2010," and the initial European Union military operations. Some of the implications of these transitions for the management of military human resources are identified. The chapter concludes by recognizing that, while much has been accomplished, there is still a great deal more to do, both with respect to rationalizing the EU's defense spending and with respect to recruiting appropriate military personnel.

Background: A World Transformed

In 1988, as the Cold War was ending, the NATO alliance had almost 5.4 million active-duty service personnel, backed up by over 7 million reservists. Of these, the United States supplied 2.2 million troops and 1.7 million reservists, the European members of NATO contributed 3.1 million active-duty servicemembers and 5.5 million reservists, and Canada the rest, with 84,000 troops and 52,000 reservists. The vast majority of these troops—with the notable exception of those from the United States, the UK, and Canada—were conscripts. Against these forces were ranged over 5 million active-duty troops from the Warsaw Pact, backed by 6.2 million reservists.[1]

However, within three years both the Warsaw Pact and Soviet Union had disappeared and a dozen years later, the numbers of armed forces in the NATO alliance had been radically transformed. From a 1988 figure of 8.6 million troops and reservists in NATO Europe, the figure had dropped by 2003 to 4.9 million, a 43 percent decrease; the corresponding U.S. figure was 2.7 million, compared to 3.9 million in 1988, a 31 percent drop.

The paradoxical reality about these forces, however, was that substantial numbers of the 12 million men and women under arms at the height of Cold War tensions virtually never saw action, whereas by 2003 their counterparts—from both the United States and the European Union (EU)—were seriously overstretched, large numbers of them being at one stage or another of the three-stage cycle of deploying, resting, or preparing to deploy. Moreover, whereas in 1989 the "peace" was kept essentially by massed conscript-based line-defenses backed by a nuclear deterrent, in 2003, crisis-management operations were carried out by professional soldiers using sophisticated conventional equipment demanding high levels of technical skills and ongoing training.

At the level of personnel and human resource management, the basic shift was from quantity to quality. As the United Kingdom's 1998 "Strategic Defence Review" stated: "defence is a highly professional, increasingly high technology, vocation." The challenge was to recruit highly motivated people, train them appropriately and to a very high standard, equip them properly, and retain both their motivation and their services.[2] This chapter examines the process whereby the EU member states, both individually and collectively, shifted their military thinking away from the fixed "legacy" weapons and systems of the Cold War years and towards the power-projection and crisis-management enablers of the present. The professional soldier of 2006 and beyond will require a range of skills—not just military

---

1. Source for military statistics: International Institute for Strategic Studies (IISS), *The Military Balance 1989–1990* (London: Brassey's, 1989), pp. 208–209. Other military statistics in this chapter are, unless otherwise stated, taken from the relevant annual volume of *The Military Balance*.

2. UK Ministry of Defense (MOD), "The Strategic Defence Review" (London: HMSO, 1998), Chapter 6, "A Policy for People," accessed at: <www.mod.uk/issues/sdr/people_policy.htm>.

skills, but also political, social, and even cultural and linguistic skills—undreamed of only two decades earlier. We have witnessed a wholesale transformation of the EU's plans, structures, weapons systems, and equipment: in short, its entire military mindset. This translates into a massive shift in the demand side of the European military-personnel equation.

The challenge of transformation was especially acute for Europe. During the Cold War, European forces were rarely deployed far from home (indeed almost never, if "home" is taken to mean Europe); they spent most of their time on exercises and virtually none of it on active combat duty. General Charles de Gaulle, justifying France's decision to spend around 40 percent of its defense budget on nuclear weapons, had coined the formula "nuclear weapons mean the absence of battle."[3] As a result, when the Gulf War overtook them in 1991, France was shocked to discover that, although its forces were among the most robustly trained and experienced in Europe, very few of them were deployable: just 15,000 out of a total armed force of 289,000. Their vaunted AMX-300 combat tanks were badly in need of servicing; only forty were combat-ready out of a notional 1,300 in service. When the lightly armed *Daguet* division finally arrived in Saudi Arabia, it found that its AMX-10RC light armored vehicles were quite literally blind to the topography of the desert theatre until equipped with U.S. global positioning (GPS) guidance systems. When, less than six months later, the Europeans were again caught off guard with the outbreak of the Balkan wars, it came as an even harsher revelation to many—even within the security community—that the Europeans were far from able, as Luxembourg's Foreign Minister Jacques Poos had imprudently implied they were, to take over responsibility for European security from the Americans.[4] They were unable even to project any forces to a region which lay, technically, within the geographical bounds of the EU itself.[5]

---

3. "Le nucléaire, c'est la non-bataille."
4. Jacques Poos uttered the optimistic words: "It is the hour of Europe, not of the USA."
5. It is often forgotten, when referring to the Balkans as "out-of-area," that the region lies inside an EU space bounded by Greece in the south, Italy in the west, and Austria in the north. In 2007, the accession of Romania and Bulgaria will complete the EU "encirclement" of the former Yugoslavia.

The basic explanation is simple. Whereas U.S. forces throughout the twentieth century had devoted massive effort—financial, technological, and logistical—to a capacity for force projection across both the world's great oceans, European forces since 1945 had been configured for line-defense across the great European plain. The West German armed forces in 1989, for instance, boasted almost 500,000 active troops, with a further 850,000 reservists. Their main equipment featured 5,000 main battle tanks, 2,136 armored infantry fighting vehicles, 3,500 armored personnel carriers, 2,500 artillery pieces, 2,700 anti-tank guided weapons, almost 5,000 air-defense guns, and 800 surface-to-air missiles. Little of this would prove useful in the new tasks of distant crisis management facing the EU in the 1990s.

Although NATO, in its new Strategic Concept of November 1991, drew attention to the need to shift focus away from massed tank and artillery battles in Central Europe to the new and more diverse crisis-management challenges of the post–Cold War world, the emphasis initially was doctrinal rather than programmatic.[6] New procurement projects have lead-times of ten to fifteen years, but few European governments were able to imagine, let alone to anticipate, the new force-projection challenges that would be facing them in the twenty-first century. All were keen to cash in on the post-1989 "peace dividend." On average, European defense budgets fell by more than 20 percent during the period between 1989 and 1998.[7] The UK immediately embarked on a series of defense reviews culminating in the 1998 "Strategic Defence Review."[8] France moved rapidly from a defense policy of rigorous national autonomy towards one geared towards integrated European operations.[9] The majority of European mili-

---

6. "The Alliance's Strategic Concept agreed by the Heads of State and Government participating in the meeting of the North Atlantic Council," Rome, November 8, 1991, available on NATO "Basic Documents" website, <www.nato.int/docu/basictxt/b911108a.htm>.

7. Budgets of France, Germany, and the UK fell by, respectively, 12 percent, 24 percent, and 28 percent during this period. Stockholm International Peace Research Institute (SIPRI) Yearbook 1999 (Stockholm: Oxford University Press/SIPRI, 1999), p. 298.

8. UK MOD, "Front Line First: The Defence Costs Study" (London: HMSO, July 1994); "Statement on the Defence Estimates: Stable Forces in a Strong Britain" (London: HMSO, May 1995); "The Strategic Defence Review" (London: HMSO, July 1998).

9. See Jolyon Howorth, "French defence reforms: national tactics for a European strategy?" Brassey's Defence Yearbook 1998 (London: Brassey's, 1998), pp.

taries, however (with the notable exceptions of Belgium and the Netherlands), remained unreformed and unchanged for the greater part of the decade. Europe, in short, revealed a dual "capabilities gap": there was a growing gap between the advanced weapons systems available to the United States military and the increasingly antiquated systems of the EU member states, and there was also a gap between those existing EU systems and the military requirements of the European Union in the post–Cold War world.[10]

In Search of a European Security and Defense Identity (ESDI)

In the early 1990s, defense planners began to address the problem of developing a serious EU military capacity that would allow the Union to assume responsibility for the new crisis-management tasks of the post–Cold War world. At a meeting at Petersberg (near Bonn) in June 1992, the Western European Union (WEU) had defined three such tasks, corresponding to three levels of combat intensity: "humanitarian and rescue tasks; peacekeeping tasks; [and] tasks of combat forces in crisis management, including peacemaking."[11] The latter task might even include high-intensity war-fighting like the Kosovo operation of 1999. This implied radical transformation of the EU's existing capacity to develop deployable, professional intervention forces geared to "out-of-area" crisis management. But where were these forces to be found?

The first task was to end conscription and to move towards all-volunteer forces (AVFs). Conscripts, it was generally recognized, tended to have limited skill-sets and, largely for political and juridical reasons, were undeployable outside of their home countries. Belgium and the Netherlands moved swiftly: Belgium announced the abolition of conscription in 1992 and ended it in 1994; the Netherlands did the same in 1993

130–151; see also Ministère de la Défense, "Livre Blanc sur la Défense 1994" (Paris: 10/18, 1994).

10. This capabilities gap was initially identified by Christopher Hill, "The Capability-Expectations Gap, or Conceptualising Europe's International Role," *Journal of Common Market Studies,* Vol. 31, No. 3 (1993).

11. The WEU, dating back to 1948, was reorganized in 1955 as the only European body with responsibility for intra-European defense liaison. Moribund for thirty years, it was reactivated in the late 1980s. Anne Deighton, ed., *Western European Union 1954–1997: Defence, Security, Integration* (Oxford: St. Antony's, 1997).

and 1996. France and Spain followed suit in 1996 after agonizing debates about the connection between conscription and democracy. In both France and Spain, the last conscripts left the armed forces in 2001. The motivations for abolishing conscription varied from country to country. Most, such as Belgium, Spain, and many central and eastern European states, sought to focus on downsizing and reduction of the military budget; others, including the Netherlands, France, and Italy, were intent on transforming their militaries into deployable forces for overseas crisis management.[12] However, by 2005, sixteen years after the end of the Cold War, only thirteen of the twenty-five EU states had moved fully to AVFs, although several others had plans to phase out conscription. (Table 2.1 summarizes the size and nature of the armed forces of the European Union's member-countries as of 2004.)

The next step was to equip these new professional forces to tackle crisis-management missions. Such a transformational process would clearly take time, but crises—in the Balkans and elsewhere—would not wait. As a stop-gap measure, the procedures known as "Berlin Plus" were devised so the EU could bridge the capabilities gap by borrowing necessary assets such as strategic lift, C4I (command, control, communications, computers, and intelligence), and logistics from the United States.[13] EU-only units could be put together from inside NATO by generating European Combined Joint Task Forces (CJTFs).[14] A European Security and Defense Identity (ESDI) was thus to be forged, "separable but not separate" from NATO and overseen politically by the WEU.

---

12. See Cindy Williams, "From Conscripts to Volunteers: NATO's Transitions to All-Volunteer Forces," *Naval War College Review*, Vol. 58, No. 1 (Winter 2005).

13. The "Berlin Plus" arrangements allowed the EU to enjoy "assured access to NATO planning" and "presumed access to NATO [i.e., U.S.] assets and capabilities," as well as a pre-designated Europeans-only chain of command. The arrangements were agreed in principle at a NATO summit in Berlin in June 1996, but it took six years of hard bargaining (the "Berlin Plus negotiations") to nail down the details. This was finally achieved in December 2002. See Jean-Yves Haine, ed., *From Laeken to Copenhagen: European Defence: Core Documents 3*, Chaillot Paper No. 57 (Paris: European Union Institute for Security Studies [EU-ISS], 2003), pp. 178–180, available at <www.iss-eu.org/chaillot/chai57e.pdf>.

14. Terry Terriff, "The CJTF Concept and the Limits of European Autonomy," in Jolyon Howorth and John T.S. Keeler, eds., *Defending Europe: The EU, NATO and the Quest for European Autonomy* (New York: Palgrave, 2003), pp. 39–60.

Table 2.1. European Armed Forces, 2004

	Professional or Conscript[a]	Number of Personnel					
		Army 2004	Navy 2004	Air Force 2004	Total in 2004[b]	Total in 1988	% Red'n 1988–2004
Austria	Conscript	33,200	—[c]	6,700	39,900	54,700	-27%
Belgium	Professional since 1994	24,800	2,450	10,250	39,200	88,300	-56%
Cyprus	Conscript	10,000	—	—	10,000	13,000	-23%
Czech Republic	Professional since 2005	16,663	—	5,609	22,272	197,000	-89%
Denmark	Conscript	12,500	3,800	4,200	21,180	29,300	-28%
Estonia	Conscript	3,429	331	193	4,934	n/a	n/a
Finland	Conscript	20,500	5,000	2,800	28,300	35,200	-20%
France	Professional since 2001	133,500	43,995	63,600	254,895	457,000	-44%
Germany	Conscript	191,350	25,650	67,500	284,500	489,000	-42%
Greece	Conscript	110,000	19,250	23,000	163,850	214,000	-23%
Hungary	Ended 2004	23,950		7,500	32,300	99,000	-67%
Ireland	Professional	8,500	1,100	860	10,460	13,200	-21%
Italy	Professional since 2005	112,000	34,000	45,875	191,875	386,000	-50%
Latvia	Plans to end 2006	1,817	685	255	5,238	n/a	n/a
Lithuania	Conscript	11,600	710	1,200	13,510	n/a	n/a
Luxembourg	Professional since 1967	900	-----	----	900	800	+12%
Malta	Professional	2,237[d]	(joint)	(joint)	2,237	1,200	+86%
Netherlands	Professional since 1996	23,150	12,130	11,050	53,130	102,200	-48%
Poland	Conscript	89,000	14,300	30,000	141,500	406,000	-65%
Portugal	Ended 2003	26,700	10,950	7,250	44,900	73,900	-39%
Slovakia	Ended 2006	12,860		5,160	20,195	n/a	n/a
Slovenia	Professional since 2004	6,550		(530)	6,550	n/a	n/a
Spain	Professional since 2001	95,600	19,455	22,750	147,255	309,500	-52%
Sweden	Conscript	13,800	7,900	5,900	27,600	67,000	-59%
UK	Professional since 1963	116,760	40,630	48,500	205,890	316,700	-35%
Norway[e]	Conscript	14,700	6,180	5,000	25,800	35,800	-28%
Turkey[e]	Conscript	402,000	52,750	60,100	514,850	635,300	-19%

Source: IISS, *The Military Balance 2005–2006*, pp. 45–150.
Bold indicates original 15 EU member states, prior to 2004.
a. Six of the EU-15 (members prior to 2004 enlargement) still field conscript armies. Half of the EU Accession states (those who became members in 2004) retain conscript armed forces but one of these (Latvia) plans to end conscription.
b. In some cases, overall numbers are in excess of the sums for the three armed forces because paramilitaries and other forces are included in the official tallies.
c. Austria and Luxembourg have no navy and Luxembourg has no air force. Of the newest ten members, joining in 2004, the Czech Republic, Cyprus, Hungary, Slovakia, and Slovenia have no navy, and Cyprus also has no air force.
d. Maltese armed forces include all three services.
e. Norway and Turkey are included here although they are not EU members, because Norway participates in the ESDP through NATO and the Berlin Plus arrangements, participates in EU joint actions, and has pledged personnel and equipment to the ESDP Rapid Reaction Force. <europa.eu.int/comm/external_relations/norway/intro/>. Turkey is included because it has a complex agreement with the EU through the EU-NATO Partnership and, if it joined the EU, would become by far the largest armed force in the Union.

In the event, these rather awkward procedures proved unsatisfactory. First, the U.S. military proved far less enthusiastic than the politicians were about "lending" hard-won high-tech assets to ill-prepared and ill-trained Europeans with little experience in the field. Second, the proposals that EU forces be "double-hatted"—available either to a NATO/U.S. commander or to a hypothetical EU commander—caused disquiet within the officer corps. Third, the Berlin Plus proposals were, to some extent, predicated on a parallel reform of NATO's overall command structure, with a view to giving more command posts to European officers. The U.S. government's reluctance in 1997 to confer on a European officer the command of NATO's southern HQ (AFSouth) in Naples effectively sank that agreement.[15] It also became clear to most actors that the WEU was too inconsequential a body to assume responsibility for political oversight of EU military missions. Thus, the challenge of improving military capacity in Europe remained essentially unaddressed throughout the 1990s. The project of generating a European security and defense identity from inside NATO proved to be a false start.

From Identity to Policy: ESDI to ESDP

The decision taken in 1998 by incoming UK Prime Minister Tony Blair, to move resolutely towards improved European capacity, broke the logjam that ESDI had been unable to shift. At a historic meeting with President Jacques Chirac in the French town of Saint-Malo, Blair moved the European defense project to a new level. The Saint-Malo Declaration of December 4, 1998, represented a triple crossing of the Rubicon which has had major consequences for European military capacity.[16] First, it conferred directly on the EU the political decision-making capacity for crisis-management missions that the WEU had manifestly been ill-equipped to assume.[17] Second, it insisted that "the Union must have the

---

15. Michael Brenner and Guillaume Parmentier, *Reconcilable Differences: U.S.-French Relations in the New Era* (Washington, D.C.: Brookings, 2002).

16. The Saint-Malo Declaration is accessible via the *ESDP Core Documents* series published by the EU's Institute for Security Studies: <www.iss-eu.org/chaillot/chai47e.pdf>, pp. 8–9.

17. For an analysis of the EU's new security and defense institutions, see Howorth and Keeler, *Defending Europe*.

capacity for autonomous action, backed up by credible military forces, the means to decide to use them, and a readiness to do so, in order to respond to international crises." The quest for autonomous EU military capacity has proceeded ever since. Third, the Declaration posited a new relationship between the EU and NATO, contributing to the "vitality of a modernized Atlantic Alliance," the precise definition of which has preoccupied planners to this day. There is little doubt that Blair's gamble was primarily motivated by a sense that, unless the European members of NATO made a concerted effort to improve their military capacity, the alliance itself would begin to unravel.[18] The shift from a relatively fruitless quest for a European military identity towards the implementation of a European security and defense policy (ESDP) was a major leap forward.[19] It was not insignificant that the initiative came from the only two EU countries with power-projection capacity. The other European countries were summoned to follow the Franco-British lead.

The British Ministry of Defence took a major role in driving forward the debate on European military transformation. The decisions taken at the EU Council in Helsinki in December 1999, leading to the establishment of a "Helsinki Headline Goal" (HHG), were inspired by a series of papers drafted in Whitehall, as were most subsequent ESDP initiatives.[20] The HHG was conceived as a rough "Force Catalogue" from which would be drawn appropriate resources for a range of hypothetical European missions, including the three main Petersberg tasks. The main elements of the Force Catalogue were to be 60,000 troops, 100 ships, and 400 aircraft, deployable within sixty days and sustainable for one year. The emphasis, however, remained focused on quantities. In a series of "Capabilities Commitment Conferences" in November 2000,

---

18. The author was informed by a senior UK Foreign Office official, in spring 2000, that the UK "would never have touched Saint-Malo with a barge-pole" had London not been convinced that this was the price of keeping the alliance in business.

19. The acronym ESDP was coined by the European Council in June 1999 to distinguish this relatively ambitious—and autonomous—EU project from the NATO-dependent mechanisms of ESDI.

20. For the Helsinki Headline Goal, see *ESDP Core Documents* series published by the EU's Institute for Security Studies: <www.iss-eu.org/chaillot/chai47e.pdf>, pp. 82–91.

November 2001, May 2003, and November 2004, this pool of resources was refined and gradually brought into shape. Following the second such conference in November 2001, EU defense officials and military planners in the Headline Goal Task Force sought to ensure at least minimal compliance with the stated objective of operationality by December 2003.

However, there were several major problems with the Helsinki Headline Goal. The first problem was the way forces were to be built up: as voluntary, bottom-up contributions. These might secure the raw numbers, but they could not guarantee the delivery, still less the mobilization, of a coherent fighting force. Instead, the key concept had to be usability. In 2005, there were still almost 1.7 million troops in uniform in Europe, but only about 10 percent were adequately trained even for serious peacekeeping operations, let alone for peacemaking, still less for warfighting. Of those 170,000, probably at most 50,000 could carry out the type of military operation needed in circumstances such as those in Iraq since 2003. Rotation requirements drop the number still more, leaving just 15,000 to 20,000 troops genuinely usable at any given time in serious military missions.[21] Yet simply increasing quantities was soon perceived as not only insufficient but inappropriate; what was required was far greater quality.

The second problem with the HHG had to do with the procurement of a new generation of strategic systems. If the EU were to engage seriously in potentially distant crisis-management operations, it needed the tools of modern force projection. The Union had identified the main areas of strategic deficiency.[22] But in order to generate an effective EU capacity in the expensive, technology-intensive areas of unmanned aerial

---

21. The Venusberg Group, *A European Defence Strategy* (Gütersloh: Bertelsmann Foundation, 2004), <www.cap.uni-muenchen.de/download/2004/2004_Venusberg_Report.pdf>.

22. The ten areas of deficiency identified at a May 2003 meeting of the EU foreign ministers in Brussels were: air-to-air refueling; combat search and rescue; headquarters; nuclear, biological, and chemical defenses; special operations forces; theater ballistic missile defense; strategic air mobility; space; unmanned aerial vehicle, surveillance, and target acquisition (UAV/STA) units; and interoperability. Antonio Missiroli, ed., "From Copenhagen to Brussels," *European Defence: Core Documents 4* (Paris: EU-ISS, 2003), p. 94. accessed at: <www.iss-eu.org/chaillot/chai67e.pdf>.

vehicles, strategic transport, and air-to-air refueling, it was not enough to rely on voluntary efforts, or even to appoint a lead nation to chair a working group. There had to be collective political agreement to drive the process forward towards agreed targets. That implied top-down leadership, pooling, and specialization. Such processes touched on sensitive issues of national sovereignty.

The third—and potentially biggest—problem with the HHG process was the absence of clear debate about the nature of the military operations the EU might aim to mount. The original thinking behind the Helsinki Headline Goal derived from experiences in Kosovo. What the EU had in mind—especially in the context of the Saint-Malo Declaration's reference to autonomous forces—was the ability to carry out a Kosovo-type operation with minimal reliance on U.S. inputs. This could be done in two ways. A Kosovo operation could have been mounted in 1999 with the EU's existing military assets, but unlike the U.S.-led operation, which depended largely on air power, it would have involved substantial numbers of ground troops and resulted in many casualties. Alternately, the EU could aim to develop a U.S.-style capacity to fight high-level network-centric warfare.[23] This would require even greater defense spending and a more significant human resources challenge. Would the price be politically acceptable? If not, would something less than a fully integrated system—what has been called a "network-enabled" capacity—be affordable? A European Network Enabling Capability (ENEC) would enable crucial functional linkages among European forces, if not a single advanced network. Consequently, the ENEC would need to be developed in parallel with a specifically European interoperability concept to ensure European interoperability throughout all operations likely to be generated by the European Security Strategy.[24] How to make such a system work remains elusive.[25] To confuse capabilities planning even further, the EU decided in 2004 that it would engage in a more extensive range of missions. Article III-309 of the EU's

---

23. See John Arquilla and David Ronfeldt, *Networks and Netwars: The Future of Terror, Crime, and Militancy* (Santa Monica, Calif.: RAND, 2001).
24. Venusberg Group, *A European Defence Strategy*, p. 12.
25. It should be noted that, in the 2003 war in Iraq, the United States and the UK fought in different geographic zones partly because their battlefield communications technologies could not be properly networked.

proposed Constitutional Treaty extended the Petersberg tasks to include *"joint disarmament operations,* humanitarian and rescue tasks, *military advice and assistance tasks, conflict prevention and* peacekeeping tasks, [and] tasks of combat forces undertaken for crisis management, including peacemaking *and post-conflict stabilization."*[26] The emphasis was firmly on those missions with both a military and a political component. The 2004 Constitutional Treaty also added the need to "contribute to the fight against terrorism." Yet that fight would require very different instruments from those needed to drive the Serbian army out of Kosovo.[27] How could Europe afford both when at the time it seemed unable to afford either? These internal contradictions at the heart of the HHG process required urgent attention.

The third EU Capabilities Conference, held in Brussels in May 2003, registered both progress and caution. On the one hand, it noted that the first phase of the European Capability Action Plan (ECAP), launched in 2001 to identify shortcomings in the HHG, had been successfully concluded, with all member states participating and nineteen panels activated to address the majority of the shortfalls.[28] On the other hand, it recognized that, "at the upper end of the spectrum of scale and intensity," significant deficiencies still existed. The conference adopted ten priority areas in which improvements needed to be ensured, either through additional contributions, or through member states' existing procurement programs.[29] The ECAP process began to shift, in summer 2003, away from sheer quantities towards more qualitative approaches and criteria. Project groups were established to focus on solutions such as leasing, multi-nationalization, and role specialization. The EU moved

---

26. Italics indicate new items added to the original (1992) Petersberg tasks. The EU's Constitutional Treaty, intended to streamline the institutional and juridical procedures of the Union, was ratified by a dozen member states in 2005 before being vetoed in referendums held in France and the Netherlands in the summer of 2005.
27. Rob de Wijk, "The Limits of Military Power," *Washington Quarterly*, Winter 2002.
28. See report of EU General Affairs and External Relations Council, Meeting of Defence Ministers, Brussels, November 19, 2002, accessible at: <www.iss-eu.org/chaillot/chai57e.pdf>, pp. 147–155.
29. The priority areas were those identified as deficiencies in the list specified at the May 2003 Brussels meeting of EU foreign ministers.

towards the recognition of "coordination responsibility" for key procurement projects: Germany took the lead on strategic airlift; Spain on air-to-air refueling; the UK on headquarters; and the Netherlands on PGMs (precision guided munitions) for delivery by EU F-16s.

From HHG to Headline Goal 2010: A Qualitative Breakthrough?

The most urgent need was soon recognized to be that of assembling a well trained, deployable, and sustainable force to meet the challenging missions of the revised Petersberg tasks. This process was facilitated by a series of informal meetings of an EU Council of Defense Ministers. In February 2002, it had been agreed that defense ministers would be authorized to meet under the aegis of the General Affairs Council (the monthly meeting of the EU foreign ministers) to discuss "certain agenda items, limited to ... military capabilities." The very fact that member states recognized the desirability of such top-down meetings constituted a major step forward. Defense ministers had previously been kept strictly subordinate to foreign ministers. Now, they were gradually becoming significant shapers of security policy. They were instrumental in helping move the debate on capacity away from the raw numbers of the HHG and towards a clear set of qualitative criteria. In addition, after the start of the Iraq War in 2003, the EU devised its first ever "Security Strategy" document, which identified the broad outlines of its military objectives.[30]

In 2004, the EU entered a new and qualitatively different stage in the process of strengthening military capabilities, with the announcement of the new Headline Goal 2010,[31] the presentation of the "battle-groups" concept, the establishment of the European Defence Agency (EDA), and the launch of the Civil-Military Planning Cell (CMPC). Defense Ministers drove forward the drafting of an "ECAP Road Map" aimed at monitoring progress in all areas of capabilities.

At the European Council meeting on June 17, 2004, Headline Goal 2010 (HG 2010) was adopted. Building on the Helsinki Headline Goal,

---

30. European Council, *A Secure Europe in a Better World*, Brussels, December 12, 2003, accessed at <ue.eu.int/uedocs/cmsUpload/78367.pdf>, frequently referred to as the 2003 Solana Strategy Paper.
31. The "Headline Goal 2010" paper of 2004 outlines European military planning until 2010; <ue.eu.int/uedocs/cmsUpload/2010%20Headline%20Goal.pdf>.

HG 2010 commits the Union "to be able by 2010 to respond to a crisis with rapid and decisive action applying a fully coherent approach to the whole spectrum of crisis management operations covered by the Treaty on the European Union." Interoperability, deployability, and sustainability are at the heart of the project. The member states identified a list of specific milestones within the 2010 horizon, including the establishment of both the European Defense Agency and the Civil-Military Planning Cell by the end of 2004; the implementation of an EU strategic lift command by 2005; the ability by 2007 to deploy force packages at high readiness broadly based on EU battle-groups; the availability of an EU aircraft carrier and associated air wing and naval escort by 2008; and "appropriate compatibility and network linkage of all communications equipment and assets" by 2010.

HG 2010, by focusing on small, rapidly deployable units capable of high-intensity warfare, successfully shifted the objective from quantity to quality. It also resolved, at least partially, the contradiction between a Kosovo-style capability and the requirements of the "war on terrorism." The newly created battle-groups, of which up to fifteen are projected for 2007, can be used for both types of operation. Battle-groups (BG) are units of 1,500 troops prepared for combat in jungle, desert, or mountain conditions, deployable within fifteen days and sustainable in the field for up to thirty days. They are defined as "the minimum militar[ily] effective, credible, rapidly deployable, coherent force package capable of stand-alone operations or for the initial phase of larger operations." The battle-group is based on a combined-arms battalion-size force and reinforced with combat support (CS) and combat service support (CSS) elements. It is associated with a force headquarters and with designated operational and strategic enablers such as strategic lift and logistics.[32] At a meeting of the Council of Defense Ministers on November 21, 2004, it was announced that thirteen battle-groups would be established, all to be operational by 2007 or sooner (a number later expanded to fifteen). (See Table 2.2.)

---

32. *European Defence: Core Documents 2004*, Chaillot Paper No. 75 (Paris: EU-ISS, 2004), p. 296, accessed at : <www.iss-eu.org/chaillot/chai75e.pdf>.

Table 2.2. EU Nation-State Participation in Fifteen New Battle-groups

Contributing nations	Target date for formation
France	2005
UK	2005
Italy	2005
Spain	2006
France, Germany, Belgium, Luxembourg, Spain	2006
France, Belgium	2006
Italy, Spain, Greece, Portugal	2006
Germany, Netherlands, Finland	2007
Germany, Czech Republic, Austria	2007
Italy, Hungary, Slovenia	2007
Poland, Germany, Slovakia, Latvia, Lithuania	2007
Sweden, Estonia, Finland, Norway[a]	2007
UK, Netherlands	2007
Greece, Bulgaria, Romania, Cyprus	2007
Czech Republic, Slovakia	2007

Note: a. Norway, although not a member of the EU, "has been actively seeking a way to be associated with the process of CFSP/ESDP policy formulation (and is today associated to the ESDP through NATO and the Berlin Plus arrangements). Norway participates in EU joint actions such as the EU police mission in Bosnia. In addition, Norway has pledged personnel and equipment to the ESDP Rapid Reaction Force." <europa.eu.int/comm/external_relations/norway/intro/>.

Member states can also offer niche capabilities; it has been agreed that Lithuania will provide a water purification unit; Greece, the Athens Sealift Coordination Centre; and France, the structure of a headquarters for a multi-national and deployable force. By 2007, the EU should have the capacity to undertake two concurrent operations, even almost simultaneously if necessary.

A European Defence Agency (EDA) subject to the authority of the European Council was called for in the draft Constitutional Treaty of August 2004. Two main reasons lay behind the change. The first was the relative failure of previous attempts to coordinate procurement and armaments cooperation, which had hitherto taken place outside the EU framework. The second reason was the accelerating reality of ESDP and the associated need to support capabilities with armaments production. The urgency of these drivers was reflected in the fact that, in June 2003, the EU agreed not to await ratification of the proposed Constitutional Treaty but to launch the EDA immediately.

The objectives of the EDA, as stated in the Constitutional Treaty, were to:

contribute to identifying the Member States' military capability objectives and evaluating observance of the capability commitments given by the Member States; promote harmonisation of operational needs and adoption of effective, compatible procurement methods; propose multilateral projects to fulfil the objectives in terms of military capabilities, ensure coordination of the programmes implemented by the Member States and management of specific cooperation programmes; support defence technology research, and coordinate and plan joint research activities and the study of technical solutions meeting future operational needs; contribute to identifying and, if necessary, implementing any useful measure for strengthening the industrial and technological base of the defence sector and for improving the effectiveness of military expenditure.[33]

The EDA is guided by a Steering Board meeting at the level of Defense Ministers, nominally headed by the Union Minister for Foreign Affairs (when that post is eventually created), and managed by a Chief Executive.[34] It offers the first real opportunity for the EU to bring its defense planning, military capability objectives, and armaments coordination in line with the urgent tasks it faces on the ground. The EU governments are thus poised to move towards more rational armaments and defense planning. The dynamics of ESDP suggest that they will progressively situate their national plans within a European framework. This will be the first step on a potentially very long road.

Another breakthrough came in 2003 in the field of operational planning. This issue had for several years pitted the UK against France. Paris had always been keen to develop autonomous EU operational planning capabilities, but London had resisted, arguing that this was an expen-

---

33. Quoted from EU *Draft Constitutional Treaty*, Article III-311. See also Burkard Schmitt, "Progress towards the European Defence Agency," EU-ISS, *Analyses*, Winter 2004.

34. After a fierce turf battle between France and the UK, Nick Witney, the former head of the UK MOD's International Security Policy Division, was named as the first Chief Executive.

sive duplication of an existing NATO capability. The UK insisted that, in the event of an "EU-only" operation (that is, without reference to NATO and without the support of NATO planning via Berlin Plus), such missions should have recourse to the national operational planning facilities of the UK at Northwood, of France at Creil and, to a lesser extent, those of Germany, Italy, and Greece. However, at a contentious defense summit among the heads of state of France, Germany, Belgium, and Luxembourg on April 29, 2003, at the height of the Iraq crisis, a decision was made to forge ahead and create an "EU" operational planning cell at a Belgian army base in Tervuren, a suburb of Brussels. This provoked outraged responses from Washington and London and briefly threatened the entire ESDP project.[35] However, later that summer, Tony Blair sought to mend fences with his European partners, and a compromise was reached involving three distinct operational planning facilities. For EU operations under Berlin Plus, a dedicated EU unit has been attached to NATO at SHAPE Headquarters in Mons, Belgium. For most "EU-only" operations, including most battle-group missions, an appropriate national headquarters will be adapted to planning for multi-national operations. For certain EU-only operations, particularly those involving combined civil and military dimensions, a dedicated and autonomous EU civil-military planning cell (CMPC) is being developed at ESDP headquarters in Brussels. This facility had grown by 2005 to around one hundred and twenty EU military personnel and began its substantive work; it should have the capacity to generate an operations center by June 2006.[36]

By the end of 2004, the EU was beginning to look like an increasingly credible potential military actor. In November 2004, the EU published its second Capability Improvement Chart, listing no fewer than sixty-four "capabilities" and their progress toward meeting qualitative readiness targets (or, in some cases, their shortcomings).[37] Significantly, some major improvements were found in areas with heavy "legacy" inputs,

---

35. IISS, "EU Operational Planning: The Politics of Defence," *Strategic Comments*, Vol. 9, No. 10 (December 2003).
36. European Council, Brussels, June 16–17, 2005, Presidency Conclusions, accessed at: <ue.eu.int/ueDocs/cms_Data/docs/pressData/fr/ec/85324.pdf>.
37. EU, Capability Improvement Chart, <ue.eu.int/uedocs/cmsUpload/DEF percent20capabilities percent20chart percent20II.pdf>.

including composite army aviation battalions and mechanized infantry battalions. Some qualitatively significant areas, such as headquarters, strategic transport, nuclear, biological, and chemical (NBC), and medical units, were recording better progress than expected. But other areas requiring substantial investment, such as intelligence, surveillance, target acquisition, and reconnaissance (ISTAR), space assets, suppression of enemy air defenses (SEAD), and PGMs, still faced serious shortfalls or needed longer time-lines for delivery.[38] The Council of Defense Ministers introduced a "Global Approach on Deployability" in 2003 to accelerate coordination of airlift and sealift centers with a view to developing an EU Movement Coordination Cell (EUMCC). Success at reaching the European Capability Action Plan (ECAP) targets set in 2001 remained dependent on meaningful political commitments by member states to invest in shortfall areas and to continue the quest for multi-national solutions. The EDA was intended to act both as a catalyst and as a benchmark.

Evaluating the First EU Military Missions

The process of defining priority areas for quality and capacity improvements was assisted by the lessons drawn from the first experiences of the EU in armed combat. On March 31, 2003, the EU launched its first-ever military operation, taking over a peacekeeping mission in the Former Yugoslav Republic of Macedonia (FYROM) from a NATO force. Operation Concordia used NATO planning under the "Berlin Plus" procedures. It deployed 357 troops, from all EU states except Ireland and Denmark and from fourteen additional nations, drawing an

---

38. Dedicated military satellite communications systems are possessed only by Italy (Sicral), France (Syracuse III), and the UK (Skynet-4). The UK and French systems are currently being upgraded. Problems of interoperability suggest an urgent need to rationalize their technical specifications for any EU mission. As for ISTAR, although the SOSTAR-X system (France, Germany, Italy, Netherlands and Spain) and the UK's ASTOR/RISTA system are under development, few believe the EU could achieve a true European battlefield surveillance capacity before the end of the decade. In unmanned aerial vehicles (UAVs), the EU is making progress but will remain for some years dependent on the United States. In space-based imagery intelligence, France's Helios system could be upgraded, but no firm Europe-wide plans are yet available.

average of just thirteen troops from each participating state. In a small and mountainous country, it succeeded in keeping the peace between bands of lightly-armed irregulars and the Macedonian "army," which boasts a defense budget less than half that of Luxembourg. This was an operation high in political symbolism and extremely modest in terms of military footprint. Concordia's primary value was that it allowed the EU to test its recently agreed procedures covering every aspect of mounting a military operation, albeit a modest one, including command and control, use-of-force policy, logistics, financing, and legal arrangements and memoranda of understanding with host nations.[39]

Then, from June to September 2003, the EU launched its first-ever autonomous operation outside of the NATO framework. Operation Artemis in the Democratic Republic of Congo offered even richer lessons about EU capabilities.[40] The mission involved rapid force projection to a distance of 6,500 kilometers into unknown and hostile terrain. The initial assessment suggests that it was a success. France was the "framework nation," supplying 1,785 of the 2,200 troops deployed. Sixteen other "troop contributing nations" were involved, offering strategic airlift (Germany, Greece, the United Kingdom, Brazil, and Canada), engineers (UK), helicopters (South Africa), and special forces (Sweden). Operational planning was conducted from the French Centre de Planification et de Conduite des Opérations (CPCO) at Creil, to which were seconded officers from thirteen other countries, thus demonstrating the potential for multi-nationalization of a national HQ. The operation exemplified rapid deployment (just seven days after UN Security Council Resolution 1484 on May 30, 2003), a single command structure, appropriately trained forces, clear rules of engagement, effective incorporation of multi-national elements, excellent inter-service cooperation, and adequate communications. NATO procedures were used throughout.

---

39. General Graham Messervy-Whiting, "The Politico-Military Structure in Brussels: Capabilities and Limits," discussion paper for the Geneva Centre for Security Policy, "Workshop on the EU and Peace Operations," September 22–23, 2003.

40. Paul Cornish, "Artemis and Coral: British Perspectives on European Union Crisis Management Operations in the Democratic Republic of Congo," unpublished report, Kings College, London, 2004.

Artemis demonstrated that the EU can undertake a peacekeeping operation on a significant scale, even at some distance from Europe.

The transfer from NATO to the EU of responsibility for the Stabilization Force (SFOR) in Bosnia-Herzegovina, in December 2004 (Operation Althea), represented an even greater test of the EU's military muscle. The initial NATO force deployed in Bosnia-Herzegovina (IFOR, December 1995) involved some 60,000 troops. It was scaled down repeatedly, to a total of 12,000 in the follow-up SFOR in January 2003. Projections for 2004 foresaw a further reduction to about 7,000 troops organized in ten battle-groups of around 750 soldiers each. Over 80 percent of the troops in NATO's SFOR were already from EU member states. Operation Althea was the EU's most ambitious military mission to date. In addition to stabilizing Bosnia-Herzegovina, Althea allowed the EU to experiment with large-scale helicopter maneuvers, combating drug-running, organizing the voluntary surrender of small arms, and undertaking liaison and observation team (LOT) activities, peace support training schemes, and psychological operations.[41] The operation exemplified the increasing demands on European soldiers for a broad range of skills and training.

Implications of EU Military Transformation for Personnel Management

The new missions, activities, and equipment that characterize the EU's military forces fifteen years after the end of the Cold War have significant consequences for numbers, recruitment, entry-level qualifications, and further training and retention of personnel across the EU. The major military nations of Europe, in the presentation of their defense reform programs, have firmly emphasized the importance and centrality of personnel management.[42] However, in the mass of policy-oriented analysis of defense transformation in Europe, there is little mention of personnel

---

41. See the Eufor website at: <www.euforbih.org/>.
42. See, for example, UK MOD, "The Strategic Defence Review," Chapter 6, "A Policy for People," accessed at: <www.mod.uk/issues/sdr/people_policy.htm>. France's "Loi de Programmation Militaire 2003–2008" similarly devotes a major section to personnel and training issues: <www.assemblee-nationale.fr/12/ta/ta0043.asp>.

or human resource issues.[43] While planners insist that personnel management is crucial, analysts continue to ignore it.

Where all-volunteer forces have been introduced, as in Spain, the Netherlands, France, and Belgium, the overall sizes of military forces have been reduced by around 50 percent. Even where conscription has been retained, the number of conscripts has dropped considerably, as in Germany, Sweden, and Poland (as shown in Table 2.1). Despite the decreases, however, recruitment of volunteers has become, for most European countries, a serious challenge. With the number of military-age citizens plunging, immigration increasingly controlled, social benefits acting as a safety-net which is not available in a country like the United States, and alternative skills-training schemes available in most countries, recruitment of between 2.5 percent and 3.0 percent of the age cohort needed to meet the targets is proving a major headache.[44] In addition, becoming a soldier is not widely perceived as a "normal" career move in the Europe of the present day. While, to date, numerical targets are just being met in most countries, this is in large part a result of aggressive armed-forces recruitment campaigns that stress the glamour, camaraderie, and travel of service life as well as the training and apprenticeship opportunities.[45]

Moreover, the numbers appear to come at the expense of quality. While most professional armed forces now stress their quest for recruits who have firm basic qualifications in mathematics and science—with engineering a highly prized qualification for officer recruits—there is little evidence that such standards for entry constitute an effective filter. Even the British and the French militaries, arguably the two most ag-

---

43. Typical is an analysis, in France's leading "glossy" magazine of defense, of the "technological revolution" that has taken place in the French army over the past ten years, featuring information systems, new-generation platforms, digitization, and other advances; "Equipements terrestres: pour une nouvelle ambition de la France en Europe," *Défense*, Vol. 99 (May–June 2002), p. 41. There is no mention of the personnel implications.
44. Williams, "From Conscripts to Volunteers"; and Chapter 3 in this volume by Rickard Sandell.
45. See, for example, the recruitment campaign put out by the French army: <www.defense.gouv.fr/sites/terre/votre_espace/recrutement_et_formation/le_recrutement_en_2004/>; or that organized by the British Ministry of Defence at: <www.army.mod.uk/careers/army_life/what_is_a_soldier.html>.

gressively "professional" armed forces in Europe, recognize that the basic qualification for joining the army is, to all intents and purposes, the fact of having reached the age of 17 or 18.[46] The emphasis everywhere is on on-the-job training: the army assesses the raw recruit's potential and orients him or her in a particular direction.

Recruitment to officer level, on the other hand, shows signs of increasingly rigorous entry qualifications in a number of countries. At the Ecole Militaire de Saint-Cyr, France's elite training school for army officers, increasing numbers of candidates have the minimum of two years or more of higher education after the baccalauréat (high school leaving certificate); the number of applicants with a university degree is also on the rise.[47] Perhaps more revealing, while ten years ago almost every officer recruit at Saint-Cyr came from a family with professional service experience, nowadays this proportion has been reduced by almost half. Similar patterns of recruitment are to be found at the UK's Sandhurst.[48] Precise data on shifts in the qualifications for either foot-soldiers or future generals are difficult to come by with any accuracy, but the signs are that the quality of officer recruits is gradually nudging upwards.

Standardization and the quest for interoperability across the continent is a growing feature of military training. Most future EU missions are likely to be multi-national, as part of a UN, NATO, or EU force. Significant standardization of equipment will have to await the effects of the European Defense Agency and the rationalization of procurement.[49] Meanwhile, language skills are highly prized, even as English is increasingly becoming the *de facto* language for multi-national force communication.

---

46. France will accept the lowest academic qualification (BEP/CAP), usually acquired by all school-leavers. The UK makes it clear that, for many jobs in the army, "a good basic standard of education" is all that is required. See, for example, <www.a.mod.uk/careers/combat/jd_aviation_groundcrew_spec.html>.
47. Author's interview with professor from Saint-Cyr, April 16, 2005. This may have something to do with the lack of attractive alternative careers for those with only two years of higher education.
48. Author's interview with Sandhurst professor, March 16, 2005.
49. It is through NATO's Partnership for Peace programs, somewhat ironically, that the majority of the EU member states are currently improving their capacity for interoperability. These programs affect formerly neutral countries such as Austria and Sweden as well as new-accession countries such as Hungary and Romania.

Table 2.3. European Forces and the Conflict Intensity Scale: U.S., EU-15, and EU + 10 Readiness for Conflict

Level of intensity	Type of operation	Countries	Required capabilities
0		Luxembourg, Malta	
1	Petersberg tasks with low intensity	Ireland, Cyprus, Estonia, Latvia, Lithuania	General purpose ground forces
2		Finland, Hungary, Slovenia, Slovakia	
3			
4	Petersberg tasks with medium intensity	Czech Republic, Poland	NBC protection, specialized forces; CIMIC (Civil-Military Coordination); Medevac
5		Austria, Belgium, Denmark, Greece, Portugal, Sweden	
6		Germany, Italy, Netherlands, Spain	
7	Advanced expeditionary warfare	France	Special forces; sea control; air support; air-to-air refueling; strategic lift; PGM; TBMD
8		UK	
9	Full scale warfare		C4ISTAR (NCW [network-centric warfare]); satellite intelligence; sensor-to-shooter network; nuclear deterrence
10		United States	

Adapted from The Venusberg Group, *A European Defence Strategy* (Gütersloh: Bertelsmann Foundation, 2004), <www.cap.uni-muenchen.de/download/2004/2004_Venusberg_Report.pdf>, Appendix 3, "The Conflict Intensity Scale," p. 68.

(Operation Artemis, which was overwhelmingly French in composition and command, was officially conducted in English.) France and a number of other countries have been pressing the EU to inaugurate a joint EU military training academy, but the resistance of other countries (notably the UK) has to date prevented this. In 2002, the first of a series of international conferences for cadets from the military academies of all EU member states (as well as for a number of observers from the U.S. military academy at West Point) was organized at Saint-Cyr; a second such conference was held in 2003 at the Belgian Royal Military Academy.

Notwithstanding these developments, the fact remains that Europe's twenty-five separate militaries are trained to very different levels of combat intensity (as shown in Table 2.3). Whereas most U.S. troops are trained to be able to cope with the requirements of full-scale warfare involving elements of C4ISTAR, satellite intelligence, sensor-to-shooter networks, and nuclear deterrence (levels 9 and 10, on the 1-to-10 scale of Table 2.3), only the UK and, to some extent, France, have forces trained to anything near this level (levels 7 and 8, advanced expeditionary warfare, involving special forces, sea control, air support, air-to-air refueling, strategic lift, precision guided munitions, and theater ballistic missile defense [TBMDs]). As for the rest, force training does not go beyond levels 4–6, giving them a capability for medium-level Petersberg peace-support tasks. A sizeable number of countries—Finland, Hungary, Ireland, Cyprus, Estonia, Latvia, Lithuania, Slovakia, and Slovenia—are unable to deal with more than the lowest-level Petersberg missions, at intensity no more than levels 1–3; Luxembourg and Malta may not be even that capable.

Conclusions

European military capacity, after almost a decade of stagnation from 1989 to 1999, has come a long way in a few short years. Progress in procurement, planning, rationalization, force transformation, and general "usability" has been impressive since the turn of the millennium. But the EU still has a long way to go before it can overcome all its shortcomings and emerge as a fully credible coordinated military actor able to carry out the full range of Petersberg tasks. The EU does not aspire to become a military power on a par with the United States, nor does it plan in terms of classical territorial defense. The crisis-management tasks it aims to carry out represent a new, professional "security firefighting" service adapted to the modern world. But the unprecedented nature of its objectives also poses one of its most difficult dilemmas: in order to embark on the type of low-casualty operations implicit in network-centric warfare, the EU would need to invest far more than is currently available in new research and development and in personnel management. That may be justifiable in the United States because the U.S. military, in addition to policing the world, is also configured to guarantee the defense of the United States. However, the more limited ambitions of ESDP rule out such spending levels in Europe. The EU is likely, therefore, to limit its interoperability aspirations to the challenges of "network-enabled" capabilities.

At the level of recruitment and training, the EU faces an enormous task of matching ends and means on the field of operations. A start has been made and progress is visible, but the challenge has only just been taken up. Above all, the EU needs to address its wasteful spending patterns. In 2004, the twenty-five EU nations spent almost US$230 billion on defense—approximately half as much as the U.S. defense budget for that year ($467 billion, as shown in Table 2.4), but almost four times the defense budget of the second biggest military spender on earth—China, at $62.5 billion—and more than that of the six next biggest spenders put together (China, Russia, Japan, Saudi Arabia, India, and South Korea, which together total $226.5 billion). (See Table 2.5.) The European Union collectively gets very little bang for this enormous amount of money. Out of that $230 billion, the EU members still attempt to fund twenty-five armies, twenty-one air forces, and eighteen navies, for no reason that is any longer obvious or clear. For as long as this duplication exists, return on investment will be sub-optimal. Just three countries in the EU—France, the UK, and Germany—together account for 61 percent of the combined EU-25 expenditure. Just four—adding Italy—account for almost 75 percent of it, or about $172 billion. The other twenty-one EU states spend, on average, under $3 billion each, less than the defense budget of Vietnam. Alone, most EU member states would be in no position even to defend their own territories.

A major rationalization of the EU's defense spending is overdue. The duplication of infrastructure and support services for these separate armed forces amounts to a huge waste of resources. It is not necessarily greater spending that is required, as is so often asserted. Wiser spending would certainly help. But only once the EU has clearly established what it hopes to achieve, with what force levels and with what state of equipment, can it have any clear idea about how much money is needed. Until then, its force transformation programs will remain incomplete.

Table 2.4. EU Member States' Defense Expenditure (2004), with Comparison to the United States

	Total US$ million	US$ per capita spending (ranking)	Percent of GDP (ranking)	Active-duty Troops (000s)
France	51,698	855 (1)	2.5 (2)	254.0
UK	49,618	823 (2)	2.3 (3)	205.0
Germany	37,790	458 (10)	1.4 (14=)	284.0
Italy	30,537	525 (7=)	1.8 (5=)	191.0
Spain	12,588	312 (12)	1.2 (20=)	147.0
Netherlands	9,607	588 (5)	1.6 (8=)	53.0
Greece	5,866	550 (6)	2.8 (1)	163.0
Sweden	5,307	590 (4)	1.5 (11=)	27.0
Poland	4,605	119 (22)	1.9 (4)	141.0
Belgium	4,361	421 (11)	1.2 (20=)	36.0
Denmark	3,558	657 (3)	1.4 (14=)	21.0
Portugal	2,830	268 (15)	1.6 (8=)	44.0
Finland	2,483	476 (9)	1.3 (18=)	28.0
Austria	2,222	271 (14)	0.8 (23=)	39.0
Czech Republic	1,976	192 (18)	1.8 (5=)	22.0
Hungary	1,530	152 (19)	1.5 (11=)	32.0
Ireland	907	228 (17)	0.5 (25)	10.0
Slovakia	729	134 (20)	1.7 (7)	20.0
Slovenia	511	254 (16)	1.6 (8=)	6.0
Lithuania	311	86 (24)	1.4 (14=)	13.0
Cyprus	227	293 (13)	1.4 (14=)	10.0
Luxembourg	243	525 (7=)	0.8 (23=)	0.9
Latvia	179	77 (25)	1.3 (18=)	5.0
Estonia	172	128 (22)	1.5 (11=)	4.0
Malta	52	131 (21)	1.0 (22)	2.0
EU-15 Totals	219,615			1,502.6
CEE-10 Totals	10,292			255.0
EU-25 Totals	229,907			1,757.6
EU-15 Average	14,641	503	1.51	
CEE-10 Average	1,029	157	1.51	
EU-25 Average	9,196	364	1.51	
Norway	4,431	968	1.8	25
Turkey	10,115	146	3.3	514
United States	455,908	1,555	3.8	1,473

Source: IISS, *The Military Balance 2005–2006.* Where troop totals differ from Table 2.1, this is due to differences in how they are calculated by the sources (IISS, *Military Balance*, in both cases). **Bold** indicates members of NATO; *italics,* accession to the EU in 2004. CEE is Central and Eastern Europe. Norway, Turkey, and United States added for comparison. Norway would rank as the biggest defense spender per capita in Europe, Turkey as the largest army with the highest percentage of GDP devoted to defense spending.

Table 2.5. World Military Expenditure, 2004

Military Spending	Expenditure in US$ million	U.S.$ per capita	% of GDP (and trend ↓ since 2003)
1. United States	455,908	1,555	3.8 ↑
2. China	62,539	48	3.7 ↓
3. Russia	61,900	429	4.3 ↓
4. France	51,698	855	2.5 ↓
5. UK	49,618	823	2.3 ↓
6. Japan	45,151	354	1.0 —
7. Germany	37,790	458	1.4 ↓
8. Italy	30,537	525	1.8 ↓
9. Saudi Arabia	20,910	810	8.8 ↓
10. India	19,647	18	3.0 ↑
11. South Korea	16,398	339	2.4 ↓
12. Australia	14,310	718	2.3 —
13. Spain	12,588	312	1.2 —
14. Canada	11,418	351	1.1 —
15. Turkey	10,115	146	3.3 ↓
16. Israel	9,682	1,561	8.2 ↓
17. Netherlands	9,607	588	1.6 —
18. Brazil	9,232	50	1.5 ↓
19. Indonesia	7,553	31	2.9 ↓
20. Taiwan	7,519	330	2.74 ↓
NATO	702,684	819	2.8 —
NATO Europe	235,358	442	1.9 —
EU 25	229,907	364	1.5 ↓
Middle East and North Africa	59,645	189	5.7 ↓
Central and South Asia	29,299	19	2.8 ↑
East Asia + Australia	180,496	85	2.0 ↓
Caribbean, Central and South America	25,659	47	1.3 ↓
Sub-Saharan Africa	8,694	13	1.7 ↓

U.S. expenditure is equal to that of the next fifteen countries combined (China to Israel); it is equal to the rest of the entire world (minus NATO Europe), totaling $456 billion. EU 25 expenditure of $229.907 billion is equal to the total of China plus Russia plus Japan plus Saudi Arabia plus India plus South Korea (which together total $226.545 billion).

Source: IISS, *The Military Balance 2004–2005*, pp. 353–358.

Chapter 3

Coping with Demography in NATO Europe

Military Recruitment in Times of Population Decline

Rickard Sandell

Demographic developments in Europe have taken a drastic turn. In just fifteen years, between 1970 and 1985, the fertility rate fell from well above the replacement level (2.1 children per mother) to well below this level in all European NATO countries other than Poland and Turkey.[1] In 1970 the average fertility in NATO Europe was about 2.6; the current level is just 1.4, and there are no immediate signs of recovery. Changes of this magnitude have serious implications. Instead of the historical pattern, in which each new generation outnumbers previous generations, the pattern has reversed since the start of the 1980s: each new generation is smaller than the previous ones.

The purpose of this chapter is to show how Europe's changing demographic trends are likely to influence the European NATO countries' defense capacities in terms of manpower. The analysis is centered on the military recruitment capacities of many European NATO countries, and how this capacity could be seriously weakened as a result of the decline in the number of births in Europe in the late 1970s and early

The author would like to thank two anonymous reviewers and the editors for their comments on an earlier version of this chapter.

1.   Poland and Turkey experienced a significant drop in their fertility rates over the same period, and since 1990 Poland's rate has been below replacement, while Turkey's rate has dropped nearly to replacement level. Thus, the trend towards lower fertility rates is present in all NATO Europe countries. <www.realinstitutoelcano.org>.

1980s. However, the analysis also provides important information to countries that use both conscription and voluntary recruitment. It provides a glimpse into a possible future recruitment scenario, should countries using only conscription as a means of recruitment decide to abandon conscription partially or in full. Even if they do not convert, population processes are still likely to influence countries' capacity to draft adequately.

The chapter is structured as follows. The next part of this chapter briefly reviews the changing demographics of Europe. Next it shows the challenges posed by the decreasing number of births in Europe for fulfilling NATO's manpower needs. The last part of the chapter addresses some of the options available to increase the effectiveness of voluntary recruitment systems and offset a too-rapid decline in militaries' numerical strength as a result of the changing demographic reality.

Changing Demographic Reality

Despite a relatively long spell of below-replacement fertility rates, the full effect of the demographic changes has so far been barely noticeable in most European countries. For example, Europe's populations are still growing. However, this growth is only the result of a rise in the number of people of reproductive age due to past population growth before the onset of the demographic transition. Because the number of people of reproductive age is increasing, the total number of births still exceeds the total number of deaths, even though the average number of births per woman is extremely low.[2]

The changing demographic reality is not just about smaller and smaller birth cohorts. While fertility has dropped to record low levels, life expectancy has risen continuously to record high levels since the end of World War II. The fact that life expectancies increase at the same time that birth rates are falling to a level under the replacement level provides an additional explanation for why Europe's populations are still experiencing some, albeit weak, population growth.

---

2.   This demographic phenomenon is known as the population momentum effect. For a formal explanation, see Samuel H. Preston, Patrick Heuveline, and Michel Guillot, *Demography: Measuring and Modelling Population Processes* (Oxford, UK: Blackwell Publishers, 2001).

Immigration is also contributing to continued population growth in Europe. In fact, since the 1990s, about 80 percent of the European Union's population growth is due to immigration.[3] The importance of immigration for population growth is likely to increase further in the first half of this century. Thus, both increased life expectancy and immigration contribute to a significant delay of the population decline that will inevitably result from a long spell of fertility rates below the replacement level.[4]

A general population decline can be expected after 2010. However, the decline is likely to be modest, and it is not until after the year 2030 that we will see a general and fast decline across Europe. Although the trend is relatively homogenous, there are some intra-European differences. Some countries are already experiencing a slight natural population decline, notably East European countries. Northern European countries are projected to see their populations peak later than Southern European countries.

This means that the major demographic problem in the coming twenty-five years is less about population decline than about a major restructuring of Europe's populations, as they go from being predominantly young populations to predominantly old, with a much more pronounced multicultural element. [5]

Initially, falling birth rates translate into a substantial numerical decrease in certain population subgroups, such as children and adolescents. In other words, demographic changes start at the bottom of the population's age structure. As time passes, the changes slowly work their way up to older age groups. If the changes are persistent—that is,

---

3. See Rickard Sandell, "Europe's Population: The Latest Trends and Their Policy Implications," *ARI*, No. 32 (2003) <www.realinstitutoelcano.org>.

4. Wolfgang Lutz, Brian C. O'Neill, and Sergei Scerbov, "Europe's Population at a Turning Point," *Science*, Vol. 299 (March 28, 2003), pp. 1991–92.

5. Note that all demographic data in this chapter referring to 2003 and beyond are projections based on a set of assumptions about future fertility and mortality rates. Hence, they indicate only one of several possible futures. The further into the future we project, the larger the element of uncertainty in the projected trends. Demographers, like economists, are only partially successful in predicting the future; much can change before 2050. This means that the data must be interpreted with great caution. However, as for the population subject to military recruitment, for the coming 20–25 years the projections are reasonably accurate, since the people in this group have already been born.

if birth rates stabilize at low or very low levels, as they have in Europe—whole generations will decrease in size compared to past generations.

For example, in 1991, the falling birth rates in Spain only affected the size of age groups under age 14. By 2004, it affected the size of all age groups under age 25. If birth rates remain at current levels, by 2050 all age groups under age 75 are likely to be substantially smaller than their present size. In 2050, those aged 75 will form the largest age cohort in the Spanish population instead of one of the smallest, as in 1991.[6] The Spanish case is not unique, but reflects a general demographic trend across most of Europe.

Since, so far, it is primarily the younger age groups—those under 18—that have become smaller, the socio-economic consequences of the demographic changes to date have been relatively insignificant. Younger age groups have limited roles in society: they are economically dependent on their parents and in general they do not work, pay taxes, fight wars, or perform other important functions in our societies. One might say that they are on standby or in training for the future. However, once they grow up, they will enter the active population and take over from their parents as breadwinners, parents, politicians, doctors, soldiers, and so on.

Most European countries have now reached the point in their demographic transition at which their younger generations—those born after the onset of the demographic transition—are beginning to leave their child and adolescent years behind and slowly start replacing their parents as the main producers of private and public goods. In other words, the new demographic reality is now entering a more socially complex phase. Thus the issue of how population developments might affect society in the near future has become more urgent. The armed forces will be one of the first institutions to feel the impact as the new reality unfolds.

Demographic Challenges for Military Recruitment

Increasingly, European countries are abandoning the concept of conscription for that of a professional military that relies on voluntary recruitment among males or, more frequently, both males and females,

6. See Rickard Sandell, "Ageing Populations: An Opportunity for Public Policy Reform," Working Paper No. 20 (Real Instituto Elcano, 2003), <www.realinstitutoelcano.org>.

who are approximately 15–29 years of age. In other words, the 15–29 age group forms an important population niche for most countries' defense capacity. As this niche is central for the analysis I conduct in this chapter, I label this cohort the armed forces' "recruitment niche."[7]

Expansion or contraction of the recruitment niche will alter the conditions under which a government and its ministry of defense can make decisions concerning the future size of the armed forces. The demographic developments discussed above are already resulting in a drastic reduction in the number of people aged 15 to 29 in most European countries. The scope of the change is such that it is likely to influence European countries' defense capacity for decades to come. To illustrate the scale of the problem, we look first at the annual changes in the size of the recruitment niche, by contrasting the size of the niche over time and among countries (see Figure 3.1).

Since there are important differences in absolute size among the countries' recruitment niches, the scale on the y-axis is set to vary across countries.[8] Hence, to get a sense of the scale of the changes depicted in Figure 3.1, it is useful to take a closer look at developments in individual countries. Germany, Italy, and Spain are example of countries with steepest declines of size of their recruitment niches. Spain, for example, had a recruitment niche size of 10 million people in 1990. In 2004, the niche was down to around 8 million, and by 2050 it is projected to decline to less than 5 million. Italy shows a similar development, down from nearly 14 million in the 1990s to 7 million around 2040. In the same period, Germany's recruitment niche drops from almost 18 million to 11 million.

---

7. Defining the armed forces "recruitment niche" as those aged 15 to 29 may seem controversial. Many countries apply a higher or a lower upper limit. For example, Spain applies age 18 as the lower limit and 28 as the upper limit; the UK's limits are 16–30. My reason for defining the recruitment niche as those aged 15–29 is due to data limitations. The fact that the age boundaries do not match each country's national restrictions should not alter the general interpretation of the findings, since the resulting size of the recruitment niche using the 15–29 interval is likely to exceed the "real" size had I restricted the niche according to national rules. Thus, the simulations based on the recruitment niche in this chapter are likely to underestimate rather than overestimate the demographic influence on recruitment.

8. The data are based on projections prepared by the U.S. Census Bureau and made available in its International Data Base online: <www.census.gov/ipc/www/idbnew.html>.

Figure 3.1. Development of the Armed Forces Recruitment Niches 1990–2050

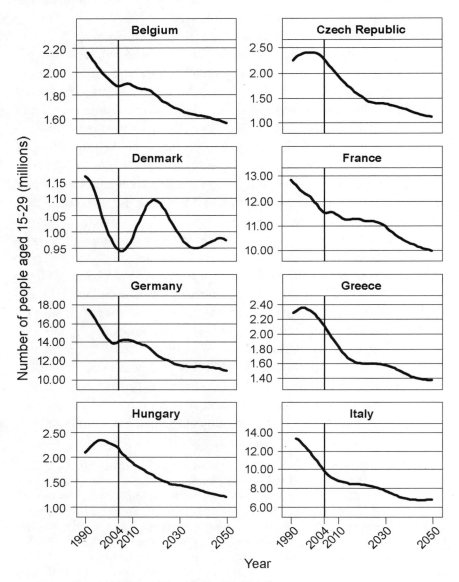

Source: U.S. Census Bureau's International Data Base

Figure 3.1 *(continued)*

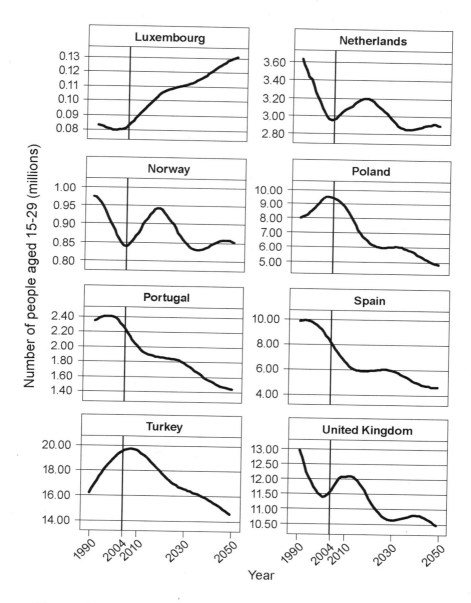

Denmark, France, the Netherlands, Norway, and the UK provide examples of countries that will see less dramatic relative declines in their recruitment niches. From a NATO perspective, it is important to notice that Turkey, too, will soon start to experience demographic developments similar to those already experienced by most other NATO member states, while the only European NATO member with a positive outlook in terms of future developments in the recruitment niche is tiny Luxembourg.

RECRUITMENT NICHE DEPENDENCY RATIO

The analysis of the previous section considers each country separately. It also examines the recruitment niche without controlling for changes in the rest of the population. This section explores important differences among countries, and assesses potential structural implications of the new demographic reality that may ultimately drive recruitment prospects and decisions about the future size of Europe's militaries.

The demographic changes faced by most NATO countries result primarily from a drop in fertility coupled with significant and continuing increases in life expectancy. Because of the nature of these two causes of demographic change, current demographic developments do not necessarily result in a decrease in absolute population. For example, in the period 1990–2050, the aggregate population decline in European NATO countries is just 3 percent. Thus, the demographic transition is and will be for some time not so much about a shrinking population as about a restructuring of Europe's population: from that of many younger people and few older people to one with few younger people and many older people.

To see what this means for military recruitment, here we expand on a concept used widely by demographers, to explore what the new demographic realities will mean for Europe's militaries. To capture the profound structural changes going on in Europe's populations, demographers use the term "dependency ratios": the number of people of working age, divided by the number of children and the aged. Dependency ratios can shed light on changes in the burden of support imposed on working-age people by a rapidly aging population. A similar concept can be useful in talking about future recruitment to the armed forces.

The primary objective for a typical armed force is to provide a sustainable defense of its nation and population. Thus, just as a society depends on its economically active population to provide for its children and elderly, a country is dependent on its military recruitment niche to ensure that it can continue to meet its defense needs. If the size of the military recruitment niche—the number of people in the appropriate age group—declines relative to the rest of the population, and if we assume that the future size of the armed forces should be at least in part related to a country's population size, then the rate of successful recruitment (in proportion to the size of the recruitment niche) has to increase to keep the military ranks filled.

This relation can be captured in a measure called the "Recruitment Niche Dependency Ratio," defined as the population under age 15 plus the population aged over 30, divided by the population between 15 and 30 years of age. An important characteristics of this measure is that it is directly comparable across countries.

Figure 3.2 shows the recruitment niche dependency ratio over time in NATO's European member states. Note that the scale on the y-axis of Figure 3.2 is the same for all countries. We can see that between now and approximately 2020–2030, all countries except Denmark, Luxembourg, the Netherlands, and Norway will pass through a phase in which the Recruitment Niche Dependency Ratio increases significantly. Thereafter the increases are more modest.

Some countries will experience more dramatic changes than others. For example, between 2004 and 2050, the Recruitment Niche Dependency Ratio for Spain would rise from 4 to just under 7 people for every person inside the Recruitment Niche. In Italy the ratio would rise from 5 to 7. Similar developments are seen in the case of the Czech Republic, Greece, Poland, and Portugal.

The dynamic behind these increases is that the number of people in the armed forces recruitment niche is shrinking rapidly as smaller birth cohorts (those born after the start of the demographic transition) enter the recruitment niche and the much larger birth cohorts preceding them leave it. Human resources targeted by military recruitment are thus a population resource in crisis, and this shortage could come to affect the armed forces recruitment capacity for much of the coming century.

Aggregating the information for all of NATO Europe gives a regional perspective on the demographic changes: over the period 2004 to 2050, NATO Europe's aggregated total recruitment niche is set to decline by 35 million people, from 105 million in 2004 to only 70 million people in 2050, increasing the dependency ratio of NATO's armed forces recruitment niche from 3.5:1 to 5.5:1.

Figure 3.2. Recruitment Niche Dependency Ratio 1990–2050

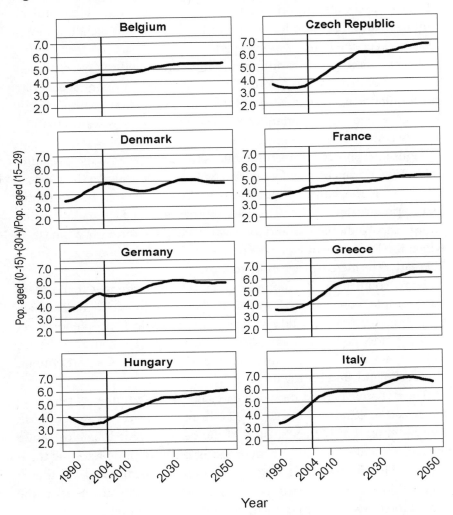

The New Demographic Reality for Military Recruitment

If the contraction of recruitment niches in all NATO Europe countries constitutes a demographic obstacle to military recruitment, the next questions are how this obstacle might influence military recruitment and how it might thus affect the capacity of the armed forces to meet the requirements for numerical strength in the future.

Figure 3.2 *(continued)*

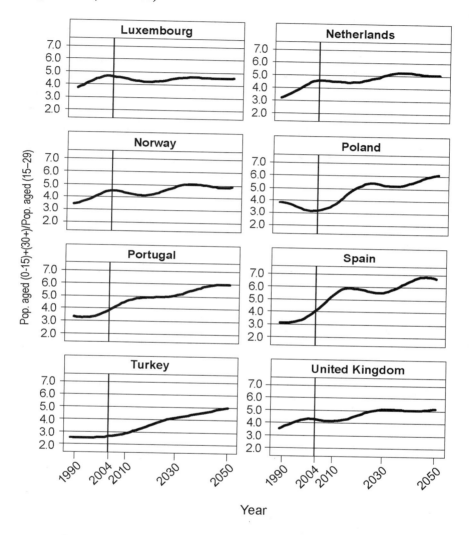

Source: U.S. Census Bureau's International Data Base

One approach to these questions is to analyze the context in which recruitment takes place. To this end I use national examples from Spain, the UK, and the Netherlands to establish a benchmark for recruitment in Europe.[9] I then use data from these three cases, and the benchmark

---

9.   There are three main reasons for choosing these three countries as a benchmark for military recruitment: their armies are fully professionalized;

provided by them, to simulate a case of hypothetical recruitment under the influence of the changing demographic conditions described above.

One can assess the demographic impact on recruitment by contrasting actual recruitment success with the size of the niche from which the recruits are recruited. This measure—the "recruitment success rate"—is the result of dividing the number of new recruits by the size of the recruitment niche. If the recruitment success rate is reasonably stable, we can assume that changes in the size of the armed forces recruitment niche will affect the total number of recruits drawn from the recruitment niche each year. The other parameter influencing recruitment needs is the force's capacity to retain those already recruited. (If many people leave the armed forces, it is necessary to raise the recruitment success rate to avoid reductions in force size.) This measure, the "exit rate," is the number of troops who leave the military in a given year, divided by the size of the armed forces. Data on the recruitment success rate and the exit rate enable us to project the variation in size of the armed forces from one year to another.

Spain is neither the largest nor the smallest of the three countries, with a population approaching 42 million people. The Spanish armed forces total about 118,000 people. The actual recruitment niche consists of all those aged 18–28, the legal age to apply for military service. The total size of Spain's recruitment niche was 6.5 million people in 2003. Its armed forces recruitment success rate fell from 3.0 per thousand in 2000 to 1.7 per thousand in 2001 and 2002, and then picked up again in 2003, reaching 2.2 per thousand.[10] On average, Spain's recruitment success rate was 2.17 per thousand for the period 2000–2003. The exit rate increased from about 9 percent in 2000 to about 14 percent in 2003, averaging 11.62 percent for the period.

---

their populations are fundamentally different in size and reflect different demographic conditions; and their military authorities report recruitment data in a transparent and comparable way.

10. Data on the Spanish armed forces in this chapter are compiled largely from information supplied in response to requests by the Spanish Congress and Senate in their sessions of questions to the Ministry of Defense, and Ministry briefings to these two bodies. Data has also been collected from the Spanish Ministry of Defense's official website, <www.mde.es>, and the recruitment office website, <www.soldados.com>. The total of 118,000 represents active-duty military personnel at all ranks, as reported by *Anuario Estadístico Militar* (Madrid: Ministry of Defense, 2003). Any faults are the author's responsibility.

The UK's population is approximately 60 million people, or about 40 percent larger than that of Spain. The UK's armed forces are also substantially larger, by approximately 75 percent, totaling about 206,000 in 2003. Since the UK has a larger population than Spain, one might expect it to have a larger recruitment niche. However, the UK also has broader age limits for entry into service; the British armed forces recruit people ages 16 to 30, compared with Spain's narrower band of 18 to 28. Thus, the UK's recruitment niche was approximately 11.5 million people in 2003 (approximately 77 percent larger than that of Spain).

Over the period 2000–2003, the UK's armed forces' recruitment success ratio (unlike that of Spain) never fell below 2.0 per thousand. However, its average recruitment success rate during that period was virtually identical to that of Spain, 2.14 per thousand. This corresponds to a yearly intake in the UK of approximately 23,000 new recruits. Over the same period, the exit rate in the UK has been more or less stable, averaging 12.12 percent.[11] Comparing the UK's recent recruitment and retention experience with that of Spain, we find that people join and leave the two countries armed forces at a fairly similar rate, but that the UK's armed forces in general have a more stable record of recruitment success and retention rates.[12]

Finally, I contrast the Spanish and the UK recruitment experiences with that of the Netherlands. With a population of approximately 16 million people, the Netherlands is the smallest of the three and it also has the smallest armed forces, with a total size of 52,000 enlisted persons. The age band for entry into service for the Netherlands armed forces runs from 17 to 29 years of age (thus falling between the bands for Spain and the UK). The Netherlands recruitment niche was approximately 2.5 million people in 2003.

Between 2000 and 2003, the Netherlands managed a recruitment success rate averaging 2.20 per thousand, practically the same rate as found in the UK and in Spain. But as in Spain, the Dutch success rate varied considerably from one year to another. The Dutch armed forces exit rate

---

11. Data on UK recruitment and exit rates are taken from the Ministry of Defence, *Annual Report and Accounts 2002/03, 2001/02, 2000/01, and 1999/2000* (London: HMSO).

12. Note that if the British age requirements had been closer to those of Spain, the UK would have needed a higher success ratio to achieve the total number of recruits reported here.

is slightly lower than that of the UK and Spain, averaging 11.03 percent for the period 2000–2003.[13]

These findings reveal some important similarities. All three countries have similar success in their recruitment efforts, being able to attract about 2 per thousand of their recruitment niche on a yearly basis. The largest differences are in exit rates, but even these differences are small. Exit rates range from 11–13 percent in all three countries.

The similarities found in recruitment success rate and exit rates for Spain, the UK, and the Netherlands make it possible to conclude that the rates are general enough to serve as a plausible benchmark for recruitment also in other countries. Applying these benchmarks for the recruitment contexts of other European NATO member countries enables us to make some general hypotheses about future recruitment scenarios, suggesting how the current and future demographic developments could affect the size of all-volunteer forces in NATO Europe.

A EUROPEAN OUTLOOK ON MILITARY RECRUITMENT: A HYPOTHETICAL CASE

The demographic issues described above are of obvious importance for countries with all-volunteer forces. Yet the success of voluntary recruitment will also be important to countries that retain a mixed model of conscription and voluntary recruitment, since the number of people they will have to draft to sustain a force of a given size will depend upon the capacity to recruit and retain voluntary soldiers.[14]

The discussion here applies even to countries that rely primarily on conscription as a means of filling the ranks, since their militaries usually have a professional core. Moreover, their ability to conscript will be influenced by the same demographic changes as voluntary recruitment will be.

Recruitment success rates in Spain, the UK, and the Netherlands suggest that future success rates in a context of voluntary recruitment to the armed forces are likely to be somewhere between 1.5 and 2.5 per thousand of a country's recruitment niche. The exit rate may be somewhere in the range of 11 to 13 percent. (This assumes that nothing drastic hap-

---

13. The data on recruitment and exits for the Netherlands was kindly made available to me by the Dutch embassy's military attaché in Spain.
14. Bernard Boëne, "La professionalisation des armées: context et raisons, impact fonctionnel et sociopolitique," *Revue Francaise de Sociologie*, Vol. 44, No. 4 (2003), pp. 647–693.

pens to modify young people's propensities to join or leave the armed forces.)

In simulating the future size of NATO Europe's militaries, controlling for demographic changes, I consider three scenarios for the period 2004 to 2050. The sole difference among the three scenarios is in the recruitment success rate. In the "low" scenario I assume that the recruitment success rate (both sexes) is constant at 1.5 per thousand; the "medium" scenario assumes that it is constant at 2.0 per thousand; and the "high" scenario assumes that it is constant at 2.5 per thousand.

For simplicity, I hold the exit rate constant at 12 percent in all three scenarios. The total size of the armed forces at the end of any given year is then calculated as follows:

$$A_{it} = A_{it-1} + ((r\beta_{i(t-1)}) - (eA_{i(t-1)}))$$

Where A_{it} is the numerical strength of the armed forces in country i at the end of any given year t, β_{it} is the size of the recruitment niche in country i in the year t, and r and e are constants representing respectively the recruitment success rate and exit rate. The value of r is given by one of the three scenarios, and the value of e is set to 0.12 (that is, 12 percent).

In projecting the size of the armed forces (A), I use the total active-duty strength as reported in *The Military Balance* under the heading "Numbers in the Armed Forces" as a baseline in this exercise (that is, I exclude reservists and paramilitary personnel).[15] Thus, for example, $A_{i(t=2003)}$ corresponds to the actual strength of the armed forces in 2003 in country i as reported in *The Military Balance 2004–2005*. From 2004 onwards, simulated scenarios apply. The results of the simulations are presented in Figure 3.3.

Each of the three recruitment scenarios reflects the assumption of a constant recruitment success ratio and constant exit ratios: the only parameter allowed to vary over time is the size of the recruitment niche. Hence, the figures show us the impact of current demographic changes, holding recruitment and exit rates constant.

---

15. International Institute for Strategic Studies (IISS), *The Military Balance*, for 1999–2000 through 2004–2005 (London: IISS, var. dates).

Figure 3.3. Three Scenarios of Future Size of Europe's Armed Force (NATO)

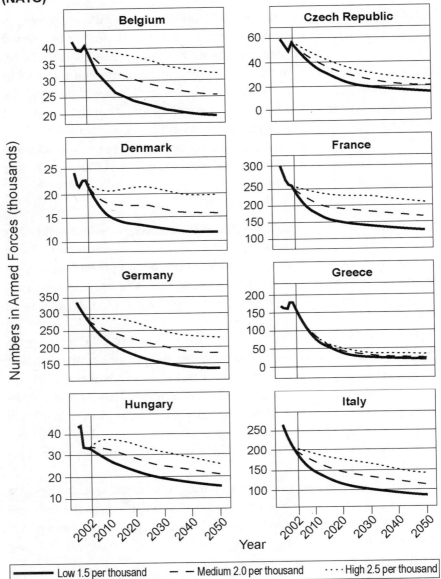

Simulations based on data from: U.S. Census Bureau's International Data Base and The Military Balance

Figure 3.3. *(continued)*

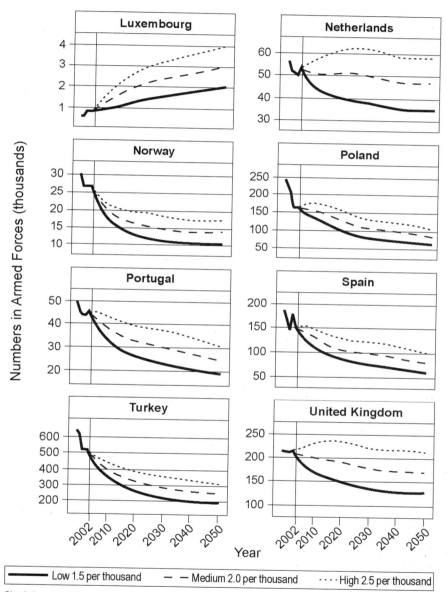

Simulations based on data from: U.S. Census Bureau's International Data Base and The Military Balance

All three scenarios provide cause for concern with regard to future military recruitment capacity in the NATO Europe area, with the exception of Luxembourg (all scenarios) and in Denmark, the Netherlands, Norway, and the UK (in the High scenario). That is, in the case where the recruitment success rate approaches 2.5 per thousand, these four countries would be able to sustain their armed forces' current size. In the other cases, if the recruitment experience of Spain, the UK, and the Netherlands are used as the benchmark for future recruitment capacity in all NATO Europe countries, the scale of the negative demographic developments of the countries' recruitment niches is such that all countries other than Luxembourg would face substantial difficulties in maintaining their current numerical strength in the future. In many cases the potential decline in numerical strength is very significant regardless of which scenario we apply.

Of course, these results cannot be accepted at face value, since some countries, such as Greece and Turkey, rely on voluntary recruitment only to a very limited degree. Yet, for countries in which conscription has formally been suspended—notably, Belgium, the Czech Republic, Hungary, Italy, Luxembourg, the Netherlands, Portugal, Spain, and the UK—the simulation is more alarming.

In the hypothetical case that recruitment in all countries of NATO Europe was voluntary, the simulation paints a harsh future for most countries, particularly if the goal is to preserve current numerical strength. In some cases, especially in those countries that have not yet taken the step towards an all-volunteer force, it might suggest that a serious discussion of future size requirements of the armed forces and the conditions for professionalization is called for before abandoning conscription altogether.

Nevertheless, as mentioned above, some countries with all-volunteer forces are likely to do fairly well in the high scenario. For example, the Netherlands and the UK would maintain their numerical strength with a recruitment success rate of 2.5 per thousand or even slightly below. The reason for this could be that countries with voluntary recruitment have already trimmed their militaries to correspond better with their actual recruitment capacity. (However, as I discuss below, maintaining a high recruitment success rate may turn out to become more difficult in the future as a result of the new demographic reality.) An additional reason why these two countries do fairly well is that their recruitment niches are likely to contract much more slowly than countries in southern Europe.

Meanwhile, France, Italy, Poland, and Spain could be in for big recruitment problems as their recruitment niches contract. Germany would face a similar challenge if it had to rely exclusively on volunteers to fill its ranks. It should be noted that these five countries accounted for 1.0 million of NATO Europe's 2.2 million active-duty troops in 2003.[16] Preserving current strength in these countries will require better than average recruitment success rates. I return to these problems in the last part of this chapter.

One could argue that it is unrealistic to assume that the recruitment success and exit rates are likely to be constant over time. Yearly fluctuations in the recruitment success and exit rates could mean that my simulation exaggerates the likely difficulties for recruitment. To explore how such fluctuations would change the picture, I assigned a random value for the parameters r (recruitment success rate) and e (exit rate) in Equation 1 on a yearly basis.[17]

As it turned out, the general conclusions from the results presented in Figure 3.3 are borne out even when the recruitment success and the exit rates are set to vary at random within their given limits on a yearly basis. This means that the general findings in Figure 3.3 are relatively robust: absent dramatic improvements in recruitment success or retention rates, armed forces across Europe are likely to shrink significantly as a result of changing demographic conditions.

Finally, Figure 3.4 shows how the three recruitment scenarios would affect the aggregate size of NATO Europe's militaries. Serious decline is likely regardless of the scenario (recruitment success rates of 1.5, 2, or 2.5 per thousand), assuming that enlistment is voluntary across NATO countries. All other things being equal (recruitment success and exit rates are constant), demographic shifts could cut the number of troops across NATO's European armed forces by 45 to 65 percent. This is well above the expected decline in the NATO countries' aggregated population, forecast at around 3 percent for the same period.

If recruitment success and retention rates were constant, as given by any of the three scenarios, Figure 3.4 suggests what level of troops

---

16. IISS, *The Military Balance 2004–2005*.
17. The yearly values for these two parameters are drawn from two random distributions with means of 0.0022 (r) and 0.125 (e) and with standard deviations of 0.00049 (r) and 0.0134 (e) respectively. The means and standard deviations are obtained from the observed values of r and e in the combined recruitment data for Spain, the UK, and the Netherlands over the period 2000 through 2003.

Figure 3.4. Aggregated Numbers in Europe's Armed Forces (NATO) Three Simulated Scenarios

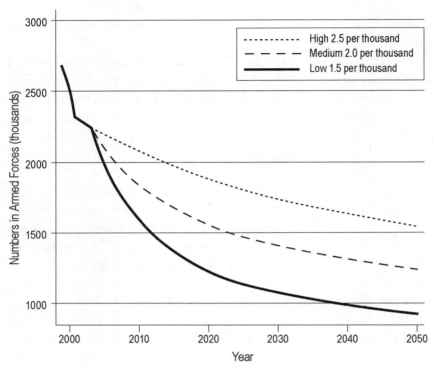

NATO Europe could aspire to, given the demographic changes over time. Increasing the number of troops would mean that the armed forces must either improve their recruitment success rate above the level stated for each scenario, or lower the exit rate. The rest of this chapter addresses some of the means and obstacles to improve the armed forces recruitment capacity and to offset the negative demographic trends I have highlighted in this section.

Reinforcing Military Recruitment Capacity

This analysis of European demographic developments and their implications for military recruitment indicates that one of the key questions for the future is what numerical strength will be required for the armed forces. Is a substantial decline acceptable? If the answer to this question is yes, then recruiting enough servicemembers in the future would be much less complicated. If the answer is no, however, then there is reason for concern.

Many have argued that NATO Europe's present forces are overly large. New concepts of operations and advances in military technology suggest that military strength and capacity are no longer purely a function of manpower.[18] Hence, a reduction in the number of troops in NATO countries is to be expected; indeed, the downsizing is already underway. However, it is less clear whether the reduced need for manpower is commensurate with the decline dictated by the changing demography in Europe.

Perhaps more importantly for military recruiters in Europe, even if it were possible to accept an additional reduction from the current levels at the scale implied by the simulations above, military recruitment may still become problematic in the coming decades. The largest obstacle for maintaining current recruitment success ratios in times of contracting recruitment niches is that the armed forces' recruitment niches overlap with recruitment niches of other important institutions such as those of higher education and the labor market. They, too, must compete for a shrinking supply of young people as a result of the current demographic developments. Since these other institutions are the preferred alternatives for many of the young people in the military's recruitment niche, competition for the decreasing number of able young people may become fiercer over time; the armed forces of Europe may be the loser in this competition.[19]

Increased competition may also affect the armed forces' capacity to retain troops, since civilian counter-offers may become increasingly attractive as non-military institutions seek to overcome the increasing scarcity of young people. Other drawbacks are easy to identify as well. The worst-case scenario is that the armed forces, being the least preferred option, will have to settle for recruiting only those who fail to qualify for positions in other sectors of society. Should this occur, na-

---

18. Martin Binkin, "Manning the American Military: Demographics and National Security," *NPG Forum Series* (1990) <www.npg.org>; and more recently NATO Secretary-General Robertson's view expressed in a press conference at the NATO Prague Summit, November 21–22, 2002; NATO Speeches, Prague, November 21, 2002, <www.nato.in>.
19. David R. Segal, Jerald G. Bachman, Peter Freedman-Doan, and Patrick M. O'Malley, "Propensity to Serve in the U.S. Military: Temporal Trends and Subgroup Differences," *Armed Forces and Society*, Vol. 25, No. 3 (1999), pp. 407–427.

tional defense capacity would be limited not only by decreasing numbers, but also by the lower quality of troops.

Several options are, however, available to the armed forces to cope with the harsher demographic reality and the increased competition implied by it. If decreasing manpower supply is not offset by lowered defense needs, the first measures to consider should be improvements in efficiency and productivity. In military terms, this implies increasing the striking power per unit or per soldier; that is, equipping and organizing a reduced number of men and women in such a way that they become capable of doing the same job that a larger contingent does today.

But improving the armed forces' efficiency and productivity is likely to be the most expensive solution. Another important drawback is that there is a limit on how much efficiency and productivity can be improved: we have yet to see an army without soldiers. A third drawback is that while these measures require very able soldiers to operate the often complicated technical equipment needed to enhance productivity and efficiency, recruiting brighter and better-trained people is likely to become more difficult as competition for such people increases. However, one could argue that in the medium and long term, recruitment that targets the brighter people might actually improve the army's recruitment capacity, since the status of the military profession would rise as a result.

A second instrumental way to deal with Europe's negative demographic developments is to expand the recruitment niche by altering the age limits. Modifying age limits is a common measure in other demographically dependent areas of our society. For example, when the future of pension systems is discussed, we often hear that because of increases in life expectancy, being 65 today is not like being 65 half a century ago, and that it should be possible to raise the statutory age for pensions. Similarly, perhaps those aged 35 may be as capable of performing modern military duties as those aged 20. Expanding the age interval could produce more recruits even at lower recruitment success rates.

However, while this choice may seem straightforward, it might have drawbacks. It is well known that successful recruitment is more likely among the youngest potential recruits. In Spain between 1997 and 1999, for example, two-thirds of all new recruits were aged 18 to 20; the number of new recruits aged 24 and above made up no more than 5 percent of the total number of new recruits.[20] The Spanish case is not likely to be an exception in this regard. The primary obstacle to recruiting people in their late twenties is that they are increasingly engaged in civilian careers; chances are that they would be reluctant to leave a job to sign up for several years of military service.

Thus it might be necessary to consider mechanisms for combining civilian careers with military careers. For example, an arrangement could be made for "military leave" parallel to the way many countries offer maternity leave. If such mechanisms existed, people might choose to sign up for military service without risking their civilian careers. This could improve the potential for recruiting people at the upper age limit of the recruitment niche.

Time and age limits are also influencing exit rates. Many armed forces struggle to determine the ideal length of service as well as the maximum age in service. Obviously, the shorter the contract, the sooner replacements must be sought, with more recruitment pressure as a consequence. Longer terms of service could have negative implications for resumption of civilian life, but in times of fast-changing demographic conditions, more flexible options as to the length of service could be an effective tool to ease recruitment pressure.

A third instrumental option to offset the demographic problem is increasing female participation in the armed forces.[21] In simulating the demographic impact on future recruitment efforts, I deliberately included people of both sexes, since armies increasingly admit women to active duty. However, while female admission to the armed forces no longer is an issue in many countries, most are failing to attract many female recruits. According to figures from 2004, female participation in NATO Europe forces averages only about 7 percent.[22] While some

---

20. Unidad de Estadística del Ejército de Tierra, *Aspirantes a Tropa y Marinería Profesional: Análisis Socioestadística* (Madrid: Direccion de servicios técnicos sección de investigación, estadística, publicaciones y cartografía: Cuartel General del Ejercito Español, 2001).

21. Mady Wechsler Segal, "Women's Military Roles Cross-nationally: Past, Present, and Future," *Gender and Society*, Vol. 9, No. 6 (1995), pp. 757–775.

22. See fact sheet prepared by the Committee on Women in the NATO Forces, "2004 Total Strength of Women in the NATO Forces," <www.nato.int/ims/2004/win/stregnth.pdf>.

countries are performing well in this regard—France at 12.79 percent and the Czech Republic at 12.3 percent, for example—Europe's armed forces overall are not yet developing the full potential of their recruitment niches.

Attracting women to the armed forces means developing mechanisms to make their participation more feasible. This implies adapting military duties, making appropriate accommodations for both sexes, and eliminating existing inequalities. In general, the armed forces must develop explicit family policies, taking into consideration the particular needs of women, in order to increase the number of women in the armed forces. This includes parental leave and child-care programs. Young men are also likely to benefit from such improvements. One of the armed forces' toughest competitors, besides the civilian labor market and higher education, is the family: both women and men are likely to turn down a job with the armed forces if their family situation is not accommodated satisfactorily.[23]

Recruiting women is not only about accommodating the particular needs of women. Few young women are likely to volunteer for service if there are frequent reports that women participating in the armed forces are subject to aggressive male behavior. While misconduct feeding this stereotype certainly is a problem in the armed forces, the armed forces may be no worse than any other institution in this regard. In fact, data on participation of women in the U.S. armed forces has indicated that women in the armed forces score higher on job satisfaction than women in civilian sectors; there is evidence that gender integration in the armed forces is more successful than in other institutions.[24] This is an important message to pass on to young females who are making life choices that could involve a military career.

There are great differences between North American and European NATO countries in terms of female participation. Both the United States and Canada have female participation rates above 10 percent; U.S. female participation is as high as 14 percent. This is a good indication that European countries could learn from how the United States and Canada

---

23. Mady Wechsler Segal, "The Military and the Family as Greedy Institutions," *Armed Forces and Society*, Vol. 13, No. 1 (1986), pp. 9–38.
24. Regina F. Titunik, "The First Wave: Gender Integration and Military Culture," *Armed Forces and Society*, Vol. 26, No. 2 (2000), pp. 229–257.

approach the problem of female recruitment and participation, in order to make more effective use of their recruitment niches.

A fourth option to consider is extending armed forces recruitment efforts to include foreigners. Immigration accounts for about 80 percent of the population growth in many European countries. The presence of immigrants is rising steadily, particularly in countries with the most problematic demographic outlook for the armed forces, including Greece, Italy, Spain, and Portugal.

This solution has already been considered by some defense ministries. For example, Spanish law allows recruitment of up to 2 percent of the total size of its armed forces from among foreigners of Hispanic origin.[25] A foreign contingent in the armed forces is obviously a sensitive matter: after all, the armed forces are traditionally a national affair, and a force with a large proportion of foreign soldiers would challenge some traditional concepts about national defense and the armed forces.

But maybe the time has come to take a different strategic view of the role of a country's armed forces and, consequently, of the nationality of its soldiers. After the end of the Cold War, there is no serious threat to the national sovereignty or territory of most NATO members, and this situation is not likely to change soon. Instead, recent military action has been limited to missions in distant lands, notably in the Balkans, Afghanistan, and Iraq, as part of larger international interventions, usually within the framework of joint NATO or UN operations. Following the change in the security outlook after September 11, 2001, more such missions will be likely in the future. Such missions, while highly dependent on the military capacity of each country, have little to do with the traditional military role of defending "homelands."

A reassessment of the strategic role of the armed forces suggests the possibility of recruiting from the fast-growing immigrant population at a time when other demographic conditions are extremely unfavorable for the recruitment of nationals. Since the new role of the armed forces has more to do with peacekeeping and nation-building in faraway places than with homeland defense, the importance of a soldier's citi-

---

25. See, for example, "Real Decreto 1244/2002, de 29 de diciembre: Reglamento de acceso de extranjeros a la condición de militar profesional de tropa y marinería" (Royal Decree 1244/2002 regulating the incorporation of foreigners in the Spanish armed forces).

zenship should not be over-emphasized. Armies participating in international operations and global peacekeeping missions should be more concerned with satisfying their need for motivated and well-trained soldiers who are willing to accept missions in remote places.

The nature of modern military activities and the professionalization of the armed forces since the late 1990s suggest that it may be time to consider at least some military activities as a job option among many other job options, from which there are no good reasons to exclude immigrant groups. Nor are there any reasons why the armed forces' immigrant contingent should be smaller than the proportion of immigrants in society as a whole. The latter issue is particularly important, since immigrants constitute the only population group that is actually growing and is likely to continue growing in most European countries over the coming decades.

However, the coming demographic changes are of such magnitude that these four instrumental measures are not likely to be enough to remedy imminent recruitment problems. The armed forces will have to deal with more fundamental aspects of their recruitment policies to be able to attract young people to a military career. The main challenge consists of addressing the mounting competition from other sectors of society as youth scarcity advances. The solution to this problem is likely to involve a mix of recruitment and retention incentives in order to compete with educational institutions and the civilian labor market.

The first incentives should be economic, but these are certainly not the only incentives available, nor even perhaps the most effective ones in the longer term.[26] Apart from offering more money, which is worth a chapter of its own, how can the armed forces improve their competitive edge and guarantee a sufficient recruitment success rate in the future? Part of the answer can be deduced from information about potential recruits' attitudes about military service.

Since the start of its transition from a conscript to a professional army, the Spanish armed forces have conducted several surveys in cooperation with the Spanish Center for Sociological Research (CIS). The CIS found on repeated occasions that around 60–65 percent of people

---

26. See, for example, Curtis L. Gilroy and Robert L. Phillips, "The All-Volunteer Army: Fifteen Years Later," *Armed Forces and Society*, Vol. 16, No. 3 (1990), pp. 329–352.

within the armed forces recruitment niche regard the decision of joining the army as a career choice; around 20–25 percent regard it as a decision based on adequate compensation; and a mere 5 percent as a means to increase their social standing.[27] Of those who had considered joining the armed forces, the main incentives that, they reported, could sway them actually to join included professional stability and promotion opportunities, the possibility of gaining civil-servant status, access to military schools, and access to security-related employment such as the national, regional, and local police forces and the Guardia Civil at the end of their military careers. People in the recruitment niche in at least some other NATO countries may hold similar opinions about military careers.

Thus, if recruitment efforts are to tap the most important motivators to joining the military, it will be necessary to address the vocational and educational aspects of joining, not just economic conditions. In doing this it should not be forgotten that the army is competing against both institutions of higher education and the labor market. Both have a record of satisfying those needs mentioned by potential recruits as crucial elements for joining the armed forces. This implies that those in charge of the battle for human resources must consider the attractiveness of the job and the education that they offer relative to what is offered by their competitors.

One way of making the educational aspects of military training more attractive, relative to civilian education, is by increasing its status, making military training directly comparable with university or vocational education by offering degrees that are equivalent to those available in civilian education. Joining the military would then be an investment in one's human capital, similar to enrollment in a university or a vocational training institute. Such measures would benefit the potential recruits as well as society, and increase the armed forces' competitive edge in the labor market. Many armed forces have already taken some steps in this direction, but this work has to progress further if it is to make military education an attractive alternative to higher education.

Many countries opting for professionalization in the armed forces are still only in the beginning of the process, and it takes time to educate both the potential recruits and civil society about the value of military

---

27. Centro de Investigaciones Sociológicas, "Encuesta N° 2447: La defensa nacional y el ejército" (2002). See also earlier editions of the same survey from 1997 onwards.

education. Even the armed forces themselves sometimes fail to make the most of the value of education in their recruitment efforts.[28]

To establish military education as an alternative to civilian education, the armed forces must recognize that they are competing with a multitude of choices offered by public and private educational institutions. This does not mean that the armed forces have to provide all of the same kinds of educational programs, but military training would do well to avoid compartmentalizing or overemphasizing the technical and security aspects of military education. Instead they could recognize and highlight skills that have both military and civilian uses, such as medicine and nursing, interpreting, administration, accounting, management, teaching and instruction, construction, environmental work, and international aid and rescue work. Offering potential recruits access to a more varied educational menu could provide them with education of value for civilian life after military training, and would thus make the armed forces a more attractive choice.

Reforms of this type would probably require reshaping the public image of the armed forces. Most young people know about the "romantic" elements of military training: handling weapons, international missions, high-risk assignments, and so on are usually what come to mind when young people think about the military, visit the official recruitment websites of many NATO countries, or watch a recruitment spot on commercial television. This is not, however, a message that would attract the broad majority of the armed forces recruitment niche. Indeed the armed forces may not actually benefit from recruits entering military service in a quest for such experiences; those who apply to the armed forces for this reason might be disappointed when confronted with the day-to-day routine of peacetime work, and the less-than-glamorous preparation required of a soldier or an officer. What most young people know less about, and what the armed forces should stress, is the concept of military training as an investment in the recruit's future that is similar, if not identical, to civilian education. In other words, recruits should be told that upon completing their military training, they will be in a significantly better position in the labor market than they were when

28. Gilroy and Phillips, "The All-Volunteer Army."

they entered the armed forces.[29] If the armed forces succeed in this task, they will be in a much better position to compete successfully for the best and the brightest in the age cohorts making up their recruitment niches.[30]

It will be equally important to emphasize the armed forces' educational capacity among the institutions, organizations, and employers that are likely to benefit from it. Marketing military education as a quality resource to its organizational beneficiaries is not so different from marketing it to the target recruitment group. Both must be made more aware of the usefulness of the training offered by the armed forces. If the demand among employers for former recruits rises, the demand for military training among potential recruits is also likely to rise.

Another group of potential recruits is made up of those who have already received extensive training elsewhere but are seeking a full-time job or a career in the armed forces, and in this way capitalize on their educational investment elsewhere. This category is crucial in countries opting for an all-volunteer force, but it is known to be the most difficult category to recruit.[31] Addressing this problem requires a critical analysis of the role of the armed forces as managers, and how they function as contractors of labor.

To become successful in attracting recruits with desired skills, it is necessary to offer prospects of promotion and interesting career opportunities. This can only be achieved if the armed forces can ensure a reasonable turnover among its higher-rank staff, to give recruits a significant opportunity to rise in the military hierarchy as vacancies

---

29. The U.S. experience has shown that this is indeed a difficult task. Moreover, the educational attainment of veterans tends to be relatively lower than for non-veterans, suggesting that in fact those who opt for a military career actually may be worse off in the medium and long term, after reentering civilian life, than those who opted for a civilian career. See Jere Cohen, Rebecca L. Warner, and David R. Segal, "Military Service and Educational Attainment in the All-Volunteer Force," *Social Science Quarterly*, Vol. 76, No. 1 (1995). Eliminating the disparity in educational attainment between those who choose to dedicate part of their life to military service and those who do not will be a key challenge.
30. Segal, et al., "Propensity to Serve in the U.S. Military."
31. Gilroy and Phillips, "The All-Volunteer Army."

emerge.[32] This is, however, problematic when the armed forces are downsizing due to changing strategic outlooks, transition from a conscript to a professional army, or other reasons. Downsizing is much easier to achieve by cutting staff at lower ranks. As a result, many countries have problems in readjusting the size of their officer contingent, with which they may have contracted on a permanent basis. Adjustments are slow, at best; this stalls turnover rates, resulting in fewer promotion opportunities for those at lower ranks, and in turn affecting career opportunities in a way that is discouraging to those who would consider joining. This greatly reduces incentives for joining the armed forces and, hence, increases the difficulties in recruiting key staff, especially those with special skills. Addressing this problem usually means offering incentives for early retirement to parts of the officer contingent, which are costly. However, it could nevertheless be an effective investment to ensure adequate replacement in the longer term, and to lower the cost of recruitment of younger people, especially those with desired skills.

Finally, some cooperative measures may be useful. The armed forces are far from alone in providing security services in today's society. Thus, when the demographic outlook is clouding the armed forces recruitment opportunities, it would be unfortunate if they should engage in competition over human resources with other organizations that are also charged with security tasks.

For example, Spain's armed forces comprise today about 118,000 people. At the same time the total number of people working in other security-related employment is about 300,000: this includes national, regional, and local police forces, the so-called Guardia Civil, and private companies offering security. It also includes special police units trained for fighting terrorism.

---

32. Sociological research has labeled this a "vacancy chain," and has shown that the presence of a vacancy chain is crucial for achieving upward mobility in large organizations. See Aage B. Sørenssen, "The Structure of Inequality and the Process of Attainment," *American Sociological Review*, Vol. 42, No. 6 (1977), pp. 965–978. See also Paul F. Hogan, Curtis J. Simon, and John T. Warner, "Sustaining the Force in an Era of Transformation," in Barbara A. Bicksler, Curtis L. Gilroy, and John T. Warner, *The All-Volunteer Force: Thirty Years of Service* (Washington, D.C.: Brassey's, 2004), on the importance of vacancy chains for the performance of military personnel.

While there certainly are differences in the services that these units are able to provide, there are also substantial overlaps. In some contexts, such as peacekeeping, it is not always clear that the armed forces are best prepared for addressing the particular needs posed by such a mission, yet it is often the armed forces that must take the responsibility for the mission even if others, for example, the Guardia Civil in the case of Spain, may be better suited for it, simply because these other bodies are not prepared for or do not consider missions abroad, or are not formally allowed to by national legislation.

In other words, the demographic outlook provides an opportunity for the national governments to consider how national, regional, and local police forces as well as paramilitary forces could work together with the armed forces both nationally and internationally to address defense and security needs and in this way reduce competition over personnel.

Cooperation of this type is not only a national issue. Wider international cooperation among different countries' armed forces might also be an attractive way to solve a growing personnel deficit. The European Union has for some time discussed the idea of launching a joint defense venture. The changing demographic outlook provides a reason to look into this possibility with renewed interest. The ways in which European armed forces are currently organized give rise to substantial overlaps in terms of capacities. Europe's armed forces might be organized in a slightly different way so that resource sharing could contribute to solving some of the personnel problems faced by national armed forces. European cooperation on military issues is not easy, but even small-scale cooperation could be a welcome contribution to ease the mounting recruitment problems highlighted in this chapter.

Concluding Remarks

The purpose of this chapter is to contribute to a much-needed debate on future recruitment problems due to a drastically changing demographic outlook. Simulations show that NATO's European forces could face a significant reduction in size as a result of current demographic developments.

Since many of the demographic trends highlighted in this paper are irreversible in the short and medium term, the only way to offset mounting demographic problems will be either to raise the recruitment success rate or lower the armed forces exit rate. However, even if the armed forces were successful in this task, the scale of the demographic problem is such that many militaries would require a recruitment success rate well above historical rates just to sustain their current numerical strength.

Setting a recruitment target for the armed forces that takes into consideration the new demographic reality is a relatively easy task; it is more difficult actually to meet it. One of the biggest problems for recruitment officers is that they are likely to face fierce competition over human resources as civilian institutions seek to attract the same young people as the armed forces. A series of measures could help militaries improve their success, including:

- instrumental measures designed to make more effective use of the available recruitment niche, and in this way cushion against the effects of contracting niche size;

- competitive measures designed to make military service more attractive and thus to offset external competition for human resources within the armed forces recruitment niches; and

- cooperative measures designed to avoid competition over human resources with other security agencies, as well as to achieve international cooperation.

The scale of the demographic problem is such that it is probably necessary to consider all three strategies simultaneously. The demographic sea change presents a serious test for any national armed forces relying on volunteer recruitment.

Chapter 4

Impact of NATO Membership on Military Service in the Baltic States

Vaidotas Urbelis

During the last decade, the armed forces of the NATO countries have been in a constant process of transformation. The alliance continues to evolve into a global military organization with the capacity to fight both traditional and new threats, such as international terrorism and proliferation of weapons of mass destruction. To be able to carry out these operations, member states including alliance newcomers are shifting towards smaller but more mobile armed forces. Transformation of the alliance and creation of new capabilities for new missions has had a profound impact upon personnel policies in Lithuania, Latvia, and Estonia. Latvia has opted for an all-volunteer force, and Lithuania and Estonia may well follow in the coming years. Development of new capabilities for the collective need plays a crucial role in determining new force structures, the role and status of military personnel in society, and personnel numbers in the various services.

NATO membership has had a huge impact upon the defense postures of Lithuania, Latvia, and Estonia, and on public perception in these countries of the armed forces and their functions. After joining the alliance, politicians started to ask new questions: What should be the role of the military in ensuring homeland security and civil defense? Should conscripts be used for collective defense operations outside the homeland territory? What is our share of responsibility in the alliance? Can armed forces be used at home or even abroad, upon the request of civilian authorities? Should border guards be trained to perform some military functions in times of crisis? New and difficult questions sparked lively discussions and provided Baltic defense planners with an opportunity to reevaluate their plans and concepts.

This chapter examines the impact of a variety of factors, both internal and external, on the military personnel policies of Lithuania, Latvia, and Estonia as well as their general public views of military service. It thus provides a broader perspective on debates over the future of the armed forces in the Baltic states and factors influencing these developments. The main theme of the chapter is that in the Baltic states, unlike other countries, external factors have played the most important role in determining force structure development, including personnel policies.

The chapter has four major sections. The first section sets the role of the Baltic states' militaries within the broader context of democratic transition and integration into Western structures. The second section assesses the implications of NATO membership and the security guarantees of Article 5 of the Washington Treaty for the development of force structures, and of the Baltic states' attitudes towards the defense model from which personnel requirements are derived. This leads to the third section, which reviews how changing threat perceptions influence personnel policies, public perceptions of compulsory military service, and military expenditures. The fourth and final section reviews the current debate over conscription and the future of professionalization of the armed forces in the Baltic states.

Impact of NATO Integration on the Role of the Military in Society

In the Baltic states, the processes of democratization and of efforts towards NATO membership ran on two parallel tracks. First, they reflected the transformation of the societies of Lithuania, Latvia, and Estonia, the development of true market economies, and the restoration of civil liberties and respect for human rights. Against this background, NATO membership was perceived as a tool to solidify and speed up the process of transformation, as it was seen that this could take place only in a nation that enjoyed credible security guarantees and could therefore devote its resources to creating favorable living conditions. In general, people perceived NATO as the winner of the Cold War, and attributed their freedom to the successful functioning of the alliance. For them, striving for NATO membership became a natural extension of their fight for freedom and democracy against dictatorship from the East.

The wish to become members of NATO thus reflected a value-driven policy of the political leaders of Lithuania, Latvia, and Estonia. At the same time it coincided with the hard-liners' view of the security situation in the region: they considered the quest for NATO membership to be a way to escape Russian influence. Pursuit of NATO membership united different factions of the Lithuanian, Latvian, and Estonian political spectrum. In Latvia, the election of October 1998 saw six parties elected to the *Saeima* (parliament). Five of these—the People's Party, the Latvian Way, the Alliance for Fatherland, Freedom/LNNK, and the New Party—declared their commitment to a western-oriented foreign policy. In Lithuania in 2001, thirteen major political parties issued a Joint Declaration confirming their adherence to the goal of integration into transatlantic structures.

Broad consensus thus emerged in the mid-1990s not only among politicians but also within society. Confidence in NATO remains very high, even though the general public views NATO and U.S. military interventions in Kosovo, Afghanistan, and Iraq as highly controversial. In each of the three countries, only a small percentage of people oppose NATO membership (mostly Russian-speaking minorities or people living in the countryside). For example, polls indicate that for the overwhelming majority of the Latvian population, membership in NATO remains the most credible guarantee of Latvia's security.[1] Similarly, 59 percent believe that the most important factor ensuring Estonia's security is NATO membership. NATO accession is supported by 66 percent of Estonians, an even higher level of support than for European Union (EU) membership (48 percent).[2]

The consensus among the political elites of the Baltic states on the major security issues has been criticized by several observers. For instance, Frank Möller wrote:

What is materializing in the Baltic states is a type of 'tunnel vision': decision-makers can only see limited ways of achieving security and refuse

---

1. Latvian Ministry of National Defense, "Public opinion," <www.mod.gov.lv/index.php?pid=13309>.
2. Factum, *Public Opinion and National Defense* (Tallinn, February 2003), p. 14; Press and Information Department, Estonian Ministry of Foreign Affairs, "Estonia Today: Support for NATO Membership," February 2004.

even to discuss alternatives. This is as much a result of their security concepts as it is a product of how they conceive the states should be.... A major result of the lack of alternatives is the absence of controversial public debate and the lack of interest or curiosity in the issue. All major political parties support the recent military policies, namely, the increase of military expenditure and integration in NATO.[3]

Möller's observation, however, fails to recognize the complexity of the value-driven, identity-driven, and interest-driven motivation toward integration with NATO. In the Baltic states, security and defense concepts are as much about identity and state-building as they are about security. Their aim is the construction of a collective self, meaning the identification of the individual with the nation, organized politically and socially as a modern, sovereign nation-state. In the Baltic states, the West is associated with prosperity, security, and democracy, whereas the East connotes poverty, unpredictability, totalitarianism, and insecurity. From the point of view of national security, the concept of the West is not associated with any particular country; rather it is linked with Western alliances and, in particular, with the EU and NATO. After regaining independence, Lithuania, like Latvia and Estonia, has been unwavering in its choice of integration with the West.[4]

Transformation of the armed forces has been an important part of the Baltic states' transition to democracy and integration into Western structures. During the last years of the Russian military presence, the reestablishment of independent military formations was a symbol of the Baltics' newly regained statehood and independence. Reestablishment of military structures was meant to solidify fragmented societies, foster patriotism, and encourage resistance to any Russian ambition to reclaim its former vassals. Conscription was also used to integrate national minorities into the civil society. Development of a democratic society,

---

3.   Frank Möller, "The Baltic States: Security, Identity, and the Identity of the State," in Dimitar Dimitrov, et al., *The Military in Transition: Restructuring and Downsizing the Armed Forces of Eastern Europe,* Brief 25 (Bonn: Bonn International Center for Conversion, 2002), pp. 48–51.

4.   Grazina Miniotaite, "The Security Policy of Lithuania and the 'Integration Dilemma'," COPRI Working Paper (Copenhagen: Copenhagen Peace Research Institute [COPRI], May 2000).

market economies, and the creation of modern armed forces went in parallel in Lithuania, Latvia, and Estonia.

Two main factors had a fundamental impact on the evolution of the armed forces in these countries. First, the development of the armed forces started from a very limited base in the early 1990s, and the military had no preconditions or preconceptions about its particular role and place in society. As a result, the institutional interests of the armed forces and their commitments to the old regime were very limited. The model for the development of a modern military in the early 1990s reflected the prevailing mood in Lithuanian, Latvian, and Estonian societies, which was to combine traditions of the past with an embrace of liberal-democratic values. Especially at the beginning of the 1990s, the main recruitment base was patriotic volunteers; for them, financial considerations played only a secondary role in their decision to join the armed forces. As a result, even though the initial units of the armed forces were created from volunteers and former officers of the Soviet army, their new structure and doctrine reflected a more "western" approach to military reform. However, there was a residual Soviet influence amongst some elements of the officer corps, which led to some resistance to "western" military norms and values.

Assistance from Western countries in the area of training and education contributed considerably to changing the attitude of the military culture. "Even in the best of circumstances, the experience of all armies suggests, it takes 10 to 15 years to 'grow' new field grade commanders and almost as long to train the non-commissioned officers—sergeants and corporals—who are the backbone of NATO-style forces."[5] Education and training therefore emerged as a key priority in the development of Lithuanian, Latvian, and Estonian armed forces, and in Western assistance to the Baltic states. Thousands of officers and civil servants of the Baltic states have undergone training in Western institutions of military education. NATO member states and Partnership for Peace (PfP) countries have also provided training and development opportunities

5. Paul Goble, "The Baltics: Analysis From Washington—Transforming Post-Communist Militaries," Radio Free Europe (RFE/RL) *Reports*, August 18, 1999.

for Baltic states' military personnel in their defense education establishments.[6]

A second major factor was that, since the core of the Baltic states' foreign and security policies was focused on integration with the West, military reforms were implemented according to NATO guidelines and accession criteria. Although NATO has not adopted formal membership criteria, there is no doubt that military performance and participation in international operations has become a de facto prerequisite for aspiring members, and remains an important way to enhance their public image in the international community. Their military performance in the international arena has become an important issue on the Baltic domestic political agenda. Military personnel programs in the Baltic states were adjusted to meet the new requirements: the Baltic states were challenged to prepare qualified military personnel for international missions according to NATO's requirements, not their own. For example, officers, non-commissioned officers, and privates must be able to speak English, use modern communication equipment, apply western doctrines, and operate in a multi-national environment.

Not surprisingly, training of qualified personnel became the first priority in Lithuania, Latvia, and Estonia. Personnel expenditure rose dramatically, taking as much as 70 percent of the overall defense budgets in the late 1990s. The three Baltic states made a deliberate decision to invest in personnel first, and only later to spend on equipment modernization programs. Quality-of-life issues emerged as a priority on the agenda of defense planners, and housing and the construction of military camps became major areas of defense expenditure. This decision has paid off: improved living and working conditions have helped make military service more attractive to young people. The armed forces now provide people with the opportunity to acquire basic computer skills and English-language training. Military service also helps integrate national minorities into civil society, especially those who previously possessed limited local language skills. Consequently, public support for the armed forces has risen substantially.

---

6. Ministry of National Defense (MND) of the Republic of Lithuania, "Defense White Paper 1999" (Vilnius: MND Publishing Centre, 1999), p. 39.

Table 4.1. Military Expenditure and Manpower Targets for NATO Invitees

2001 population in millions	Military expenditures in 2002		Military expenditures as share of GDP		Military manpower	
	Change from 1997	$ million	2001	Target percent (year)	2001 (except as shown)	Declared target (year)
Bulgaria 8.12	+16%	339	2.6%	2.8 (2003)	65,000 (2002)	45,000 (2004)
Estonia 1.35	+81%	91.4	1.77%	2.0 (2002)	8,642	Constant
Latvia 2.34	+125%	88.3	1.2%	2.0 (2003)	5,410	Constant
Lithuania 3.49	+163%	212	1.8%	2.0 (2002)	8,150 (2002)	Constant
Romania 22.40	-18%	985	2.5%	2.38 (2003)	164,000 (2000)	112,000 (2003); 75,000 (2007)
Slovakia 5.41	-1%	386	1.9%	1.89 (2002) 2.0 (2006)	42,600	24,500 (2006)
Slovenia 1.99	-1%	265	1.4%	1.5 (2002)	10,000 (1998)	7,700 (2004)

Source: "NATO Enlargement: The successful candidates," background paper for *SIPRI Yearbook 2003* <web.sipri.org/contents/milap/milex/bgpapers/mex_nato_invitees.pdf>. Dollar figures in constant (2000) prices and exchange-rates.

The drive towards NATO membership also resulted in increased defense spending in the Baltic states. (See Table 4.1.) In order to boost their political image in the NATO countries, in the late 1990s the Baltic states established "2 percent for defense" as a political benchmark. Given that the number of personnel in the armed forces remained at approximately the same level between 2001 and 2005, these increases in defense expenditure have allowed the Baltic states to allocate more resources to training and quality of life. Despite huge progress, however, development of policies and the expenditure of funds for pay, housing, benefits, and family services remain underdeveloped in all of the Baltic states.

Impact of Changing Concepts on Force Structure

NATO membership and Article 5 security guarantees had huge effects on defense concepts and military structures in the Baltic states. As new members of the strongest military alliance in the world, Lithuania, Latvia, and Estonia each had to re-evaluate its entire defense posture and adjust its defense from a purely national to a collective orientation. Before the invitation to join NATO, defense of the Baltic states was based on the principle of total defense. As described by Talvas Jundzis:

[It was] primarily based on numerically small defense forces and units of volunteers as territorial reserves. If required the infantry units [would] be supplemented by a mobilized reserve whose manning is provided for by the compulsory service system and militarized volunteer units. If occupation occurs, [the expectation is to] engage in guerrilla warfare and civilian non-military resistance, to deprive the aggressor of an unlawful governing mechanism and prevent it from really controlling the country.[7]

This strategy was centered on a huge mobilizable reserve comprising people who had undergone compulsory military training. It was estimated that, altogether, the Baltic states in times of general war could mobilize more than one million men at arms, able to fight a guerrilla war and to resist massive aggression from an outside power. Large conscript-based armed forces were thus prepared for total war, but they possessed few capabilities for acting in the international environment, nor did such a system require countries to develop sophisticated social-guarantee systems for their military personnel.

A fear of outside aggression, albeit on smaller scale, remains today. For instance, Latvian President Vaira Vike-Freiberga has on several occasions expressed concern over Russia's foreign policy, and has warned of the possibility that Russia might use force against its neighbors at some point in the future. Former Latvian Minister of Defense Girts Kristovskis has even described Belarus as a potential adversary of Latvia.[8] The Soviet Union, and its successor the Russian Federation, have always

---

7.   Talvas Jundzis, "Baltic States: Cooperation on Security and Integration into the European Security System," NATO fellowship report <www.nato.int/acad/fellow/94-96/jundzis/03-02.htm>.
8.   William Horsley, "Latvia Fears Russian Attack," *BBC News*, April 30, 2000.

been perceived by all three countries as the main threat to their sovereignty and territorial integrity. Although good-neighborly relations have been declared to be a foreign-policy priority, the perception of the potential threat, related to uncertainty about Russia's internal political situation and its external policies, has remained.

Polls confirm that the public in the Baltic states is concerned about a potential threat from the East. After NATO enlargement, however, fear of Russian aggression decreased dramatically. In 2003, the probability of direct military threat was considered in Latvia to be very low; only 9.6 percent said they feared aggression from an outside power.[9] The public views terrorism as a more significant threat.[10] Internal threats, such as drugs and criminality, are seen as most dangerous by more of the population (68.9 percent and 54.3 percent, respectively) than terrorism and military threats (22.6 percent and 9.6 percent, respectively). Almost as threatening, in the view of the Latvian population, are economic crises and natural disasters. Similarly, a military attack against Estonia is seen as highly unlikely, with only 16 percent of Estonia's population believing that such a threat exists.[11] The dominant point of view expressed by the general public in all three Baltic states is that their armed forces would be unable to withstand a large-scale military invasion by a major power. Consequently, the armed forces are viewed as a part of collective efforts to ensure security guarantees and preserve transatlantic links, rather than as an element of national power.

The concept of total defense and self-reliance was modified after accession to the NATO alliance in 2004. Becoming part of the world's strongest military alliance pushed countries to review their defense planning principles and concentrate their resources on areas that are necessary for NATO. Planning need no longer be based on the assumption that, in case of crisis or war, no allies would send reinforcements to the Baltic states. Instead, Lithuania, Latvia, and Estonia must prepare forces to act together with forces of other NATO countries. There is no need to keep a big structure of armed forces; it is enough to have small deployable and sustainable armed forces. Thus, the priority should be on devel-

---

9.   Baltic News Service, "Du trečdaliai latvių—už profesionalią kariuomenę" (Two-thirds of Latvians—for professional armed forces), May 25, 2003.
10. Latvian Ministry of National Defense, "Public opinion."
11. Factum, *Public Opinion and National Defense*, p. 16.

opment of the capabilities necessary for acting with allies. Only in this way can Lithuania, Latvia, and Estonia use their human and financial resources to achieve the best results for themselves and for NATO.

All three Baltic states quickly undertook steps to adjust their defense plans to the new requirements. In 2003, Lithuanian Minister of Defense Linas Linkevicius noted that, "due to their history, the Baltic states should feel vulnerable to traditional military threats," but nevertheless,

we are among those who argue that NATO must transform itself from an immobile defense alliance in the heart of Europe into a flexible and rapidly reactive force capable of intervention wherever needed to prevent a conflict rather than to stop one that already started.... This implies a major shift in our planning assumptions from a reactive Cold War–type defensive posture to a proactive planning that would enable timely action.[12]

A slimmer force structure means a decrease in the planned number of armed-forces personnel in each of the Baltic states, from the previously planned ten-brigade structure to just one or two brigades each. Plans for reservists were adapted accordingly: the planned size of reserve units was diminished by 400 percent across the Baltic states, and attention has shifted from light infantry to specialist training. The number of reservists has been reduced dramatically; for example, Lithuania reduced its planned pool of 100,000 active-duty reservists to just 10,000. These changes did not mean an actual decrease in the number of military personnel in regular units; this number stays at almost the same level. Reductions were made by cutting the number of conscripts and reservists; the number of professionals—voluntary, paid members of the military—will actually be slightly higher in the future. (See Table 4.2.)

After 2005, none of the Baltic states plan major changes in the size of their armed forces; the numbers are likely to remain at approximately the same level for a decade or more. The armed forces of each country will consist of one regular Infantry Brigade (known as LITBRIG, LATBRIG, and ESTBRIG), and one brigade-size Home Guard (reserve) unit to reinforce active units in times of crises. Infantry units will be the largest part of the force structure. A small Logistics Command will support deployments of

---

12. Linas Linkevicius, "Life after Enlargement," keynote speech at Vilnius Roundtable, Northeast European Security after 2004, "Dual Enlargement: The End of History?" June 6 and 7, 2003.

Table 4.2. Changing Plans for Numbers of Military Personnel in the Baltic States

	1995 actual	1995 plans for 2000		2000 plans for 2010		Actual, 2005	
	Full-time regulars	Planned regular	Part-time volunteers	War-time mobiliz-ation	Total man-power incl. mobilized reserve	Full-time regulars	War-time mobiliz-ation
Estonia	3,100	8,000	8,000	28,000	45,000	5,500	16,000
Latvia	2,875	9,000	16,285	20,000	50,000	4,900	16,000
Lithuania	5,035	27,500	10,400	24,000	100,000	12,000	19,000

Source: T. Jundzis, "Baltic States: Cooperation on Security and Integration into the European Security System," <www.nato.int/acad/fellow/94-96/jundzis/03-02.htm>; NATO Parliamentary Assembly Annual Tour, Estonia, Latvia, Lithuania, August 31–September 10, 2000, Secretariat Report, International Secretariat, October 2000, <www.naa.be/archivedpub/trip/00annualtour.asp>; International Institute for Strategic Studies (IISS), *Military Balance 2003/2004* (New York: IISS/Oxford University Press, 2004); Ministry of Defense, Republic of Estonia, Department of Defense Policy and Planning, *Estonian Defense Forces 2003–2006.*

forces in international operations. The Navy and Air Force will remain small and mostly professional, with a very small number of conscripts.

Each Baltic state has agreed with NATO that it will prepare and maintain one battalion-size task force that could be used for deployment in crisis-response operations. In order to implement that promise, Lithuania, for example, is giving the greatest share of its attention to the Motorized Infantry Brigade, of which one battalion can be deployed outside Lithuanian territory for Article 5 operations. Stinger air-defense weapon systems and the Javelin medium-range anti-tank weapon system, to be delivered to the rapid-reaction brigade in coming years, will improve the unit's combat capabilities. According to the "Estonian Defense Review," Estonia's army will consist of one active infantry brigade with one rapid-reaction Estonian Battalion (ESTBAT) that could participate in NATO missions, plus a second high-readiness battalion for internal missions. The full brigade will be operational in 2006 and will include four reserve battalions and reserve support units.[13]

A crucial issue in the integration into NATO became that of finding a national "niche" in the structures of the alliance forces. Lithuania, Lat-

---

13. "Invited NATO Members' Progress on Military Reforms," 146 DSCFC 03 E, <www.nato-pa.int/Default.asp?SHORTCUT=364 >.

via, and Estonia decided to concentrate their efforts on providing specialist groups in such fields as military engineering and medicine, to help share the burden with other members of NATO more effectively. Such capabilities are already receiving increasing attention in the Baltic states. All of the deployable units will be manned largely by professionals and will be certified using criteria adopted by NATO. In practical terms, this means that all military personnel will have to comply with rules and regulations similar to those applicable to other members of the alliance.

National laws of all three Baltic states forbid the use of conscripts for international deployments. This placed the military planners of the Baltic states under pressure to plan for international operations using entirely professional units, and allocating to them the largest share of resources; as a result, the units with conscripts were left with territorial defense responsibility, for which they remained poorly trained and equipped.

The decision to make almost the entire force structure deployable was made only after formal NATO membership. Major obstacles remain on the path toward full implementation of the new defense models. Because the adoption of a professional personnel model is closely linked with the new defense plans, such obstacles may slow down the planned changes in personnel policies as well.

First, all Baltic states still have a significant constituency that believes the territorial defense model is more appropriate than creation of capabilities for the alliance. In particular, some see NATO's force structure and interoperability requirements as both excessively costly and incompatible with current national defense structures.[14] Second, transatlantic disagreements over Iraq and other issues put the Baltic states into a controversial situation: the volatile geostrategic environment, they say, emphasizes the need for alliance members to preserve their capabilities to fight conventional threats. On the other hand, Baltic military planners are under pressure from NATO's leaders and advisers to transform their old defense postures rapidly and to move from a territorial force towards an expeditionary force model. This move requires developing

---

14. G. Kesa, "The Estonian Defense Forces: Modernising Defense," in Anthony Forster, Timothy Edmunds, and Andrew Cottey, eds., "Transforming Postcommunist Militaries: Professionalisation of Armed Forces in Central and Eastern Europe," Working Paper No. 30, University of Sussex, 2001.

new sets of military capabilities and, even more importantly, new thinking about the security environment and threat perception.

Armed Forces and the Public Debate

During the early 1990s, changing threat perceptions and an almost universal political consensus on major security and defense-policy goals brought with them a public disengagement from discussions on military matters. The changing structure and missions of the armed forces were seen to be part of "high politics" in which the general public had little interest; there was very little public concern over defense issues. The 1999 Kosovo campaign found public support for the armed forces and for integration into the alliance at a low point.

There were several important reasons for the erosion of the status of the armed forces in society during the early 1990s. The first years of independence were characterized by economic and financial crises. As a result of internal disputes and clashes, and the inability of senior defense officials and other leaders to deal effectively with defense issues, officers and serving personnel—many of whom volunteered for service in the burst of patriotic enthusiasm that followed independence—grew increasingly discontented. Insufficient funding for military clothing, housing, and salaries worsened the situation. The popularity of military service declined, and the number of qualified and skilled staff opting to leave for the more lucrative commercial sector grew significantly.[15]

Throughout most of the 1990s, the defense budgets of the Baltic states suffered severe shortfalls, described by Latvia's former defense minister, Janis Trapans:

At the outset, the country had to extricate itself from the rubble of a collapsed Soviet economic structure. The government's annual budget was small. Social needs claimed a large share of what was on hand. Because there was no reliable inflow of the government's revenues and therefore

---

15. Gintaras Tamulaitis, "National Security and Defense Policy of the Lithuanian State," Research Paper 26 (Geneva: United Nations Institute for Disarmament Research [UNIDIR], 1994).

no dependable projection for expenditures, money available to various ministries could be delayed or reduced at short notice.[16]

Consequently, defense planners in the Baltic states lived with "survival budgets" that sufficed only to keep the defense establishment afloat. Members of the military were underpaid and their social needs were not addressed by the government. (See Figure 4.1.)

The residual negative associations with the Soviet army, along with a poor understanding of the role of new national defense structures, also influenced the general opinion of the military. Former Chief of Staff of Estonia's Defense Forces, Ants Laaneots, recalls that:

In 1992, when we made an attempt to create a general list of Estonian officers with professional military background, we found only 431 names, including 16 officers who had acquired experience [by serving with] western armies. The rest had a background in the Soviet armed forces. We only managed to include about 60 people out of the whole group in actual service [in Estonia], which was an insignificant number compared with our real need.[17]

Against this backdrop, both the military as an institution and the military as a career were bound to be unpopular. In 1993, it was noted that Lithuania's military forces suffered from a chronic lack of popular prestige.[18] A 1994 opinion poll in Latvia ranked the military eighteenth in a list of desired careers.[19]

---

16. Janis Trapans, "Criteria for Success or Failure in Security Sector Reform: The Case of Latvia," Working Paper Series No. 17 (Geneva Centre for the Democratic Control of the Armed Forces, 2002), p. 13.

17. Ants Laaneots, "Democratic Control of Armed Forces: The Case of Estonia," presentation at the conference on "Civil-Military Relations and Defense Planning: Challenges for Central and Eastern Europe in the New Era," Kiev, 2000.

18. R.A. Vitas, "Civil-Military Relations in Lithuania," in C.P. Danopoulus and D. Zirker, eds., Civil-Military Relations in the Soviet and Yugoslav Successor States (Boulder, Colo.: Westview Press, 1996), p. 73.

19. I. Viksne, "Democratic Control of Armed Forces in Latvia," in A. Cottey, T. Edmunds, and A. Forster, eds., Guarding the Guards in Central and Eastern Europe (London: Palgrave, 2001).

Figure 4.1. Military Expenditures in the Baltic States (in constant US$ millions)

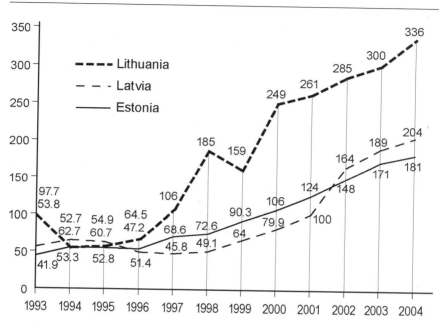

Source: SIPRI project on military expenditures, *The SIPRI Military Expenditure Database* <first.sipri.org/non_first/login_milex.php>. For 2004, information from official website of the Ministry of Defense for each of the three Baltic countries.

This situation has changed. A 2003 poll showed that, of all state institutions, the Lithuanian armed forces ranked third in popularity in public opinion polls, surpassed only by the mass media and the church.[20] The Lithuanian armed forces are trusted by 65 percent of the total population (18 percent have no opinion).[21] The popularity of the Latvian Armed Forces increased from 9.8 percent in 1999 to 21.3 percent in 2002. Only the church and the mass media received higher confidence ratings than

20. Polls are conducted by Vilmorus (polling organization) and results are published monthly in the biggest Lithuanian daily, *Lietuvos Rytas*. The economic crisis of 1999 saw the LAF's resurgent popularity become somewhat dented.

21. Baltijos tyrimai, "Lietuvos gyventojų nuomonė apie Lietuvos kariuomenę" (Baltic Survey, Public opinion about the Lithuanian armed forces), survey released in June 2003.

the military.[22] The Estonian Defense Forces are trusted by 75 percent of all respondents, who rank them the fourth most reliable state institution (behind the president, the Border Guard, and the Bank of Estonia).[23] Consistent with the improved image of the military as an institution, the military profession has become a desirable career. An increasing number of conscripts express the wish to remain in the armed forces, and competition to enter military academies is also increasing.

Several developments have contributed to the improved public attitude towards the armed forces. First, the governments have worked to present information to the public on security policy and the armed forces. Senior officials now appear more frequently on television and in major newspapers than they did in the past, and relations with the mass media have improved significantly. Secondly, Western observers and officials have frequently praised the successful evolution of the Baltic states' armed forces, and their positive opinions have been reflected in Lithuanian, Latvian, and Estonian society. The training and discipline of the armed forces have improved significantly, and participation in international peace operations and training exercises has demonstrated their growing military capability.

Third, economic and political developments have brought more support for defense. Economies in the Baltic states are improving and parliamentary decisions on appropriations are no longer dominated by social needs. Politicians have declared membership in NATO to be a foreign-policy priority, and their ambitious political pronouncements have had to be matched with allocation of additional resources to defense. For example, NATO has informally indicated that candidate countries should devote 2 percent of their gross domestic product (GDP) to defense. According to Latvia's former defense minister, Janis Trapans, "when cabinets and parliamentary committees divided the budget, a strong argument that Latvia's Defense Ministry made [was] the '2 percent for NATO' [argument]."[24] Perhaps it is not surprising,

---

22. Viksne, "Democratic Control of Armed Forces in Latvia."
23. Press and Information Department, Estonian Ministry of Foreign Affairs, "Estonia Today: Support for NATO Membership," February 2004; Factum, *Public Opinion and National Defense*, p. 10.
24. Trapans, "Criteria for Success or Failure in Security Sector Reform," p. 14.

then, that increases in defense expenditures have been supported by the general public. In Latvia, a large proportion of the population thinks that the defense budget should be increased further; in 2001 this was the opinion of 45.7 percent of those surveyed.[25]

Despite increases in defense budgets and wages, the Lithuanian, Latvian, and Estonian militaries still do not enjoy social benefits comparable to members of the militaries of the other members of the alliance. Apart from government-provided housing or housing allowances, other forms of support are less developed or non-existent. Such perquisites as allowances for boarding school for service families whose mobility would otherwise disrupt their children's education; medical care; scholarships or other educational support for children; family assistance programs; recreational facilities and discount travel; or openings in child-care centers for military families are basically not available in Lithuania, Latvia, or Estonia.

If the trend towards professionalization continues, Lithuania, Latvia, and Estonia will in the future face the same challenges as other European countries that deploy personnel for military missions abroad. Because "new missions and frequent deployments can be a strain on military families," they will need "improved support and benefits to help them cope with the problems that arise while the service member is deployed and to offset some of the negatives of frequent deployments."[26]

Increasing participation by the Baltic states in international operations will force them to allocate more resources and attention to pay,

---

25. Latvian Ministry of National Defense, "Public opinion," <www.mod.lv>. In 2002, 30 percent of people surveyed in Estonia and 32 percent of those surveyed in Lithuania thought that defense budgets should be increased. Only 10 percent in Latvia and 14 percent in Estonia, but 47 percent in Lithuania, thought that defense budgets should be decreased (26 percent in Latvia and 48 percent in Estonia thought it should stay the same). Ibid.; Factum, *Public Opinion and National Defense*, p. 19; Baltijos tyrimai, "Lietuvos gyventojų nuomonė apie Lietuvos kariuomenę" (Baltic Survey, Public opinion about the Lithuanian Armed Forces), survey released in June 2003.
26. Deborah Clay-Mendez and Cindy Williams, "Recruit the Soldier, Retain the Family—Then Hire a Contractor: A Cautionary Tale from the U.S. Experience with an All Volunteer Force," paper prepared for conference on "Building Military Capability: The Transformation of Personnel Policies," Brussels, June 13–15, 2004. See also Chapter 10 in this volume by Deborah Clay-Mendez.

housing, family benefits, and other quality-of-life programs for military personnel. Otherwise, they will not be able to attract and keep enough qualified personnel to do the job, and could fail to meet their international commitments.

Changing Attitude towards Compulsory Military Service

Increasing participation in international operations and the protection afforded by NATO security guarantees have provided the Baltic states with a solid basis for rethinking their policies on conscription and compulsory military service. Decisions to create small, mobile forces that could contribute to alliance missions have changed how people perceive the functions of the armed forces and their role in society. Expeditionary warfare requires a different quality of military forces and new models of recruitment. New requirements and new missions call for soldiers who are not only well-trained in military terms, but also well educated and aware of international relations, fluent in foreign languages, and expert in civil-military relations: in other words, true professionals.

The "total defense" concept previously applied by Lithuania, Latvia, and Estonia required large mobilizable reserves to reinforce active units. A conscription system was essential to prepare each and every citizen to fight or to resist aggression by non-military means. In reality, the Baltic states never fully implemented this concept; the youth were unwilling to spend a year in the armed forces. The Ministries of Defense have never had enough human and material resources for the extensive training programs and preparation of infrastructure that would be required to deal with all the draftees who would serve under a system of truly universal service. On paper, the plans looked impressive, but in reality less than 10–25 percent of young males aged 18 served as conscripts in the Baltic states' armed forces.

There were many reasons for this. According to the chief of Lithuania's Draft Agency, Major General (retired) Jonas Andriškevičius, in 2002, 48 percent of Lithuania's young people who appeared before the draft agency's examiners were identified as not suitable for military service for health reasons. Corruption in the health system was mostly to blame. Others were students, or had small children, or helped their elderly parents, or for other reasons were exempt from compulsory military service. In total, only one of seven Lithuanian citizens at the age of 19 actually reports for compulsory military service. Germany provides a sharp contrast: there, two out of three young people in the relevant age group perform military or alternative national service; 96 percent of young Germans in the relevant age cohort report for service, compared to just 62 percent for Lithuania.[27] The words "universal" and "compulsory" thus in this case lose much of their meaning. Moreover, downsizing of the armed forces, with the creation of high-readiness units, has eroded the rationale for retaining conscription.

In Lithuania, public support for a professional military is increasing; in 2003, more than half of the population (53 percent) declared its support for ending conscription.[28] Of those polled, however, 68 percent declared their support for the proposition that "the armed forces are necessary because only there can young people be taught how to defend our country."[29] This inconsistency reflects two distinct trends in the society: on the one hand, the general public wishes to preserve the armed forces as a state-building institution, while on the other, the absence of a visible military threat and the existence of NATO security guarantees strengthen arguments against conscription. Although the trend is similar in Estonia, the majority of Estonians still consider it important to preserve a universal military obligation: this view is upheld by 60 percent of the population. A majority of Estonian citizens believe that all young men should still be required to complete military service; the shift to professional armed forces was supported only by a third of survey respondents.[30]

During the period 2000–2002, support for fully professional armed forces was highest in Latvia; the majority of the Latvian population expressed the belief that the state's armed forces should be based on professional, rather than conscripted, armed forces. According to a 1999

---

27. A. Gurevičius, "Geriausi kareiviai—studentais netapę vaikinai" (The best military [members] are young people who failed to enter universities), *Respublika*, November 10, 2003; D.K. Burmeister, *The German Model of Conscription: Compulsory Military Service in the 21st Century*, Conference on "Recruiting Models for the Armed Forces in the 21st Century," Copenhagen, April 7–8, 2003.

28. "Baltijos tyrimai Lietuvos gyventojų nuomonė apie Lietuvos kariuomenę" (Public opinion about the Lithuanian armed forces), survey released in June 2003. In the same poll, 28 percent disagreed and 19 percent had no opinion on this subject.

29. Ibid. The poll found 24 percent against and 8 percent with no opinion.

30. "Estonia Today: Support for NATO Membership."

survey, 66 percent of the Latvian population already supported creation of a professional military.[31] A survey conducted three years later revealed that this proportion had not changed; only 21.9 percent of Latvians supported conscription in 2002.[32] (The main argument of supporters was that conscription helps to prepare citizens to resist foreign invasion.) This was a big change from 1994, when 71.5 percent of the population surveyed believed a national army to be essential, and only 15.9 percent opposed it.[33]

Latvia was the first Baltic state to announce the official abolition of conscription. The "State Defense Concept," approved by the Latvian Cabinet of Ministers on September 30, 2003, and accepted by the Latvian *Saeima* on November 13, 2003, declared that the policy of mandatory military service in the Latvian Armed Forces would cease by the end of 2006. Several reasons were given for this move. First, the armed forces had to meet the demands of the current security situation, which requires quality (for participation in multi-national operations), and not quantity (for national defense). The second reason was the high level of public support for a professional military. The third was that membership in NATO provides security guarantees to Latvia, while imposing an obligation to ensure the country's readiness for collective security within the scope of the alliance.

Lithuania and Estonia may very well follow Latvia's example and end military conscription in the future. Their laws already prohibit deployment of conscripts to international operations. The Lithuanian and Estonian armed forces today need to enlist only about 10–20 percent of all members of the "recruitment niche" of 19-to-27-year-olds. The system is not very stringent and conscription easy to avoid. For example, for a small fee, any young man can receive a health exemption statement from a doctor to present to the military draft board. Membership in the European Union provides young people with opportunities to obtain education abroad and salaries well above those of even professional members of the military. For these reasons, the Lithuanian and

---

31. "Latvian Ministry of National Defense, "Public opinion," <www.mod.lv>.
32. Baltic News Service "Du trečdaliai latvių—už profesionalią kariuomenę" (Two-thirds of Latvians: for professional armed forces), May 25, 2003.
33. Jundzis, "Baltic States: Cooperation on Security and Integration."

Table 4.3. Comparison of Average Monthly Salaries in Lithuania and Estonia (in Euros)

	Lithuania	Estonia
Average civilian salary	360	470
Armed forces: average salary of private	350	270–340
Armed forces: average salary of captain	830–950	660–830
In addition each member of the military receives:		
— food allowance	100	60
— accommodation allowance	60–120	45–85

Source: Data provided by Lithuanian and Estonian Ministries of Defense.

Estonian systems can already be described as temporary and based on "voluntary conscription." A political decision to abandon such systems seems very likely to be made in the next few years.

The course of the conscription debate in Lithuania and Estonia will depend considerably on the success of the Latvian transition. The Latvian decision to abandon conscription will certainly improve its military capabilities, but many challenges lie ahead. In order to attract more skilled people to join the military in 2004, the Latvian government increased salaries for military professionals by 30 percent, and it is likely to increase them even more in the future. (See also Table 4.3.) Personnel expenditures already account for more than 50 percent of the defense budget; absent additional reductions in force size, further increases in pay and benefits would eat into spending for deployment capabilities and could ruin modernization plans.

Although in the Baltic states, population growth is negative (nearly the lowest in the world) and overall population is decreasing, the current trend towards professionalization is not likely to be complicated by the worsening demographic situation.[34] Lithuania's population growth rate is negative at –0.23 percent (number 220 of 232 countries), while that of Estonia is –0.49 percent (at 224), and Latvia lower still at –0.73 percent (230). However, it will take about a decade for the declining population to result

---

34. CIA Factbook, map and graph, "Europe: People: Population growth rate," <www.nationmaster.com>.

in a smaller recruitment base for these countries. According to the Lithuanian Recruitment Agency, the number of 18-year-olds will increase from 25,000 in 2004 to 29,000 in 2009; afterwards it will go down to 18,000 in 2019. Moreover, even if all three Baltic states decide to abolish conscription and to create fully professional armed forces, a recruitment success rate of 2 percent will provide more than enough volunteers to satisfy the armed forces' needs. At least until 2019, the armed forces in Lithuania and Estonia must recruit or conscript at most only 3,000 military personnel annually in order to satisfy their defense needs. (See Table 4.4.)

Ultimately, the decision to abandon conscription will be a political question, not a military one. The unwillingness or inability of governmental agencies to enforce conscription legislation strictly has meant that conscripts are more like "volunteer conscripts," and thus this issue has not yet come on to the political agenda. However, in the future Lithuania and Estonia are likely to resume public debate on the professionalization of their armed forces.

Conclusion

After joining NATO, the military establishments in the Baltic states began to face all of these new challenges. Membership required reevaluating defense concepts and adopting collective thinking about national defense. This task has not yet been fully implemented in concrete military plans and doctrines, although substantial progress has been made. NATO's role here was indispensable: allies provided not only the specification of requirements but also the instruments to meet those requirements. Engagement, initially, in NATO's Partnership for Peace and later in other NATO initiatives has had a significant impact. These processes required all of the new NATO members to adopt detailed defense planning standards and practices for operating within NATO. They also prompted the decision by Lithuania, Latvia, and Estonia to focus on capabilities for collective defense, rather than for defense of their own territory. Defense reforms in Lithuania, Latvia, and Estonia derived from their desire to join NATO.

In parallel to the changing defense concepts, new personnel policies were adopted. From under-trained, under-paid, and under-equipped forces, the Lithuanian, Latvian, and Estonian armed forces emerged as equal partners of the other members of the alliance. Conscription is slowly fading away; the armed forces are becoming leaner but more capable, and

Table 4.4. Demographic Bases of the Baltics' Militaries

	Lithuania	Latvia	Estonia
Military-eligible manpower—those fit for military service, age 19–27	738,602	466,659	257,386
New military-eligible manpower each year (those reaching military age of 19 years annually)	28,300	19,209	10,884
Potential new recruits annually after professionalization, if recruitment success rate (the number of new recruits divided by the size of the recruitment niche) is 2 percent	14,800	9,500	5,100
Required recruitment each year, assuming exit rate of 15 percent (number who leave military each year): (15 percent of wartime structure)	2,850	2,400	2,400
Percentage of new recruits that must come from annual military-eligible manpower pool (assuming that all recruits come from this pool)	10%	12%	22%
Percentage of military among total population	0.54%	0.68%	1.6%

Source: CIA Factbook, map and graph, "Europe: People: Population growth rate," <www.nationmaster.com>. The calculations in this table are based on Rickard Sandell, "Coping with Demography: Military Recruitment in Times of Population Decline," paper prepared for the conference "Building Military Capability: The Transformation of Personnel Policies," held in Brussels June 13–15, 2004; see also Chapter 3 by Rickard Sandell in this volume.

they are being used more widely. Armed forces units now spend most of their time in international operations or preparing for new deployments. More active participation in NATO activities and out-of-area operation will keep constant pressure upon decisionmakers in Vilnius, Riga, and Tallinn to invest more in military personnel. They will need to adopt new social programs, today almost non-existent, to recruit the best and most suitable people to the armed forces. Although training and basic infrastructure development issues will not continue to dominate Baltic defense planners' agenda, recruitment enhancement and retention procedures will require more attention. The Baltic states have enough human and financial resources to perform this task, but the speed of success will largely depend on the transatlantic political agenda, the successful functioning of the alliance, and the credibility of its security guarantees.

Part II
The Choice of Personnel Model

Chapter 5

The Economic Case for All-Volunteer Forces

John T. Warner and Sebastian Negrusa

The fall of the Berlin Wall and the resulting reduction in required forces has caused many countries of Europe to reconsider how they acquire military manpower. France and Spain ended conscription in 2001, Portugal in 2003, Hungary in 2004, and Italy in 2005. Among the ten countries invited to join NATO in 2004, Latvia, Romania, Slovakia, and Slovenia have all ended conscription or plan to phase it out by 2008 or sooner. However, a number of other European countries plan to continue conscription, including Denmark, Norway, Germany, Greece, Turkey, Bulgaria, and Poland.

The decisions of European countries to end conscription will no doubt involve many political, social, and historical considerations, but economic considerations will play a critical role. The economic considerations are two-fold. First, does an all-volunteer force (AVF) have lower or higher real resource cost than a force of equal effectiveness (not necessarily equal size) obtained with conscription? Second, is an AVF more equitable than a draft? When the Gates Commission recommended in 1970 that the United States end conscription (which it did in 1973), it answered both questions in the affirmative.[1]

This chapter has three purposes. The first is to describe the economic theory of the choice about whether to procure military manpower by conscription or through volunteers. The second is to consider some of the critics' typical objections to a volunteer force and see whether those

---

1. *Report of the President's Commission on an All-Volunteer Armed Force* (Washington, D.C.: U.S. Government Printing Office [U.S. GPO], 1970); here-

concerns have been realized in the United States. The third is to examine the choices of European countries about whether to end conscription in light of the economic model presented in the chapter.

The Economics of Military Manpower Procurement

From the time the Gates Commission recommended an end to the draft in the United States, a number of economists have studied the economics of military manpower procurement.[2] The general view among these economists was that an AVF is always cheaper than a draft, not in government budget terms but in terms of the real resource (social) cost to the country. Nobel Prize winning economist Milton Friedman played an influential role in the U.S. decision to end conscription, both as a member of the Gates Commission and through his *Newsweek* column and other public writings. Recent work, however, suggests that the economic case for a volunteer force is not as clear-cut as previously thought.[3] In fact, in some economic models, there are cases in which conscription has a lower social cost than an equally capable volunteer force. Here, we describe one such model, the Warner-Asch analysis, because it is the most complete of the three recent analyses.[4]

---

after referred to as the Gates Commission report.

2. W. Oi, "The Costs and Implications of an All-Volunteer Force," in Sol Tax, ed., *The Draft* (Chicago: University of Chicago Press, 1967), pp. 221–251; W. Oi, "The Economic Cost of the Draft," *American Economic Review*, Vol. 57, No. 2 (1967), pp. 39–62; W.L. Hansen and B. Weisbrod, "Economics of a Military Draft," *Quarterly Journal of Economics*, Vol. 81, No. 3 (1967), pp. 395–421; Milton Friedman, "Why Not a Volunteer Army?" in Tax, *The Draft*, pp. 200–207; S. Altman and R. Barro, "Officer Supply: The Impact of Pay, the Draft, and the Vietnam War," *American Economic Review*, Vol. 61, No. 4 (1971), pp. 649–664.

3. D. Lee and R. McKenzie, "Reexamination of the Relative Efficiency of the Draft and the All-Volunteer Army," *Southern Economic Journal*, Vol. 59 (1992), pp. 644–654; T. Ross, "Raising an Army: A Positive Theory of Military Recruitment," *Journal of Law and Economics*, Vol. 37, No. 1 (1994), pp. 101–131; J. Warner and B. Asch, "The Economic Theory of the Military Draft Reconsidered," *Defence and Peace Economics*, Vol. 7 (1996), pp. 297–312.

4. The Warner-Asch analysis explicitly analyzed productivity differences between volunteer and draft forces and the factors that tend to make volunteer forces more productive. The Lee-McKenzie and Ross analyses assumed forces of equal size and did not consider potential differences in productiv-

EFFICIENCY ISSUES

We begin with the real resource costs (or social costs) of a military force: the opportunity cost, or value in forgone uses, of all of the resources an economy uses in the provision of a military force. There are costs associated with developing, procuring, operating, and maintaining hardware; providing the manpower to operate the hardware; and deploying the force. The analysis of military manpower procurement focuses on the second of these costs, but these various costs may be interrelated. There are four manpower costs associated with supplying a military force:

- opportunity costs of the personnel in the force;

- social costs associated with efforts to evade military service;

- cost of recruiting and training;

- deadweight tax losses associated with raising tax revenues to pay the force.

OPPORTUNITY COSTS. Opportunity cost is what society gives up elsewhere because individuals are in uniform rather than engaged in civilian pursuits. Opportunity cost is the sum of what military personnel would have produced and earned if they had been in the civilian sector rather than the military sector (W^C) and the net value that personnel place on the non-pecuniary aspects of civilian life (τ): $OC = W^C + \tau$. The supply curve of military personnel is based on opportunity cost, as shown in Figure 5.1. The supply curve arrays individuals by their opportunity costs from lowest (OC_{MIN}) to highest (OC_{MAX}). Each point on the curve shows how many individuals would be willing to join at a given military wage (W^M).

---

ity. The Gates Commission's analysis focused mainly on cost, although the Commission estimated a volunteer force to be about 10 percent more productive, primarily as a result of lower turnover and the implied need for a smaller training establishment. More is said about productivity differences below.

Figure 5.1. Enlistment Outcomes and Social Costs in a Volunteer System and a Random Lottery Draft, No Evasion Costs

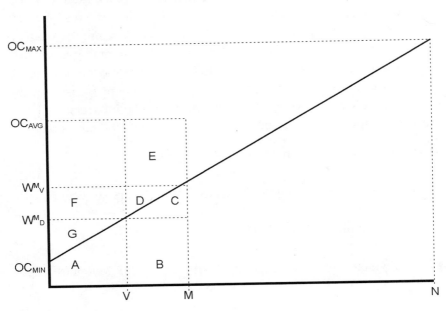

Key:
W^M_D = draft wage, W^M_V = volunteer wage, OC_{MIN} = minimum opportunity cost in population, OC_{MAX} = maximum opportunity cost in population, OC_{AVG} = average opportunity cost of individuals with opportunity cost above W^M_D, V = number of volunteers, M = total number of recruits, and N = population eligible for military service.

The position and slope of the curve are affected by civilian wage opportunities, non-pecuniary factors, and the military recruiting effort. For example, general productivity growth that raises all civilian-sector wage opportunities proportionately increases everyone's opportunity costs and shifts supply to the left. A wave of patriotism or improvements in the conditions of military life would shift it to the right. The slope of the supply curve is based on the variation in opportunity costs among the N individuals eligible for military service. If all individuals have the same opportunity cost, the supply curve would be horizontal. But more variation in either civilian wage opportunities or in preferences for civilian over military life lowers OC_{MIN} and raises OC_{MAX}, and thereby increases the slope of the military supply curve. The result is that enlistment is less responsive to changes in the military wage (the supply curve is less elastic) and a larger pay increase is needed to elicit a given change in enlistment.[5]

As the U.S. experience indicates, the supply curve shown in Figure 5.1 can be shifted outward by a more intensive recruiting effort.[6] The primary recruiting resources in the United States are recruiters and advertising, for which the U.S. Department of Defense spends over $1 billion annually. Through information and persuasion, recruiters and advertising can influence youth preferences and thereby expand the number of individuals willing to join the military at a given wage W^M. Pay policy under the volunteer force is not independent of recruiting costs, because a more intensive recruiting effort can substitute for higher pay. But if there are diminishing returns to recruiting resources, then the costs of recruiters and advertising, like payroll costs, rise exponentially with respect to the number of recruits (M). Furthermore, with diminishing returns there exists a unique, cost-minimizing combination of pay and recruiting resources for each desired number of recruits. Evidence for the United States indicates that there are, indeed, diminishing returns to recruiting resources.[7]

Suppose a country needs a force of size M. Under a volunteer system, it must pay a wage of W^M_V to induce M individuals to join, given the resources devoted to recruiting. The M volunteers are individuals whose opportunity costs of military service are less than or equal to W^M_V. The opportunity cost of the whole force is the sum of the opportunity costs of the M volunteers (area A+B+C in Figure 5.1).

In the case of a draft, the government sets a lower wage (W^M_D) and consequently attracts only V (< M) volunteers. The military must therefore draft M-V individuals from the pool of N-V (non-volunteers) in

---

5. Elasticity measures the responsiveness of enlistment supply to military wages and is defined as $\varepsilon = \%\Delta E / \%\Delta W^M$. An elasticity of 1, for instance, indicates that a 10 percent increase in military pay is associated with a 10 percent increase in enlistment.

6. See J. Warner and B. Asch, "The Economics of Military Manpower," in Keith Hartley and Todd Sandler, eds., *Handbook of Defense Economics* (New York: North-Holland, 1995).

7. Evidence for the United States is reviewed in Warner and Asch, "The Economics of Military Manpower." Estimates indicate that a 10 percent expansion of the recruiter force raises enlistments by about 5 percent, while a 10 percent increase in advertising raises enlistments by less than 1 percent.

order to provide a force of size M (where N is the population of individuals eligible for military service). Drafts can take many forms. One form is a pure lottery draft in which all individuals eligible for military service have an equal chance of being selected for military service. Therefore, in a random lottery draft, M-V draftees are selected at random from the pool of N-V individuals. The average opportunity cost (OC$_{AVG}$) of a randomly selected draftee will be the average opportunity cost of the N-V draft-eligible non-volunteers. Because individuals are selected at random, the average opportunity cost of the M-V draftees will also equal OC$_{AVG}$, which in turn exceeds the opportunity costs of the M-V marginal volunteers. As a result, the opportunity cost of a draft force exceeds the opportunity cost of a volunteer force. In Figure 5.1, the opportunity cost of a draft force is A+B+C+D+E, so in a random lottery draft, the opportunity cost of the draft force exceeds the cost of a volunteer force by area D+E.

Methods of conscription other than by pure random lottery can reduce the excess opportunity cost of a draft force. The U.S. World War I draft was by "lowest value drafted first."[8] Draft boards in World War I exempted those who had the highest value in the civilian sector and conscripted those with the lowest value in the civilian sector. Of course, civilian wages do not fully reflect individuals' opportunity costs, which include a the non-pecuniary preference factor τ. But if civilian wages and the non-pecuniary preference factor τ are unrelated, a least-value-drafted-first system will tend to conscript the same individuals who would have served in the volunteer system and therefore reduces the excess opportunity cost of the draft force over a volunteer force. While such a system reduces the excess opportunity cost of a draft force, it does so by shifting the burden of providing for a military force from the general taxpayer to the conscripts with the poorest civilian opportunities. It raises obvious equity issues and is the reason why more recent drafts in the United States (and perhaps elsewhere) have been lottery-based.

---

8. R. Cooper, "Military Manpower Procurement: Equity, Efficiency, and National Security," in Martin Anderson, ed., *Registration and the Draft: Proceedings of the Hoover-Rochester Conference on the All-Volunteer Force* (Stanford, Calif.: Hoover Press, 1982), pp. 343–376.

EVASION COSTS. The second cost associated with conscription arises from the fact that individuals may expend resources to evade it and the government must expend resources to prevent this evasion.[9] Individuals will seek to evade conscription if the personal benefits from doing so exceed the costs. Consider first the benefits. In a pure lottery draft, each individual's probability of being drafted is the ratio of the number to be drafted to the pool of non-volunteers: $\Pi = (M-V)/(N-V)$. Let θ be the probability that the government can prevent evasion and $1-\theta$ be the probability of successful evasion. The benefit to successful evasion is $(1-\theta)\Pi\,\delta(OC - W^M_D)$. This expression weights the net gain from evasion, $OC\text{-}W^M_D$, by the product of the probability of being drafted and the probability of successful evasion. The benefit to evasion thus rises with the threat of conscription and with the likelihood of successful evasion.

The gain to evasion is multiplied by another term, δ, that accounts for other influences such as the length of service under conscription (which might vary from months to years) and the fact that draft evaders may be forced into shadow labor markets that do not provide the same civilian opportunities that are available without evasion. A small value of δ due to a short enlistment period or a large wage penalty in shadow labor markets reduces the gain from evasion.

Now consider the costs of evasion. One cost is the direct cost (C_e) of moving underground or going to another country. Another cost is the penalty the individual will suffer if unsuccessful, denoted by the term J. The penalty might include jail time and possible loss of future earnings due to a prison record. The full expected cost of evasion is thus $C_e + \theta J$.

Evasion occurs if $C_e + \theta J < (1-\theta)\Pi\delta(OC - W^M_D)$ and reduces the total population of available individuals from N to θN (see Figure 5.2).

If the cost of evasion is the same for everyone, then the individuals with the highest opportunity costs seek to evade the draft. Furthermore, individuals seek to evade the draft either because they have high civilian wage opportunities or because they have high positive values of the non-pecuniary preference factor τ. It is clear from the condition for evasion activity that such activities will increase, the higher the probability

9. L. Sjaastad and R. Hansen, "The Conscription Tax: An Empirical Analysis," in *Studies Prepared for the President's Commission on an All-Volunteer Armed Force,* Vol. II (Washington, D.C.: U.S. GPO, 1970).

Figure 5.2. Enlistment Outcomes and Social Costs in a Volunteer System and a Random Lottery Draft (With Evasion Costs)

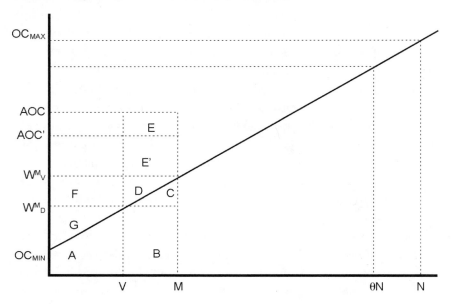

of being drafted (Π), and the higher the probability of successful evasion $(1-\theta)$. Notice, though, from Figure 5.2 that if $(1-\theta)N$ individuals successfully evade the draft, the opportunity cost of those remaining in the draft pool declines by the difference of the areas E and E'.

The social cost of evasion is $C_e(N-N') + C_G$ where $N-N'$ is the number of individuals who attempt evasion and C_G are the costs to the government of preventing it.[10] Such costs include monitoring the borders to prevent draft dodgers from leaving the country, and prosecuting and incarcerating them. C_G is a function of θ (the probability of detecting and preventing evasion) and of the size of the draft pool ($P = N-V$). Thus, $C_G=C_G(\theta, P, F)$. Government costs increase as the desired level of evasion prevention (θ) increases and as the size of the draft pool P increases. That is, to achieve a given success in evasion prevention, costs must increase as the size of the pool to be monitored increases.

---

10. $N-N'$ is the number of individuals who attempt evasion and $(1-\theta)N$ is the number who are successful. $N-N'$ exceeds $(1-\theta)N$ if some evasion is unsuccessful.

How much will the government spend to prevent evasion and how much evasion will occur? To answer this question, notice that the government's cost of staffing the military force is the military payroll plus the cost of evasion prevention: $W^M_D M + C_G$. The government will choose the level of military pay under the draft (W^M_D) and the level of draft evasion expenditures (C_G) to minimize total cost. But notice that this affects the mix of the force between volunteers and draftees; as W^M_D increases, volunteers increase and the required number of conscripts declines. When evasion is easy to stop, the government will increase C_G while at the same time reduce the military wage W^M_D. Costly and difficult prevention of evasion requires the government to reduce evasion prevention expenditures but increase the military wage. Thus the optimal wage level under the draft—and therefore the mix of the force between volunteers and draftees—is determined (at least in part) by the ease of detecting and preventing evasion.

Two extreme cases help illustrate these ideas. First, if the government could prevent evasion without cost, θ would equal 1 and C_G would equal 0. In this case, there would be no evasion and the situation would be as depicted in Figure 5.1. If there is no evasion, this implies that the government can set a very low (subsistence) level of military pay. Consequently, the force will comprise a high ratio of draftees to volunteers. At the other extreme, suppose that individuals can evade the draft at no cost ($C_e = 0$). Then, as long as θ is less than 1, everyone with an opportunity cost above W^M_D would evade the draft and the pool of military-eligible individuals would shrink to V. In this case, the draft is impossible to enforce and the government must resort to a volunteer system to sustain a force of size M (by increasing military pay to W^M_V). The real world is, of course, between these two extremes, but they serve to set the bounds on evasion costs, the level of pay during a draft, and the mix of volunteers and conscripts.

RECRUITING AND TRAINING COSTS. Under a draft, the resources devoted to recruiting are minimal and the main recruiting cost is the cost of testing recruits for the purposes of screening out unqualified prospects and assigning those who are enlisted to appropriate occupations. A volunteer force requires a more substantial recruiting effort to provide information to prospective recruits and entice them to join. If there are diminishing returns to recruiting resources, the costs of recruiters and advertising, like payroll costs, will rise exponentially with respect to the number of recruits (M).

Personnel who enter military service can serve for one term or many terms and the terms themselves can vary. In the European countries that currently have a conscripted force, terms of service for draftees range from 6 months to 15 months. In the United States prior to 1973, draftees served for two years. But the higher pay required to implement a volunteer force induces volunteers to join for longer initial terms and re-enlist at much higher rates. The average length of enlistment in the United States is now about 4.5 years. One advantage of longer initial enlistments and higher retention is reduced turnover and lower training costs. The annual turnover rate in the U.S. enlisted force during the draft was about 21 percent; today it is around 15 percent.[11]

DEADWEIGHT TAX-LOSS COST. The budgetary cost of a military force is not a real cost per se. Governments derive the means to pay personnel from taxes on their citizens, which represents a pure transfer from taxpayers to military personnel. However, there is a real cost associated with taxation. Higher taxes cause individuals and businesses to distort economic decisions, such as decisions regarding saving versus consumption, or work versus leisure. An estimate of the economic loss in the United States from tax distortions (known as "deadweight tax losses") is about 30 cents per dollar of tax revenue.[12] The deadweight tax loss due to a military force is proportional to the military payroll. Because the payroll associated with a volunteer force of a given size is always larger than the payroll of a draft force of equal size, the deadweight tax loss associated with the volunteer force is larger. Furthermore, under a volunteer force the military must raise pay when it wants to expand the force, something it does not have to do under conscription. As a result, the military payroll and the deadweight tax loss due to that payroll rise exponentially under a volunteer force. But these costs

11. J. Warner and B. Asch, "The Record and Prospects of the All-Volunteer Military in the United States," *Journal of Economic Perspectives*, Vol. 15, No. 2 (2001), pp. 169–192.

12. E. Browning, "On the Marginal Welfare Cost of Taxation," *American Economic Review*, Vol. 77, No. 1 (1987), pp. 11–23.

Figure 5.3. Total Costs of Draft and Volunteer Forces

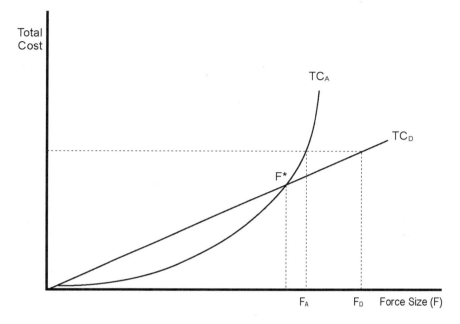

Key: TC_A = total cost of a volunteer force, TC_D = total cost of conscripted force, F_A = volunteer force size, and F_D = draft force size.

rise only linearly under a draft, due to the fact that additional personnel may be brought in under compulsion, without raising the wage.

FACTORS INFLUENCING THE CROSSOVER POINT

Figure 5.3 displays the sum of the four costs of a military force as a function of force size. Due to the exponential rise in the deadweight tax cost of the volunteer force, its cost rises faster with force size than does the cost of a draft force. Below (above) the force size F*, a volunteer force has lower (higher) social cost. The crossover point F* at which a draft force becomes cheaper than an equally-sized volunteer force is a function of several factors.

If more individuals are willing to join the military at a given military wage, the supply curve in Figure 5.1 shifts to the right. Such an increase in supply reduces the opportunity cost and the deadweight tax cost of staffing a military force by voluntary means relative to the cost of staffing it by conscription. TC_A (the total cost of a volunteer army) shifts outward relative to TC_D (the total cost of a draft) and F* increases. An increase in the responsiveness (elasticity) of supply to pay (where the supply curve in Figure 5.1 becomes flatter) has the same effect.

An increase in the ease of draft avoidance and an increase in the government's cost of preventing it will tend to increase the total costs of a draft system and push the crossover point F* to the right. When evasion costs become extremely high, the total cost of a draft will exceed the total cost of an AVF at every force size. The ease of evasion and the high cost of detecting and preventing it, as European borders have become more open and the circulation of individuals is almost completely free, may explain why some European countries have ended conscription or are contemplating its end. The countries that do not plan to end conscription, such as Turkey, may be the ones into which and out of which mobility may be more difficult.

The draft wage is not an independent variable in the model. It is negatively related to θ (the probability that the government can prevent draft evasion). So if θ is low, the draft wage must be high, as the government minimizes total budgetary costs. The higher the draft wage, the higher the number of volunteers and therefore the fewer people need to be drafted. Under most circumstances F* will move to the right, making the case for a volunteer system more compelling. The crossover point F* moves rightward because the increase in wage costs under a draft is higher than the reduction in C_G (cost of preventing evasion) plus the opportunity-cost gain as a result of evasion.

Recruiting costs under a draft are likely to be proportional to the number of recruits, therefore maintaining the linearity of the TC_D curve in Figure 5.3. But recruiting costs under a volunteer force rise faster than force size, as discussed above. Recruiting costs therefore increase the slope and convexity of the TC_A curve in Figure 5.3. The cross-over point F* moves further left the more the TC_A curve rises due to recruiting costs.

However, training costs have the opposite effect. The reduced turnover of personnel in the case of a volunteer force decreases total training costs relative to a force of equal size procured under conscription. When the per-capita cost of training increases, F* moves to the right. This seems to reflect the case in the majority of European countries, which now face a very low risk of armed conflicts on their territory. Increasingly, the main mission of their armed forces is not to defend the national borders (in which case training costs are relatively low), but rather to manage conflicts and maintain peace outside their territories, missions that tend to require special training with higher costs.

The one cost that is larger at every force size for an all-volunteer force arises from the deadweight loss of taxation. A higher deadweight loss per unit of tax revenue collected tends to reduce the force size at which a draft force becomes the cheaper choice. Variations in the deadweight loss from taxation from one European country to another may be a factor causing F* to vary by country.

For countries with youth cohorts that are small relative to the size of the overall population, the problem of procuring military manpower is more difficult, as Rickard Sandell points out in Chapter 3. Especially when the required force is large relative to the youth cohort, the crossover point is moved to the left. It is hard to recruit, on a voluntary basis, what might turn out to be the majority of the people reaching military age each year. Therefore, from this point of view, a draft may be cheaper for countries that maintain militaries that are large relative to the size of their populations, such as Lithuania.[13]

THE PRODUCTIVITY OF DRAFT AND VOLUNTEER FORCES

Proponents of conscription often argue that a draft (at least a random-lottery draft) will induce service by the more able individuals in society: those individuals who have higher opportunity costs of service and who would not serve without conscription. They argue that a draft force will, as a result, be more productive than a volunteer force of comparable size. Empirical evidence from the United States, however, suggests that the quality of military entrants increased after the termination of the draft.

In any case, every other consideration points to higher productivity, and therefore a smaller required force size, in a volunteer system than a draft system. To begin with, draft forces are typically characterized by short enlistments and high turnover, a result of which is that individuals and units in draft forces are typically less capable than individuals and units in similarly sized volunteer forces.[14] One reason for lower individual productivity is that draftees have less time on the job to learn

---

13. Christopher Jehn and Zachary Selden, "The End of Conscription in Europe?" *Contemporary Economic Policy*, Vol. 20, No. 2 (2002), pp. 93–100.
14. Terms of enlistment in most European countries are typically a year or less. During the draft in the United States, the term of enlistment for conscripts was two years. The Israeli army currently requires conscripts to serve for three years.

their duties well than volunteers do. Studies of the U.S. experience overwhelmingly show a significant return to on-the-job training and experience.[15] The second is that draftees are typically less motivated than volunteers. An efficiently designed military compensation system will motivate volunteer forces to work hard and effectively.[16] In contrast, incentives to motivate draftees must be negative in nature, such as bad-conduct discharges for poor performance, or oriented toward positive post-service rewards for successful completion of an enlistment, such as educational benefits.

Unit productivity, too, is typically lower in militaries characterized by high turnover, which is likely to be the case in conscripted militaries. Shorter durations of service and higher turnover degrade unit cohesion, reduce teamwork, and hamper unit effectiveness.

In the United States and elsewhere, weapons systems and other military hardware have become increasingly sophisticated. More complicated equipment typically requires better trained and more experienced personnel to operate and maintain effectively. Technological improvements embodied in new hardware tend to increase the productivity of a volunteer force relative to a draft force.

Another source of productivity difference is that the type of force has implications for military strategy and tactics. A draft force typically requires more supervision and top-down control than a volunteer force, in which junior personnel are more motivated to perform well in hopes of being promoted. We speculate that the ability to push responsibility further down the chain of command in a volunteer force compared to a draft force will make volunteer forces more flexible on the battlefield and better suited to prevalent concepts of military transformation.

---

15. Warner and Asch, "The Economics of Military Manpower," summarized these studies.
16. B. Asch and J. Warner, "A Theory of Compensation and Personnel Policy in Hierarchical Organizations with Application to the United States Military," *Journal of Labor Economics*, Vol. 19, No. 3 (2001), pp. 523–562. They show how an effectively designed compensation system helps retain able personnel and reward performance.

PROCUREMENT SYSTEM CHOICE

If efficiency is the only criterion for choosing a system of military man-power procurement, the optimal policy will be to select the method that delivers the desired military capability at the lowest real resource cost. In terms of Figure 5.3, if the desired capability requires a force to the left of F* (the force size at which a conscripted force becomes cheaper than a volunteer force), the optimal system will unambiguously be the volunteer system, for two reasons. First, at any force level to the left of F*, the volunteer force has lower real cost than a draft force of equal size. Second, if the volunteer force is more productive, the required volunteer force will be smaller than the required draft force. Factors that push the crossover point F* to the right, as discussed above, increase the range of force sizes over which the volunteer system unambiguously dominates the draft system.

To the right of F*, the choice is ambiguous. In Figure 5.3, if volunteer force F_A has the same capability as draft force F_D, society would be indifferent between the two on efficiency grounds since they would entail the same total resource cost. But if the volunteer force required to deliver the same capability as draft force F_D is smaller than F_A, society would prefer the volunteer system on efficiency grounds; if it is larger, then society will prefer the draft.

EQUITY ISSUES

Although economists tend to focus on efficiency issues, the fairness question of who should bear the burden of national defense occupied center stage in the U.S. debate about conscription during the 1960s. Advocates of conscription and advocates of a volunteer force have very different concepts about what constitutes equity in the provision of a military force:

The debate between the draft and volunteerism often seems to begin and end with the concepts of individual freedom to choose within the state, and individual responsibility to the state. These concepts clash. If a person is obligated to serve, the concept of individual freedom is violated. If a person is free to choose, the concept of responsibility to the state is violated.[17]

---

17. James Hosek, "Commentary," in J. Eric Fredland, Curtis Gilroy, Roger D.

In Europe, where conscription was almost universal prior to 1990, the prevailing view was that all citizens had a moral obligation to defend the state and that such obligations outweighed individual freedom and rights within the state.[18]

Balancing the broad concepts of individual freedom and of obligation to the state involves ethical judgments beyond the scope of economics. But economics does offer some insights about the consequences of conscription and volunteerism for the distribution of income and for the distribution of the burden of paying for national defense. Conscription in fact promotes a less equal distribution of income and tends to place the burden of paying for national defense on lower-income groups. Benjamin Franklin recognized this point two centuries ago:

But if, as I suppose is often the case, the sailor who is pressed and obliged to serve for the defence of this trade at the rate of 25s. a month, could have £3.15s, in the merchant service, you take from him 50s. a month; if you have 100,000 in your service, you rob that honest part of society and their poor families of £250,000 per month, or three million per year.... But it may be said, to give the king's seamen merchant's wages would cost the nation too much, and call for more taxes. The question will then amount to this; whether it be just in a community, that the richer part should compel the poor to fight for them and their properties for such wages as they think fit to allow, and punish them if they refuse?[19]

Implicit in Franklin's statement is the regressive nature of the conscription tax. This tax is particularly regressive when conscription selects for service the same individuals who would have served in the volunteer system (as did the "least value drafted first" system during World War I). Couple the fact that conscription reduces the need for tax revenues with the fact that the income tax systems of most developed countries are progressive, and it is clear that conscription tends to reduce the income tax obligations of higher-income individuals and families relative to the tax obligations of lesser-income individuals and

---

Little, and W.S. Sellman, eds., *Professionals on the Front Line: Two Decades of the All-Volunteer Force* (Washington, D.C.: Brassey's, 1996), pp. 117–124, at 118.
18. Jehn and Selden, "The End of Conscription in Europe?"
19. This quotation is taken from the Gates Commission report, p. 24. The original source was not provided.

families.[20] Conscription therefore reduces the progressivity of the tax system two ways: by collecting more implicit taxes from conscripts and volunteers, and by collecting (proportionately) fewer direct taxes from higher-income individuals and families.

The move in recent drafts to limit exemptions and deferments and instead to conscript by lottery derives from the general recognition that the draft tax tends to be regressive. But a lottery raises other equity issues. If conscription applies to men only, families with daughters and families without any children can avoid the conscription tax, but could not avoid a general income tax to pay for an AVF. Because conscription is a tax on labor, it narrows the tax base: recipients of capital income avoid paying for defense under conscription, but not under a volunteer system.

Although a lottery draft is more equitable than other forms of taxation, in that everyone has an equal chance of selection, random assignment of a tax burden would clearly not be fair either. The obvious inequity increases as the number to be drafted falls in relation to the pool of draft-eligible individuals. At the height of the Vietnam War, the United States military was enlisting a number equivalent to one-third of male youth turning 18 years old each year.[21] When conscription ended in 1973, this figure had declined to 20 percent; today about 9.1 percent enlist.[22] Despite the fact that the Vietnam War was an unpopular war and military pay was very low at that time, about half of annual accessions were volunteers. So even if the United States were to return to a draft, it would be unlikely to draft more than five percent of each 18-year-old male youth cohort. And unless accompanied by a pay reduction or a significant expansion of force size, conscription of even 5 percent of each male youth cohort would require rejection of some qualified volunteers. Adding women to the pool of potential conscripts would make the fraction to be drafted small indeed.

---

20. According to 2001 data from the U.S. Internal Revenue Service, the top 1 percent of taxpayers pay one-third of the individual income tax collections in the United States; the top 5 percent pay 53 percent and the top 10 percent pay 66 percent.
21. Oi, "The Costs and Implications of an All-Volunteer Force."
22. Warner and Asch, "The Record and Prospects of the All-Volunteer Military in the United States."

Many advocates of conscription propose solving the inequity of imposing the draft tax on a limited fraction of the population by requiring all youth to participate in some form of national service.[23] Almost 2 million males and 2 million females turn 18 years old in the United States each year. Requiring all males or all teenagers to participate in some form of national service just to maintain equity with the small fraction that might be required to serve in the military would be extremely costly and, in the opinion of many observers, would provide little social benefit.

An equity issue that proponents of conscription tend to ignore involves equity within the military. Even under conscription, militaries typically need to attract many highly skilled personnel, such as pilots, doctors, lawyers, and engineers, and to retain them for longer periods of service. Although the United States has drafted doctors and other professionals from time to time, conscription is not a very efficient means of acquiring the services of such personnel. Even with conscription of the unskilled, it is likely that professionals would have to be recruited by voluntary means, that is, by paying them market-clearing wages. In addition to receiving market wages, the more highly skilled personnel typically have better working conditions and less exposure to danger. (An exception might be pilots, but part of their pay is compensation for the extra risks they bear.) An equity issue is whether it is fair to attract the more highly skilled by voluntary means while at the same time paying draftees less than their opportunity costs and exposing them to more danger and harsher working conditions.

Evidence from the U.S. Experience with an AVF

During the debate over conscription in the United States, critics expressed a number of concerns about a volunteer force that some in Europe share today. These include concerns that:

- a volunteer force will not attract recruits of sufficient ability to perform military tasks well, and the force will be of low quality;

---

23. Twenty-five years ago, economist Milton Friedman and Congressman Pete McCloskey engaged in an entertaining if heated debate about national service. Anderson, *Registration and the Draft: Proceedings of the Hoover-Rochester Conference on the All-Volunteer Force.*

- a volunteer force will not be representative of the society at large;

- recruiting and retention will be too unresponsive to pay to make an AVF feasible;

- recruiting and retention will be too responsive to the state of the economy to sustain the force during boom periods.

Consider first the issue of recruit quality. Recruit quality has varied considerably during the period of the U.S. AVF, but not always in the directions that worry its critics. Recruit quality in the United States is commonly measured by the distribution of scores on the Armed Forces Qualification Test (AFQT) and by the percent of recruits considered to be "high-quality." Recruits are placed into aptitude categories on the basis of AFQT score. The nationally-normed percentiles are: I (93–100), II (65–92), IIIA (50–64), IIIB (31–49), IV (10–30), and V (0–9). The armed forces are legally prohibited from taking individuals scoring in the lowest aptitude category V. Of course, cognitive ability is not the only characteristic a soldier needs to perform his or her job well. Nevertheless, studies indicate that AFQT score is a strong predictor of the job performance of U.S. military personnel.[24]

Table 5.1 shows the aptitude group distribution of enlisted accessions during three draft years—1952, 1957, and 1968—and at five-year intervals beginning in 1973. For comparison, the top row also shows the aptitude group distribution of the overall 1980 male youth population, when the Armed Services Vocational Aptitude Battery (ASVAB) was administered to a nationally representative sample of American youth.[25] (Unfortunately, the breakdown of group III into its IIIA and IIIB subcategories is not available for either the 1980 male youth population or the three draft-era years.)

---

24. David Armor and Paul Sackett, "Manpower Quality in the All-Volunteer Force," in Barbara Bicksler, Curtis L. Gilroy, and John T. Warner, eds., *The All-Volunteer Force: Thirty Years of Service* (Washington, D.C.: Brassey's, 2004), pp. 90–109.
25. The AFQT score is derived from the verbal and math components of the ASVAB.

Table 5.1. Aptitude Distribution of U.S. Accessions

	Iª (93–100)	II (65–92)	ALL III (31–64)	IIIA (50–64)	IIIB (31–49)	IV (10–30)	V (<10)	Average AFQTᵇ
1980 Male Youth	5	35	29			23	8	52
Enlistees								
1952	6	22	32			39	0	49
1957	8	25	43			24	0	54
1968	6	32	38			25	0	55
AVF begins								
1973	4	31	52	24	28	13		56
1978ᶜ	5	23	43	16	28	29		51
1983	6	31	52	21	32	11		57
1988	4	36	55	26	28	5		59
1993	4	38	56	29	28	1		61
1998	4	35	60	29	31	1		59

a. Numbers in parentheses are AFQT percentile ranges.

b. AFQT averages for 1988, 1993, and 1998 computed from raw enlistment contract records supplied by U.S. Department of Defense, Defense Manpower Data Center. Means for earlier years were estimated as sum of within-aptitude group average AFQT times percent in aptitude group. Within-aptitude AFQT averages were constructed from Army enlistment data for 1987–98. For corroboration, estimated averages were constructed for years 1988, 1993, and 1998 and in all three cases were within one percentage point of the actual average.

c. 1978 data corrected for misnorming.

Sources: Aptitude frequencies for 1980 male youth and for 1952, 1957, and 1968 enlistees are from *Profile of American Youth*, Office of the Assistant Secretary of Defense (Manpower, Reserve Affairs, and Logistics), 1982. Data for 1973 through 1993 are from *Population Representation in the Military Services, Fiscal Year 97*, Office of the Assistant Secretary of Defense (Force Management Policy), November 1998. Fiscal Year 1998 data were provided by the Defense Manpower Data Center.

The comparisons in Table 5.1 are striking. In most years of the all-volunteer force, about 4 percent of the accessions have come from aptitude group I, slightly lower than the 5 percent of the male youth population in this category and much lower than the draft-era range of 6–8 percent. But the AVF has attracted a higher share than the overall population of recruits from aptitude group II, especially since 1988. The biggest change has been the increase in accessions from aptitude group III and the virtual elimination of accessions from group IV. The draft generated slightly more highly able recruits (aptitude group I) than the

AVF, but also many more low-scoring recruits (group IV). Average AFQT has risen during the AVF (last column of Table 5.1).[26]

The educational attainment of U.S. enlisted accessions has improved remarkably since the inception of the all-volunteer force. In 1973, less than two-thirds of accessions had high school diplomas. By contrast, since 1984, high-school graduates have comprised 90 percent or more of total accessions for all services together. On most dimensions, U.S. forces are more qualified today than they were during the draft. Concerns expressed during the 1960s draft debate that the volunteer force would be a low-quality force have not materialized.

The second concern was that volunteers would not be representative of the society at large, in terms of either income group or of race. Consider, first, representation by income group. To study the issue of the representation by income group, Warner and Simon examined the cumulative distribution of U.S. military recruits by family income decile over the FY 1988–98 period. Recruits were arrayed by the median family income in the 5-digit zip code of residence. If the population of recruits were perfectly representative of different income classes, the cumulative distributions would lie along a 45-degree line along which, for example, 10 percent of recruits would be drawn from the 10 percent least wealthy families, 20 percent from the 20 percent least wealthy families, and so on. In fact, recruits are slightly less likely to come from wealthier families. The distribution for the Marine Corps is closest to the 45-degree line, followed by the Air Force, Navy, and Army, although the overall

---

26. The movement toward a greater number of high-quality accessions was not a smooth one. Table 5.1 shows that the proportion of group II and group III recruits actually dropped substantially from 1973 to 1978, rebounding after that time. More detailed data shows that "high-quality accessions"—defined as those with a high school diploma who score 50 or above (I, II, or IIIA) on the AFQT—rose at the start of the volunteer force from 42.8 percent in 1973 to 48.6 percent in 1976 and then plummeted to 27.1 percent in 1977 and 33 percent in 1978. The quality decline was not, however, recognized at the time: a new version of the ASVAB test, introduced in 1977, was mis-normed. As a result, many recruits who should have been placed into aptitude group IV were erroneously placed in higher aptitude categories. Reports from recruiting stations painted a rosy recruiting picture, even as actual recruit quality declined. The problem was discovered in 1980, and later corrected, after the armed forces training commands complained about recruits' poor performance in training.

differences among the services are small. The broad picture emerges that U.S. military recruits are not concentrated in the lower part of the income distribution and are in fact broadly representative of all parts of the income distribution. Since the distributions are based only on enlisted recruits, it is likely that inclusion of officers, who are more likely to come from higher-income families, would equalize the distribution further.

On the issue of racial representation, the Gates Commission predicted that black representation in the U.S. armed forces would increase from 14 percent of the enlisted force under the draft to only 15 percent in a volunteer force.[27] In fact, representation of African Americans in the U.S. armed forces has increased to about 20 percent. Thus blacks are somewhat overrepresented in the enlisted force in comparison with their representation in the population (12.6 percent). Hispanics, however, are underrepresented. At the start of the all-volunteer force, Hispanics made up less than 2 percent of the enlisted force. While their share of the enlisted force has grown to about 10 percent, rapid population growth has pushed their share of the overall population to over 14 percent. Overall, however, minority-group representation in the U.S. armed forces is broadly representative of their share of the overall population.

The third concern, the belief that recruiting and retention would be so insensitive to military pay that a volunteer force could not be sustained at any feasible cost, has proved incorrect. Collectively, many studies of U.S. military recruiting and retention have found that both are quite sensitive to military pay.[28] The sensitivity of recruiting to pay is revealed in Figure 5.4, which shows high-quality recruits (having a high-school diploma and scoring in group I, II, or IIIA) as a percentage of total recruits over time, along with an index of military pay relative to civilian wages. While the high-quality series has trended upward over time, swings in it coincide with swings in relative pay. Faced with recruiting shortfalls in the late 1990s, U.S. military personnel received pay increases in excess of civilian wage increases in both 2001 and 2002. Recruiting rebounded in response to these pay increases.

---

27. Gates Commission report, pp. 149–150.
28. Studies summarized in Warner and Asch, "The Economics of Military Manpower."

Figure 5.4. Percent High Quality Recruits, Civilian Unemployment Rate, and Relative Pay at Entry (Each Series Normalized to 1.0 in 1974)

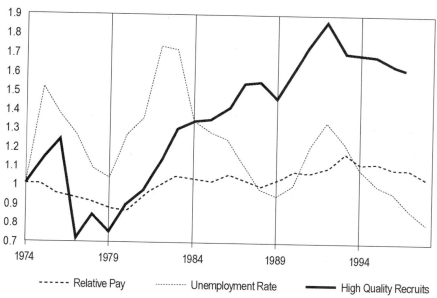

Of interest is how U.S. military personnel cost and military pay stand in comparison to the compensation of others. Table 5.2 shows the Regular Military Compensation (RMC) for all U.S. military personnel (officers and enlisted). RMC is the salary-equivalent of basic pay plus allowances for food and housing. In fiscal year 2003, average U.S. RMC was about $45,000 per capita. Adding retirement benefits and other special and incentive pays raised the cost to about $57,000 per person. Thus U.S. military personnel are paid somewhat better than full-time U.S. workers, on average. In fact, RMC stands at about the 60th–70th percentile of earnings of full-year-round civilian male workers with similar education and experience. The evidence indicates that the U.S. military has been able to attract a well-qualified, socially-representative force with levels of pay comparable to those of many Americans.

Table 5.2. U.S. Active Force Compensation in FY 2003

	Total (billion)	Average	Share
Basic Pay	$39.68	$28,513	50%
Basic Allowance for Housing (BAH)	$15.85	$11,390	20%
Basic Allowance for Subsistence (BAS)	$3.85	$2,770	5%
Tax Advantage	$3.89	$2,797	5%
Total of Regular Military Compensation (RMC)	**$63.28**	**$45,470**	**80%**
Special and Incentive (S&I) Pays	$3.42	$2,460	4%
Other Allowances	$1.52	$1,091	2%
Retired Pay Accrual	$10.67	$7,670	14%
TOTAL	**$78.90**	**$56,691**	**100%**

Source: Items of RMC calculated from Selected Military Compensation Tables, Office of the Under Secretary of Defense (Personnel and Readiness), January 1, 2003. Other items from FY 2003 DoD Budget.

One lesson learned over the years of the AVF is that recruiting and retention are sensitive to the business cycle, as Bernard Rostker and Curtis Gilroy discuss in Chapter 9. Periods of recruiting and retention difficulty do coincide with booms in the economy, as Figure 5.4 illustrates for the case of recruiting. Conversely, recruiting and retention improve during periods of economic slack. U.S. military personnel managers have learned to deal with these fluctuations through the judicious use of enlistment bonuses and other incentives.[29]

Application of the Theory to European Choices

The model discussed above identifies a number of factors that will influence whether a country will prefer a volunteer force to conscription. Tables 5.3 and 5.4 provide information about members and prospective members of NATO that helps explain their decisions to keep or end conscription. Table 5.3 shows NATO members' defense spending as a percentage of Gross Domestic Product (GDP) in the periods 1980–84 and

29. For some evidence on this point, see John T. Warner, Curtis Simon, and Deborah Payne, "The Military Recruiting Productivity Slowdown: The Roles of Resources, Opportunity Cost and the Tastes of Youth," *Defence and Peace Economics*, Vol. 14, No. 5 (2003), pp. 329–342.

2003, as well as defense manpower (uniformed military plus civilian) as a percentage of the labor force in the same periods.

Table 5.4 shows the active force size in the member and prospective member countries in 2003 and provides other data including number of conscripts, conscripts as a percentage of the active force, the male population fit for military service, the force as a percentage of the male population, and each country's conscription plans.

DEMAND FOR DEFENSE

Among the factors influencing a choice between conscription and an AVF, first and foremost is a country's demand for military manpower. The fall of the Berlin Wall and the reduced threat of war between NATO countries and former Warsaw Pact countries enabled the countries in NATO and its invited members to reduce defense spending and force levels. As Table 5.3 shows, defense spending in the NATO countries of Europe fell from an average of 3.5 percent of GDP in 1980–84 to 2.0 percent of GDP in 2003. U.S. defense spending fell from 5.3 percent of GDP to 3.5 percent of GDP over the same period. The model discussed above indicates that when, as reflected in Table 5.3, the demand for defense declines and required force size falls, a volunteer force becomes cheaper relative to conscription after all social costs are included. Decision-makers in European countries choosing to terminate conscription probably understood this fact, at least intuitively.

Table 5.4 shows the active force size in different countries as a percentage of the male population aged 15–49 that is estimated to meet military entrance standards. Figure 5.5 shows this percentage for each country, grouping the countries by their intended method of manpower procurement. Greece and Turkey, the two countries with the highest manpower requirement relative to the relevant population, plan to maintain conscription. The average percentage of force requirement from total manpower inventory for the countries that have decided to keep conscription is 3.22. The average for the countries that currently have, or plan to implement, a volunteer force is 1.68. Figure 5.5 reveals a tendency for countries with larger military manpower requirements to keep conscription.

Table 5.3. Measures of Defense Effort by Selected NATO Members, 1980–1984 and 2003

Country	Defense Expenditures as a Percent of GDP		Defense Manpower as a Percent of Labor Force[a]	
	1980–1984	2003	1980–1984	2003
Belgium	3.2	1.3	2.8	1.0
Czech Republic	—[b]	2.2	—	1.1
Denmark	2.4	1.6	1.5	1.0
France	4.0	2.6	2.8	1.6
Germany	3.3	1.4	2.4	0.9
Greece	5.4	4.2	6.1	5.1
Hungary	—	1.9	—	1.4
Italy	2.1	1.9	2.5	1.5
Luxembourg	1.0	0.9	0.9	0.8
Netherlands	3.0	1.6	2.5	0.9
Norway	2.7	2.0	2.5	1.4
Poland	—	2.0	—	1.2
Portugal	2.9	2.1	2.5	1.4
Spain	2.3	1.2	2.9	0.9
Turkey	4.0	4.8	4.6	3.9
United Kingdom	5.2	2.4	2.1	1.1
NATO Europe Average	3.5	2.0	2.8	1.6
Canada	2.0	1.2	1.0	0.5
United States	5.6	3.5	2.9	1.5
North America	5.3	3.4	2.7	1.4
NATO Total	4.5	2.7	2.7	1.5

Note: a. Includes uniformed military personnel and civilian personnel.

b. — indicates not a NATO member at the time.

Source: NATO website <www.nato.int/docu/pr/2003/table3.pdf>.

Table 5.4. NATO Members and Invitees, Active Force Size, Conscripts, and Population Fit for Military Service, 2003

	Active Force Size (000)	Number of Conscripts (000)	Conscripts as Percent of Force	Manpower Inventory[a] (000)	Force per Manpower Inventory	Conscription Intention
Belgium	39	0	0	2,059	1.89%	Ended 1994
Bulgaria	51	45	88	1,551	3.29%	Keep
Canada	60	0	0	7,158	0.84%	None
Czech Rep.	40	19	48	2,002	2.00%	Ended 2005
Denmark	23	6	26	1,095	2.10%	Keep
Estonia	6	1	16	283	2.12%	Keep
France	259	0	0	12,079	2.14%	Ended 2001
Germany	283	93	33	17,400	1.63%	Keep
Greece	178	98	55	2,026	8.78%	Keep
Hungary	33	23	70	2,027	1.63%	Ended 2005
Italy	200	40	20	12,349	1.62%	End 2007
Latvia	5	2	40	466	1.07%	End 2008
Lithuania	13	5	38	736	1.77%	Keep
Luxembourg	1	0	0%	94	1.06%	None
Netherlands	53	0	0	3,537	1.50%	Ended 1996
Norway	27	15	56	911	2.96%	Keep
Poland	163	81	50	8,078	2.02%	Keep
Portugal	45	9	20	2,018	2.23%	Ended 2003
Romania	97	30	31	4,974	1.95%	End 2007
Slovakia	22	8	36	1,136	1.94%	End 2006
Slovenia	7	1	14	413	1.69%	Ended 2004
Spain	151	0	0	8,392	1.80%	Ended 2001
Turkey	515	391	76	11,801	4.36%	Keep
UK	213	0	0	12,354	1.72%	None
USA	1,434	0	0	73,598	1.95%	None

a. Manpower inventory comprises males fit for military, that is, those age 15–49 who are expected to meet entrance standards.

Sources: Cindy Williams, "Filling NATO's Ranks: Military Personnel Policies in Transition," Report of Transatlantic Roundtable, September 8–9, 2003; IISS, *Military Balance 2003*; and <www.nationmaster.com>.

It is clear, however, that downsizing brought about by the end of the Cold War is not the only factor influencing the choice between conscription or an AVF. Figure 5.5 indicates that many of the countries deciding, at least for the present, to maintain conscription have a demand for manpower comparable to that of many of the countries preferring voluntarism, including the UK and United States (which both have forces equal to about 2 percent of the fit male population). Other factors identified by the analysis above may be affecting the decision, such as productivity, cost of draft evasion, equity issues, deadweight tax loss, and supply and military pay factors.

PRODUCTIVITY DIFFERENCES

Prior to the collapse of Communism, the military forces of some Scandinavian members of NATO were forces whose purpose was homeland defense. Rather than maintain large active forces, these NATO members conscripted a large percentage of the male youth population for short periods of training and then required these personnel to undergo periodic refresher training. For example, Norway had a reserve force over ten times the size of its active force.[30]

Large forces might be necessary for homeland defense against a potential invasion, but they are not as useful in the roles and missions that NATO has embraced as priorities in recent years. Aside from legal restrictions that prohibit many European countries from deploying short-term conscripts outside of their borders,[31] rapid-deployment and peacekeeping are activities that require training and skill-sets beyond the scope given to conscripts. Furthermore, volunteerism allows individual countries within NATO to specialize in the performance of specific tasks within the overall NATO mission in ways that could not be accomplished in armies in which draftees predominate (as discussed in Chapter 2 by Jolyon Howorth).

---

30. Table 3 of Jehn and Selden, "The End of Conscription in Europe?"
31. Cindy Williams, "Filling NATO's Ranks: Military Personnel Policies in Transition," Report of Transatlantic Roundtable, September 8–9, 2003.

Figure 5.5: Active Force as a Percent of Males Aged 15–49 Fit for Military Service (Selected Countries)

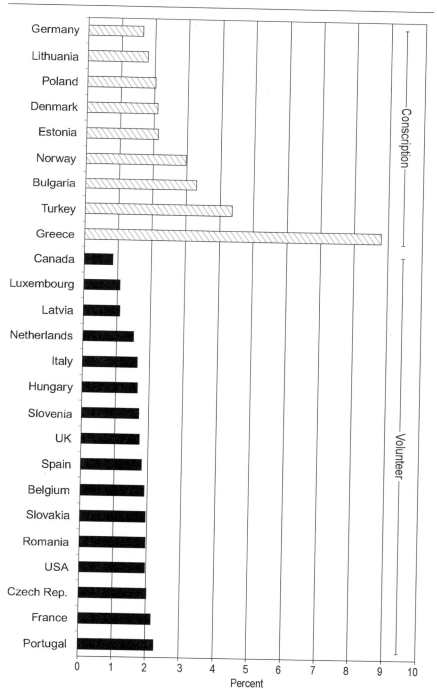

Apart from NATO, members of the European Union (EU) have given the concept of a cohesive European army serious consideration.[32] The European Union seeks a more active role in the world, and to this end it strives for a unity of action while complementing NATO missions.[33] But in order to become complementary with NATO (and U.S.) forces, the European troops must increase their productivity, and this objective is more likely to be achieved by becoming fully professional. This way, it is argued, the Europeans will become better partners of the Americans in the future.

DRAFT EVASION AND ITS COSTS

Conscription has a long tradition in Europe and has been well accepted there, especially in countries with almost universal conscription for training in militia-based homeland defense forces. When the belief that citizens have a moral obligation to defend the state is universal, draft evasion is less likely. Periods of high external threat are likely to reinforce this belief, especially when most citizens believe that national survival is at stake. Evasion becomes more likely with a decline in external threats and in the belief that conscription is necessary for national survival. Across most countries of Europe, the social acceptability of conscription seems to be at higher levels than in the United States. This might be part of the reason why some countries in Europe still maintain the draft. However, after the fall of communism, the perceived level of military threat declined across Europe. As a result, it is likely that both the demand for security and the belief that citizens have a moral obligation to serve have decreased, making evasion more likely.

---

32. For some time, the French have advocated an EU rapid deployment force that could respond to contingencies of vital interest to EU members. The British endorsed the concept at the Saint-Malo Summit of 1998. Joint Declaration issued at the British-French Summit, Saint-Malo, France, December 3–4, 1998, <www.atlanterhavskomiteen.no/publikasjoner/sp/99/4-99.htm>.

33. "In strengthening the solidarity between the member states of the European Union, in order that Europe can make its voice heard in world affairs, while acting in conformity with our respective obligations in NATO, we are contributing to the vitality of a modernized Atlantic Alliance which is the foundation of the collective defense of its members." Joint Declaration issued at the British-French Summit, Saint-Malo, France, December 3–4, 1998. See Chapter 2 by Jolyon Howorth.

Evasion may be easier in some countries than others. Countries with porous borders, from which migration is easier, may find evasion more difficult to detect and prevent. Such is likely to be the case among NATO countries in the core of Europe and future NATO countries such as Romania on the eastern border of NATO. Countries from which migration is more difficult, such as Turkey, will have a lower cost of enforcing conscription.

EQUITY ISSUES

When conscription is not universal, it is more likely to be seen as inequitable. The other inequity factor is the size of the conscription "tax." Because the required enlistment period for conscripts in most European countries was typically less than a year, the conscription tax was lower there than in the United States, where conscripts served for two years.[34] Both of these factors reduced the inequities of conscription in Europe. But declining force requirements and the need to have fewer personnel who serve for longer periods has brought home the inequities to European publics. In Spain, for example, the Partido Popular won an absolute majority in the Spanish Congress in 1997 after it promised to end conscription.[35]

DEADWEIGHT TAX LOSS CONSIDERATIONS

Probably the most subtle factor influencing a country's choice about how to procure military manpower is the deadweight loss from taxation. Countries with less developed tax systems, in which the costs of collecting taxes and the economic distortions from taxation are high, will have a lower cost of conscription relative to volunteerism. In terms of Figure 5.3, the crossover point F* will come at a lower force size in such countries. Several cases illustrate this idea. Denmark and Norway, two countries planning to continue conscription, already have high levels of taxation; deadweight tax losses due to additional direct taxation may be high in those countries, tilting the balance away from a volunteer force. By contrast, due to its less developed system of direct taxation and difficulty in collecting direct taxes, Turkey has relied heavily on the inflation tax (by printing money to finance government spending), and

---

34. Table 2 of Jehn and Selden, "The End of Conscription in Europe?"
35. Jehn and Selden, "The End of Conscription in Europe?"

may have found that collecting taxes implicitly through conscription, as well as through inflation, was easier than collecting taxes directly.

The dramatically declining shares of GDP represented by national defense revealed in Table 5.3 indicate that the deadweight tax cost of national defense is now lower throughout Europe than it was at the height of the Cold War. This fact alone will make countries more able to raise military pay to competitive levels and eliminate conscription.

SUPPLY FACTORS AND COMPETITIVE MILITARY PAY LEVELS

The success of a volunteer force will depend in large part on the sensitivity of recruiting and retention to military compensation. Recruiting and retention in the United States have been found to be sensitive to compensation, and the United States has been able to attract and retain a volunteer force by setting military compensation at about the 70th percentile of earnings of comparably educated males with similar levels of experience in the workforce. Is the U.S. experience likely to carry over to Europe? While the data required for a thorough analysis of this question are unavailable, we believe that the answer is yes. Anecdotal evidence from Romania supports this belief.

In Romania, the 2003 payroll expenditure for 66,275 permanent active-duty military personnel and 26,150 civilian personnel employed in the defense establishment was $246 million.[36] Thirty thousand conscripts added another $80 million, for a personnel cost of about $326 million. In 2003, Romanian conscripts were paid about $10 per month in cash and provided with food and housing.[37] Thus, total draftee compensation was roughly $80 per month. But Romania pays its volunteers more than its conscripts. For example, in 2004, privates who were volunteers were paid between $191 and $317 per month depending upon experience.[38]

Whether Romania will be able to sustain an adequate number of volunteers with this pay structure depends on how it compares with opportunities in the civilian sector. The average monthly income of male workers in

---

36. Table 5.4 shows a force size of 97,000, which includes conscripts and active-duty military, while the figures given here (totaling 92,425) comprise permanent active-duty military personnel and civilians but not conscripts.
37. Converted from Romanian leu to U.S. dollars at current exchange rates.
38. Constructed from data provided in *Monitor Official of Romania*, No. 347 (1999); and No. 4 (2004).

the Romanian economy in 2004 was about \$183 per month.[39] It is apparent that the pay levels for Romanian military personnel are better than the average earnings in most sectors of the Romanian economy. Unless there is a strong aversion to military service among Romanian youth, it is quite likely that, with sufficient attention to recruiters and advertising, these pay levels will prove attractive to volunteers.[40] Even with these improved pay levels, the planned strength reductions and elimination of conscription will allow Romania to reduce its military manpower outlays from \$326 million in 2003 to \$300 million by 2006.

Conclusion

Our review of the economics of conscription and of the movement toward volunteer forces in a number of European countries in light of economic theory suggests that the decisions of many European countries to end conscription are both efficient and equitable:

- volunteer forces have lower real resource costs than conscripted forces over a fairly wide range of force sizes, and the post–Cold War downsizing has put many countries in that range;

- changing roles and missions of European militaries have reduced the usefulness of conscripted forces and increased the value of better-trained, professional forces;

- European voters are now more acutely aware of the inequities of selective, less-than-universal conscription.

European countries are naturally concerned about other consequences of conscription, including the social representation of the military. While these concerns are real, evidence from the United States suggests that they are not likely to be of such magnitude as to sway the decision based on economic costs and benefits.

---

39. National Bank of Romania, <www.bnr.ro>, *Secțiunea statistică a Buletinului lunar,* September 2005.

40. The U.S. military devotes significant resources to recruiters and advertising. Warner, Simon, and Payne, "The Military Recruiting Productivity Slowdown." Given the small size of most European countries compared to the United States, as well as the concentration of their populations in a few large cities, resources devoted to recruiters and advertising are likely to be relatively lower.

Chapter 6

The New Danish Model

Limited Conscription and Deployable Professionals

Bertel Heurlin

This chapter aims to describe and explain the recent transformation of the Danish armed forces, with specific emphasis on the question of conscription versus an all-volunteer professional force. For one hundred and fifty years, Danish defense relied heavily on conscription. As in most other countries of Europe, this way of organizing the armed forces faced serious challenges and obstacles after the end of the Cold War: conscription is not consistent with preparing to face the new kinds of international threats. There is, however, a broader context in which conscription must be evaluated, which has led Denmark to choose to retain a form of conscription. There is thus potential benefit to other nations in looking at the Danish defense system.

The analysis in this chapter reviews the Danish defense model from the bipolar world of the Cold War era, and the changes that were made after the Cold War ended and unipolarity prevailed. It then reviews how the new strategic and international environment after September 11, 2001, influenced the new Danish model.[1] These defense policy de-

---

1. Sources of useful background and information for this chapter include: H.C. Bjerg, *Forsvar for Værnepligten* (København: Landsforeningen Værn om Danmark, 1996); H.C. Bjerg, "Den danske værnepligts historie," in "Se lige ud! Værnepligten til debat"(Debate: Bjerg, Østergaard, and Engell), *Folk og Forsvar* (1999), pp. 9–32; Hans Branner and Morten Kelstrup, eds., *Denmark's Policy towards Europe after 1945: History, Theory and Options* (Odense: Odense University Press, 2000); Anja Dalgaard-Nielsen, "Homeland Security and the Role of Armed Forces: A Scandinavian Perspective," in Thomas Jäger, ed., *Die Transatlantischen Beziehungen* (Wiesbaden: VS Verlag für Sozialwissenshaft, 2005); Lene Hansen and Ole Wæver, eds., *European Integration and Na-*

velopments are assessed in light of the work of Kjell Goldmann about the conflicts between democracy and security policy.[2]

The Danish Conscription Dilemma

During the Cold War, conscription was the cornerstone of Danish defense. After its end, Denmark was quick to adapt to the new international environment. In the late 1990s, Chief of Defense Christian Hvidt could, with only a bit of exaggeration, declare that, "We have a professional defense, based on conscripts."[3]

With the attacks of September 11, 2001, and with new signals from the international security system, Denmark faced the dilemma of whether to keep or abandon conscription. An increasing number of countries in Europe were in the process of suspending or even abolishing conscription and creating all-volunteer forces (AVFs). NATO was recommending

---

tional Identity: The Challenges of the Nordic States (London: Routledge, 2002); Bertel Heurlin, "Denmark: A New Activism in Foreign and Security Policy," in Christopher Hill, ed., The Actors in Europe's Foreign Policy (London: Routledge, 1996), pp. 166–185; Heurlin, Global, Regional and National Security (Copenhagen: Danish Institute of International Affairs, 2001); Heurlin, Riget, Magten og Militæret (The kingdom, the power and the military) (Aarhus: Aarhus Universitetsforlag, 2004); Jørgen Lyng, ed., Ved forenede kræfter. Forsvarets øverste ledelse (Vedbæk: Nyt Nordisk Forlag Arnold Busck, 2000); Nikolaj Petersen, Dansk udenrigspolitisk historie 1973–2003, bind 5 (København: Danmarks Nationalleksikon, 2004); Mikkel Vedby Rasmussen, "What is the Use of It? Danish Strategic Culture and the Utility of Armed Forces," Cooperation and Conflict, 2005; Henning Sørensen, "Conscription in Scandinavia During the Last Quarter Century: Developments and Arguments," Armed Forces and Society, Vol. 26, No. 2 (2000), pp. 313–334; Henning Sørensen, Belysning af mulighederne for og konsekvenserne af civilsamfundspligt i Danmark, DUPI Reports No. 8 (København: Dansk Udenrigspolitisk Institut, 2001); Uffe Østergård, "Værnepligt og Nationalstaten," Fokus (København: Dansk Udenrigspolitisk Institut), No. 5 (1998), p. 199.

2. Kjell Goldmann, Democracy and Foreign Policy: The Case of Sweden (Aldershot: Gower Publishing, 1986). See also Bertel Heurlin, "Revolution in Danish Military Affairs? Professionalism and Network Centric Warfare," in Kristina Spohr Readman, ed., Building Sustainable and Effective Military Capabilities: A Systemic Comparison of Professional and Conscript Forces, NATO Science Series V, Vol. 45 (Amsterdam: IOS Press, 2004), pp. 109–122.

3. Heurlin, Riget, Magten og Militæret (The kingdom, the power and the military), p. 241.

AVFs. New and potential NATO members were trying to "skip a generation of military development," aiming at an advanced defense to meet new security challenges. This implied getting rid of the old Cold-War territorial defense concept, which relied heavily on mass armies of conscripts.[4] So there were significant reasons to reconsider the Danish model and whether to take the final step and fully give up conscription.

There were, however, also many reasons to keep conscription. In Denmark, strong political forces urge retention of conscription. Conscription is included in the Constitution of Denmark, which states that every man capable of bearing arms is obliged to participate in the defense of the fatherland. Conscription supports a democratic defense that is embedded in society, and a society that is not separated from its military forces. It ensures a democratic and transparent defense, directly supervised and controlled by the population. It is a guard against lowering the threshold for a government's international use of the armed forces, as it would be politically easier to deploy an AVF than a force that relies upon draftees.[5] It is considered an important part of Denmark's identity as a nation, and a guardian of national cohesion and integrity.

Conscription also plays a major role in a broader political context relating to Denmark's self-understanding. It functions as a societal, cultural, and national melting pot for the population of male youth. It serves as a social equalizer. It helps to produce and spread shared human values and Danish values. Conscription guarantees that personnel will be recruited from all segments of society. It emphasizes the duty to defend the homeland.

Thus Denmark faced the choice of whether to abandon conscription, at the cost of losing valuable and positive features while gaining some advantages. Among the advantages to Denmark of an all-volunteer professional force would be the opportunity to take part in the revolution in military affairs, to develop the capacity for international first-in-first-out capabilities, and to demonstrate that Denmark is an effective interna-

---

4.   Bertel Heurlin and Mikkel Vedby Rasmussen, eds., *Challenges and Capabilities: NATO in the Twenty-first Century* (Copenhagen: Danish Institute for International Studies, 2003).
5.   See Pertti Joenniemi, "Farewell to Conscription? The Case of Denmark," in Pertti Joenniemi, ed., *The New Face of European Conscription* (London: Ashgate, forthcoming 2006).

tional military intervention partner of, particularly, the United States, NATO, and the UN.

The solution to the dilemma was to keep the Danish model but in a new configuration. In 2004 it was decided to reorganize the Danish armed forces and reduce the general term of conscription by more than half, from the former period of eight to twelve months, depending on the services, to just four months, this term to be followed by a three-year period during which a former conscript would be subject to recall.

This transformation of Denmark's defense involved a radical decision to eliminate comprehensive mobilization forces, which meant giving up territorial defense as it had traditionally been understood. The resources that had been devoted to sustaining a mobilization force, which would be of no use in the new international political-strategic environment, could be released to strengthen the two new main pillars of Danish defense: deployable forces for international intervention and forces for "total defense" (the Danish version of "homeland security"). The main aim for the political as well as the military establishment was to have more military forces able to take part in operational missions, and to have more "boots on the ground." The mantra was "back to soldiering," leaving behind the Cold War "defense as a mere symbol."[6] What happened to conscription was part of the most profound transformation of the Danish armed forces since the end of World War II.

Changes with the End of the Cold War

Fundamental change in Denmark's defense program began with the end of the Cold War. The new international setting altered Denmark's position. Structurally, bipolarity had been replaced by unipolarity as the United States emerged as the only superpower. Cold War–era security founded upon a balance of power had ceased to exist. Attempts at cooperative security under the guidance of the United States prevailed. Regionalization on a global scale had taken the place of the global East-West conflict. Closed and rather narrow conceptions of security were replaced by open, extended conceptions including "soft security" issues

---

6. Heurlin, *Riget, Magten og Militæret* (The kingdom, the power and the military).

such as environmental threats, international crime, immigration, food security, epidemics, and natural disasters. Instead of a concrete and well-known threat, the emerging threats were unknown challenges, instability, and chaos.

The NATO concept of collective defense and deterrence was maintained in theory; however, the main task of its military forces would now be to secure the new world order and the regional internal European order. This required the ability to conduct international military interventions. These new conditions had several impacts on Danish foreign and security policy: where, during the Cold War, Denmark had been seen as an exposed East-West front-line state, now it was in the rear and extremely safe. The 1997 Danish defense commission could declare that "in the coming ten years there will be no direct, conventional military threat to Denmark."[7] Denmark's efforts to manage tensions between the Nordic countries and the Soviet Union during the Cold War could now be directed toward trying to make the Baltic Sea area into a zone of stability, democracy, and prosperity. This created new possibilities for Denmark: even a small state, in the new world order, could pursue a great-power policy of activism and could internationalize, regionalize, and militarize its foreign policy. The obvious challenge for Denmark, as a small state losing its strategic importance as a Cold War front-line state, was to avoid marginalization, by playing the role of producer of security instead of consumer of security as it had during the Cold War. Denmark could now take a leading role within NATO.

This meant that, after the end of the Cold War, Denmark had to work hard both regionally and internationally. Its tool was international activism. Leaving behind its NATO policy of the 1980s, in which it constantly insisted on footnotes to the nuclear policy of the alliance, Denmark could move to the forefront of security policy and defense policy, by participating in the Gulf War of 1991 and the Kosovo War in 1999, and being constantly active in peacekeeping and peace enforcement missions, not least in the Balkans. Regionally, Denmark could take political, military, diplomatic, and organizational action to support the new democracies in the Baltic Sea area.

---

7. See Summary of Report from the Defense Commission of 1997, <www.fmn.dk>.

Accordingly, Danish defense underwent considerable change aimed at improving its ability to contribute to international military activities. The Danish International Brigade (DIB) was established in 1992; its objective was the capability for permanent deployment of military forces of one thousand soldiers as part of international missions. The force structure, the organizational structure, and the structure of military equipment were subject to considerable changes. However, fundamental transformation, which would have escaped the legacy of the Cold War by exclusively focusing on international missions, failed to materialize.[8]

The Bruun Report: Changes after September 11, 2001

New developments in the international system created the foundation for more change. The attacks of September 11, 2001, triggered a rethinking of the role and mission of military forces. The era of symmetric great-power wars was clearly over. Asymmetric wars, network-centric wars, and "politically correct" or normative wars—those international wars that were legitimized by the international community or at least by a powerful part of it—were high on the agenda.

In reaction to these challenges, Denmark took some unusual steps. Denmark's long-term (3–5 year) defense plans are traditionally negotiated among the main parties that normally are part of shifting multi-party coalition governments.[9] Confronted with political, technological, or strategic challenges, the government may set up a defense commission of political leaders, military people, and civilian experts to conduct a thorough investigation of the critical issues as the basis for a new defense conciliation agreement.[10] This happened in 1988–89 in connection with the sea changes around the end of the Cold War, and again in

---

8. Heurlin, *Riget, Magten og Militæret* (The kingdom, the power and the military).
9. The Center-Right minority government of 2004 depended upon the support of the right-wing nationalistic Danish People's Party. This coalition group sought to retain conscription. The opposition parties, including the Social Democrats, aimed at ending it or at least reconsidering the concept.
10. A comprehensive analysis is found in Heurlin, *Riget, Magten og Militæret* (The kingdom, the power and the military).

1997–98 in connection with consolidating the new role of military forces in the post–Cold War period.

Approaching the end of the 2000–2004 defense agreement period, the possible appointment of a new defense commission was therefore on the agenda. Shifts in the international strategic and political setting after September 11, 2001, were evident, and profound modification of Denmark's military forces was clearly necessary. But no defense commission was established to dig deep into the issues. Instead, the "Bruun Group," a small, fast working group of officials from foreign and military services, plus a few independent experts, was established in spring 2003 to undertake a rapid analysis of the new security and defense situation. By September 2003, it was to present a survey of Denmark's position, possibilities, and prospects in the new security area and on this basis suggest the basic lines of development for Danish defense policy.[11]

The Bruun Report of September 2003 established the basis for future rapid changes in the Danish armed forces. The report stated the fundamental objectives of Danish foreign policy: to further Denmark's freedom, security, interests, and prosperity, and to further normative values such as the international rule of law, human rights, and democracy. Danish security policy would be aimed at upholding the sovereignty of Denmark; at countering direct as well as indirect threats to Danish territory and Danish citizens; and at furthering international peace and security through preventing conflicts and war, peacekeeping and peace enforcement activities, and measures to promote stability.

Most of these objectives are familiar and traditional objectives. The new one is the individualization of security expressed in the emphasis on the threat to the individual Danish citizen; this reflects the increasing threat of terrorist attacks. The Bruun Report also emphasized that Danish security policy must be flexible and adaptable in order to be able to react quickly and effectively to future changes in the threat spectrum.

The new framework for security policy is characterized by globalization, by transformation of military technology, and by transformation of the international security situation, including the enlargement of NATO and the European Union (EU). The conventional military threat against Denmark has disappeared for the foreseeable future and thus there is no

---

11. See Danish Ministry of Defense (MOD) website at <www.forsvaret.dk>.

more need for territorial defense. Even if a conventional threat should, in the distant future, reappear, territorial defense would probably be very different from that of the Cold War.[12]

BRUUN REPORT RECOMMENDATIONS

These circumstances led the Bruun Report to recommend a Danish defense consisting of two pillars. One pillar is to provide for "total defense," or homeland security, meaning securing the society and its citizens, including defending against and coping with terrorist acts and their consequences. The second pillar is to have internationally deployable military capacities. Denmark should base its defense planning on capabilities, which signifies a focus upon how a potential adversary would fight rather than who or where this potential adversary could be. Dynamic force planning is required, with the ability for rapid adaptation and reaction to new challenges in an international environment characterized by unpredictable and asymmetrical threats.

The Bruun Report acknowledged that the use of conscripts for mobilization-based armed forces in wartime, as planned during the Cold War, has lost most of its relevance. One dimension is, however, still considered important. During the Cold War, much of the population received training in disciplines that, after September 11, became increasingly crucial, such as guarding, first aid, operations during catastrophes, and defense against nuclear, biological, and chemical warfare. Thus, as part of "total defense," there is still a need for conscription in order to have an available pool of manpower with such training. Conscription can also be an important tool for recruitment into the professional forces: by requiring large numbers of young men to become familiar with military life (even for just a few months), the draft can create a pool of potential volunteers to serve for longer periods.

Although the Bruun Report was influenced by U.S. political and strategic thinking, such as the concepts of "homeland security," capability-based defense planning, and the "revolution in military affairs" (now often referred to in NATO and the United States as "transformation"), clearly only the United States has the resources to transform all its armed forces to exploit fully these military-technological develop-

---

12. Bruun Report (Bruun-rapporten), September 2003, <www.forsvaret.dk>, p. 37.

ments. There are limits for a small country like Denmark, but the aspirations are high. The political vision of the 2005–09 Defense Plan, following the recommendations of the Bruun Report, was for specialized Danish armed forces, able to deliver clearly defined, deployable, and high-quality military capacities, ready for action across a full spectrum of tasks, including the "sharp end" of the spectrum—high-intensity conventional warfare—as well as low-intensity tasks such as peacekeeping.

Decision-making: The Defense Command Proposal

The Bruun Report became the conceptual and practical basis for the process of negotiating the next five-year defense plan. An unusual procedure followed. Immediately after the publication of the Bruun Report, the Danish Defense Command, which had been represented in the Bruun Group, released its own vision for a transformed Danish defense. Chief of Defense General Jesper Helsø presented the main points of the so-called "K-Paper," or Capability Paper, of the Danish Defense Command.[13] Although the Capability Paper itself was confidential, the main issues were made public through his presentation and on the Internet.

Thus the Defense Command took the initiative, introducing a fairly far-reaching proposal for the transformation of the armed forces, rather than waiting to react to input from the government and the political parties. This suggested that Defense Command was familiar with the new concepts and ideas being discussed by the defense-oriented political community, and that it intended to appear daring, visionary, and able. Fully aware of the need to transform, its leaders knew that a draft consisting primarily of minor changes to be implemented over time would have been regarded as foot-dragging, which in the end would be politically punished.

The solution—a proposal including comprehensive transformations—was, in that climate of domestic and international politics, destined to be a success. The fundamental situation was practically an issue of survival for Denmark's defense capability: the political choice was between radical transformation or starving: "use it or lose it."

---

13. See the "K-notatet" ("K-Paper" or Capability Paper), August 2003, <www.forsvaret.dk>.

The main message in the draft of the Defense Command was that radical reform of defense was necessary. The last four long-term defense plans (1989, 1992, 1995, and 1999) had taken ever-increasing bites out of the fundamental structure of the armed forces. This could not go on. Defense Command's answer was total elimination of the territorial defense: it would give up the mobilization force structure, reduce conscription to a minimum, specialize, and prioritize. It would introduce the armed forces as a fighting force on the front line of international deployable intervention forces and as a critical component in a new Danish foreign policy that would emphasize active engagement in world affairs.

Two Pillars: Total Defense and Deployable Forces

The fundamental concept of Danish policy, following from the Bruun Report and the K-Paper, was to divide Danish defense in two parts: total defense and expeditionary forces. Total defense has to do with assuring the security of Danish society, its members, and its facilities against terror and other threats. To strengthen homeland security, an expanded concept of "total defense" is foreseen, making use of the military draft. Increased cooperation and integration between the armed forces and other national authorities is intended. The objective is, in case of an extensive catastrophe, to augment fire brigades, police, and civil defense with 5,000 members of the military for a period of seven nights and days. The number of total-defense personnel is based on worst-case scenarios, such as an attack on the Copenhagen airport or the Copenhagen Metro, major accidents, or environmental disasters. The main activities would be guarding and securing sites, rescue, dealing with nuclear, biological, and chemical (NBC) material, and providing assistance to civilian professionals. Being able at all times to mobilize a total personnel of 5,000 requires a pool of 15,000. This number is to be achieved by introducing a three-year "mobilization" or recall requirement after the four-month conscription period. This relatively short time ensures that troops are fresh and recently trained; no re-training would be needed.[14] (See Figure 6.1.)

---

14. Based upon author's conversations at the Ministry of Defense, May 2004.

Figure 6.1. Military Training after the Danish Defense Reform of 2004

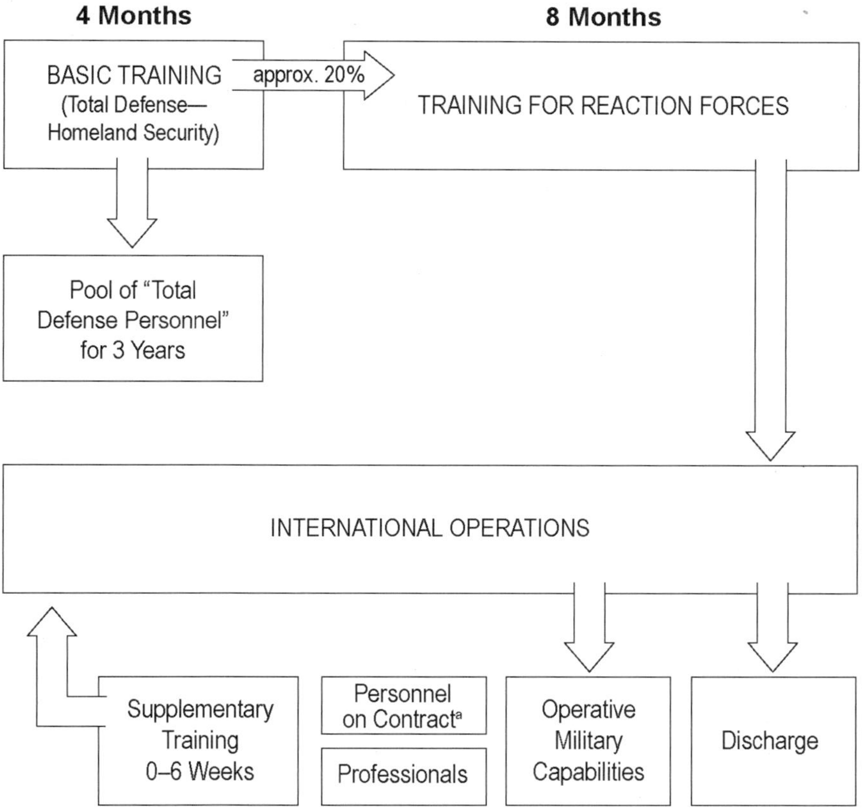

4 Months   8 Months

BASIC TRAINING   approx. 20%
(Total Defense—
Homeland Security)

TRAINING FOR REACTION FORCES

Pool of "Total
Defense Personnel"
for 3 Years

INTERNATIONAL OPERATIONS

Supplementary
Training
0–6 Weeks

Personnel
on Contract[a]

Professionals

Operative
Military
Capabilities

Discharge

Source: "Folk & Forsvar," March 2005.
Note a. Six weeks of maintenance training annually.

The expeditionary forces would be charged with stabilizing international order to promote fundamental human rights and global values such as freedom and democracy. Denmark's expeditionary forces must be organized according to the demands of the new global situation: international war is now not just a possibility, but a daily fact of life. Danish military forces, in order not to be marginalized internationally, must have the capability to be among the first to the fight, and to take their place in the front line. To fulfill this obligation, Danish forces must adapt to the revolution in military affairs, including network-centric warfare, with technological transformation and "leaner but meaner" armed forces.[15] To join international missions at the sharp end of the spectrum, Denmark must comply with the requirements for the NATO Response Force (NRF). Denmark's forces must be ready for immediate action, fully deployable, and sustainable, that is, supported logistically and able to fight the full range of missions. They must, accordingly, be equipped with advanced equipment based on modern technology, which will require increased investment in sophisticated and reliable military equipment.

Denmark's objective is to be able, at any time, to deploy 2,000 soldiers to international missions (1,500 from the army and 500 from the navy and the air force).[16] To sustain this level it will be necessary, according to the usual three-to-one rule, to have a pool of at least 6,000 deployable soldiers.

AVF AND CONSCRIPTION: THE NEW DANISH DEFENSE MODEL

This led Denmark to the crucial question of whether to rely on an all-volunteer force or conscription. Volunteer, professional troops are required for expeditionary, rapidly deployable armed forces with modern sophisticated equipment.

Conscription might also be necessary, however, for homeland security or total defense. Responding to man-made or natural catastrophes could require vast numbers of personnel. They need not necessarily be fully trained as soldiers; they could be citizens in uniform with rudimentary instruction in policing, rescue, firefighting, patrolling, and guarding. Denmark's total-defense soldiers, trained for only four months, are hardly soldiers at all. They may handle a weapon, but they are not trained to fight in a regular war; officially they are often not even referred to as soldiers, but rather as "total defense personnel."

---

15. Denmark did not previously attempt to meet the requirements of the "revolution in military affairs," but it now makes RMA a priority.

16. This objective was introduced by the Danish Prime Minister Anders Fogh Rasmussen in a speech at the Danish Defense Academy, November 2003. This was the first time a Danish prime minister had ever visited the Academy.

The Danish solution, announced as the new Danish Model, is that the AVF-conscription dilemma is not a real dilemma. It is not a question of "either-or" but of "both-and." Denmark has it both ways: on the one hand, the solution keeps the virtues of conscription, especially those attributable to recruiting from a broad spectrum of Danish society, the military's function as a social melting pot, and incorporating values of democracy and civil society in military institutions. And on the other hand, this solution permits Denmark to live up to the technological requirements of the revolution in military affairs and network-centric warfare, which require a professional military.

This new model has received positive attention, as well as some questions, outside Denmark. For example, within NATO, there have especially been questions regarding the four-month term of conscription. Some argue that at least a year is needed to train a soldier. The answer, however, is that these people are not soldiers: they are able to protect, to guard, and to carry out minor military operations at the platoon level. They function as personnel for total defense, and as a recruiting pool for the volunteer force, which consists of career professionals and of servicemembers who sign up for a limited, multi-year contract, or extend for a series of such contracts. So, despite the general anti-conscription attitude of NATO, the NATO Secretary-General has indicated that the Danish model definitely is a step in the right direction.[17] The Danish model is certainly meeting the requirements of NATO and addressing the challenges of the revolution in military affairs and network-centric warfare.

BUDGET IMPACT

Does the Danish model require increased military expenditure? Among the conditions for the 2004–2009 defense agreement was a political agreement to keep the budget unchanged. Earlier estimates of the added costs for introducing a full AVF in Denmark were very high; in 1998, for example, it was estimated at 4 billion Danish Kroner, equivalent to one-fourth of the defense budget. When this figure was presented, then Defense Minister Hans Hækkerup declared, "hereby

---

17. According to author's interviews at the Danish MOD.

Figure 6.2. Conscripts and Professional Soldiers in the Danish Armed Forces, Selected Years 1982–2009

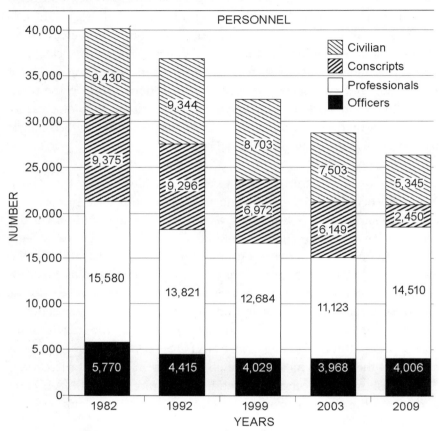

Source: Danish Defense Command, 2005.

this idea died."[18] Maybe the estimate was an exaggeration, but it reflected the fact that the costs of maintaining large mobilization forces on a non-conscription basis would be very high.

The concept was that abandoning the mobilization force structure, which had no military relevance in the new security environment, would allow Denmark to transfer the resources thus saved to the new two-pillar concept of increased deployable forces and effective total-defense forces. Because the new four-month conscription term would

18. Heurlin, *Riget, Magten og Militæret* (The kingdom, the power and the military), p. 112.

supply plenty of people for total defense while continuing to bolster recruitment for the deployable forces, there would be no increase in expenses.

FUTURE ISSUES

In what direction will the future configuration of the Danish armed forces develop, looking at the composition of professional soldiers, including personnel on contracts? In the coldest days of the Cold War—say, in 1982—almost one-third of the armed forces (not counting civilian employees) were conscripts. By contrast, in 2009, the share of conscripts will be around one-eighth, a remarkable reduction. As Figure 6.2 shows, the rollback of conscription is not complete, nor is it supposed to be. Conscription remains a way of recruiting willing and able young men (women are not obligated to serve, but since 1998 they may enlist). The main problem will be to get enough young people to volunteer for a career in the armed forces, as soldiers on contract, as long-term professional soldiers, or as officers.[19]

The basic need is, in the first instance, to hire able young people to serve in the armed forces. A fundamental rationale for maintaining conscription is for recruiting. Yet even the total-defense force is expected to require only about 20 percent of Denmark's young men turning draft age each year. To ensure that every young man gets at least some introduction to the armed forces, Denmark has instituted a compulsory one-day call-up for each year's cohort of young men in various centers around the country. Women may volunteer. This one-day session functions partly to provide information on the armed forces, aimed at recruitment, but also it takes the place of having each young person come up before a draft selection board. Judging from the comprehensive efforts by the military institutions to make these one-day sessions work well, the Danish military sees this kind of "draft" as highly important.

A more general issue of the future has to do with the argument that conscription is incompatible with the RMA, or more specifically with network-centric warfare. The notion of leaner but meaner armed forces

---

19. The military establishment will, according to the author's interviews in the Danish MOD, tend to seek professional soldiers, because soldiers on contract are known to become less willing to be sent to international operations after their first term, or after time goes by.

suggests "the fewer soldiers the better," in contrast to the mass armies of the Cold War. The view that quality is superior to quantity is generally accepted in the Danish military establishment. But there are considerations that contradict this common view. First, high technology does not necessarily require long or intensive training. Sound technology choices and good human-system interfaces can make advanced technology easier to use, not harder. To the armed forces, the main problem of technology is not training, but a question of economy, priority, and investment in high-tech equipment. Second, to meet the requirements for total defense or homeland security, quantity in many ways is more crucial than quality.

In the long run, in actual practice, conscription in its traditional format might disappear. If enough volunteers sign up for military service, beginning with the four months of basic total-defense service, conscription will become unneeded. If not, conscription will function as a tool for recruiting to the AVF, in this way ensuring that all segments of society are represented in the military forces, and also securing a broad pool for recruiting potential officers.

Democracy and Foreign Policy

Why has Denmark in effect given up conscription despite all its praised virtues? First, conscription still exists, based on a lottery, but it covers less than 20 percent of the male population. So proponents can claim that military service is still rooted in Danish society, and that it still establishes the valuable democratic and human connection between military and society. Second, in case of severe changes in the international environment and the return of the old conventional threats, there are traditions and procedures to build upon.

The Swedish political scientist Kjell Goldmann offers an explanation for this development based on a model of the relationship between democracy and foreign policy.[20] Democracy, he argues, is incompatible with foreign policy and security policy due to three factors: supreme interest, bargaining, and remoteness. Supreme interest has to do with the vital question of survival; here, the particular interests of political

---

20. Goldmann, *Democracy and Foreign Policy.*

parties are subordinated. Bargaining with foreign countries is not a matter for diverging points of view emanating from party politics; it must be done in unison, and often with secrecy. Remoteness is a factor, in that foreign policy issues are far away, and do not have a direct influence upon the individual voter. Defense policy, at least as it was practiced during the Cold War, shares this characteristic. So, Goldmann says, democracy has difficulty influencing foreign and security policy.

The political landscape can thus be described in Goldmann's terms: during the Cold War, the supreme interest was at stake for countries on both sides of the East-West conflict; that is, their very existence was threatened. A devastating war, even Armageddon, could break out at any time. Millions of soldiers and tens of thousands of nuclear-tipped missiles were ready to go into action as soon as the orders came. Bargaining was a critical part of East-West relations, primarily dealing with arms control and disarmament. Analytically seen, a virtual war took place, with constant introduction of new and more advanced weapons systems on both sides, and a parallel process of arms control negotiations, which had remarkable results. Bargaining was thus an essential element of the foreign-policy agenda. As concerns the factor of remoteness, the situation during the Cold War was rather strange: despite the high alert and readiness of the military forces, the situation fostered and required a certain restraint. Nobody wanted a war, which would inevitably develop into a disastrous nuclear war. This was exactly the reason for conducting a "virtual war."[21] So, in this way, military preparedness with mass armies and weapons of mass destruction gained a certain kind of remoteness: the military was there for deterrence, not for fighting. Not a shot was fired directly between NATO and the Warsaw Pact during the Cold War. The military forces could be considered symbols or virtual forces, and "World War III" was remote. This state of affairs had an enormous influence upon conscription: a world war was a possibility, but with low probability; societies were, in a way, mobilized; survival was at stake, and mass armies were trained. The soldiers were ready to die for their countries and maybe also for an ideal, but still it was a virtual war, not a shooting war.

---

21. See Heurlin, *Global, Regional and National Security*; and Heurlin, *Riget, Magten og Militæret* (The kingdom, the power and the military).

All of this changed with the end of the Cold War. The supreme threat to survival disappeared. Wars were no longer survival wars or symmetric wars. Great-power wars had disappeared. Instead, small wars, civil wars, and asymmetric wars were on the agenda. "Politically correct" or normative wars became dominant, fought on behalf of the international community in order to secure stability, foster human rights, and prevent crimes against humanity. The biggest difference is that war has now become not just a probability, but a reality. Soldiers are now not just trained to fight, they do in fact fight. This implies a new issue of identity: if one is willing to die for one's own country, is one also willing to die for the international community?

One might say that, supported by the new world order and unipolarity, not only a "revolution in military affairs" but also a "revolution in societal affairs" has taken place. This revolution has to do with the emerging new role of the individual. Never before has the individual citizen, all over the world, been able to exert such comprehensive influence: as a political actor (due to democracy), as an economic actor (due to the market economy), and as a social actor (due to civil society). Together with the disappearance of threats to the supreme existential interest, this signifies a new relation between conscription and citizenship.[22] Conscription is, in this view, no longer tied to citizenship nor attached to the nexus between the state and the nation, but instead has more to do with giving individuals an opportunity to serve in an international or trans-national context, with the state performing a mediating role. It could be argued that the tradition of the citizen-soldier, with conscription providing a crucial link between the state and the nation, is fading and that instead a new post-national constellation, one that is at the same time individual and trans-national, is evolving.[23]

Arms control and disarmament bargaining as it took place during the Cold War has also disappeared. War is not necessarily something to be avoided: on the contrary, some normative wars are seen as necessary and must be fought. In an asymmetric strategic environment, bargaining has been replaced by coercion: demanding explicit efforts by international lawbreakers, ordering regime change, and issuing ultimatums.

---

22. See Joenniemi, "Farewell to Conscription? The Case of Denmark."
23. Ibid., p. 2.

Finally, remoteness is no longer relevant, due to internationalization and globalization, together with new information and communication technologies. The globe has become one single political, technological, and military battlefield. Global regulation is a need, and regulation can be pursued by internationally accepted military means.

In Goldmann's terms, the impacts of the supreme existential interest, of bargaining, and of remoteness have diminished. Democracy can thus take a larger role in foreign and security policy. This general explanation affects not just Denmark's armed forces, but those of many other countries as well. Increasing democratic processes in the post-modern world—involving new political, economic, and social roles for the individual—will tend to bring conscription into question and generally to foster the emergence of all-volunteer armed forces.

Conclusion

Danish defense is now undergoing its most fundamental transformation in many years. In the absence of any conventional military threat to Denmark in the foreseeable future, Denmark has chosen to get rid of the capacity for territorial defense offered by mass-mobilized forces, and to set up instead a two-pillar system that provides for deployable forces and for homeland security. It thus is moving from having "an irrelevant defense to a relevant defense."[24]

Implicit in these changes is that the Danish defense organization can now rely more on political choice—namely where, how, and why to intervene—rather than on response to well-recognized massive military threats from a strong hostile bloc. The need for territorial defense is gone, and with it the need for mobilization forces and, in turn, the military need for conscription, except to provide a recruiting pool for the AVF. In the long run, conscription may become unnecessary if enough young people volunteer. To the Danish political community and to the general population, this seems to be the best of all worlds: Denmark can still claim to have armed forces that are based on conscription, while avoiding some political and societal costs by having abandoned conscription in practice.

---

24. Danish Chief of Defense Jesper Helsø, quoted in *Folk and Forsvar*, No. 1 (March 2005), p. 1.

Denmark's two-pillar solution, comprising both deployable forces and homeland security, places a priority on a first-in-first-out force that applies the advances of the revolution in military affairs and engages in close military cooperation both with the United States and, perhaps eventually, with the EU.[25] Denmark has moved away from being a détente-oriented and even pacifist country, in particular by widening its strategic alliance with the United States; it is one of the few European states actively participating in the U.S. war in Iraq and in the postwar efforts there.

Denmark will increasingly seek to use its military power as an instrument of foreign policy to avoid international marginalization. One might say that Denmark has "militarized" its foreign policy, but this "militarization" is limited to cooperative activities with NATO, the United Nations, and ad-hoc coalitions involving the United States. Setting the number of deployable soldiers at 2000, to be constantly available for international missions, is a genuine political choice. In some tactical and strategic situations, such numbers, although small, could be decisive. Thus, this is a political signal that Denmark, although it is a small state, is willing and able to play a significant international role. In relation to NATO requirements and to the international efforts of the larger members of NATO, Denmark is fairly well positioned. Able to deploy 40 percent of its total military forces and having up to 8 percent actually deployed internationally at most times, Denmark is at the top in meeting the NATO objective for individual countries. By these measures, it surpasses even Great Britain and Germany.[26]

Given these factors, the new Danish defense program reflected in the June 10, 2004, five-year defense plan can justifiably be called "a new Danish Model."[27] Credit is due to the government's willingness to com-

---

25. Due to one of its four "opt-outs" of the Maastricht Treaty, Denmark does not participate in European Union military cooperation. These opt-outs were established to make the treaty more acceptable to the Danish people, who had rejected the treaty in a 1992 referendum; the Danes voted yes one year later to a specific Danish "opt-out" version of the treaty. It is the aim of the Danish government to get rid of the European Defense opt-outs, but this would require a new referendum.

26. According to the Danish Chief of Defense, quoted in *Folk and Forsvar*, No. 1 (March 2005), p. 1.

27. See website of the Danish Armed Forces at <www.forsvaret.dk>.

promise, and especially to the military's far-seeing preparations for a radical transformation of the Danish defense community.

Defense policy thus to a great extent reflects domestic policy: the exact shape and content of the armed forces are determined by many decision-makers who have varying views and varying influence upon the final outcome. Unlike domestic policy, however, the vital decisions will be subject to the possibilities and constraints of the international setting. In the final analysis, states will be rewarded or punished according to how well their defense policy responds to the structural conditions of the international system. It is against this standard that Denmark's New Defense Model will have to be judged.[28]

---

28. See Birthe Hansen and Bertel Heurlin, eds., *The New World Order: Contrasting Theories* (London: Macmillan, 2000).

Chapter 7

General Conscription and Wartime Reserve in Finland

Hannu Herranen

Finland, unlike many other European countries, has decided to retain general conscription and territorial defense as key elements of its defense. In today's world, a nation that builds its military defense on general conscription and territorial defense may be seen as clinging to outdated ideas about security, and perhaps even perceived as risking military ineffectiveness. Professional armed forces have been introduced into many European countries. The need for such a development is explained by, for example, the changed nature of crises and wars, advanced technology, military integration, and the perception that professional armies are more effective than armies of conscripts. Increasing international cooperation also affects the way in which national defense is organized in the twenty-first century.

The Finnish view, however, diverges from the mainstream European way of thought, turning on demographic, geographic, geopolitical, and economic factors, as well as Finland's historical background and the will of its population.

Armed forces that rely on general conscription may not be able to generate all of the capabilities required for some of the international crisis-management tasks or traditional military operations carried out by coalitions. However, this does not mean that conscription cannot potentially generate the capabilities required for an independent national defense. However, apart from the capability issue, which is addressed below, general conscription does generate a number of undeniably positive factors.

This chapter first reviews some of the reasons that Finland has opted to retain conscription; these reasons are found in history, geography, and culture as well as budgetary constraints. There is a brief comparison with how some of Finland's neighbors have changed their conscription practices. Finland's concept of "Total Defense," based on self-reliance and the use of conscripts and reserves, is explained. The conscription and reserve systems are then detailed. Finland's participation in international crisis-management is outlined. The costs of the conscription system are reviewed, and the quality of a military based on conscription is then assessed. The chapter concludes with a review of some of the issues that could affect Finland's choice to retain conscription in the future.

Why Conscription for Finland?

Finland, at roughly 330,000 square kilometers, is one of Europe's medium-size countries. Its geopolitical location and its moderate population of some 5 million people, as well as economic realities, set some constraints on how the national defense is organized.[1] The fact that a very high proportion of its people share a common language and a common religion can be viewed as unusual strengths, but a cross-section of the population is otherwise similar to that of other countries in Western Europe.[2]

History has shaped Finns' opinions on the importance of national defense and how it should be organized. For five hundred years, Finland was a battleground between Sweden and Russia. After the Russo-Swedish war of 1808–09, Finland was annexed by Russia, but during the turmoil of the Russian Revolution, Finland declared itself an independent state in 1917. After World War II broke out in early September 1939, Finland was invited to send a representative to Moscow to discuss "important questions of mutual interest," but in late October, the Soviets began to move troops towards Finland's eastern border. Negotiations soon broke off, and on November 30, 1939, the Winter War, as it is called in Finland, began. Despite heroic defense efforts, Finns

---

1. Finland's GDP per capita in 2003 was approximately €27,000.
2. About 93 percent of the population speaks Finnish as their native tongue; the second official language is Swedish, spoken by approximately 6 percent of the population as their native language. About 85 percent of the population are members of the Lutheran church.

were forced to sign an armistice on March 13, 1940, in which the Soviet Union annexed about 10 percent of Finland's land.

Finland was able to preserve its independence, first against the Soviet Union and then against Germany. In all of the European countries that took part in the "shooting war" of World War II, only three capitals were not occupied: London, Moscow, and Finland's capital, Helsinki. However, this freedom came at a high cost: between 1939 and 1945, Finland lost some 85,500 troops killed in action.[3]

After the tragic events of World War II, Finland decided to opt out of the great-power controversies and to pursue a policy of non-alliance, while actively contributing to peace support operations, especially under the auspices of the United Nations.

The deep-rooted principle of self-reliance among Finns thus grows out of this recent history: their will to defend their country has often been tested as Finland has either remained alone or has been left alone in situations crucial to her survival. As Defense Minister Seppo Kääriäinen put it: "The defense of Finland in all situations must rely on the Finns themselves. The ability to defend our own country and its citizens remains the foremost task of national military defense."[4]

A complete understanding of why Finland has retained general conscription should also take account of its politico-military culture and special features.[5] A study by Arto Nokkala points out that, because Finland has had little immigration, a united and dominant national culture emphasizing communality prevails in Finland; other sub-cultures have only a marginal position. Although globalization has penetrated Finland, it has not yet changed Finnish perceptions of the country's military and social needs and possibilities. The special relationship between the Defense Forces and Finnish society has been close throughout

---

3.   This number represented 2.2 percent of the total population. Sotatieteen Laitos (Institute of Military Science, Editorial staff), *Toinen Maailmansota* (World War II) (Porvoo, Finland: WSOY, 1994). The estimate of Soviet losses on the Finnish Front for 1939–44 is about 500,000. *Suomi Sodassa* (Finland at war) (Keuruu, Finland: Otava, 1983).

4.   Defense Minister Seppo Kääriäinen's web column on January 22, 2004, "The Territorial Defense," <www.defmin.fi>.

5.   Kari Laitinen and Arto Nokkala, "Suomalainen asevelvollisuus— historiaa, haasteita ja tulevaisuutta" (Finnish conscription—history, challenges and future), *Puolustusministeriö*, No. 1 (Saarijärvi: Gummerus, 2005).

the period of independence, and the operation of the Defense Forces continues to affect wide circles in society.

In spite of the great losses it inflicted, World War II did not upset this culture in Finland. The country resisted invasion and did not consider itself to be fighting "on the wrong side," as did some Eastern European countries that were left within the Soviet sphere of influence. Nor did the collapse of Communism at the turn of the 1990s have much effect on Finland's culture and values.

As Nokkala notes, the military and the military community are presently visible but not prominent in Finnish society. Military persons are generally interviewed as security-policy experts in the news media, and the garrisons interact closely with the surrounding civil society. Those serving in the military profession are appreciated but not in an overemphasized way. Military professionals have the right to vote in elections, but not the right to be members of political parties or to be candidates in parliamentary elections while in office. This limitation is considered to increase the social acceptability of the Defense Forces.

Nokkala points out that, because Finland's extensive conscription system includes almost the whole male population, the society has continuous control of the Defense Forces, and its operations must reflect trends in the dominant culture. For instance, almost all male members of Parliament are reservists who have done their conscript service. Top business executives and other influential persons in society have strong ties to the country's armed forces for similar reasons.

General conscription also has psychological significance. A shared obligation strengthens the commitment of citizens to national defense and is an important factor in enhancing the will to defend the country and to work for it during peacetime. Conscript service is seen as a kind of "social university" and a great equalizer, where all male citizens, regardless of their wealth or social status, are treated equally. It thus contributes to Finland's basic democratic values.

The system provides an opportunity for the younger generations to build upon the accomplishments of the previous generations and to further their legacy. The Finnish national character is represented in the way by which the military leads and how Finns prefer to be led: with fairness, honesty, and tolerance.

COMPARISON WITH CONSCRIPTION IN FINLAND'S NEIGHBORING COUNTRIES

Armies based on conscription are only about 200 years old. Recent social and military developments have raised questions about conscription, and a move towards professional armies can be seen in many European countries, especially after the end of the Cold War era. Among others, France, the Netherlands, Belgium, and Spain have given up general conscription.[6]

None of the Nordic countries of Sweden, Norway, and Denmark, with which Finland is often compared, has yet totally relinquished the conscription system. Of these countries, Denmark has moved closest to a professional army in conjunction with its NATO membership; it has shortened the term of conscript service from 8–12 months to just four months, and trains only about 20 percent of the male age group subject to conscription, in contrast to some 80 percent in Finland.[7] Sweden now trains only some 25 percent of each annual age cohort. Its recent security policy guidelines suggest that Sweden plans to discontinue its national defense and will concentrate on international crisis management.

NATO member Norway trains roughly one-third of each annual age group cohort.[8] Most of the conscripts will be trained for 6 to 12 months as operational troops; some of them are given four months of training geared toward Home Guard duties. A more selective call-up system has been proposed in Norway.

In the armed forces of the Baltic countries of Estonia, Lithuania, and Latvia, an increasingly professional core is complemented by conscript service and by a small reserve that is also based on conscription.[9] In Russia, the number of professional soldiers has increased to a certain extent, but the goal of professionalization has not been reached, mainly for economic reasons.

---

6. Laitinen and Nokkala, "Suomalainen asevelvollisuus—historiaa, haasteita ja tulevaisuutta" (Finnish conscription—history, challenges and future), pp. 121–126.
7. See Chapter 6 by Bertel Heurlin in this volume.
8. The total number of trained conscripts is some 9,500 (35 percent of the annual age-group cohort).
9. See Chapter 4 by Vaidotas Urbelis in this volume.

In Finland, by contrast, the importance of general conscription to national defense has rarely been questioned, and general conscription is strongly supported by its citizens. Finns have been surveyed on their willingness to retain general conscription, to alter it, or to transfer entirely to professional armed forces. Results from the years 2001–05 show that approximately 80 percent of Finns want to keep the system as it is, while only about 10 percent would like to diminish the total number of those militarily trained, and just 7–8 percent would prefer to replace general conscription altogether with a fully professional military.[10]

Self-reliance at Home: Finland's Concept of Total Defense

Finland's national defense is based on the doctrine of territorial defense, in which territorial forces, thoroughly familiar with their home areas, are formed of reservists during a wartime mobilization. They are responsible for defending their area or, in low-intensity crises, for providing assistance to civilian authorities. Supported by territorial forces, operational troops are used for the most demanding military operations such as protecting the most vital infrastructure, counter-attacks, or anti-terrorist activities.

Approximately 97 percent of wartime troops are reservists; the rest are professionals. Wartime totals have recently been reduced to about half of what they were in the 1970s.[11] The main reasons for this were economic, and in particular the objective of devoting resources to furnishing the troops with equipment sufficient both in quality and quantity. In spite of the reductions, Finland's wartime military force would still be one of the continent's largest.

---

10. The Advisory Board for Defense Information ABDI, Publications and documents, Bulletins and reports, November 24, 2005, p. 24 <www.defmin.fi>.

11. In the 1970s the total wartime strength was targeted at some 750,000; in the 1980s about 530,000; and in the 1990s about 430,000 troops. Finnish defense of the 2010s and 2020s will be based on a total strength of 350,000 soldiers. "White Paper on Finnish Security and Defense Policy 2004," <www.defmin.fi/>, Publications and Documents, Finnish Defense and Security Policy (hereafter cited as "White Paper" 2004), pp. 105–107. According to non-classified data, Sweden's wartime strength is 61,000 (31,000 operational troops plus 30,000 Home Guard); that of Norway 78,000 (28,000 plus 50,000); that of Germany, 685,000; and that of Poland, 375,000.

A large wartime troop structure is necessary because of Finland's military non-alliance and its choice to maintain a territorial defense. The territorial defense doctrine is regarded as appropriate for responding to the following crises and threat scenarios:

- a regional crisis that might have effects on Finland;

- political, economic, or military pressure, which might include a threat of military force or even limited use of military force;

- use of military force in the form of a strategic strike, or an attack beginning with a strategic strike aimed at seizing territory.[12]

Finnish defense planning has as its starting point the worst-case scenario, that of a large-scale military invasion. Over the last five to ten years, the prevention of low-intensity crises and other emergency situations such as natural disasters, threats targeted at information systems, and terrorism have been stressed in preparations and planning. The threat of terrorism is especially emphasized.

The most recent Security and Defense Policy Report ("White Paper"), published by the Ministry of Defense in September 2004, reaffirmed these basic guidelines, which have been followed for years. The "White Paper" states that Finland must maintain and develop its defense capability as a militarily non-allied country, and must monitor the changes in its security environment, especially those occurring in Northern Europe; that Finland must be able to guarantee its freedom of action under all circumstances; that a credible national defense must aim at preventing security threats from developing against the Finnish territory; and that Finland's defense capability should be developed so that the entire country can be defended. General conscription and territorial defense, discussed next, are among the instruments of this "total defense" capability.[13]

The Conscription and Reserve System in Finland

Since 1918, Finland's national military defense has been based on general conscription. Over the course of decades, the system has been

---

12. "White Paper" 2004, p. 104.
13. Ibid., pp. 8–9.

adapted both legislatively and functionally to emerging challenges and national resources. General conscription continues to be the cornerstone of Finnish defense.

According to national legislation, every Finnish citizen is obligated to participate or assist in national defense.[14] Finnish males are liable for national service. Military service lasts six, nine, or twelve months, depending on what special training is taken. Under law, required military service can take place only within national borders. All Finns serving on international assignments are professional soldiers or reservists who have signed a contract on a voluntary basis, have undertaken extra training, and have agreed to a longer term of service.

The group that is called up annually comprises about 30,000 eighteen-year-old male citizens. Approximately 98 percent of them participate in call-up events that are organized each autumn. Another 1.5 percent participate in later call-ups, while approximately one in two hundred of the men liable for national service are never reached, for one reason or another. About 85 percent of all young men in that age group are assigned to military service. As some young men do not serve, for medical, mental health, or ethical reasons, only some 82 percent of that age group serves. Approximately 8 percent of that age group are exempted from military service for medical reasons, while some 7 percent choose the civilian service alternative.[15] Some young men are allowed to defer their military service to a later time due to ongoing studies, personal economic situation, or other important personal reasons. Deferments of service can be allowed up to the age of 28. Nobody begins service immediately after the call-up: actual military service for those not deferred begins within two years of the call-up.

During the call-ups, which are organized by the military provinces in various municipalities around Finland, participants' physical fitness and mental health are examined. Basic psychological tests, aimed at

---

14. The Constitution of Finland, June 11, 1999. According to the Constitution female citizens are obliged to participate in all types of civilian defense tasks, for example, as labor conscripts.

15. Even though national service is compulsory for men, it is easy to transfer to the alternative civil service; it is enough simply to express a desire to do so. Approximately 2,000 young men each year choose the civil service option, mainly for religious or ethical reasons. *Defense Staff Conscription Division Statistics 1999–2003.*

measuring their aptitude for training and education, are conducted. The tests are the same for everyone.

More than 80 percent of men in each age group successfully complete their military service. This level is expected to stay the same for at least the next ten years.[16] The high number of those having completed their military service enables an appropriate age structure in wartime troop structures, which are predominantly made up of reservists.

TRAINING

Because personnel are the most important resource for Finland's national defense, the system for training personnel is continuously developing to meet changing requirements. All conscripts receive similar basic training, whether they are in the army, the navy, or the air force. Tests are carried out to select suitable conscripts for leadership positions as platoon and squad leaders or for special training for various rank-and-file duties such as missile experts (marksmen), tank drivers, or radar operators. Personal preference and skills acquired in civilian life are also taken into consideration.

After the special training period, there is field training for every conscript. Conscript leaders from the previous contingent, assisted and guided by professional staff, train and lead the conscripts from the new contingent and form them into platoons. The conscripts' training culminates in combat exercises and live-fire exercises. During their military service, conscripts do not do maintenance jobs or other support tasks: they are in military training during their entire service time.

All those who have completed their military service as conscripts become reservists; almost all reservists are assigned to tasks in a wartime unit that correspond to the training they received as conscripts. Only reservists in essential occupations, for example, key leaders of civilian administration and industry, civilian logistic personnel, or members of the police corps, are not assigned to wartime units.

---

16. About 400 women also apply for and receive armed training as conscripts on a voluntary basis and are then placed within wartime troop units and can be mobilized with their male colleagues, if needed.

Figure 7.1. Training Concept for Conscripts and Reservists

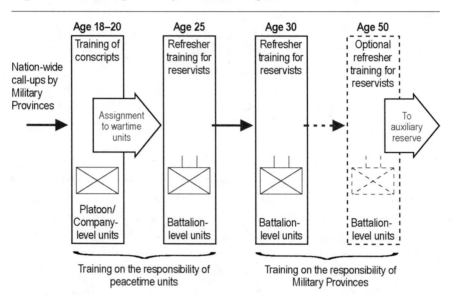

Training on the responsibility of peacetime units

Training on the responsibility of Military Provinces

After completing conscript service, reservists undergo two to three refresher training periods at intervals of about five years (see Figure 7.1).[17] Reservists train in battalions and in larger units. The aim is to make use of the special training reservists may have from their civilian education and careers, such as skills in information technology. Every year, some 30,000 reservists take part in refresher courses.

The refresher training courses are conducted as wartime unit exercises, mostly at the battalion level. In these exercises, reservist leaders train and lead their own wartime units, supported by professional military personnel. Refresher training for wartime units is organized once every five years on average, but the most important units and personnel, such as special guard companies, surface-to-air missile batteries, and units that are responsible for the mobilization, participate in refresher courses more frequently. Participation in refresher training is

17. For a time, deferments and a shortage of financial resources reduced the efficiency of the reserve exercise system. The economic recession in the 1990s and the ever-increasing costs of defense matériel drove down the number of refresher courses. After a dip in 1998–99, however, the number and quality of the exercises have bounced back to acceptable levels.

compulsory but a reservist may apply for deferment.[18] Based on participation in exercises and thus on increasing competence, reservists in the rank and file can be promoted to warrant officers, and those in the reserve officer corps may be promoted up to the rank of major. In some cases promotion may also be based on professional skills acquired in civilian life.

The Army peacetime units are only training centers for both conscripts and reserves. The Air Force and Navy bases have broad wartime obligations as well. There are high proportions of professional personnel in the Navy and the Air Force units, and they can be regarded as almost comparable to a professional armed force. A relatively small number of conscripts are trained in these forces at any given time; they mainly perform support functions.

THE MILITARY COMMAND STRUCTURE

The president of the Republic of Finland is the Supreme Commander of the Defense Forces in both war and peace. He or she issues to the Defense Forces their orders concerning strategic tasks, decides on significant changes in military readiness, and has the sole authority to promote military officers. In cooperation with Parliament, the president decides on war and peace. Parliament enacts laws on national defense; its various parliamentary committees supervise the activity of the armed forces. The civilian-run Ministry of Defense is responsible for setting basic policy, managing the defense budget, and coordinating parliamentary control of the armed forces.

The Chief of Defense (CHOD), a four-star general, reports both to the president of Finland and the Minister of Defense. The CHOD, aided by the Defense Staff, leads the Defense Forces, comprising the Army, the Navy, and the Air Force. Neither the CHOD nor the Defense Staff are included in the organization of the Ministry of Defense.

---

18. The main reasons for granting deferments are academic studies and economic and family reasons. According to the Defense Staff data, deferments for reservists' health cause an average annual loss of up to some 15 percent from refresher training. The Defense Forces have attempted to remedy this situation with pre-exercise medical check-ups of reservists and by drawing up individual fitness improvement plans.

During peacetime, command and administration of the Defense Forces is organized into military commands, military provinces, and brigade or regiment-level units.[19] The regional commanders are responsible for the military readiness of their regions and for cooperation with civil authorities. There is no significant change in the command and administration system when readiness is raised to wartime levels.

The peacetime strength of the Defense Forces amounts to approximately 16,500 professional personnel (soldiers and civilians), plus about 30,000 conscripts annually. The strength is periodically increased by reservists who attend annual refresher courses. Among the professional personnel are 3,600 officers, 3,600 warrant officers (NCOs), 1,700 enlisted personnel, and 7,600 civilians. These personnel are in charge of operating the highest echelons, training conscripts, maintaining equipment, and providing routine sustainment services.

WARTIME OR MOBILIZATION STRUCTURE

The strength of the wartime Defense Forces is approximately 350,000 men and women.[20] The troops are divided into a territorial component of about 250,000 and an operational component of about 100,000.[21] In practice, almost all wartime territorial forces intended for the military defense of Finland are formed by the military provinces; each military province leads the mobilization and calls up troops from the trained reserve in its province. Each military province is also in charge of defense planning for its area.

The system is very traditional, but very flexible. In mobilization, the peacetime headquarters and establishments are reinforced with reservists to bring them up to their wartime strength. The peacetime brigade-

---

19. The 2004 White Paper set a requirement to simplify the structure so that, from the start of 2008, the military regional commands will be disbanded and the country divided into seven military provinces and peacetime brigade/regiment-level units. "White Paper" 2004, pp. 121–123.

20. Some 285,000 troops are designated for the Army, 25,000 for the Navy, and approximately 35,000 for the Air Force.

21. Operational troops are the core of national defense—the youngest, best equipped, and best-trained reservists—and can perform the most demanding combat tasks all over the country. Territorial troops comprise older reservists and are mainly responsible for protecting vital objectives and combat support activities in their home area.

and regiment-level units mobilize most of the wartime operational troops. All wartime troops are reservists, not conscripts in training.

Three brigades of the peacetime Army have been designated "readiness formations" that have greater readiness to mobilize reserve troops rapidly. In addition, the Navy and Air Force units can, because of their structure and personnel, be mobilized rapidly. During mobilization, the training of conscripts may continue in the training centers; only after training would they be deployed as wartime troops.

The material readiness of the territorial troops has been improved by increasing their mobility, protection, firepower, and capability for assistance to civilian authorities in low-intensity crises. Special attention has been paid to developing a capability for joint situational awareness for all services, utilizing Finland's particular expertise in communications technologies.

The functional aspect of defense is also constantly being developed, and is increasingly migrating toward defending democratic values, vital targets, and functions, instead of defending large land areas.

Finland's total defense consists of civilian as well as military components. The territorial defense doctrine is only one part of the national total defense, which consists of military defense, economic security, internal security including rescue service, border control, policing and public law and order, infrastructure such as electricity, water supply, and the like, public health, and defense information services. There is a clear division of labor, supported by legislation, between the military and the civilian component: civil authorities such as police, health care, and rescue services take care of citizens' domestic or everyday security and welfare, while the Defense Forces are responsible for preventing and repelling external threats. The security of Finland's citizens is also supported by a system of stockpiles maintained by the Ministry of Trade and Industry, including raw materials, bread grain, fuel, medicine, fertilizer, and the like. The Frontier Guard and Customs authorities, which are subordinate to the Ministry of the Interior, are responsible for border security. Despite the division of labor, there is significant cooperation among these various authorities. Recently this cooperation has been substantially increased by precautions against so-called new threats.

Finland's total defense is supported by voluntary organizations. Some 12,000 Finns who are liable for national service participate in additional voluntary exercises. About 16,000 other citizens participate in security training organized by the National Defense Training Association (Maanpuolustuskoulutus ry), for some of which they pay a fee. Voluntary exercises and security training are short-term events, normally conducted over the weekend, and the focus is usually on skills related to citizens' everyday security, such as first aid, orienteering, and the like.

Finland's International Participation: Military Crisis Management

Conscription produces a large reserve that can be drawn upon for the Finnish contribution to international crisis management. Finland has participated in international peacekeeping and crisis-management operations since 1956.[22] During the five decades since then, more than 45,000 Finns have served in operations led by the United Nations, NATO, the European Union, and the Organization for Security and Cooperation in Europe (OSCE). Approximately 90 percent of personnel in the Finnish contingents are reservists who have signed a contract for 6–12 months. The rest of Finland's troops are professional officers in active service and special personnel, such as engineers, mechanics, or legal advisers.

According to Finnish law, conscripts cannot be used in crisis-management operations, but they can participate in international exercises. At any given time, a maximum of 2,000 troops can be deployed abroad. All of them must volunteer to do so under a special contract. In practice, the average number of Finnish troops deployed abroad in recent years has been approximately 1,000. It has been Finland's aim to send to international operations each year: one battalion, one or two detached companies, and one, two, or three CIMIC (civil-military cooperation) detachments, together with staff and liaison officers. Table 7.1 shows the Finnish contribution to international crisis-management op-

---

22. Finland's national security and defense policy states that: "The Government's goal is to promote sustainable development, stability and security in the international community and to strengthen Finland's international position. The Government will support a more effective United Nations and other structures of broad-based international cooperation with a view to enhancing democracy, respect for human rights, and the rule of law. Finland is an active Member State of the European Union and promotes strengthening of the common foreign and security policy and transatlantic cooperation." Government platform on the Finnish government website, <www.valtioneuvosto.fi/hallitus/hallitusohjelma/en.jsp>, p. 4.

Table 7.1. Finland's Participation in International Crisis Management in 2000–2004 (Number of Troops)

	2000	2001	2002	2003	2004
SFOR (Stabilization Force, Bosnia-Herzegovina)	117	115	80	80	
KFOR (Kosovo Force)	820	820	820	820	700
ISAF (International Security Assistance Force, Afghanistan)			50	50	82
EUFOR (European Union Force, Bosnia-Herzegovina)					200
UNMEE (United Nations Mission in Ethiopia and Eritrea)					185
UNTSO (United Nations Truce Supervision Organization)	12	15	15	14	14
	949	**950**	**965**	**964**	**1181**
SOURCE: Defense Staff International Division statistics.					

erations in recent years. In proportion to its population of five million, Finland's contribution is high, and Finland has good reason to consider itself "a great power in crisis management." Finland intends to participate in the European Union battle-group concept with two detachments of some 200 troops each; this will, accordingly, diminish Finland's contribution to other crisis-management activities. The annual expenditure for international crisis-management operations, covered jointly by the Ministry of Defense and the Ministry for Foreign Affairs, is approximately 100 million euros.

Military crisis-management contingents consist of active-duty professional military personnel and of selected reservist volunteers who have signed contracts. When conscripts apply for crisis-management training, they also commit themselves to serve for one year, to participate in international crisis-management exercises during their national service, and to be called for crisis-management operations when in reserve. One of the peacetime army units, the Pori Brigade, specializes in international crisis-management training. It is also possible for those who have completed their conscript service in other peacetime units to apply for international duties.

Reservists may volunteer in response to advertisements in the news media. Some specialists are personally asked by Pori Brigade or the Finnish International Center (FINCENT) to apply.[23] Personnel are selected on the basis of testing; after supplementary training, they are deployed to international operations. When reservists are assigned to a crisis-management contingent, their civilian trade or profession as well as military or other leadership training is taken into consideration. Professionals are in overall command of the contingent, and are partly responsible for certain specialist duties such as intelligence and legal services, but otherwise reservist subordinates are led by reservist leaders.

Due in part to its large and well-motivated reserve and sound civilian education, Finland has not had difficulty finding troops for international assignments. For every Finn serving in international crisis-management operations, three to four volunteers are waiting to be called upon. Service in military crisis-management operations is respected.

Compensation and Manpower Costs

Finland has chosen conscription in part because it would not be able to afford the higher cost of a professional army. Depending on the duration of service, conscripts are paid a modest daily allowance of €3.6–8.25. The total budgetary cost for one conscript per day is an average of €37. The total cost for one trained conscript amounts to €9,500 on average, including matériel costs associated with training. Married conscripts' families are assisted financially during the period of service with housing allowances and welfare and other benefits.

When taking part in refresher training, reservists receive daily pay from the government that is approximately ten times what conscripts receive. The employer can deduct that amount from the person's salary but, perhaps reflecting the positive public attitude toward reserve training, many employers do not do so. Together with their food, accommodation, health care, subsidized travel, daily allowance, and payroll costs, the average cost per day is €117.

---

23. Since 2001, the Finnish International Center has taken the lead on all Finnish Defense Forces peace support operations including recruiting, equipping, and providing command and control.

Some Finnish universities and most vocational colleges give credit for the completion of a longer conscript service period or special training. Depending on the area of study and what special training is received, a student who has completed his or her conscript service can be granted credits toward a degree or have the service recognized as practical training, for example, by showing a service certificate or a portfolio built up during leadership training. Successful completion of conscript service is also a significant advantage when applying for a job.

One of the remaining challenges for Finland is to improve the socio-economic status of reservists and conscripts. The defense establishment is working on proposals for, among other things, raising reservist pay and conscript allowances and increasing the number of free vacation trips during leave.

SAVINGS FROM CONSCRIPTION ARE AVAILABLE FOR PROCUREMENT

Finland's defense budget for 2004 was €1,885 billion.[24] The defense expenditures for 2004 represent some 1.4 percent of GDP (if military pensions are included, in accordance with NATO definitions). Investment in major equipment (excluding R&D) accounted for about 26.6 percent of total defense expenditure in 2003; in 2004, the amount was 26.8 percent and in 2005 it was 25.8 percent. This figure is expected to rise to 28.3 percent in 2006, and then to about 29 percent until 2008.

According to the 2004 "White Paper," the budget share of the defense branch will be set according to the government's 2005–2008 expected expenditure framework. Defense spending will then remain constant in real terms during the years 2009–2012, with approximately one-third used for procurement. It is assumed that the expected rise in matériel costs will be offset by increases in maintenance efficiency.[25]

A defense budget that Finland can afford would not support the formation and sustainment of a big enough professional army to give Finland a credible military defense all by itself. Faced with similar challenges, Denmark and Norway have based their defense solution on

---

24. The 2004 defense budget included: payroll costs of €704 million; procurement of defense equipment, €573 million; other operational costs, €422 million; upkeep of conscripts, €143 million; equipment and administration, €43 million.
25. "White Paper" 2004, p. 130.

NATO partnership, while Sweden, whose defense solution most resembles that of Finland, spends almost three times as much for its national defense.

For comparison, Denmark spends about 1.3 percent of its GDP for all defense costs, Norway about 2 percent, and Sweden 1.9 percent. Finland, at 1.4 percent of GDP, is not very different; however, it gets a lot more "bang for the buck" due to the higher proportion it can spend on matériel procurement. In total spending—not just per-capita costs— Finland is a relatively high defense spender on procurement, even compared to all European NATO countries. This is only possible because general conscription is economically favorable for Finland.

Since Finland has chosen to remain militarily non-allied, it must spend money on hardware which, if it were a member of an alliance, would be regarded as redundant. This has been a conscious choice. It may sound somewhat old-fashioned to speak about the "sacrifice" conscripts make when they serve the country during their military service. However, given the meager benefits Finns award their conscripts, the term "sacrifice" has real meaning. In countries where most members of the armed forces are full-time professionals, servicemembers get considerably greater allowances and therefore these countries cannot spend as much on procurement.

Measuring defense as a share of GNP has been criticized in Finland on the grounds that general conscription imposes alternative expenses that do not show in defense expenditure statistics. The argument is that persons performing their military service could otherwise be productive in the civilian labor market or by increasing their competitiveness through study. (See Chapter 5 in this volume by John Warner and Sebastian Negrusa.) Because conscription acquires human resources at lower cost than in the open market, and because conscripts' service time can therefore be viewed as a loss in overall civilian production, it is argued that these alternative expenditures should be estimated and accounted for.

Finnish defense expenditures comprise 2.09 percent of GNP if opportunity costs are taken into account in this way.[26] Even this percentage

---

26. Kari Alho, Ville Kaitila, and Markku Kotilainen, *An International Comparison of Defense Expenditure* (Helsinki: The Research Institute of the Finnish Economy, 2003), pp. 57–59. In their model, alternative expenditures are esti-

puts Finland in the middle of OECD countries. Due to its high unemployment, Finland's total defense expenditures, when measured this way, are above those of the other neutral European nations, but remain very slightly lower than small NATO countries' average expenditures.[27]

Does the Finnish System Generate High-quality Personnel?

Conscription is often said to result in a lesser capability than professional armed forces. In Finland, however, the military training given to conscripts and reservists, good and modern equipment, and Finland's special advantages produce the desired results. Finnish peacekeepers have repeatedly shown the world the professional skill and capability of Finnish reserve troops.

Finland views its conscripts as troops in training; it does not plan to fight a war with conscripts or send them abroad for crisis-management operations. The national service is only the first stage, during which a person liable for military service gets the basis for his or her special training. One would be ready for significant defense tasks only after having completed one or two reserve refresher training courses.

While quality may be assessed domestically, using internationally accepted methods and standards, credibility is determined abroad. Finnish reservists serving as contract personnel in peace support operations led by the United Nations, the European Union, and NATO compare very favorably with other countries' full-time professionals. Finland's reserve troops are generally better educated academically. Most of them are slightly older and have already held civilian jobs in which they have accrued skills and competencies other than just military training. They are thus well-rounded troops who possess a high degree of initiative and are capable of solving complex problems without explicit orders

---

mated by correcting the average annual number of conscripts by the median annual unemployment and by inserting this into the total employment. However, even the authors of this accounting model from a respected Finnish research institute concede that the model greatly simplifies the situation and generalizes or simply ignores certain relevant factors.

27. Alho, Kaitila, and Kotilainen, *An International Comparison of Defense Expenditure*, pp. 63–64. In 2004, the unemployment rate in Finland was the highest of all Nordic countries, about 8–9 per cent (which was equal to the average for the Euro area). <www.stat.fi>.

from their officers. This is not often typical of other professional armed forces' personnel who, although they may be very well trained in their specific fields of expertise, tend to be less interested in what is outside their own narrow areas of competence.

Finland was the first non-NATO country chosen to lead a multi-national brigade in Kosovo; this is a sign that NATO finds Finland's training system and performance credible, even though only a handful of its crisis-management troops are professionals and most of the troops are reservists. These are the same people who would defend Finland if needed.

What Lies Ahead

The decline of the military confrontation between East and West in Europe and the fact that the world is becoming increasingly globalized and networked have diminished the role of the nation-state and have altered public views on security. As a result, certain tasks traditionally regarded as nation-state tasks are being and have been transferred to supra-national institutions, including some aspects of national security. At the same time, unification and globalization create new security threats, and in this circumstance membership in a multi-national community gives citizens a stronger sense of security.

Meanwhile, national armed forces are subjected to ever greater demands for economic efficiency and specialization. This has led many nations to form fully professional armed forces and to abolish general conscription altogether. Increases in international cooperation and in defense technology have created greater demands for language proficiency as well as other professional skills that cannot be acquired during conscript service or refresher training.

The Finnish will to defend the nation is still supported by all sectors of the population, and the general attitude toward national defense is positive; however, security needs and previously self-evident values and attitudes will be influenced by changing security challenges and changing values and attitudes. Membership in the European Union, in particular, has increased Finns' sense of security during the last decade. Today, however, changes in security structures and so-called new threats are challenging this arrangement.

As many European nations question the relevance and even efficacy of general conscription, there will be a continuing need to make the case for the Finnish defense solution, both nationally and internationally. Based on opinion polls, the average Finn is less concerned about the probability of major war than with everyday threats such as illness, accidents, and natural disasters, and perhaps with the threat of international terrorism. However, veterans of World War II are still around to remind Finland that not so long ago, it was thrust into a major war alone, badly prepared, and ill-equipped.

Unlike many European countries, Finns still feel that general conscription can contribute credibly to security even as attitudes and the security environment change.[28] As long as there is no real trust in the political and military-security guarantees provided by the international community, national preparedness is seen as essential, but economic constraints mean that maintaining a large enough fully professional military is impracticable for a non-allied country such as Finland.

Many future factors will undoubtedly present challenges for conscription. The development of international crisis-management cooperation and Defense Forces capability, and the increasingly technical nature of defense equipment, have meant an increase in the proportion of professional personnel in the most important wartime forces such as electronic warfare formations, maintenance units, and command echelons. Information system warfare, information management and other technological fields, new duties and new techniques in helicopter operations, electronic intelligence and surveillance, modern training methods, and increased international duties will all require additional resources. Technological advances, in particular, will require a degree of user training that cannot be provided during the short periods of conscript military service or reservist refresher courses.

Some factors could seriously challenge general conscription and the territorial defense doctrine in either Finnish society or in the Defense Forces. The biggest change would arise from a perception of permanent and positive developments and the stabilization of the security situation in Finland's near neighborhood. Another factor, almost as significant, would be a decision by Finland to abolish its policy of non-alliance, or a marked increase in the credibility of the European Union security struc-

---

28. "Finns' Opinions on Foreign and Security Policy, Defence, and Security Issues," ABDI Reports 1/2005, at <www.defmin.fi>, November 24, 2005, pp. 18, 23–27 and 35, 36.

tures. However, even NATO membership would not necessarily mean that Finland would give up either of the basic pillars of its defense.[29] The main questions would largely hinge on Finland's ability to maintain a substantial national defense and, simultaneously, to be able to live up to the requirements set by the military alliance.

Demographic factors in Finland will not require an end to general conscription. The size of the male population is sufficient to maintain wartime troop levels at 350,000 well into the future.[30] The annual intake is even large enough to allow Finland to reduce the share of young people trained in the military without a significant increase in the average age of wartime troops. Tightening of requirements in call-ups, so that slightly fewer conscripts would be assigned to military service, has occasionally been discussed: this would make it possible to filter out those conscripts who would probably be discharged in the early phases of their military service anyway. However, wishing to retain the egalitarian character of universal military service, Finns have thus far been unwilling to take this road.

A predicted labor shortage in the 2010s and 2020s will increase competition for skilled workers and thus may put pressure on conscription, or at least on the duration of military service, starting with the beginning of the next decade.[31] Preliminary work is being done to improve benefits and compensation for conscripts and reservists, which would make it possible to respond better to changes in the future.

For any nation, however, the main cornerstone of national defense is a strong will to defend the nation; without this no nation can prevail, regardless of how much money it spends. Annual studies show that the will of Finns to defend their country has remained very high through-

---

29. Ministry of Defense, "Effects of a possible membership in a military alliance on development of the Finnish system and defense administration," April 27, 2004, <www.defmin.fi>, Settlements.

30. The number of men participating in call-ups will vary between 34,000 and 29,000 during the years 2006–2020. Initially, the number will be approximately 32,000, but will stabilize at less than 30,000 at the end of the period. *Statistical Yearbook of Finland* (Keuruu: Statistics Finland, 2000).

31. It has been estimated that there are not enough skilled workers willing to move to Finland from the new member states of the European Union to alleviate the problem. There are, however, no conclusive estimates on the dimension of the labor shortage.

out the decades.[32] Their confidence in the Defense Forces is extremely high, and their confidence in Finland's ability to cope in a war fought with conventional forces has been stable. For now, most Finnish citizens continue to view conscription as the best basis for Finland's military defense.

---

32. Studies conducted between 1990 and 2005 showed that an average of 76 percent of all Finns thought that if Finland were attacked, Finns should take up arms in defense, even if the outcome were uncertain. This percentage has remained fairly steady. An even larger percentage of Finns would be willing to participate in national defense according to their skills and abilities if Finland were attacked. ABDI, November 24, 2005, p. 27, <www.defmin.fi/>; and ibid., July 5, 2004.

Chapter 8

An All-Volunteer Force in Disguise

On the Transformation of the Armed Forces in Germany

Gerhard Kümmel

Like so many other militaries all over the world, the German armed forces are currently undergoing major change. Indeed, the depth and intensity of this change is so profound that in Germany, the talk is no longer merely of reform, but of a substantial transformation of the Bundeswehr. This chapter moves from the general to the specific—from general information about the Bundeswehr to a discussion of the specific issues of manpower and conscription. It starts by briefly outlining the stimuli for change and then sketches the history of the Bundeswehr from the 1950s onward to illustrate the significant change the military has undergone. This is followed by a description of the transformation process the Bundeswehr is currently undergoing with a focus on conscription and other manpower issues. I conclude that the transformation of the military in Germany might very well go even farther than currently envisaged. While Germany may retain the institution of conscription, which is enshrined in its political-military culture, in practice, conscription has already become a fiction, and it can be expected to become even less real in the future.

Drivers of Transformation

In the post–World War II era, the development of the nuclear bomb and the onset of the Cold War forced military people to shift from war-fighting to deterrence. The resulting change to the military profession was fundamental.[1] Soldiers turned, in Michel Martin's apt phrase, from warriors to managers and technicians.[2] If war should occur despite deterrence, it would basically mean inter-state war starting with conventional weapons and escalating to nuclear weapons. A mass army based on conscription was the format that was widely used. With the end of the East-West conflict, the outlook changed dramatically again. One reason is that, in the era of globalization, the security of any country can be influenced and threatened by events and developments in faraway places. The security policies of each country must, therefore, take the global aspects of security into consideration. Armed forces must adapt and prepare accordingly.

Globalization has also increased the public's sense of international responsibility and solidarity. Modern mass media and means of communication serve to disseminate knowledge of the life, the cultures, the living standards, and also the plights of people in other parts of the globe, which may elicit a humanitarian impulse, a sense that "something must be done."[3] Since the end of the East-West conflict, therefore, such selective humanitarianism has prompted a substantial increase in the number of military missions or "operations other than war" (OOTW). As a consequence, as Figure 8.1 shows, the number of European and NATO soldiers deployed in out-of-area operations has risen substantially since 1991.

De-escalation, peacekeeping, and peace-support operations and humanitarian interventions are consistent with the "civilianization" of the military, and as such are acceptable to segments of society that otherwise have pacifist or anti-military views. But they pose a substantial challenge to the armed forces, extending the task profile of the military beyond deterrence, defense, and attack:

---

1. Cathy Downes, "To Be or Not to Be a Profession: The Military Case," *Defence Analysis*, Vol. 1, No. 3 (1985), pp. 147–171, p. 156.
2. Michel L. Martin, *Warriors to Managers: The French Military Establishment Since 1945* (Chapel Hill: University of North Carolina Press, 1981).
3. Christopher Dandeker, "New Times for the Military: Some Sociological Remarks on the Changing Role and Structure of the Armed Forces of the Advanced Societies," in Giuseppe Caforio, ed., *The Sociology of the Military* (Cheltenham, U.K. and Northampton, Mass.: Edward Elgar, 1998), pp. 573–590, 579; Gerhard Kümmel, "Untiefen des Menschenrechts-Diskurses," *WeltTrends*, No. 31, Vol. 9 (2001), pp. 101–117.

Figure 8.1. Soldiers in Out-of-Area Missions, 1980–2002

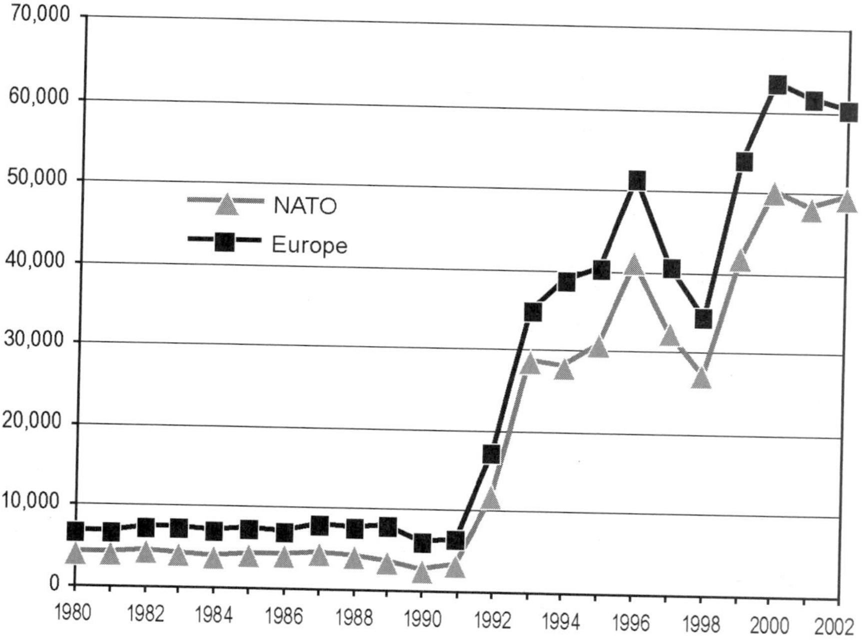

Note: Europe here comprises 35 European countries excluding the city-states of Cyprus and Malta, parts of the former Yugoslavia, Bosnia-Herzegovina, and states without armies such as Liechtenstein and Iceland.

SOURCE: Ines-Jacqueline Werkner, *Allgemeine Trends und Entwicklungslinien in den europäischen Wehrsystemen*, SOWI Working Paper 134 (Strausberg: SOWI, 2003), p. 10.

In military operations other than war, ... soldiers [must] ... know how to fight, how to establish local security, how to deal with the local adversaries, and how to cooperate with local partners and civilian international relief organisations.... [This] requires nothing less than a new self-perception of the military profession.... The new functions and the non-traditional roles of the soldier as streetworker, policeman and diplomat complement the traditional roles of the soldier as warrior, defender and attacker.[4]

---

4. Gerhard Kümmel, "A Soldier is a Soldier is a Soldier!? The Military and Its Soldiers in an Era of Globalization," in Giuseppe Caforio, ed., *Handbook of the Sociology of the Military* (New York: Kluwer Academic/Plenum Publish-

Quite a few of today's military missions do not resemble traditional inter-state war. Conflicts emerging since the early 1990s increasingly stem from rifts between various segments of society within states, and from state structures falling apart. Fought on a sub-state level, these are often asymmetrical wars between relatively weak governments and relatively strong anti-government forces and may, because of their potential and actual spillover effects, require intervention and military operations other than war by interested actors. The defense ministries and the armed forces of the world have adapted accordingly.

The militaries have also had to adapt to the constraints of national budgets and the widespread diminution of direct military threat: the 1990s were marked in many countries by cuts in defense and military budgets and considerable reductions in military manpower. Reductions have also been propelled by national demographic and social developments. The demographic revolution described in Chapter 3 by Rickard Sandell, marked by decreasing birth rates and increasing life expectancy, is accompanied by changing values.[5] Whereas military values put emphasis on authority, obedience, duty, community, comradeship, discipline, patriotism, and giving, civilian values increasingly stress individuality, self-fulfillment, autonomy, cosmopolitanism, and taking. As a result, a "demilitarization of societies" is taking place.[6]

At the same time, however, military tasks have expanded to involve more frequent deployments in military missions of various new kinds. To respond to this, the armed forces must make organizational and

---

ers, 2003), pp. 417–433, p. 432.

5. Ronald Inglehart, *The Silent Revolution: Changing Values and Political Styles Among Western Publics* (Princeton, N.J.: Princeton University Press, 1977); Ronald Inglehart, *Culture Shift in Advanced Industrial Society* (Princeton, N.J.: Princeton University Press, 1990); Ronald Inglehart, *Modernization and Postmodernization: Cultural, Economic and Political Change in 43 Societies* (Princeton, N.J.: Princeton University Press, 1997); Ulrich Beck, *Risikogesellschaft. Auf dem Weg in eine andere Moderne* (Frankfurt am Main: Suhrkamp, 1986); Anthony Giddens, *The Consequences of Modernity* (Stanford, Calif.: Stanford University Press, 1990).

6. Karl W. Haltiner, "Die Demilitarisierung der europäischen Gesellschaften und die Remilitarisierung ihrer Streitkräfte," in Thomas Jäger, Gerhard Kümmel, Marika Lerch, and Thomas Noetzel, eds., *Sicherheit und Freiheit. Außenpolitische, innenpolitische und ideengeschichtliche Perspektiven. Festschrift für Wilfried von Bredow* (Baden-Baden: Nomos, 2004), pp. 226–241.

structural changes. Militaries seek to use high-tech warfare as much as possible instead of putting boots on the ground. For example, the revolution in military affairs (RMA) involves efforts to give soldiers more sophisticated high-tech weapons and equipment to reduce the risk to individual soldiers. Through the use of outsourcing, privatization, and other market-economic approaches, many militaries seek to become smaller, more flexible, more modular, leaner, and more professional.[7]

The rise of peace-enforcement missions in the 1990s and the asymmetric threats in the military operations in Afghanistan and Iraq have reinforced this trend. This might be called the "remilitarization" of the military, and the increasing professionalization implies a shift from conscription to an all-volunteer force. Such a shift has been implemented or planned by many countries, as Cindy Williams discusses in Chapter 1.

The German Case

Germany might appear to deviate from the mainstream, because it still adheres to conscription. However, military transformation has engulfed the Bundeswehr as it has the rest of Europe: it just has not done so with regard to the draft. Germany's past helps explain why conscription remains an essential element of its political-military culture.

THE BUNDESWEHR OF THE BONN REPUBLIC

After World War II, Germany was demilitarized, and the German military was publicly discredited because of its active promotion of the war and its involvement in the Holocaust.[8] But the Cold War and the threat perceptions following the outbreak of the Korean War eased the way for the rearmament of Germany and creation of the Bundeswehr. However, these steps were by no means universally approved by the German public. The *"Ohne Mich"* (Without me) movement tried to prevent rearmament and

---

7. Christopher Dandeker, "Flexible Forces for the Twenty-First Century," Report No. 1, *Facing Uncertainty* (Karlstad: Swedish National Defense College, Department of Leadership, 1999).

8. This section is based on Wilfried von Bredow, *Demokratie und Streitkräfte. Militär, Staat und Gesellschaft in der Bundesrepublik Deutschland* (Wiesbaden: Westdeutscher Verlag, 2000); Detlef Bald, *Militär und Gesellschaft 1945–1990. Die Bundeswehr der Bonner Republik* (Baden-Baden: Nomos, 1994); Detlef Bald, *Die Bundeswehr. Eine kritische Geschichte 1955–2005* (Munich: Beck, 2005).

the establishment of armed forces. In a public opinion poll of February 1955, 42 percent of West Germans opposed establishing armed forces, while just 39 percent were in favor.[9] This opposition force, however, was driven to the margins of political discourse by the anti-communism then prevailing, and by the perception of the Soviet Union as a war-prone adversary. Thus the armed forces, created after 1955 with defense as their core mission, soon met with broader public approval. Those who advocated the dissolution of the Bundeswehr dropped from 43 percent in October 1956 to 30 percent just four months later, in February 1957, and to 23 percent by July 1961.[10] The perception of a communist threat from the East persuaded Germany's partners and allies in the Western European Union (WEU) and in NATO to agree to allow Germany to establish one of the biggest mass armies in Europe.[11]

Well into the early 1960s, when the Berlin Wall was erected, the guiding principle was that the armed forces of the new Germany should not resemble the German armed forces of the past, which were widely perceived as militaristic and indifferent to human rights. The military in Germany was, therefore, explicitly made subject both to Germany's constitution (Basic Law, *Grundgesetz*) and to the Charter of the United Nations. Germany's Basic Law was meant to establish political and democratic civilian control of the armed forces. During the 1960s, Germany experienced a fundamental and far-reaching shift in its political culture, as students—those who came to be called the "1968-ers"— questioned the older generation about Germany's National Socialist past and especially about the Holocaust.

This impulse towards political participation, transparency, and public debate did not leave the armed forces unaffected. In the second half of the 1960s the Bundeswehr, too, experienced a sort of democratization. General Wolf Graf von Baudissin was particularly responsible for giving the

---

9.   Elisabeth Noelle and Erich Peter Neumann, eds., *Jahrbuch der öffentlichen Meinung 1947–1955* (Allensbach: Verlag für Demoskopie, 1956), p. 366.

10. Elisabeth Noelle and Erich Peter Neumann, eds., *Jahrbuch der öffentlichen Meinung 1958–1964* (Allensbach and Bonn: Verlag für Demoskopie, 1965), p. 470.

11. Article 24, Paragraph 2 of the German constitution (the Basic Law, *Grundgesetz*), explicitly opens the possibility for Germany to participate in a system of collective security. Thus, membership in NATO and the WEU was permitted by the constitution.

Bundeswehr what was to become its new philosophy and guiding principles: *Innere Führung* (Leadership and Civic Education) and the ideal of a "citizen in uniform."[12] Thus, for example, soldiers may run as candidates for elections and may join political parties and unions. *Innere Führung* implies that soldiers have fundamental rights and responsibilities guaranteed by the constitution and by international human rights standards. Thus, for example, a soldier is required to treat both fellow-soldiers and adversaries in a civilized manner. *Innere Führung* also entails the right and responsibility of the individual soldier to object to orders that violate Germany's Basic Law or international human rights law. "The concept of *Innere Führung* has made the Bundeswehr an integral and natural component of our state order and society."[13] Despite the arguments of some critics that *Innere Führung* could degrade military effectiveness, it has considerable support in German politics and in German society at large.

To secure the rights of individual soldiers, the German government created the position of the Defense Commissioner of the German Parliament (*Wehrbeauftragter des Deutschen Bundestages*). Recognizing that higher education for officers would be useful to assure that soldiers would know more about their own society, the Department of Defense established Bundeswehr universities in Hamburg and in Munich. Accordingly, since the early 1970s, the overwhelming majority of officers in Germany have an academic education and a university degree, thus exemplifying the ideal of the soldier-scholar.

At the same time, there was also a shift in NATO's strategy of massive retaliation as it was superseded by flexible response. The ensuing NATO decision to deploy U.S. cruise missiles and Pershing II missiles on European soil met with unprecedented opposition, triggered in part by the fact that Central Europe, and Germany in particular, could become not just a military theater but also the target of intermediate-range nuclear missiles.[14] An influential and politically active peace movement challenged

---

12. Wolf Graf von Baudissin, *Soldat für den Frieden. Entwürfe für eine zeitgemäße Bundeswehr* (Munich: Piper, 1969).

13. German Department of Defense, *Weißbuch 1004. Weißbuch zur Sicherheit der Bundesrepublik Deutschland und zur Lage und Zukunft der Bundeswehr* (Bonn: BMVg, 1994), p. 136.

14. Elisabeth Noelle-Neumann and Edgar Piel, eds., *Allensbacher Jahrbuch der Demoskopie 1978–1983* (Munich: K.G. Saur, 1983), p. 633; Elisabeth Noelle-

the government by presenting alternative strategies of defense, raised doubts on ecological grounds about the use of nuclear energy, began to organize a new party (the Green Party), and took the debate to the streets. In the late 1970s and early 1980s, huge demonstrations took place and military barracks were blocked by demonstrators.

The discussion was characterized by extreme polarization. Yet resistance was primarily in opposition to military strategy and to nuclear weapons, rather than to the military as such. In fact, despite the prevalence of negative attitudes towards nuclear armaments, the Bundeswehr gained in respect: positive attitudes rose from 34 percent in 1971 to 47 percent in 1980, while negative attitudes decreased from 28 percent to 16 percent.[15]

The missile controversy also affected the governing Social Democratic Party (SPD). Helmut Schmidt lost the backing of considerable parts of his own party that refused to agree to the deployment of the U.S. missiles. The coalition of the Social Democratic Party and the Liberal Party (FDP) broke up. Helmut Kohl and the Conservative Party (CDU), in a coalition with the liberals, decided to deploy the American missiles. In the second half of the 1980s, polarization of German society on this issue eased somewhat, as hopes for a worldwide political detente were increased by the new approach to security politics of Soviet leader Mikhail Gorbachev and by the Intermediate Nuclear Forces (INF) Treaty. In 1987, no less than 65 percent of the German population thought that the prospects for a superpower rapprochement and detente at that time were much better than in the past.[16]

THE BUNDESWEHR OF THE BERLIN REPUBLIC

With the collapse of the bipolar international order in 1989–90, Germany found itself in a situation that most other Western societies also faced. The sudden disappearance of the enemy triggered high expectations for

---

Neumann and Renate Köcher, eds., *Allensbacher Jahrbuch der Demoskopie 1984–1992* (Allensbach: Verlag für Demoskopie, 1993), p. 1064.

15. Noelle-Neumann and Piel, *Allensbacher Jahrbuch der Demoskopie 1978–1983*, p. 325; Noelle-Neumann and Köcher, *Allensbacher Jahrbuch der Demoskopie 1984–1992*, p. 1060.

16. Noelle-Neumann and Köcher, *Allensbacher Jahrbuch der Demoskopie 1984–1992*, p. 1065.

Table 8.1. German Military Personnel, 1975–2005

	1975–76	1980–81	1985–86	1990–91	1995–96	2001–02	2004–05
Population	62.6 million	61.7 million	61.1 million	76.9 million	81.1 million	82.4 million	82.5 million
Armed Forces	495,000[a]	495,000	485,800	476,300	339,900[a]	296,000	284,500
Army	345,000	335,200	340,800	335,000	234,000	203,200	191,350
Air Force	111,000	106,000	108,700	103,700	75,300	67,300	67,500
Navy	39,000	36,500	36,300	37,600	28,500	25,500	25,650
Conscripts	227,000	225,000	228,850	203,000	137,300	107,000	94,500
Reserves	1.2 million	750,000	770,000	1.0 million	414,700	390,300	358,650

Source: International Institute for Strategic Studies (IISS), *The Military Balance* (London: Brassey's and Oxford University Press for IISS, various dates 1975–2004).

Note a. These totals reflect some 20,000 paramilitary border troops.

a more harmonious and peaceful world order in which Germany could act as a typical "civilian power."[17] There would be little room, it was hoped, for armed forces or organized violence, and the United Nations would gradually develop into a world government. The percentage of Germans who thought that Germany still needed armed forces declined from 75 percent in 1984 to 57 percent in 1990 and 1991.[18]

This represented a unique challenge for the military as German reunification—the incorporation of the former German Democratic Republic (GDR)—also meant the integration of the National People's Army (Nationale Volksarmee, NVA) into the Bundeswehr. The Bundeswehr had been preparing to downsize both the number of personnel and the number of garrisons substantially, by 30–35 percent each (see Table 8.1), and the incorporation of former NVA soldiers threatened to complicate that task. In the end, however, only about 10,000 of the 90,000 NVA soldiers of October 2, 1990, were brought in to the Bundeswehr.[19]

---

17. See, e.g., Knut Kirste and Hanns W. Maull, "Zivilmacht und Rollentheorie," in *Zeitschrift für Internationale Beziehungen*, Vol. 3, No. 2 (1996), pp. 283–312.
18. Noelle-Neumann and Köcher, *Allensbacher Jahrbuch der Demoskopie 1984–1992*, p. 1050.
19. Heiko Biehl, Thomas Bulmahn, and Nina Leonhard, "Die Bundeswehr als Armee der Einheit: Eine ambivalente Bilanz," in Gerhard Kümmel and

Downsizing was also aggravated by the emerging new international landscape: it became apparent quite soon after the fall of the Berlin Wall and the Iron Curtain that military conflict would continue to be a fact of life. This implied that, in its foreign, security, and military policy, the reunited and now fully sovereign Germany would have to respond and adapt to the risks and challenges of the new international environment, and assume a more international orientation. In particular, Germany's allies expected the Bundeswehr to participate actively in joint military actions. This led to an intense debate in Germany and within its armed forces over the legitimacy of participating in military combat missions outside national and alliance borders, even within the framework of the United Nations or the OSCE (Organization for Security and Coopera- tion in Europe). Some viewed this as Germany's contribution to the management of international relations, furthering Germany's interest in international stability and international order and securing international human rights. Others, however, argued that it risked a militarization of German politics and society. When the government declared that peacekeeping and peace enforcement operations as well as out-of-area operations were consistent with Germany's constitution as contribu- tions to international security, it was sued. In July 1994, however, the Federal Constitutional Court (*Bundesverfassungsgericht*) largely con- firmed the government's interpretation of the Basic Law.[20] Thus, the Bundeswehr went to Somalia in 1993–94, and then took part in missions to the Balkans and Afghanistan. Operations beyond the NATO area have become common: in 2005, a total of 6,400 German soldiers could be

Sabine Collmer, eds., *Soldat—Militär—Politik—Gesellschaft: Facetten militär- bezogener sozialwissenschaftlicher Forschung. Liber amicorum für Paul Klein* (Baden-Baden: Nomos, 2003), pp. 199–228.

20. Karl-Heinz Börner, "The Future of German Operations Outside NATO," *Parameters*, Vol. 26, No. 1 (1996), pp. 62–72; Robert H. Dorff, "Germany and Peace Support Operations: Policy after the Karlsruhe Decision," *Parameters*, Vol. 26, No. 1 (1996), pp. 73–90. For the positions of the various German par- ties concerning the interpretation of the Basic Law in the early 1990s, see John S. Duffield, *World Power Forsaken: Political Culture, International Institu- tions, and German Security Policy after Unification* (Stanford, Calif.: Stanford University Press, 1998), pp. 173–221.

found on duty in Afghanistan (ISAF), the Balkans, Georgia, Sudan, and elsewhere.[21]

This was the result of a protracted process that involved public and political debate, and three watershed events in particular.[22] The first was the Gulf War in 1990–91. The conservative-liberal Kohl-Genscher administration did not participate militarily in the U.S.-led alliance against Saddam Hussein's Iraq, citing constitutional rather than political reasons to restrain Bundeswehr operations to NATO territory. However, Germany served as a major financial sponsor of this endeavor. During this debate, there appeared the beginning of changes in German public opinion, which had hitherto strongly opposed any German military participation in out-of-area missions. The human rights violations by Saddam Hussein and the acts of ethnic cleansing in the Balkans prompted serious debate in the peace movement and in the Green Party; an increasing segment of society argued that, under certain circumstances, the use of violence could be justified. Opinion polls from the early 1990s show that a majority of the German population accepted that Germany had to take on more responsibility in securing peace worldwide; many also agreed that the Bundeswehr should participate in UN missions to monitor ceasefire agreements and assist police forces.[23]

This view was reinforced by the second and third events: the civil war, atrocities, and acts of ethnic cleansing in the Balkans and the precarious humanitarian situation in Somalia triggered another debate over the question of deployment of German soldiers and Bundeswehr participation in out-of-area missions. The result was that German soldiers took part in the humanitarian military operation authorized by the United Nations in Somalia, in the UN peace enforcement mission in

---

21. See the complete list in <www.bundeswehr.de/C1256EF4002AED30/CurrentBaseLink/W264VFT2439INFODE >, retrieved December 16, 2005.

22. Michael Schwab-Trapp, *Kriegsdiskurse. Die politische Kultur des Krieges im Wandel 1991–1999* (Opladen: Leske and Budrich, 2002); Martin Florack, *Kriegsbegründungen. Sicherheitspolitische Kultur in Deutschland nach dem Kalten Krieg* (Marburg: Tectum, 2005).

23. Zoltán Juhász, "German Public Opinion and the Use of Force in the Early 1990s," in Philip Everts and Pierangelo Isernia, eds., *Public Opinion and the International Use of Force* (London and New York: Routledge, 2001), pp. 57–85, at p. 67.

Bosnia, and the NATO peace enforcement mission in Kosovo. The constitutional arguments that had been raised before the 1990–91 Gulf War were overtaken by political arguments in the latter two events.

Support for the use of force in Yugoslavia, for example, was not limited to the political élite, as Zoltán Juhász points out, but was widespread among the German population, especially in the western Bundesländer (states).[24] Even so, there were mass demonstrations in Germany against the NATO bombings in Yugoslavia, especially at the beginning of the air attacks, and public support declined, temporarily but noticeably, after the inadvertent NATO bombings of the Chinese embassy and civilian targets. The generally broad public support for the Kosovo mission is especially noteworthy, since the national security policy of united Germany continues to be characterized not only by a strong commitment to multilateralism but also by a "culture of reticence" that emphasizes the use of non-military means to achieve security. German public opinion on military and security matters is strongly influenced by this reluctance to use military force, which also explains German society's preference for humanitarian and peacekeeping missions over peace-enforcement or combat missions.

In terms of civil-military relations, the growing overall willingness to use military means is of considerable importance because it reflects a more positive attitude towards the military within segments of society that have hitherto been anti-military. In addition, particular events have led to peaks in societal sympathy. For example, positive attitudes rose from 76 percent in 1997 to 84 percent in 1999, after the Bundeswehr provided disaster relief following huge floods near the river Oder, and remained at 80–86 percent in 2000–2003.[25]

---

24. The German populations in the Eastern parts of Germany and those in the Western parts differ considerably in their views concerning out-of-area missions of the Bundeswehr and Germany's foreign and security policy. See Juhász, "German Public Opinion and the Use of Force in the Early 1990s"; and especially Biehl, Bulmahn, and Leonhard, "Die Bundeswehr als Armee der Einheit: Eine ambivalente Bilanz," pp. 199–228.
25. Annual Population Surveys, 1997–2005, of the Bundeswehr Institute of Social Research (SOWI).

THE TRANSFORMATION OF THE BUNDESWEHR

Since it was clear that a military that was designed for Cold War conflicts would be inappropriate for the altered military challenges of the late twentieth century, Germany has sought to cope with the new security and political environment by various means. Along with promoting international military cooperation and military multi-nationalism, Germany initiated a comprehensive reform of its armed forces to make the military more flexible, more effective, and more compatible with its international partners, and at the same time more cost-effective. A series of major statements by the Department of Defense in the 1990s documents this endeavor. The goal of this transformation is to make the Bundeswehr cost-effectively ready for the challenges of the twenty-first century, with its diffusion of threats and heightened perceptions of insecurity in the wake of the terrorist attacks of September 11, 2001:

At present, and in the foreseeable future, there is no conventional threat to the German territory.... [and thus] the security situation calls for a security and defense policy that is geared to the prevention and containment of crises and conflicts ... based on common action with allies and partners ... [even] beyond NATO territory.[26]

This requires substantial modification of the military's task profile. The transformation of the Bundeswehr is proceeding on various levels. Germany's military budget experienced a significant decline during the 1990s; this changed nominally, towards the end of the decade, due to military missions abroad. Since 1990, there has been an overall net decrease in the military budget, as well as a decline in the military budget as a share of Germany's gross domestic product (GDP), as shown in Table 8.2.

---

26. Defense Policy Guidelines promulgated by Secretary of Defense Peter Struck (SPD) on March 21, 2003, German Department of Defense, *Defense Policy Guidelines* (Berlin: BMVg, 2003), pp. 4ff.

Table 8.2. German Military Expenditures, 1988–2004

Year	In billion Euro (at current prices)	In billion US$ (at constant 2003 prices and exchange rates)	As share of Germany's Gross Domestic Product (GDP)
1988	31.5	48.7	2.9%
1989	32.3	48.6	2.8%
1990	35.0	51.2	2.8%
1991	33.5	48.3	2.2%
1992	33.5	45.9	2.1%
1993	31.5	41.3	1.9%
1994	30.1	38.5	1.7%
1995	30.2	37.9	1.7%
1996	30.0	37.1	1.6%
1997	29.5	35.8	1.6%
1998	29.8	35.9	1.5%
1999	30.6	36.6	1.5%
2000	30.6	36.0	1.5%
2001	30.6	35.4	1.5%
2002	31.2	35.5	1.5%
2003	31.0	34.8	1.4%
2004	30.5	33.9	n.a.

Source: The Stockholm International Peace Research Institute (SIPRI), *Military Expenditure Database for Germany*, <first.sipri.org/non_first/result_milex.php?send>, retrieved January 13, 2006. Data for 2005 is not available.

Germany's current plan includes increasing procurement expenditures to improve capability for the "more probable tasks of international conflict prevention and crisis management"; such capabilities would include "command and control, intelligence collection and reconnaissance, mobility, effective engagement, support and sustainability, survivability and protection." In particular, the Bundeswehr seeks to acquire new capabilities for "strategic deployment, global reconnaissance and efficient, [and] interoperable command and control systems

Table 8.3. Germany's Investment and Manpower, by Service, to 2010

Services	Investment in million Euro	Share of total investment	Manpower	Share of total manpower
Army	13,168	27.9%	105,000	42%
Air Force	26,276	55.6%	44,500	17.5%
Navy	5,332	11.3%	19,000	7.5%
All Services	2,450	5.2%	—a	—
Total	47,226	100.0%	252,500	100.0%

Source: Sascha Lange, *Neue Bundeswehr auf altem Sockel. Wege aus dem Dilemma,* SWP-Studie S 2 (Berlin: Stiftung Wissenschaft und Politik, 2005), p. 14.

a. In the category "Manpower," Lange does not list 84,000 soldiers, or 33 percent of total manpower, who are assigned to the Armed Forces Base (Streitkräftebasis, SKB) and the medical service.

and means."[27] These equipment plans are quite ambitious since the combined costs of the current and planned procurement amount to more than 47 billion Euros (see Table 8.3).[28]

Cost-effectiveness, then, is of utmost importance and is meant to be accomplished through a closer cooperation between industry and the Bundeswehr, for example, by outsourcing and privatization of mobility and vehicle management, supply of uniforms, real estate management, guarding of military facilities, maintenance of armored vehicles, and information technology. Further privatization and outsourcing possibilities, for example, of responsibility for feeding soldiers, are currently being analyzed, and this process is likely to gain momentum. Further on, major savings and an increase in cost-effectiveness are expected from downsizing the military.[29] This puts manpower issues and the issue of conscription on the agenda.

27. German Department of Defense, *Defense Policy Guidelines*, pp. 5, 20.

28. Sascha Lange, *Neue Bundeswehr auf altem Sockel. Wege aus dem Dilemma,* SWP-Studie S 2 (Berlin: Stiftung Wissenschaft und Politik, 2005), pp. 7, 10.

29. From a total of 258,000 in 1960, the Bundeswehr rose to 437,000 members in 1965 and peaked at 495,000 in 1985; in 1990 it dipped to 459,000 then rose briefly to 476,000 in 1991 before declining to 445,000 in 1992, 345,000 in 1995, 319,000 in 2000, and 257,000 in 2004. German Department of Defense figures.

MANPOWER ISSUES AND CONSCRIPTION

Downsizing the military and reducing its institutional presence in the country includes the closure of a significant number of military sites, which will reduce the number of military sites to 392 by 2010.[30] The average number of billets per military site will increase from about 800 in 2003–04 to 900 by 2010.[31]

By 2010, the Bundeswehr will have a military force of 252,500 soldiers. These are both male and female soldiers because, since 2000, women are eligible for any classification and trade within the armed forces.[32] This figure includes 195,000 career servicemembers and shorter- and longer-service volunteers serving from two to twenty years; 25,000 extended-volunteer-service conscripts serving up to a maximum of 23 months in total; 30,000 conscripts with nine-month terms; and 2,500 reservists on exercise. All will be allocated to one of three force categories: the 35,000 soldiers allocated to the Operational Force category will be prepared to conduct militarily demanding peace-enforcement operations against a militarily organized enemy as a prerequisite for later and generally less demanding peace stabilization operations. The goal for the 70,000 soldiers in the Stabilization Forces category is to have up to 14,000 soldiers each in up to five different simultaneous military operations. These military missions are typically longer-term multi-national peace-stabilization operations of low to medium intensity. The main task of the soldiers in the third category, Support Forces, is to assist and support in the preparation for and conduct of military operations by the Operational and Stabilization Forces, both at home and abroad. The category of Support Forces consists of 147,500

---

30. German Department of Defense, *Die Stationierung der Bundeswehr in Deutschland* (Berlin: BMVg, 2004); see also German Secretary of Defense, *Die Bundeswehr der Zukunft. Ressortkonzept Stationierung* (Berlin: BMVg, 2001).

31. German Department of Defense, *Die Stationierung der Bundeswehr in Deutschland*, pp. 16ff.

32. Currently, there are about 12,000 female soldiers who represent more than 6 percent of the non-conscript military personnel. Gerhard Kümmel, "Integrating the 'Other': The Bundeswehr and Women Soldiers," in Giuseppe Caforio and Gerhard Kümmel, eds., *Military Missions and their Implications Reconsidered: The Aftermath of September 11th* (Amsterdam: Elsevier, 2005), pp. 343–368.

soldiers including 39,000 positions reserved for training purposes as well as 2,500 reservists.

The number of civilians working for the Bundeswehr, mostly in administrative roles, will be down to 75,000 by 2010 from about 125,000 at the turn of the century. Whereas the reduction in the number of military personnel is well advanced and has already almost reached the level envisaged for 2010, the reduction of civilian personnel has just started.[33]

As these data show, conscription will accompany the Bundeswehr well into the future. Conscription is an institution that is politically and culturally engrained in German society. It has been considered by the German political class and the media to be one of the best means to prevent the military from moving too far away from society and to ensure close contact between the armed forces and society. Conscription has also, to be sure, been used by authoritarian and dictatorial political regimes: the Third Reich introduced conscription right after the National Socialists took power. Nevertheless, since the French Revolution and the *levée en masse*, conscription has widely been viewed in democratic political systems as a useful instrument to secure the relationship between the armed forces and society, and to prevent an estrangement or isolation of the military from society with possibly disastrous consequences.

Every male person with German citizenship at the age of 18 is liable for conscription. Formal requests for an early call-up can be made at the age of 17, if the parents or persons having parental authority agree. As a consequence, there are some 17-year-old conscripts in the Bundeswehr, leaving Germany open to charges of employing child soldiers. In peacetime, the draft term is nine months long; liability for conscription ends at the age of 45 or, in an emergency, at age 60. Non-commissioned officers and officers are no longer subject to conscription once they turn 60. In general, men are drafted until the age of 23. Payment is, depending on rank, between €245 and €300 per month.

There are, however, always people who do not want to be drafted and there are several ways to pursue this. Apart from trying to manipulate the cognitive and physical evaluation by which draftees' fitness and aptitude for military service are assessed, a potential draftee may invoke the Law on Conscription. Under this law, one may be exempt from mili-

---

33. German Department of Defense, *Grundzüge der Konzeption der*

tary service, without conscientious objection, because of a commitment to perform some respected alternative service, such as firefighting or in the fields of disaster prevention and control. Since such alternative service requires one to serve only a few days per month, its term is for several years (six, at present). Finally, there is conscientious objection. The Basic Law, Article 4, Paragraph 3, guarantees the right of the individual to be exempt from military service because of conscientious objection and to perform civilian or community service instead. Thus conscientious objection, the ensuing community service in civilian institutions, and alternative service have been permanent parts of the German military system. (See Figure 8.2.)

In socio-economic and educational terms, the conscientious objectors are mostly better educated than the average for their age group, which suggests that better-educated youth are under-represented in the Bundeswehr. Conscientious objection has often been perceived as less deserving of respect than military service.[34] During the 1970s, 1980s, and 1990s, however, the number of those who chose conscientious objection increased (see Figure 8.2) due to domestic developments, especially the democratization of society and developments in security politics and military strategy. Conscientious objectors began to receive more respect from the public.[35] In the 1990s, the number of conscientious objectors reached new highs, their numbers doubling between 1990 and 1998.

Bundeswehr (Berlin: BMVg, 2004).

34. In a public opinion survey in the summer of 1968, 45 percent of the German population held the opinion that conscientious objectors only wanted to dodge military service, while just 31 percent thought this to be a genuinely conscientious decision (18 percent were undecided). Elisabeth Noelle and Erich Peter Neumann, eds., *Jahrbuch der öffentlichen Meinung 1968–1973* (Allensbach and Bonn: Verlag für Demoskopie, 1974), p. 499.

35. Those surveyed who said that they had "much respect" for conscientious objectors increased from 39 percent in 1971 to 45 percent in 1976, 59 percent in 1981, and 79 percent in 1990, while those who said that they had "little respect" declined from 42 percent in 1971 to 36 percent (1976), then to 31 percent (1981), and just 15 percent in 1990. The rest said that it depended upon the circumstances. Noelle-Neumann and Köcher, *Allensbacher Jahrbuch der Demoskopie 1984–1992*, p. 1057.

Figure 8.2. Petitions Filed for Conscientious Objection, 1958–2004

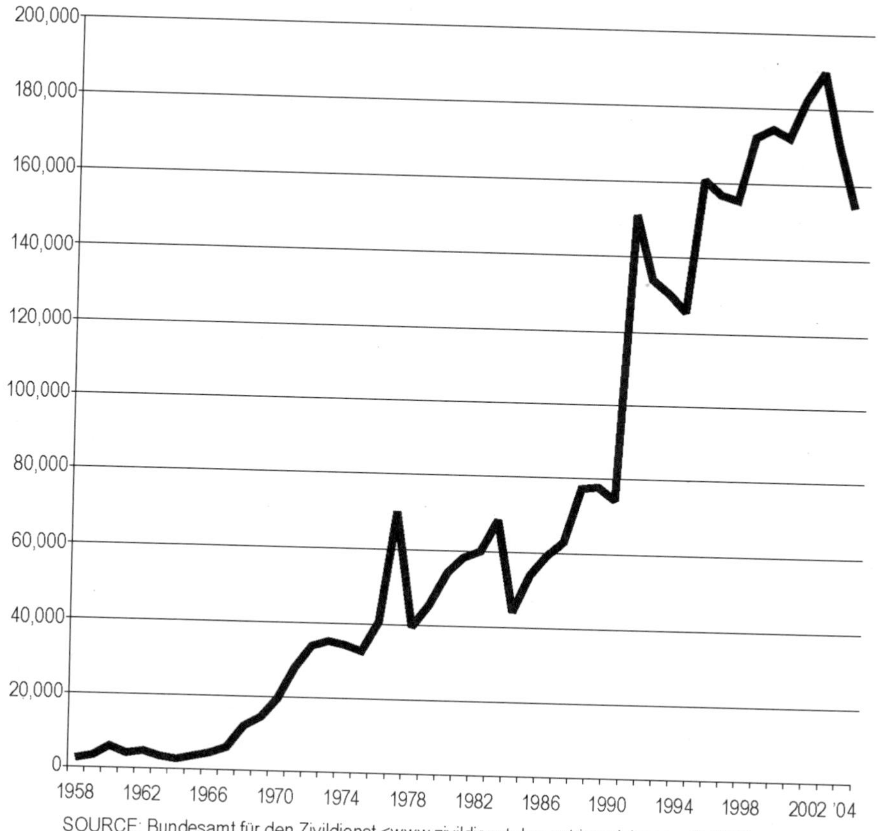

SOURCE: Bundesamt für den Zivildienst <www.zivildienst.de>, retrieved January 9, 2006.

This rise can be traced to the change in the actual activities of the Bundeswehr. During the Cold War, the military had been designed, structured, manned, equipped, and trained to deter or, in the unlikely event that deterrence failed, to fight the mass Warsaw Pact armies. In a sense, these military missions were somewhat "virtual" during the Cold War. Afterward, however, the Bundeswehr began to prepare for and to conduct actual operations, which involved real threats to the life and security of individual soldiers. Germany's armed forces have thus undergone a transition, from a military force that never really expected to be deployed in missions where it must fight, to a military with new missions involving active engagement and participation in armed conflict. The military profession has, in short, become more dangerous. Thus, in

Table 8.4. Duration of Community and Military Service (in months)

	Military service	Community service
April 1957–March 1961	12	—
April 1961–March 1962	12	21
April 1962–June 1962	15	21
July 1962–December 1972	18	27
January 1973–December 1983	15	16
January 1984–September 1990	15	20
October 1990–December 1995	12	15
January 1996–June 2000	10	13
July 2000–December 2001	10	11
January 2002–September 2004	9	10
Since October 2004	9	9

Source: Adapted from <www.kampagne.de/Themen/Wehrpflicht/Dauer_Wehrdienst_Zivildienst.php >; retrieved January 9, 2006.

Note: There was no provision for alternative service or conscientious objection April 1957 to March 1961.

a German society in the midst of a value shift, with rising individualization and post-modern and post-materialistic values, the reasons and motives cited for conscientious objection have changed substantially. It is no longer simply a matter of conscience to choose conscientious objector status: "Cost-benefit considerations are of primary importance. Many view civilian service as entailing less risk and fewer constraints on freedom."[36]

Over the years, the term of conscription as well as that of community service has changed considerably. As Table 8.4 suggests, alternative community service previously lasted up to one-third longer than military service. In recent years, however, especially from mid-2000 onwards, the difference has decreased; the terms of military and community service were equalized in October 2004.

36. Bernhard Fleckenstein, "Germany: Forerunner of a Postnational Military?," in Charles C. Moskos, John Allen Williams, and David R. Segal, eds., *The Postmodern Military: Armed Forces After the Cold War* (New York and Oxford: Oxford University Press, 2000), pp. 80–100, 89.

Germany has obviously not abolished conscription as many other countries have done since 1990; it has only reduced the duration of service, and it intends to retain conscription in the future. The official rationale is that it is "indispensable ... for the operational readiness, effectiveness and economic efficiency of the Bundeswehr," and that, in addition, protecting Germany and its citizens may require the "ability to reconstitute for national defense as well as to provide support in the event of natural disasters and emergencies."[37]

Along with the political argument for securing good civil-military relations and attaching the military to the democratic system, and the military argument of providing reconstitution capabilities in the event of an emergency, there is also a personnel argument for conscription based on recruitment needs.[38] The Department of Defense acknowledges that conscription is a valued recruitment base: in recent years, about half of the career soldiers and many of the shorter-term (2–8 years) and longer-term (8–20 years) volunteers have been recruited from among those serving as conscripts.[39]

Critics, however, reject all three arguments, claiming that an all-volunteer force is not necessarily incompatible with society and democracy, and that reconstitution as well as recruiting could be secured without conscription. Furthermore, they argue, conscription is anachronistic, because new missions require professional personnel. For example, it is argued that, "other than providing for an easily accessible pool

---

37. German Department of Defense, *Defense Policy Guidelines*, p. 5.
38. On this debate see, e.g., German Department of Defense, *Wehrpflicht im 21. Jahrhundert. Mehr Sicherheit für alle* (Berlin: BMVg, 2002); Matthias Sehmsdorf, *Wehrpflicht- versus Freiwilligenarmee. Ausgewählte ökonomische Aspekte des Wehrsystems* (Hamburg: Verlag Dr. Kovac, 1998); Jürgen Groß and Dieter S. Lutz, eds., *Wehrpflicht ausgedient* (Baden-Baden: Nomos, 1998); Andreas Prüfert, ed., *Hat die allgemeine Wehrpflicht in Deutschland eine Zukunft? Zur Debatte um die künftige Wehrstruktur* (Baden-Baden: Nomos, 2003); Ines-Jacqueline Werkner, *Wehrpflicht oder Freiwilligenarmee? Wehrstrukturentscheidungen im europäischen Vergleich* (Frankfurt am Main: Peter Lang, 2006).
39. Lieutenant Colonel Burmeister, *Hat die Wehrpflicht eine Zukunft? Ein Beitrag zur aktuellen Diskussion* (Berlin: Wissenschaftliche Dienste des Deutschen Bundestages, 2003), p. 12; The Press and Information Office of the Federal Government in Cooperation with the Federal Ministry of Defense, *German Security Policy and the Bundeswehr* (Bonn: BMVg, 1997), p. 27.

for recruiting volunteers, conscription represents a severe handicap for improving both the quantity and quality of Germany's CRO [crisis response operations] capability, especially since there is little hope for a significant increase in defense funding."[40] Indeed, Germany does not employ any conscripts in its international military operations. If a draftee wants to join an international mission, he must become an extended-volunteer-service conscript serving between 10 to 23 months. In addition, economic analyses have found that an All-Volunteer Force of about 200,000 soldiers would meet crisis response operations standards and would also be cheaper than a conscript army.[41]

The Department of Defense has responded to this in several ways. First, it has reduced the duration of conscription successively, from eighteen months in the late 1970s to nine months at present (see Table 8.4 above). Second, it has cut the number of conscripts in the armed forces, and it plans to reduce the conscription ratio within the armed forces even more drastically in the years to come. During the Cold War, West Germany maintained a peacetime strength of up to almost half a million soldiers, with conscripts constituting about 45 percent of the force (see Table 8.1 above).[42] By contrast, the plan for 2010 is to have 30,000 conscripts in a total force of 252,500 soldiers, or just 12 percent of the force. This could be described as "pseudo-conscription" or an "all-volunteer force in disguise." This creates a dilemma for Germany: on the one hand, general

---

40. Reiner K. Huber, "On the Linkage of Force Capability and Conscription: Implications for German Defense Reform," paper presented at the Transatlantic Roundtable on "Filling NATO's Ranks: Military Personnel Policies in Transition," at the Transatlantic Center of the German Marshall Fund of the United States, Brussels, Belgium, September 8–9, 2003, p. 9.

41. Reiner K. Huber and Bernhardt Schmidt, "Limits of German Defence Reform: Results of Parametric Analyses for the Commission 'Common Security and Future of the Bundeswehr'," *Journal of the Operational Research Society*, Vol. 55 (2004), pp. 350–360. See also Reiner K. Huber, *Bericht zur Studie Datengrundlagen zur Entwicklung von Strategieoptionen für die Weiterentwicklung der Bundeswehr* (Munich: Institut für Angewandte Systemforschung und Operations Research, 2000); Jürgen Schnell and Gabriele Straub, *Zur ökonomischen Effizienz der Wehrpflicht am Beispiel der Bundeswehr—ist eine Wehrpflichtarmee "billiger" und "effizienter" als eine Freiwilligenarmee? Teilstudie H der Studien zur Zukunft der Bundeswehr* (Munich: Bundeswehr University, 2000).

42. Huber, "On the Linkage of Force Capability and Conscription," p. 1.

Table 8.5. Military Aptitude Tests in Germany, 1994–2004

Year	Number of individuals taking military aptitude tests	Passed (percent)
1994	318,797	79.3
1995	395,514	86.8
1996	418,181	89.5
1997	427,521	88.9
1998	417,805	88.6
1999	395,646	88.1
2000	381,484	87.4
2001	370,792	83.7
2002	365,957	84.7
2003	363,311	84.8
2004	369,745	80.4

Source: Peter Tobiassen, "Jeder Zweite muss nicht mehr dienen," *Wehrgerechtigkeit 2005. Eine umfassende Auswertung aktueller statistischer Angaben des Bundesministeriums der Verteidigung* (Bockhorn: Zentralstelle für Recht und Schutz der Kriegsdienstverweigerer aus Gewissensgründen, 2005), p. 10.

conscription is officially supported, while on the other hand, the need for conscripts in practice has been much lower than the number of potential candidates, which raises issues of draft equity and whether general conscription has become a sort of selective service.

The Department of Defense reacted to this by changing the Conscription Law in the fall of 2004. It redefined the criteria by which somebody is eligible for the draft. The upper age limit for being drafted has been reduced from 25 to 23 years of age, and candidates are exempt from conscription if they are married or if they have to care for a child or children. Most importantly, the aptitude testing system has been redefined and rearranged in such a way that the pool of candidates for conscription has become smaller (see Table 8.5).

The modification of the aptitude testing system has already created an imbalance vis-à-vis the civilian service, as the number of young men performing community service increasingly surpasses the number of young men in military service (see Table 8.6). For 2005, the Federal Office for Community Service (*Bundesamt für den Zivildienst*) expected to have about 105,000 conscientious objectors for 79,000 community-service billets. By

Table 8.6. Military, Community, and Alternative Service Performed in Germany

Year of birth	Registered male youth (total)	Military service (percent of total)	Community and alternative service (percent of total)	No service (percent of total)
1979	416,034	132,889 (31.9%)	139,883 (33.6%)	143,262 (34.4%)
1980	440,158	127,821 (29.0%)	145,053 (33.0%)	167,284 (38.0%)
1981	439,725	114,866 (26.1%)	137,887 (31.4%)	186,972 (42.5%)
1982	444,468	94,047 (21.2%)	125,455 (28.2%)	224,966 (50.6%)
1983	434,181	66,798 (15.4%))	101,326 (23.3%)	266,057 (61.3%)

Source: Tobiassen, "Jeder Zweite muss nicht mehr dienen," p. 21.

contrast, the Department of Defense wanted to draft only 66,700 men in 2005 and to reduce this number further to 55,000 annually from 2007 onwards.[43] As a result, a number of lawsuits seek to establish whether this form of "adapted" conscription is still consistent with Germany's Basic Law or whether it violates principles of equity by being a form of selective or fictitious conscription. At present, these lawsuits are still pending as the cases have been transferred to the German Constitutional Court. The final judgment may overturn the present regulations. However, public opinion in general still supports conscription.[44]

At the same time, people are aware that something needs to be done. In opinion polls, keeping the status quo meets with the least agreement (36 percent of those surveyed in 2003). There is considerable support for creating an all-volunteer force (46 percent) and even more (52 percent) for institutionalizing general service, that is, a universal requirement for either civilian or military service by all young males.[45] However, a majority of the political class and the media continue to favor conscription. Many have expressed concerns over recent U.S. recruitment problems. Germany could expect similar recruitment problems, based on eco-

---

43. *KDV-Aktuell*, No. 1 (September 1, 2004), p. 10.
44. The percentage of the public surveyed who have a positive attitude toward conscription was 73–74 percent most years between 1997 and 2003, reaching highs of 78 percent (1998) and 80 percent (1999) and a low of 69 percent in 2002. Annual SOWI Population Surveys.
45. 2003 SOWI Population Survey.

nomic analysis: an all-volunteer force of 200,000 men and women is said to pose a recruitment requirement of 30,000–40,000 people annually.[46] Nevertheless, it might very well be that, if the courts do not interfere, conscription will not be altered very much, especially as the Bundeswehr has already been facing recruitment problems.

To manage recruitment problems and to counterbalance the fact that the military profession has become more dangerous, the Department of Defense has increased its public relations efforts. This involves advertising with posters in public places, open houses or "Days of Open Doors" (*Tage der offenen Tür*) in local units, unit visits, and ads in newspapers, on radio, and on television. Increasingly these efforts also include internships with the military, exhibitions such as "Our Army," "Our Navy," and "Our Air Force," and information on the Internet.[47] The current slogan is thought to appeal to the targeted group, age 14 and over, not with national or patriotic sentiments, as one might think, but rather with a cosmopolitan sense: "Mission: Peace" (*Auftrag: Frieden*). In addition, the Bundeswehr has intensified its advertising events in schools through a "youth officers" program, and has established the "Girls' Day" project to attract young women.

The Department of Defense has also launched an "Attraction Program" (*Attraktivitätsprogramm*) to increase the appeal of becoming a soldier and to create incentives to choose a military career. This includes reform of the Vocational Advancement Service (*Berufsförderungsdienst, BFD*), the agency that provides support for the transition at the end of a military career (not for conscripts) to a civilian career. The Bundeswehr also offers incentives to enlist, by providing training and education for degrees that can be used in civilian jobs, and by increasing payment and promotion prospects.[48]

---

46. Huber and Schmidt, "Limits of German Defence Reform," pp. 350–360. See also Huber, *Bericht zur Studie Datengrundlagen zur Entwicklung von Strategieoptionen für die Weiterentwicklung der Bundeswehr*; Schnell and Straub, *Zur ökonomischen Effizienz der Wehrpflicht am Beispiel der Bundeswehr*.

47. In addition to the overall website of the armed forces at <www.bundeswehr.de>, the Department has established a special website for recruiting purposes, <www.bundeswehr-karriere.de>, with web radio, chat, and other features.

48. For example, the military has increased pay for squadron officers to the A12 payment level. The armed forces have also created improvements in

Similar incentives are also directed towards non-commissioned officers, where a profound restructuring of career paths has taken place. Here, the age for becoming a sergeant first class (starting with an A8 payment of around €1,780 per month) was reduced from 33 to 31 years. The average age for becoming a sergeant major (receiving an initial A9 payment of about €1,900 per month) was lowered from 47 to 42 years. Opportunities for senior non-commissioned officers to become career soldiers have been improved. The entrance payment for rank-and-file volunteers (privates) has been increased up to the A3 payment level (starting at €1,520 per month). In 2002 alone, about 42,000 soldiers profited from these improvements in payment and promotion.[49]

Lastly, the Bundeswehr has put considerable energy into enhancing the military's attractiveness for job seekers. It has taken steps to improve the situation for families, for example, by establishing family centers. The Law on Pursuing Equity for Soldiers (*Soldatengleichstellungsdurchsetzungsgesetz*), which went into effect in January 2005, offers soldiers, both male and female, the possibility of working part-time in flexible arrangements. This is also meant to increase retention, as are increased efforts in internal advertising.

By these measures, the Bundeswehr has somewhat alleviated its recruitment problems. It has also benefited from extending its recruitment pool to women much more than in the past. Starting in the mid-1970s, when access to the military was first granted to women, female soldier candidates were restricted to the medical field. In 2000, however, the Bundeswehr was fully opened to women, which led to a substantial increase in the number of female soldiers. Thus, by now, women have come to constitute a very valuable personnel resource for the Bundeswehr at large: they make up about 14–17 percent of applications for non-commissioned officers and rank-and-file career paths, and about 10–14

---

more than 2,600 billets in the A12–A14 pay grades (mostly captains and majors), with initial payments between €2,560 and €2,970 per month respectively (not counting extra payments for family status), and in more than 170 billets in the A15–A16 pay grades (lieutenant colonels and colonels), with payments between €3,870 and €4,300 per month respectively.

49. German Department of Defense, *Bundeswehr 2002. Sachstand und Perspektiven* (Bonn: BMVg, 2002), pp. 29–33.

percent of officer applications.[50] Nevertheless, the Bundeswehr has not yet alleviated its recruitment problems to the desired level.

This means that recruiting still remains somewhat problematic. It is expected that recruitment problems will become worse in the years to come, beyond just those areas where problems are already quite severe, such as in aeronautics and information technology where the military faces stiff competition from private industry. Recruiting problems will be exacerbated by the declining average physical condition of young males. In addition, a substantial decrease in the number of recruits from the economically distressed new provinces (*Bundesländer*) is expected, due to decreasing birth rates. As these provinces have been a significant source of recruits, military personnel planners are looking quite grimly at the future. Further efforts will be needed and further incentives will have to be developed.

Conclusion

Whether all of these measures will be sufficient and effective is an open question. The main issue is that transformation rests on a shaky financial foundation. Despite the imbalances and inconsistencies, reform and the transformation process are likely to continue. In the end, it is the people within the organization—their talents, skills, and motivation—who make an organization work, and it is the larger society whose backing is needed for the successful transformation of the organization itself and for the accomplishment of its tasks. Herein may lie the greatest challenge of the transformation in the years ahead.

With regard to manpower issues and personnel, transformation implies a massive reduction in the overall number of soldiers. A closer look, however, reveals that this is basically due to the substantial reduction in the number of conscripts; the numbers of shorter-service and longer-service volunteers and career soldiers are actually increasing. This means that conscription will become increasingly hollow and fictitious. At the beginning of the twenty-first century, the Bundeswehr is, in fact, an all-volunteer force in disguise.

---

50. Defense Commissioner of the German Parliament, *Jahresbericht 2004. Drucksache 15/5000: Unterrichtung durch den Wehrbeauftragten* (Berlin: Deutscher Bundestag, 2005), pp. 9ff.

Part III
The Transition to
All-Volunteer Forces

Chapter 9

The Transition to an All-Volunteer Force

The U.S. Experience

Bernard D. Rostker and Curtis L. Gilroy

When the United States moved to an all-volunteer force (AVF) in 1973, it was after much public debate about how the United States should procure its military manpower—by continuing conscription or instead instituting a volunteer military. The dominant theme of the debate was summed up by the title of a 1966 landmark study by the Presidential Advisory Commission on Selective Service: *In Pursuit of Equity: Who Serves When Not All Serve?*[1] Indeed, the major theme of the President's Commission on an All-Volunteer Armed Force in 1970 (the Gates Commission) was the inequity of the draft. Its finding that the draft was inherently unfair provided the final push toward an all-volunteer force for the United States.[2]

In this chapter, we first review the context of the U.S. transition to an AVF. Next, we examine reasons for its success, including aspects of re-

The authors thank Robert Clark, Major Angela Giddings, Anita Hattiangadi, Lieutenant Colonel John Jessup, Aline Quester, Cindy Williams, and John Warner for helpful comments on earlier drafts of this paper.

1.   Marshall Burke, *In Pursuit of Equity: Who Serves When Not All Serve?* Report of the National Advisory Commission on Selective Service (Washington, D.C.: U.S. Government Printing Office [U.S. GPO], 1967).
2.   Thomas Gates, *Report of the President's Commission on an All-Volunteer Armed Force* (Washington, D.C.: President's Commission on an All-Volunteer Armed Force, 1970). The Commission was known as the Gates Commission after its chairman, former secretary of defense, Thomas Gates. Hereafter cited as Gates Commission Report.

cruiting, personnel, retention, and force structure. We believe that the lessons of the U.S. transition to an AVF are potentially useful to other countries facing similar choices.

The Right Time for Change

Through most of its history, America's military was staffed by volunteers. Historically, the draft was only used to obtain military personnel during major wars requiring very large armies, such as the Civil War (1861–1865), World War I, and World War II. Accordingly, the draft was suspended after World War II for eighteen months. However, it was reinstated at the beginning of the Cold War, and lasted for another twenty-five years, through the Korean conflict and most of the Vietnam War. Thus, the United States has had conscription for only thirty-five years of its history, and nearly all of those years were in the twentieth century.

The American people generally accepted the draft when service was universal or nearly so, but public acceptance began to change in the mid-1960s for several reasons. The first reason was a combination of shifting demographics and changes in the military's demand for personnel. The size of the eligible population of young men reaching draft age each year was so large and the needs of the military so small in comparison that, in practice, the draft was no longer universal. It also meant that obtaining enough volunteers was possible at budget levels that were seen as acceptable.[3] At the height of the postwar draft era, the military needed one out of every three young men to sustain the force; today, it needs only about one out of twenty young men and women. Another reason was the rising voice of conservatives and libertarians who questioned the moral and economic rationale for conscription. They argued that the state had no right to take the services of young men involuntarily and without their consent. Under a draft in which not all served, how could the nation ask some to bear the burden of military service when others could escape that responsibility? Finally, the growing unpopularity of the Vietnam War strengthened arguments about the unfairness of a draft.

---

3. John T. Warner and Beth J. Asch, "The Record and Prospects of the All-Volunteer Military in the United States," *Journal of Economic Perspectives*, Vol. 15, No. 2 (2001), pp. 169–92.

Economic considerations also played a critical role in bringing about an all-volunteer force. The Gates Commission presented a new paradigm for evaluating military organizations. It addressed the demand for and supply of manpower, attrition and retention, and the mix of career and non-career personnel in the context of management efficiency and personal equity. The Commission concluded that a pay increase raising military earnings to a level comparable to what was found in the civilian sector would be adequate to sustain a force of the desired size, and that the resulting budgetary increases would be mostly offset by substantial savings because many of the draft's inefficiencies would be eliminated (as discussed in some detail in Chapter 5 by John Warner and Sebastian Negrusa). As a result, proponents of an all-volunteer force were able to muster persuasive economic arguments at a time when the need for change was strongly felt and demographics made change feasible. These factors were critical for the Gates Commission's recommendation: "We unanimously believe that the nation's interest will be better served by an all-volunteer force, supported by an effective stand-by draft, than by a mixed force of volunteers and conscripts."[4]

FOUR BROAD REASONS FOR THE SUCCESS OF THE ALL-VOLUNTEER FORCE

It would be less than honest to report that the U.S. transition to an all-volunteer force was smooth and swift. It was not. Mistakes were made and, in some cases, the same mistakes were made more than once. In fact, seven years after the inception of the volunteer military, some still called for a return to the draft on both moral and efficiency grounds. Some still believed that every young man had a moral obligation to serve in the military, while others were concerned that the United States was attracting a low-quality force in which minorities, the poor, and the uneducated were over-represented. The situation was so dire that former President Richard Nixon, the person most responsible for the nation's move to a volunteer military, concluded in 1980, "I considered the end of the draft in 1973 to be one of the major achievements of my administration. Now seven years later, I have reluctantly concluded that we should reintroduce the draft.... The volunteer army has failed to

---

4.   Gates Commission Report, letter of transmittal from Thomas S. Gates to the President, February 20, 1970.

Figure 9.1. Total U.S. Military Force, FY 2004

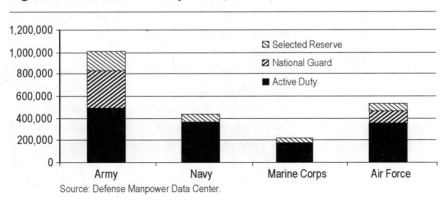

Source: Defense Manpower Data Center.

provide enough personnel of the caliber we need."[5] This view was short-lived, however; Congress soon breathed new life into the volunteer military with significant increases in personnel budgets.

It would take, however, another ten years of concerted effort and the crucible of the Gulf War before the all-volunteer force was considered a success. Nixon could then rightly acknowledge the "dramatic improvement in the quality of the men and women who joined the armed forces. Consequently," he concluded, "I endorse the all-volunteer Army approach without qualification."[6]

Today, the U.S. military force totals 2.26 million men and women—1.41 million in the active-duty force and 850,000 in the reserve forces. The reserves comprise about 400,000 Army, Navy, Marine Corps, and Air Force selected reservists, and 450,000 uniformed personnel in the Army and Air National Guard (Figure 9.1).[7] To sustain this force in fiscal year 2004, the military recruited about 183,000 active-duty and 118,000 reserve enlisted members, and commissioned about 17,600 active-duty officers

5.   Richard Nixon, *The Real War* (New York: Warner Books, 1980).

6.   Richard Nixon, personal letter to John C. Whitaker, November 4, 1993, as cited in Bernard D. Rostker, *I Want You: The Evolution of the All-Volunteer Force*, MG-265-OSD (Santa Monica, Calif.: RAND, 2006).

7.   These numbers do not include the Coast Guard active forces (30,000) and reserve forces (7,000), nor the Individual Ready Reserve and Individual National Guard, which together form a manpower pool of 280,000 trained people who are available for mobilization, but who do not train regularly in military units or receive a regular paycheck.

Table 9.1. Total Military Enlisted Recruits and Officer Commissions, FY 2004

	Active Duty		National Guard and Reserve	
	Enlisted	Officer	Enlisted	Officer
Army	77,586	7,136	81,503	5,843
Navy	39,871	4,213	11,246	1,852
Marine Corps	31,006	1,275	8,248	713
Air Force	34,362	4,937	17,180	2,709
Total DoD	**182,825**	**17,561**	**118,177**	**11,117**

Source: Official figures reported by the Services to the Office of the Under Secretary of Defense for Personnel and Readiness, Accession Policy and Reserve Manpower and Personnel Directorates.

and 11,000 reserve force officers (see Table 9.1). The Army, having the largest force, has the greatest recruiting requirements. For the all-volunteer force to succeed, the Army must succeed.

Although this chapter emphasizes recruiting, recruiting is really a derivative of personnel retention and force structure. For a constant force end-strength, yearly military accessions must equal yearly separations. Effective recruiting programs mean little if other parts of the military establishment are ineffective; if there is an increase in the number of people who leave service, recruiters have to work that much harder to achieve higher recruiting goals to make up for increased separations. Effective recruiting also means finding recruits with the characteristics to be successful soldiers, sailors, marines, and airmen. In short, a successful volunteer military begins with recruiting—the engine of the all-volunteer force.

The last thirty years of the U.S. experience with a volunteer military suggest that there are four broad reasons for its success, which countries moving to a volunteer force would do well to consider. They are:

- commitment to leadership;
- understanding the issues and the need for research;
- skill in management; and
- adequate budgets.

In the rest of this chapter, we examine each of these factors in turn.[8]

---

8. For a more in-depth treatment of these and other issues, see Rostker, *I Want You: The Evolution of the All-Volunteer Force.*

Commitment to Leadership

Leadership at the highest levels of the government is critical to a nation's transition to a volunteer military. The all-volunteer force would not have come about in the United States when it did without the leadership of President Richard Nixon. In 1968, as a candidate for president, Nixon publicly declared his support for an all-volunteer force. In a 1968 radio address that year, he said:

Today all across our country we face a crisis of confidence. Nowhere is it more acute than among our young people. They recognize the draft as an infringement on their liberty—which it is. To them, it represents a government insensitive to their rights—a government callous to their status as free men. They ask for justice—and they deserve it.[9]

Within weeks of taking office, Nixon began planning a volunteer military. On March 27, 1969, he announced the formation of the Gates Commission, charging it "to develop a comprehensive plan for eliminating conscription and moving toward an all-volunteer armed force."[10]

The Gates Commission was greatly influenced by one of its members, Professor Milton Friedman of the University of Chicago. He was an articulate spokesmen for the view that the draft was "inconsistent with a free society."[11] It is now generally agreed that Friedman—later a Nobel laureate—was the intellectual father of the modern U.S. all-volunteer force.

Nixon had a very strong secretary of defense in Melvin Laird. As a former member of Congress, Laird knew how to work with Congress. At critical points, he personally interceded with his former colleagues who would not otherwise have supported the volunteer military. Even before the Gates Commission reported its recommendations in 1970, Laird established the Project Volunteer Committee at the Pentagon to develop a com-

---

9. Richard M. Nixon, "The All-Volunteer Armed Force: A Radio Address, October 17, 1968," in Harry A. Marmion, ed., *The Case Against a Volunteer Army* (Chicago: Quadrangle Books, 1971), pp. 75–82.
10. President of the United States, "Statement by the President Announcing a Commission on an All-Volunteer Armed Force," March 27, 1969, in *Gates Commission Report*.
11. Milton Friedman, "Statement by Professor Milton Friedman," March 9, 1967, Hearing before the 90th Cong., 1st Sess., Vol. 113.

prehensive action program for moving towards a volunteer force and to provide the day-to-day management of its operation.[12] His philosophy was to have the four services be the prime agents to implement the all-volunteer force, each developing its own proposed programs and recommendations for approval. The Department did not need, nor did it want to establish, a new office to manage the all-volunteer force; the services would have to make the volunteer military work.

During this critical period, the uniformed leadership of the military services was supportive. A senior Defense Department official warned, however, that "there is one thing only that can keep the All-Volunteer Force from being a success, and that is a lack of complete and positive commitment on the part of those [civilian and military leaders] responsible for its operation."[13]

The very early years of the volunteer military were uncertain, yet it was ultimately successful. Following the Gates Commission's recommendations, the volunteer force was given adequate resources. Congress enacted the largest pay raise ever (over 60 percent) to provide new recruits with pay comparable to that of their civilian peers. Policymakers in the administration and the Congress, as well as civilian and military leaders in the Defense Department, carefully monitored its progress. But its success during the first four years lulled many into complacency. Personnel budgets were soon cut and military pay fell significantly behind civilian pay. As a result, recruiting dropped sharply, putting the all-volunteer force in jeopardy. It took heroic Congressional efforts in the early 1980s to push through large pay raises again (25 percent over two years), and this action—over the initial objections of the White House—is generally credited with saving the all-volunteer force at that time. The early success of the AVF had been taken for granted; this was the first hard lesson to be learned.

When Ronald Reagan took office as president in 1981, he directed his new secretary of defense, Caspar Weinberger, to form a defense manpower task force to review all military manpower issues and make pro-

---

12. Melvin Laird, "Project Volunteer (Committee)," Memorandum to Secretaries of the Military Departments, Chairman of the Joint Chiefs of Staff, and Assistant Secretaries of Defense, April 10, 1969.
13. Roger T. Kelley, "Memorandum to Deputy Secretary of Defense," May 31, 1973.

posals to increase the effectiveness of the active and reserve forces. The task force concluded that, although "the recruiting and retention of qualified personnel for the Armed Forces had deteriorated [in the late 1970s] to the point where many were questioning the effectiveness of the All-Volunteer Force," there had been "a dramatic improvement during the past two years." In fact, the report continued:

the fiscal year just completed, FY 1982, has been the best year for recruiting and retention that the All-Volunteer Force has ever experienced.... The Task Force is confident that the higher active and reserve strengths planned for the next five years can be achieved without the resumption of the draft.[14]

Weinberger played a very important part in the success of the volunteer military, displaying strong leadership, particularly regarding the role of women. Reflecting on the first decade of the all-volunteer force, Weinberger said, "The most rewarding development we have seen in our armed forces over the past decade has been the tremendous expansion of opportunities for women."[15] He made his intention clear in a major policy statement: "This Department must aggressively break down those remaining barriers that prevent us from making the fullest use of the capabilities of women in providing for our national defense."[16]

The increased involvement of women was important to the transition to a volunteer force in the United States. The Gates Commission and others had overlooked their potential interest and participation in the military.[17] Women had, during the draft era, been held by Congress

14. Caspar W. Weinberger, *Military Manpower Task Force: A Report to the President on the Status and Prospects of the All-Volunteer Force* (Washington, D.C.: U.S. GPO, 1982), p. i.

15. Caspar W. Weinberger, "The All-Volunteer Force in the 1980s: DoD Perspective," in William Bowman, Roger Little, and G. Thomas Sicilia, eds., *The All-Volunteer Force after a Decade: Retrospect and Prospect* (New York: Pergamon-Brassey's, 1986).

16. Caspar Weinberger, "Women in the Military," Memorandum to Secretaries of the Military Departments, January 14, 1986.

17. Aline O. Quester and Curtis L. Gilroy, "Women and Minorities in America's Volunteer Military," *Contemporary Economic Policy,* Vol. 20, No. 2 (April 2002), pp. 111–121.

Figure 9.2. Women in the Enlisted Force, FY 1973–2004

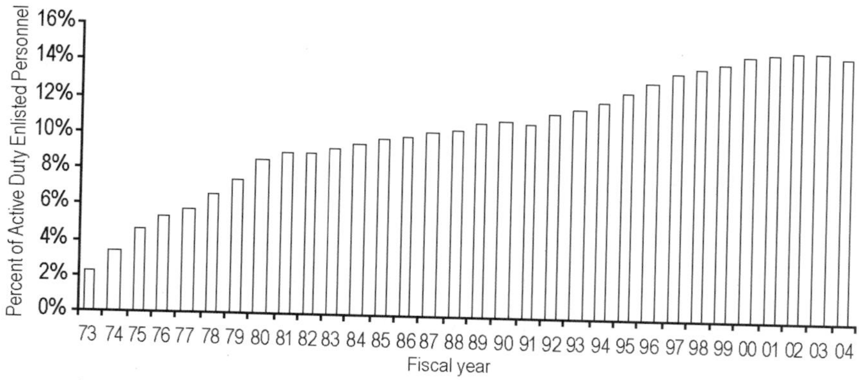

Source: Defense Manpower Data Center

to a maximum of 2 percent of each service; in 1967, new legislation made it possible to increase the number of women in the military significantly. By 1983, when Weinberger spoke, women made up 9 percent of the enlisted force; by 2004, women accounted for 15 percent of the enlisted force (see Figure 9.2), and about 18 percent of new recruits.

While national leadership was necessary to establish the all-volunteer force and to ensure its adequate funding, it was the individual services that really had to make the AVF work. The first task was to figure out how to recruit soldiers, sailors, marines, and airmen. In the early 1980s, that task fell most heavily on Army General Maxwell Thurman. Many considered him to be the single most important military leader in the history of the all-volunteer force. Although Thurman would be the first to acknowledge that increasing pay levels and educational benefits made the Army more attractive to youth, his leadership was also a key factor.[18] He recognized, more than any other uniformed leader, that the military had to compete aggressively for youth in the civilian labor market, and that to do so it needed the right tools: flexible policy "levers" based on market research and statistical analysis.

At a conference marking the twentieth anniversary of the U.S. All-Volunteer Force, General Thurman catalogued the actions that turned

---

18. Curtis L. Gilroy, Robert L. Phillips, and John D. Blair, "The All-Volunteer Army: Fifteen Years Later," *Armed Forces and Society*, Vol. 16, No. 3 (1990), pp. 329–350.

the Army's recruiting failures of the late 1970s into the successes of the 1980s.[19] He emphasized the need for quality recruits and a quality force; the importance of highly trained and professional recruiters who are accountable for achieving their recruiting goals; and the importance of an effective advertising campaign to attract high-quality youth. He saw the need for an efficient information system for assigning individuals to military jobs, and emphasized realistic and rigorous training against meaningful standards. He identified effective leadership by a sizable Non-Commissioned Officer (NCO) corps as the backbone of the fighting force. Pay comparability, educational incentives, and adequate recruiting resources were among the requirements he stressed for a successful volunteer military: if the Army failed to recruit and retain the necessary number and quality of personnel, the all-volunteer force as a whole would fail.

There was also successful activity in the other services. In the Marine Corps, "systematic recruiting"—a standardized process for all Marine Corps recruiters—was instituted. This efficient and successful management system has six components: tracking and recording recruit information, establishing critical connections and contacts, maintaining contacts with recruits and families, performing outreach, emphasizing core values, and ensuring quality recruiting personnel and quality recruits. These procedures, drafted by Brigadier General Alexander McMillan in 1977, have worked very well for the Marine Corps and are still in use today.[20]

Understanding the Issues and the Need for Research

Research had been a critical part of the all-volunteer force from its beginning. The research staff of the Gates Commission was largely drawn from economists who had experience working on military manpower and civilian labor-market issues. Before that, from World War I to the

19. Maxwell R. Thurman, "On Being All You Can Be: A Recruiting Perspective," in J. Eric Fredland, Curtis L. Gilroy, Roger D. Little, and W.S. Sellman, eds., *Professionals on the Front Line: Two Decades of the All-Volunteer Force* (Washington, D.C.: Brassey's, 1996).
20. Anita U. Hattiangadi, Gary Lee, and Aline O. Quester, *Recruiting Hispanics: The Marine Corps Experience* (Alexandria, Va.: Center for Naval Analyses, 2004).

late 1960s, military personnel issues had generally been the realm of psychologists, psychometricians, and sociologists.

For the psychologists and psychometricians, the basic questions were selection and classification of personnel: who would be selected from the pool of potentially available young men and women and, once selected, for which jobs would each be best qualified? Beginning with World War I, their efforts brought aptitude testing into the American mainstream and intelligence quotients (IQ) to the public consciousness. Psychological screening became critical in World War II for selecting and classifying Navy and Army aircrews, and is considered to be one of the triumphs of applied psychology. The development of the Armed Services Vocational Aptitude Battery (ASVAB), the military's modern selection and classification test, is highly respected by the educational and psychological testing community. A whole section of the American Psychological Association today is devoted to the field of military psychology. Sociologists and anthropologists studied group dynamics, relations between civilian society and the military, and social relations within the military. Sociologists emphasized the relationship between the military and society, as well as the internal social organization and effectiveness of alternative military organizations.

The Pentagon leadership, however, began to recognize that development and sustainment of an all-volunteer force went beyond the realms of psychology and sociology. For economists, military manpower was a relatively new field. When the results of early studies were presented at the 1966 annual meeting of the American Economics Association, one commentator declared that there could "hardly be a better subject for economic analysis than comparative methods for the recruitment of military manpower" because the problem offered "both micro- and macroeconomic aspects" to study.[21] Economists came to dominate the debate about the all-volunteer force and staffed key management positions in the Pentagon for the next several decades. Yet it took an interdisciplinary approach by the analytic community to prove that an all-volunteer force would work.

---

21. George H. Hildebrand, "Discussion," *American Economic Review*, Vol. 57, No. 2 (1967), p. 63.

Figure 9.3. Performance of First-Term Recruits by Aptitude Category

Source: U.S. Department of Defense (1992).

Note: For reporting purposes, scores on the AFQT are divided into five aptitude categories or percentile ranges: V, 1–9; IV, 10–30; III, 31–64; II, 65–92; and I, 93–99. Category III is often divided into subcategories IIIA (percentiles 50–64) and IIIB (percentiles 31–49). The upper half of the AFQT comprises categories I, II, and IIIA. By law, non-high school graduates in category IV and all individuals in category V are ineligible to enlist.

THE EARLY FOCUS

Early research focused on manning the all-volunteer force, in terms not of quantity, but of quality. At the center of this research was the finding that high-quality personnel were essential to the success of a volunteer military. The psychology community described two dimensions of quality that were important: education, reflected by completion of a high school diploma, and aptitude, reflected by a score in the upper half of the military's enlistment examination, the Armed Forces Qualification Test (AFQT).

These two quality dimensions are significant. First, high school graduates have been found to be more likely to complete their initial term of service and are thus a better training investment. About 80 percent of recruits with a diploma complete their initial three-year enlistment term, compared to only 50 percent of those who did not complete high school. For those who received alternate credentials—including those schooled at home—only 60 percent, on average, complete three years of service.

Second, recruits who score above the 50th percentile on the AFQT are easier to train and will perform better on the job. As Figure 9.3 shows, initial aptitude is a good predictor of on-the-job performance based on thirty occupational specialties across the four services. The Figure summarizes a multi-year Department of Defense research project, the results of which were validated by the National Academy of Sciences. Performance for all personnel improves with experience, as one would expect, but as Figure 9.3 shows, high-quality personnel have consistently higher performance scores at all levels of experience. As members gain experience, initial aptitude remains an extremely important predictor of performance. The highest-aptitude personnel enter the military at a performance level that is higher than the level of the lowest-aptitude personnel even after three years of service.

A body of statistical evidence confirms this relationship.[22] For example, high-aptitude Army soldiers operating PATRIOT missile batteries are better at hitting enemy aircraft and defending assets than soldiers who scored lower.[23] Communication equipment operators who scored higher are better at both radio operation and repair.[24] Tank crews composed of soldiers with high scores have significantly higher performance on firing ranges.[25] Navy ships with a greater proportion of high-scoring crewmembers experienced less ship downtime.[26]

Having the data to measure the relationship between a person's aptitude and actual performance helped the military to defend its need for quality recruits and a quality force. But it was difficult to determine how much quality was enough. The more appropriate question, however,

---

22. This evidence is summarized in Paul Hogan, Curtis Simon, and John Warner, "Sustaining the Force in an Era of Transition," in Barbara Bicksler, Curtis L. Gilroy, and John T. Warner, eds., *The All-Volunteer Force: Thirty Years of Service* (Washington, D.C.: Brassey's, 2004); and Curtis L. Gilroy and W.S. Sellman, "Recruiting and Sustaining a Quality Army: A Review of the Evidence," in Robert L. Phillips and Maxwell R. Thurman, eds., *Future Soldiers and the Quality Imperative* (Ft. Knox, Ky.: U.S. Army Recruiting Command, 1995).
23. B.R. Orvis, M. Childress, and J.M. Polich, *Effect of Personnel Quality on the Performance of Patriot Air Defense System Operators*, R-3901-A (Santa Monica, Calif.: RAND, 1992).
24. John Winkler, Judy Fernandez, and Michael Polich, *Effect of Aptitude on the Performance of Army Communications Operators*, R-4143-A (Santa Monica, Calif.: RAND, 1992).
25. Barry D. Scribner, D. Alton Smith, Robert H. Baldwin, and Robert L. Phillips, "Are Smart Tankers Better: AFQT and Military Productivity," *Armed Forces and Society*, Vol. 12, No. 2 (1986), pp. 193–206.
26. Aline O. Quester, *Enlisted Crew Quality and Ship Material Readiness*, RM-88-254 (Alexandria, Va.: Center for Naval Analyses, 1989).

Figure 9.4. Aptitude and Education Attainment of Active-duty Recruits, FY 1973–2004

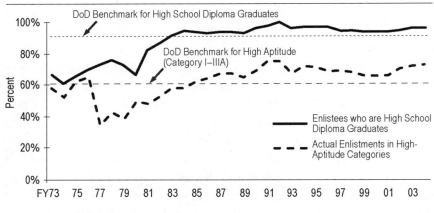

Source: U.S. DoD.

Note: Between 1976 and 1979, recruiting budgets were drastically cut and there was misnorming of the military enlistment test, both of which adversely affected recruiting. See below, footnote 47.

was how much quality the U.S. could afford. This required tradeoff analyses between performance, on the one hand, and costs of recruiting, training, and attrition on the other.[27] This, in turn, allowed the military to determine, for example, the extent to which quality would fall and performance would deteriorate if recruiting budgets were cut. To maximize job performance and minimize costs, the Department of Defense set benchmarks for enlistment at 90 percent or more high school diploma graduates and 60 percent or more scoring above the 50th percentile on the AFQT.[28] The services have recruited at or above these benchmarks for the past twenty years (see Figure 9.4).

A high-quality force, including a high-quality non-commissioned officer corps, depends upon quality recruits. Quality begets quality in two respects. High-quality recruits are more likely to stay if conditions of service are attractive, and quality recruits are more attracted to service if they see other high-quality individuals in the ranks. But the military

27. Bert F. Green and Anne S. Mavor, eds., *Modeling Cost and Performance for Military Enlistment* (Washington, D.C.: National Academy Press, 1994).

28. These benchmarks were established in 1993 and validated in 2000. See *Review of Minimum Active Enlisted Recruit Quality Benchmarks: Do They Remain Valid?* Report to Congress (Washington, D.C.: Office of the Assistant Secretary of Defense, Force Management Policy, March 2000).

must commit to paying for quality. How to attract a quality force is the subject of the next section.

THE RECRUITING CHALLENGE

Recruiting a quality force requires a thorough understanding of why people enlist, which can be discerned by the collection of comprehensive data and the construction of statistical models. But the rigors of formal analysis were a point of contention during the early transition to the volunteer force. Decision-makers were reluctant to wait for the research and analytical community to provide answers. Policy-makers were anxious to go ahead and try new programs, and then modify or drop them if they proved to be ineffective. The approach, at first, was experimental rather than analytical.[29] This was not the approach that should have been taken; data collection and analysis should have come before program implementation.

It did not take long, however, for the Department of Defense to see the need for a data center to develop and maintain computerized personnel files for analysis and reporting. Each of the services collected its own data, and in 1974, DoD established the Defense Manpower Data Center as a central repository for comprehensive historical time-series data and longitudinal information on all military personnel, and as a clearinghouse for administrative records and survey data collected on the military force and the civilian population. In addition, because the Department of Defense lacked sufficient and timely research to guide and support formulation of manpower and personnel policy, the Defense Manpower Studies Center was established at the RAND Corporation in 1976 as a Federally Funded Research and Development Center (FFRDC). Its mandate was to conduct interdisciplinary studies and analyses identified as high priorities in support of DoD-wide manpower policy decisions. The services also established their own research centers, both independent organizations and government civilian research institutes.[30]

---

29. Gus C. Lee and Geoffrey Y. Parker, *Ending the Draft—The Story of the All Volunteer Force* (Washington, D.C.: Human Resources Research Organization, 1977).

30. Today, the Department of Defense works closely with other FFRDCs such as the Center for Naval Analyses and the Institute for Defense Analysis, as well as universities, laboratories, and other research organizations, to

One important survey conducted by the Defense Manpower Data Center was the Youth Attitude Tracking Study, an annual national survey of military-eligible youth between 16 and 21 years of age begun in the mid-1970s. Managers of the all-volunteer force use the survey to track changes in the answers to the "propensity to enlist" question— "How likely is it that you would serve in the military?" This survey became the barometer for predicting military enlistment. A series of RAND studies published in the 1980s found, not surprisingly, that a higher propensity to enlist makes recruiting easier.[31] However, the studies also found that not everyone with a high propensity enlists, and that almost half of those who do enlist were likely to have expressed disinclination earlier.

The important determinants of the supply of high-quality recruits have been categorized into three groups: environmental factors, recruiting resources, and recruiting policy variables.[32] Environmental factors include the size and characteristics of the youth population, the civilian unemployment rate, and civilian earnings relative to military pay; these are factors over which the Department has little control. Recruiting resources include the number of recruiters and the amount of advertising. Recruiting policy variables comprise enlistment bonuses, educational benefits for college, and recruiter goals. Other factors such as propensity to enlist and the effects of influencers on youth, such as parents, teachers, and coaches, can also be important determinants.

Some of these factors were included in the earlier studies of enlistment supply. For example, one of the early models pointed out that the eligible youth population consists of segments or "groups of individuals who make [similar] decisions regarding school, work, and military service" and that "knowing how enlistment determinants differ by market segment should aid the efforts both of recruiters and enlistment policy-

study ways in which it can improve the efficiency and effectiveness of the volunteer military.

31. These studies were summarized in Bruce R. Orvis, Martin T. Gahart, Alvin K. Ludwig, and Karl F. Schutz, *Validity and Usefulness of Enlistment Intention Information* (Santa Monica, Calif.: RAND, 1992).

32. John T. Warner, Curtis J. Simon, and Deborah M. Payne, *Enlistment Supply in the 1990s: A Study of the Navy College Fund and Other Enlistment Incentive Programs* (Arlington, Va.: Defense Manpower Data Center, 2001).

makers."[33] It examined how these choices are made and provided some insights as to the potential drawing power of educational benefits as an incentive to enlist.

A 1982 study of the effectiveness of alternative educational benefit plans on enlistments was based on controlled experiments across the country.[34] Four alternative plans were offered to new recruits, and their enlistment behavior was observed. A similar empirical technique was used in 1986 to test how much different bonus amounts could expand the recruiting market, channel new recruits into particular occupational specialties, or lead to different lengths of initial enlistment.[35] This study pointed to recruiters as among the most important elements in the recruiting process. Work reflecting significant advances in econometric theory rigorously examined the way in which recruiters respond to quotas assigned them.[36]

Most of this early research focused on the Army, which had the highest recruiting goals and was at greatest risk of not achieving them. A model to provide monthly forecasts of Army enlistments one to two years in the future provided Army leadership with an "early warning" indicator of potential recruiting difficulty.[37]

A summary of fifteen empirical studies of enlistment supply that have shaped current U.S. military personnel policies (eleven of them

---

33. James R. Hosek and Christine E. Peterson, *Enlistment Decisions of Young Men* (Santa Monica, Calif.: RAND, 1985).

34. J. Michael Polich, Richard L. Fernandez, and Bruce R. Orvis, *Enlistment Effects of Military Educational Benefits* (Santa Monica, Calif.: RAND, 1982).

35. J. Michael Polich, James N. Dertouzos, and S. James Press, *The Enlistment Bonus Experiment* (Santa Monica, Calif.: RAND, 1986).

36. James N. Dertouzos, "Recruiter Incentives and the Marginal Cost of Accessions," in Barry E. Goodstadt, G. Thomas Sicilia, and H. Wallace Sinaiko, eds., *Proceedings of the Joint Service Workshop on Recruiter Productivity* (Washington, D.C.: Office of the Assistant Secretary of Defense [Manpower, Reserve Affairs and Logistics], 1983); and Thomas Daula and David Smith, "Estimating Supply Models for the U.S. Army," in R. Ehrenberg, ed., *Research in Labor Economics* (Greenwich, Conn.: JAI Press, 1985), pp. 261–309.

37. Charles Dale and Curtis Gilroy, "Enlistments in the All-Volunteer Force: Note," *American Economic Review,* Vol. 75, No. 3 (1985), pp. 547–51. For current enlistment forecasts, see Lawrence Goldberg and Dennis Kimko, *An Army Enlistment Early Warning System* (Alexandria, Va.: Institute for Defense Analysis, 2003).

focusing on the Army) estimated the effect that various levels of re-sources devoted to recruiting and related programs and policies have on the enlistment of high-quality recruits. The authors conclude that "even though they examine a wide range of time periods, and use dif-ferent cross-sectional units of observation, theoretical frameworks, and methodologies … the estimated effects of most variables are reasonably close to one another."[38]

Estimates based on a model by Warner, Simon, and Payne covering the 1989–1997 period are summarized in Table 9.2. The estimated effect on high-quality enlistments is expressed as a percent change as a result of a 10 percent increase in each factor. For example, the table shows that a 10 percent increase in the civilian unemployment rate would increase the Army's high-quality enlistments by 2.6 percent. The estimated effect of pay is considerably larger: a 10 percent increase in military pay rela-tive to civilian pay is predicted to increase Army enlistments by over 10 percent. Each 10 percent increase in the number of recruiters would in-crease high-quality enlistments by 3.8–5.7 percent, varying by service. Increases in advertising, bonuses, educational benefits, and recruiting goals are all associated with increases in enlistments. In terms of demo-graphic factors, military enlistments decline with increases in family income and college attendance: the higher the family income and pro-portion of youth going to college, the lower enlistments will be. But enlistments are higher in geographic areas where the percentage of vet-erans, blacks, or Hispanics in the population is high.

This model is vital for formulating cost-effective plans to sustain the volunteer military, as it compares the effects of important factors on the enlistment decision. Its estimates are used directly to shape policy, and indirectly as input to other models that conduct cost-tradeoff analyses. It is an example that other countries might find useful to help analyze the determinants of youth decisions to enlist in their militaries.

The Department of Defense recognized the importance of systemati-cally collecting survey and administrative-record data, building eco-nomic and statistical models that are theoretically sound and empirically defensible, conducting experiments to test the efficacy of alternative programs, and formulating policies on the basis of quantita-

---

38. Warner, Simon, and Payne, *Enlistment Supply in the 1990s*, p. 73.

Table 9.2. Impact of Selected Factors on the Enlistment of High-quality Enlisted Recruits

For 10% increase in this factor —	— enlistment changes by percentage shown			
	Army	Navy	Marine Corps	Air Force
Unemployment	2.6	2.9	2.8	2.3
Military Pay Relative to Civilian Pay	10.5	11.7	3.8	6.7
Recruiters	5.0	5.7	4.3	3.8
Advertising Expenditures	1.6	0.8	a	a
Enlistment Bonuses	1.2	a	b	b
Educational Benefits	0.5	0.2	b	b
Recruiting Goals	1.5	4.1	0.5	4.3
Demographic and other factors: c				
— Family Income	-7.2	-7.8	-4.0	-6.2
— College Attendance	-8.7	-10.1	-8.9	-11.7
— Percent Veteran	14.4	14.8	11.0	9.7
— Percent Black	4.9	14.9	3.3	a
— Percent Hispanic	5.7	14.2	5.2	3.7

Source: Warner, Simon, and Payne, *Enlistment Supply in the 1990s*, p. 36.

a. Not statistically significant.

b. Factor not included in the analysis.

c. Demographic and other factors—family income, college attendance and percent veteran, black, and Hispanic—were estimated at the state level.

tive evidence. Ten years after the volunteer military started, General Thurman remarked:

As we look back on the first decade of the All-Volunteer Force, I feel that we have learned how to make it work. *We have found the levers to pull.* We have determined the influences of bonuses and education incentives. We have seen the power of effective advertising.... In short, we have a better understanding of the supply of available youth, the recruiting environment, and the use of recruiting resources.[39]

39. Maxwell R. Thurman, "Sustaining the All-Volunteer Force 1983–1992: The Second Decade," in Bowman, Little, and Sicilia, *The All-Volunteer Force after a Decade*, pp. 266–285 (emphasis added). Although the discussion in this

Skill in Management

The transition from a conscripted force to a volunteer military presents special challenges to civilian leaders as well as the military services. In the United States, the individual services—the Army, Navy, Marine Corps, and Air Force—established their own policies within the context of overall policy guidance set by the Department of Defense. A number of technical lessons have helped the United States manage its volunteer military, and may prove useful for countries making the transition to a volunteer force.

First, the military had to learn how to recruit. Each of the services began by understanding the population base from which volunteers could be recruited: the approximately 25 million youth 18–24 years of age in the United States. The United States can be much more selective in taking volunteers than conscripts: the volunteer military is of higher quality than the U.S. draft force of over thirty years ago; it is also of higher quality than the average civilian population of today from which it is drawn. The United States has emphasized quality because high-quality recruits have been found to be the most cost-effective. In fiscal year 2004, 95 percent of new recruits were high school diploma graduates and 73 percent scored above average on the enlistment test (see Table 9.3). For comparison, note that less than 80 percent of American youth have a high school diploma and, by definition, only 50 percent of the youth population scores in the upper half of the AFQT.

Other screens winnow the size of the eligible civilian population. Medical standards are the most significant. Screens for moral behavior such as police records and arrests for drug and alcohol abuse are also important. All together, medical and moral issues as well as family status (such as having dependents) make nearly 60 percent of the civilian population ineligible for enlistment even before consideration of aptitude and high school graduation.

---

chapter has focused on recruiting studies, a substantial body of published research has examined retention and its relationship to pay and other factors. For a review of the models and empirical results related to military retention, see John T. Warner and Beth J. Asch, "The Economics of Military Manpower," in Keith Hartley and Todd Sandler, eds., *Handbook of Defense Economics*, Vol. I (New York: Elsevier, 1995), pp. 348–398.

Table 9.3. Quality of Active-duty Enlisted Recruits, FY 2004

	Percent high school diploma graduate	Percent Testing above 50th Percentile (AFQT I, II, IIIA)	Percent Testing Below 30th Percentile (AFQT IV)
Army	92	72	<1
Navy	96	70	0
Marine Corps	97	69	<1
Air Force	99	82	0
All Services	**95**	**73**	**<1**
U.S. Youth Population	**80**	**50**	**30**

Source: Official figures reported by the Services to the Office of the Under Secretary of Defense for Personnel and Readiness, Accession Policy Directorate.

The second lesson is that quality goals for enlistees must be established; in the United States, they are now based on AFQT test scores and high school graduation status. If leadership does not set standards, subordinates will, and they may not be consistent with leadership's desires and military needs.

Third, a professional, highly trained, and highly motivated recruiting staff must be developed. The U.S. military may be called an "all-volunteer force" but it is, in reality, an "all-recruited force."[40] Currently about 15,000 recruiters across the United States represent the four services. Each one is responsible, on average, for about twelve new enlisted recruits each year. Recruiters are assigned goals in terms of quantity and quality of recruits, and are held accountable for achieving these goals through a management system often characterized by face-to-face meetings between the recruiters and their supervisors.

Fourth, an independent military enlistment processing organization must be established to administer enlistment tests and physical examinations to potential recruits, determine whether they meet certain character standards, and undertake background checks with law enforcement and citizenship authorities. Enlistment tests are used not only to select individuals for military service, but also to classify and

40. Thurman, "On Being All You Can Be," p. 55.

assign them to military jobs for which they are most qualified and in which they are most interested.

Fifth, an advertising strategy must be developed to help expand the recruiting base. With a volunteer force, the government needs to explain to youth the benefits and opportunities of military service. For many young people, it is a worthwhile professional career; for others, it is a noble job for a shorter period of time, perhaps between high school and a civilian job or university. Advertising conveys a variety of messages to youth: the military offers money for education, bonuses to enlist in certain occupations or for enlistment tours of different lengths, career opportunities with civilian relevance, work in a high-technology environment, and good preparation for adulthood. Advertising also portrays the intangibles of the military such as service to country, honor, courage, commitment, and a setting in which to learn discipline and to mature. Another purpose of advertising is to develop and maintain a positive public image of the military. In the United States, the military is typically the most respected institution,[41] but influencers of youth such as parents and teachers do not always view the armed services as a desirable option for youth. In 2004, DoD spent nearly $400 million on enlisted recruitment advertising. A small proportion of this advertising is joint and applies to all the services, but most of the advertising is service-specific. The United States has found that such a combination of advertising is most effective.

Sixth, military pay must be set so that it is comparable to what prospective recruits and military members could earn in the civilian sector. Pay is a significant enlistment incentive. It is not, by itself, sufficient to guarantee success of an AVF, but without the perception of a fair and equitable pay package, a volunteer force is guaranteed to fail. Looking back over the 1970s, General Thurman noted that when the United States was "unable to pay competitive salaries, we lost the heart of our NCO corps and, with it, the mid-level troop [and] technical leadership we needed."[42] Setting pay correctly takes constant vigilance. To this end, the U.S. Congress directs the Department of Defense to study military pay every four years to ensure that pay is adequate to recruit and

---

41. See, for example, the Gallup polls <www.Gallup.com> and the Harris polls at <www.harrisinteractive.com>.

42. Maxwell R. Thurman, "Sustaining the All-Volunteer Force 1983–1992: The Second Decade," p. 274.

Figure 9.5. Comparison of Enlisted Pay with Civilian Earnings, 2000 and 2004

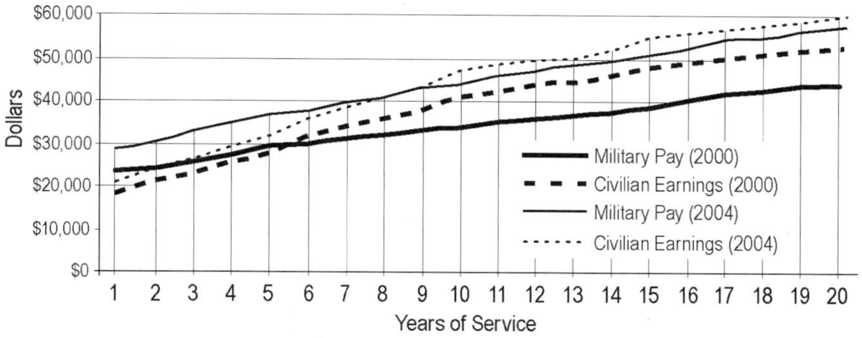

Source: Office of the Under Secretary of Defense for Personnel and Readiness, Compensation Directorate.

retain the force. The most recent study found that the military was not paying a high enough premium to sustain the educated force it had.[43] This laid the groundwork for the largest "catch-up" pay raise in over twenty years, targeted both to officers and enlisted members in various grades. Figure 9.5 depicts a comparison of enlisted military pay with the earnings of similarly educated and otherwise comparable civilians over a twenty-year career. Comparing the 2000 lines with the 2004 lines shows that the gap between military and civilian pay has closed considerably.[44] This study also called for more balance and flexibility in the compensation system: balance between basic pay and special and incentive pays, and flexibility to respond to changing circumstances for more effective force shaping.

Seventh, specific monetary incentives are needed to motivate individuals to enlist and reenlist. Enlistment and reenlistment bonuses and special pays, while generally effective in expanding the market, are especially important for channeling individuals to hard-to-fill occupations,

43. U.S. Department of Defense, *The Ninth Quadrennial Review of Military Compensation* (Washington, D.C.: Office of the Under Secretary of Defense for Personnel and Readiness, 2002).

44. For a technical description of how the pay comparisons were calculated, see U.S. Department of Defense, *The Ninth Quadrennial Review of Military Compensation*.

hazardous-duty assignments, and undesirable locations. Educational benefits are provided to recruits as another incentive. Members can use these while in service or after they leave the military to further their education and training for a civilian job. In the United States, DoD sets the overall guidance for these bonuses, special pays, and benefits, while the individual services determine eligibility according to their specific needs.

Eighth, it is crucial to develop challenging career paths. The United States needed to develop its training and in-service professional military education, and to offer rewarding assignments to keep the most highly qualified and best-trained personnel. The United States also had to ensure that members believed that the promotion system was fair and that it was based solely on merit and performance. Under the AVF, the force is more senior and experienced than under the draft: in the Army, for example, careerists now make up over 40 percent of the active enlisted force. This contrasts sharply with about 20 percent in the latter years of the draft era.

Ninth, a quality non-commissioned officer (NCO) corps is essential to provide both troop and technical leadership to the enlisted force. As the quality of enlisted accessions increased in the volunteer military, and as pay was set at competitive levels to ensure career opportunities for talented personnel, the United States found that the quality of the NCOs also increased. The impact of education, both military and civilian, for these NCOs, and the importance placed upon it for career progression, was a product of the emphasis placed on the entrance-level quality of accessions. The better educated the NCO corps, the better the NCOs perform, and this, in turn, creates stronger competition for advancement and retention. The U.S. experience has been that emphasizing quality at the accession point and ensuring competitive pay and attractive career paths result in a high-quality NCO corps.

Finally, the U.S. experience has shown that quality-of-life benefits, such as housing, child care, health benefits, family advocacy programs, and military stores (particularly in remote locations) are essential to a volunteer force. Although the military recruits *individuals*, it retains *families*: family considerations are important in the individual's reenlistment decision. It took the United States a long time to recognize the importance of quality-of-life and family issues.

Adequate Budgets

The final major factor in the eventual success of the U.S. all-volunteer force is that, over time, the United States has ensured that there are adequate resources to support it. The defense budget must be large enough to support pay raises that keep pace with both inflation and civilian-sector pay increases; to supply resources for recruiting including support for advertising, recruiters, bonuses, and educational benefits; and to fund the military retirement program and quality-of-life initiatives. On various occasions, military pay has been allowed to fall too far behind civilian earnings, and sometimes recruiting and other programs have been reduced too much. Each time, recruiting and retention suffered, and the viability of the AVF was threatened. This was because policymakers did not understand the fragile relationship between recruiting and economic factors—specifically, the aspects of the labor market in which the military competes for manpower, and the ways in which pecuniary and nonpecuniary incentives allocate labor supply. The story of what happened after the early success of the all-volunteer force is instructive.

In the early years, the U.S. volunteer force was successful primarily because it was given adequate resources. Following the Gates Commission's recommendations, Congress enacted a pay raise of over 60 percent in 1972 to provide new recruits with pay comparable to their civilian peers. Recruiting resources were increased to place more recruiters across the country, to enhance recruiting facilities, and to expand and improve advertising. Educational benefits for servicemembers were still generous and were attractive incentives. A growing youth population and rising civilian unemployment in those early years together resulted in a richer manpower pool from which the services—particularly the Army—could draw.

By 1977—four years into the volunteer military—circumstances had changed. If uncertainty and some early success characterized the early years of the AVF, overconfidence characterized the next several years. Educational benefits, a popular incentive, were reduced, while the level of military compensation was allowed to fall so far behind civilian pay that it was inadequate to attract and retain the numbers and quality of the people needed. Recruiting resources were thought to be more than adequate and were cut. Years later, General Thurman noted, "Recruiting resources as a whole [had been] thought to be at least adequate, if not excessive, and became targets for cost-cutting."[45] This was at a time when the economy was robust and youth unemployment was low. Rather than cutting recruiting budgets in a tight labor market, resources should have been increased to be effective in this challenging recruiting environment. The recruiting difficulties that resulted should not have come as any surprise: by 1979, all four services failed to achieve their recruiting goals. The Army and Marine Corps suffered most; the Army fell short of its recruiting mission by 17 percent.[46] The quality of recruits fell precipitously (as shown in Figure 9.4). For the Marine Corps, only 37 percent of new recruits were high quality; for the Army that figure was a dismal 25 percent, a sharp contrast to today's figures for the Marine Corps (66 percent) and the Army (67 percent).[47] During the late 1970s and early 1980s, the quality of new recruits was far below what are now considered the minimum levels established by the DoD.

The Gates Commission had predicted that the Army would have the greatest difficulty in obtaining volunteers. "Voluntary enlisted deficits are the highest in the Army. This ... is to be expected given that entry level pay is lowest for enlisted personnel and that the nonmonetary conditions of service are less attractive in the Army than in the other three services."[48] The White House under President Jimmy Carter was more concerned with fighting inflation and holding down the overall size of the federal budget than in military recruiting and compensation.

To remedy the situation, Congress legislated two large pay raises for the military—11.7 percent in 1980 and 14.3 percent in 1981—to help restore military-civilian pay comparability. The goal was to raise basic pay

---

45. Thurman, "Sustaining the All-Volunteer Force 1983–1992: The Second Decade," p. 269.
46. Gilroy, Phillips, and Blair, "The All-Volunteer Army: Fifteen Years Later."
47. Quality also fell because of the mis-norming of the Armed Services Vocational Aptitude Battery (ASVAB). The scoring algorithm for interpreting applicants' test performance was flawed; that is, scores at the lower end of the distribution were artificially inflated, resulting in the enlistment of over 400,000 low-quality recruits between 1976 and 1980 who should not have been permitted to enlist.
48. Gates Commission Report, p. 56.

Figure 9.6. Recruiting Budgets and High-quality Active-duty Enlistments, FY 1976–2004

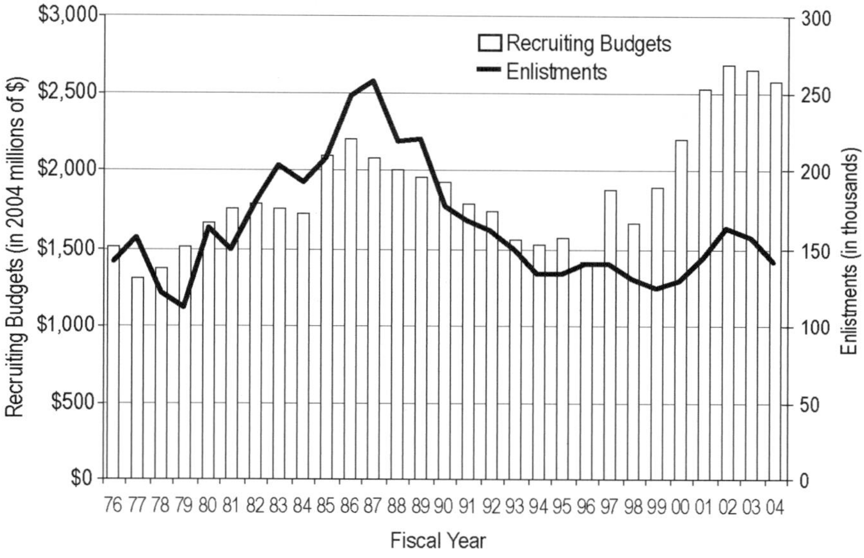

Source: Recruiting budget figures reported by the Services to the Office of the Under Secretary of Defense for Personnel and Readiness, Accession Policy Directorate. Enlistment data from the Defense Manpower Data Center.

Note: High-quality enlistments are defined as those recruits who both possess a high school diploma and score in the upper half of the Armed Forces Qualification Test.

of all servicemembers to a level that would allow the Army to meet its manpower objectives. According to the Gates Commission, "The evidence is overwhelming that, if compensation is set at levels which satisfy Army requirements, the other services will be able to attract enough qualified volunteers to meet their respective requirements."[49]

Not just inadequate military pay, but inadequate recruitment budgets, had contributed to the problems of the late 1970s. The same mistake was made in the late 1990s, when the United States again became overconfident and cut recruiting budgets too much at a time when the economy was strong and unemployment low. The U.S. military had just undergone a 25 percent drawdown of its active-duty force. Recruiting resources were cut as the recruiting mission was reduced. Unfortunately, budgets were

49. Ibid., p. 57.

cut too much and, with unemployment reaching a thirty-year low of 4 percent, the services found it difficult to achieve their recruiting goals: the Army missed its goals in 1998 and 1999, while the Navy missed its goal in 1998 and the Air Force in 1999. There is a close relationship between enlistments and recruiting budgets, as shown in Figure 9.6, but the Department of Defense neglected these trends in the latter years of the 1970s and again in the 1990s. It took a large infusion of resources to correct this oversight in 1978 and 1979 before recruiting turned around in 1980. It took even larger increases in 1998 and 1999 before recruiting rebounded in 2000. In fiscal year 2004, the United States spent $2.6 billion to recruit 182,825 active-duty men and women into the military.

After a decade's experience with the AVF, General Thurman noted that "the quality of the enlistee tracks with the expenditure of recruiting resources. We must understand this relationship ... and so too must the Congress."[50] Twenty years later, former Deputy Secretary of Defense John P. White pointed out that:

it takes some time for the system to detect any important shifts in program effectiveness. Monitoring mechanisms are weak and imperfect, leading to an unfortunate lag between changes in conditions and changes in policy.... Once the remedies are fashioned there is a further, inevitable, lag in the time it takes to make either internal, programmatic adjustments or legislative changes such as authorizing a pay increase.[51]

White was particularly sensitive to the problem because, as a senior decision-maker in the Carter administration, he had been unable to convince the president to increase military pay in 1978 when it was obvious to most that it needed to be increased. The clear message from the experience of the late 1970s, White noted, was that a volunteer military "requires an on-going institutional commitment to assure its continued success." The experience in the late 1990s proved that the United States had not yet learned this lesson well enough.

---

50. Thurman, "Sustaining the All-Volunteer Force 1983–1992: The Second Decade," p. 274.

51. John P. White, "Reflections on Managing the All-Volunteer Force: Past and Future," in Bicksler, Gilroy, and Warner, *The All-Volunteer Force: Thirty Years of Service*, pp. 33–44.

Looking Ahead

In January 2001, departing Secretary of Defense William Cohen remarked that:

On countless occasions I've been asked by foreign leaders, "How can our military be more like America's?" I'll repeat here today what I've said time and time again. It's not our training, although our training is the most rigorous in the world. It's not our technology, although ours is the most advanced in the world. And it's not our tactics, although ours is the most revolutionary in the world. We have the finest military on Earth because we have the finest people on Earth, because we recruit and we retain the best that America has to offer.[52]

In October 2004, Secretary of Defense Donald Rumsfeld wrote that "a draft simply is not needed." Noting that there are "295 million people in the United States of America and ... some 2.6 million active and reserve forces serving," Rumsfeld said:

We are capable of attracting and retaining the people we need, through the proper use of pay and other incentives.... In danger zones across the globe, the all-volunteer, professional force is performing superbly—as typified in operations in Afghanistan and Iraq.... These men and women ... are committed, enthusiastic, and proud to be contributing to the defense of the nation. Most importantly, they want to be doing what they are doing. Every single one of them stepped forward, raised their hand, and said, "I'm ready. I want to serve."[53]

When the draft ceased to mean universal service, it lost its legitimacy. Although other countries have maintained the universality of their conscription systems by reducing terms of service to fit their demographics and their budgets, as well as their national public opinion, this was not an alternative for the United States, given the worldwide military commitments it had accepted after World War II. The alternative to the draft—the all-volunteer force—has been a resounding

---

52. William Cohen, *Farewell to Armed Forces* (Washington, D.C.: Department of Defense, 2001).
53. Donald Rumsfeld, letter to the Honorable Duncan Hunter, Chairman, Committee on Armed Services, U.S. House of Representatives, October 5, 2004.

success. It has resulted in a professional career-oriented military that has proven itself on battlefields throughout the world. It is a force that is generally representative of American society and has provided outstanding employment opportunities for groups that had long been excluded from the mainstream of society.[54] It is a leading employer of women, with equal pay for equal work. It is the most racially integrated institution in America.[55] It is a resilient and flexible force that has integrated full-time active-duty soldiers with their part-time civilian reserve counterparts to form a truly total force. Moreover, this has been done within an affordable budget and with a competitive wage. Today, people join because they want to join, not because someone is forcing them to serve. The American people do not favor a return to the draft; seven out of ten are opposed.[56] A survey of teenagers found that 86 percent of them think the United States should not return to a draft; about 70 percent are not even worried about being drafted.[57]

As demonstrated over the past thirty years, the all-volunteer force is in some ways a fragile institution. From time to time, inattention to the economic environment, ignorance of the adverse effects of budget cuts on recruiting, and insensitivity to the needs of servicemembers and their families have resulted in declining enlistments and low quality of recruits. Today, the fragile nature of the all-volunteer force comes from extended operations in Iraq and Afghanistan. Those charged with managing the force must be vigilant; the knowledge gained from over thirty years will contribute to ensuring the continued success of our all-volunteer force.

---

54. Sue E. Berryman, *Who Serves? The Persistent Myth of the Underclass Army* (Boulder, Colo.: Westview Press, 1988); and Tim Kane, *Who Bears the Burden? Demographic Characteristics of U.S. Military Recruits Before and After 9/11* (Washington, D.C.: The Heritage Foundation, 2005).

55. Charles C. Moskos and John Sibley Butler, *All That We Can Be: Black Leadership and Racial Integration the Army Way* (New York: Twentieth Century Fund, Inc., 1996); Quester and Gilroy, "Women and Minorities in America's Volunteer Military."

56. Ipsos Poll taken between June 20 and 22, 2005. See <www.ap-ipsosresults.com>.

57. Gallup Poll taken between January and February 2005. See <www.Gallup.com>.

Chapter 10

Cash and In-kind Compensation Policies for a Volunteer Force

Deborah Clay-Mendez

A successful volunteer force requires a compensation package of cash and in-kind benefits sufficient not only to attract high-quality recruits but to also retain experienced, trained personnel. Because many older, experienced personnel are likely to have families, this means that the compensation package must provide a way of life acceptable to families. A compensation system that works well for a force of young conscripts may not be adequate to support a volunteer force.

Since the end of the Cold War, twelve of NATO's twenty-six member states have ended military conscription or announced plans to phase it out and introduce a volunteer force. Other NATO states plan to maintain a conscript force for homeland defense but are increasing their reliance on volunteer personnel for other missions. With volunteer personnel, NATO states can create professional, highly trained units capable of deploying for alliance operations ranging from peacekeeping on Europe's periphery to combat operations abroad. As the importance of volunteers increases, many nations are reassessing their systems for rewarding military service.

Before they commit to new compensation programs, these nations have the opportunity to examine the experiences of their NATO colleagues. Some European governments are looking at aspects of the U.S. system for ideas to improve the quality of life for military families.[1] France has expanded family assistance programs, including help with searching for schools, and is considering a new initiative to provide, at

---

1. For a comprehensive review of military family policies in NATO states, see Cindy Williams, "From Conscripts to Volunteers: NATO's Transition to

government expense, family housing near military installations. Germany and Belgium are opening child-care centers for military families, and the Netherlands is considering such a move.[2] Romania is building new housing for military families.

Each NATO member has its own historical, economic, and social environment. Thus, many of the issues faced by the U.S. military compensation system will not be relevant to other nations. For example, the cost of military health care—a growing problem for the U.S. military—is less likely to be an issue in Western European nations that offer universal health care to their citizens and that do not have a history of maintaining large networks of military hospitals in peacetime. Yet while the specifics of the U.S. experience are unique, its successes and failures may still provide some useful insights into compensation policies for other volunteer forces.

This chapter examines the compensation package offered by the U.S. military. It describes the overall size of the package and its heavy reliance on in-kind and deferred benefits in lieu of cash pays. It then describes how that system, with its emphasis on family-friendly in-kind benefits, expanded in the early years of the Cold War, survived the introduction of the all-volunteer force in the 1970s, and continues to develop today. It reviews some of the advantages and disadvantages of in-kind and deferred benefits relative to cash pays, and identifies some of the unintended consequences of relying on those benefits. In the United States, one unintended consequence is that military personnel have become unnecessarily costly relative to non-military personnel. This reduces the level of military capability that the United States can provide for any given level of resources and provides an incentive for decision-makers to rely on civilians and contractors even when military "boots on the ground" would be more effective. The chapter then goes on to look at alternatives to the current system in the United States and obstacles to change. It concludes by offering five broad lessons of the U.S. experience.

All-Volunteer Forces," *Naval War College Review*, Vol. 58, No. 1 (Winter 2005). 2. Ministry of Defense Netherlands, "Summary of the Defence White Paper 2000" <www.mindef.nl/nieuws/media/170701_whitepaper2000.html>, p. 19; Transatlantic Roundtable on "Filling NATO's Ranks: Military Personnel Policies in Transition," at the Transatlantic Center of the German Marshall Fund of the United States, Brussels, Belgium, September 8–9, 2003.

The Mix of Cash, Deferred, and In-kind Compensation

The U.S. military, which relies on a mix of pay, bonuses, and educational benefits to recruit high-quality enlistees, offers an even wider range of deferred cash and in-kind benefits to retain those already in the force. Roughly 58 percent of active-duty servicemembers are married or have dependents, and family-friendly in-kind benefits play a large role in the military's compensation package.

The nonpartisan Congressional Budget Office (CBO) estimates that the average annual compensation cost per active-duty servicemember was $99,000 in 2002.[3] This is for a force comprising 16 percent officers and 84 percent enlisted personnel. The CBO cost estimate reflects the costs borne by the U.S. government for all forms of compensation (cash, in-kind, and deferred benefits). It does not include the cost of training soldiers or reimbursing them or their families for moving between assignments. Nor does it include costs that do not appear in the federal budget, such as forgone local sales taxes and the cost of the interest and risk the government bears because it has resources invested in housing developments, child-care facilities, and retail ventures at military bases. In contrast, the median annual cost to private employers in the United States for full-time male workers over age 16 was on the order of $49,000, including $13,000 in non-cash benefits.[4]

The high quality of military personnel and the sacrifices and risks of military life explain a portion of the $99,000: military service may command a premium compared to civilian jobs. But another reason that the United States pays so much is that, on average, less than half, or just $43,000 of the $99,000, is cash that the servicemember can spend immediately as he or she chooses (see Figure 10.1). The bulk of active-duty compensation, $56,000 per servicemember, consists of deferred compensation,

---

3. Congressional Budget Office, *Military Compensation: Balancing Cash and Noncash Benefits*, Economic and Budget Issue Brief, January 16, 2004.
4. Strict comparability might suggest comparisons of medians, or of averages. However, no estimate of the median military compensation package (including in-kind and deferred benefits) is available. However, because the military includes neither the richest nor the poorest workers in the United States, a comparison between the average military compensation package and the median civilian package may be more useful than a comparison based solely on averages.

Figure 10.1. Active-duty Compensation

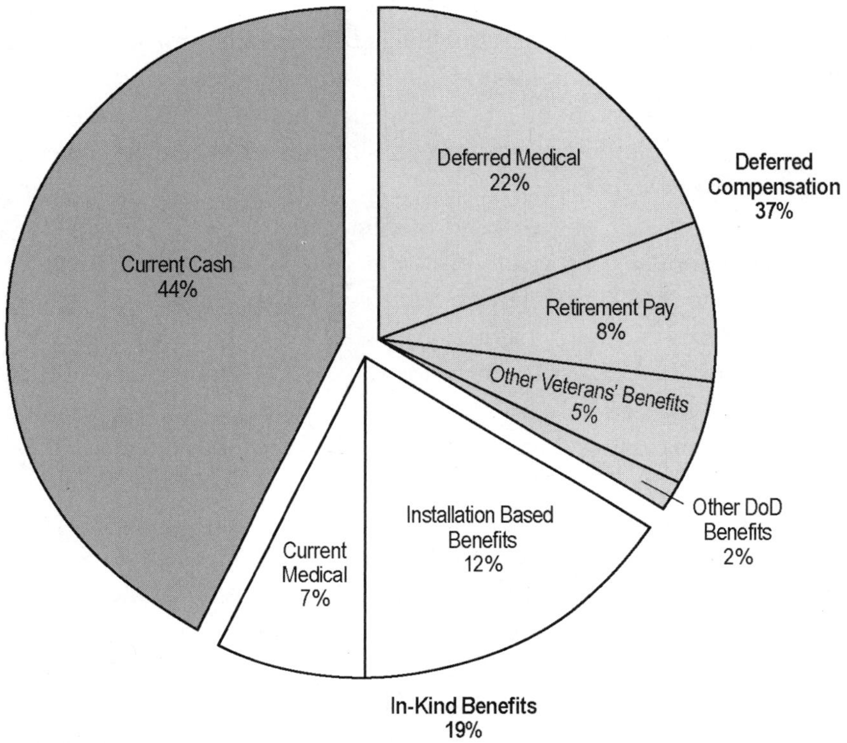

Source: Based on data from Congressional Budget Office.

available only to veterans, military retirees, or their dependents, or of other benefits that, although available to active-duty servicemembers and their families, are provided in kind rather than in cash.

Servicemembers generally value the in-kind and deferred benefits offered by the military, and in some cases those benefits are more cost-effective than cash pay. Nonetheless, the inability of servicemembers to choose between cash and in-kind benefits means that there is no way to ensure that the value they place on the deferred or in-kind benefits equals or exceeds the costs that the government incurs in providing them. If the value of the benefits to servicemembers is less than their cost, the government may be spending more than is necessary to attract and retain personnel. In addition, many of the costs of the in-kind or deferred benefits fall outside of DoD's military personnel budget and, as a result, military decision-makers may disregard or even be unaware of the full cost.

DEFERRED COMPENSATION

Deferred compensation—the cash and in-kind benefits provided after separation to former servicemembers and their dependents—accounts for roughly $37,000 of the $99,000. This figure includes benefits for which all military veterans are eligible—such as low-cost home mortgages—as well as the retirement pay, survivor benefits, and retiree health-care benefits available to military retirees or their dependents. In the U.S. military, active-duty servicemembers who have served at least twenty years are eligible for an immediate retirement annuity and lifetime health care for themselves and their dependents, while those who leave before twenty years do not get any military retirement benefits.

IN-KIND BENEFITS

The in-kind benefits DoD provides to active-duty servicemembers and their families account for an additional $19,000. Some of those benefits, such as gyms, serve both married and single servicemembers. Yet many of the benefits provided at military installations, including subsidized child-care centers, grocery stores, and housing, are valued the most by members who have families. For example, junior enlisted personnel who are single live on military bases in dormitory-style barracks, while DoD provides married personnel—regardless of rank—with either on-base family housing units or cash housing allowances. About a third of the married personnel live in the on-base units, which are a particularly attractive benefit for junior enlisted members with large families because the services assign the units based on family size as well as rank. The other two-thirds of married personnel, as well as single senior personnel, receive cash housing allowances. The cash housing allowance is larger for those with dependents; thus cash compensation can vary substantially based on family status.

Child-care centers on bases are an increasingly important benefit. DoD operates over 800 child-care centers at 300 military installations, relying on government employees to provide high-quality, subsidized care to over 64,000 children below the age of 6.[5] Waiting lists for the on-base child-care centers are often long, as parents pay, on average, only

---

5. Department of Defense, *Overview of the Military Child Development System*, at <www.militaryhomefront.dod>, January, 2006.

half of the center's operating costs and none of its capital costs. Junior personnel and parents of small infants pay an even smaller share of the cost. In addition, to ensure high-quality education for the school-age dependents of military personnel, the Department of Defense operates 299 elementary and secondary schools, serving 102,000 children of military personnel.[6] Together with the U.S. Department of Education, it also provides supplemental funding (in lieu of local property taxes, which military families living on federal land do not pay) to local schools that have a high proportion of military dependents.

Subsidized retail activities are another in-kind benefit. DoD employs roughly 18,000 civil servants to run a system of 275 military commissaries, or on-base grocery stores. The commissary system is, in effect, one of the largest supermarket chains in the United States. Another 80,000 federal civilians work in DoD's networks of on-base general merchandise stores, gas stations, fast-food outlets, home furnishing stores, movie theaters, and golf courses. The goal of these DoD-controlled facilities is not just to provide military families who are assigned to isolated locations with access to goods and services, but to provide all military families with access to goods and services at below-market prices. The facilities are able to offer below-market prices because of a combination of funds appropriated directly to them by the Congress, indirect appropriations in the form of maintenance, transportation, and utilities provided by the military services, tax subsidies in the form of exemptions from state and local sales and excise taxes, and access to government capital at no interest charge.[7]

HEALTH CARE

Health care is the single most costly in-kind benefit that U.S. servicemembers and their families receive. When costs are calculated on an accrual basis, DoD and the Department of Veterans Affairs spend $29,000 each year per active-duty member on health care.[8] These funds

---

6. Department of Defense Education Activity, <www.dodea.edu/commun ications/dodeafacts.htm>, November 4, 2004.
7. Congressional Budget Office, *The Costs and Benefits of Retail Activities at Military Bases*, October 1997.
8. The accrual cost of future benefits is the amount that DoD would need to set aside each year for active-duty members in order to fully fund those fu-

pay for the operation of DoD and Veterans' Administration (VA) hospitals and clinics as well as for the care that DoD and the VA purchase from the private sector on behalf of current and former military personnel and their beneficiaries. Active-duty personnel, who are typically young and healthy, account for only about 10 percent of these costs. The accrual cost of caring for active-duty personnel when they become veterans or retirees accounts for another 53 percent, and the current and future costs of caring for the dependents of military personnel account for the remaining 37 percent.

Origin of the Military System of Lifetime and Family Benefits

The military sector in the United States is more paternalistic and supportive of current and former employees and their families than is the civilian sector, and this may make sense, given the unique rigors and risks of military life. Nonetheless, this system of family-friendly benefits evolved in parallel to a civilian society in which—for good or ill— civilian workers often pay the full cost of their child care, depend on employers for health insurance that may involve high premiums as well as co-payments, and—except when suffering severe financial need—do not receive family assistance from the government, nor subsidies of the cost of goods and services.[9] How did the military develop a system so different from that faced by the U.S. population as a whole?

Supporters of deferred and in-kind benefits often cite their deep roots in military tradition. As early as the 1800s, the military provided housing to commanding officers at frontier installations and soldiers relied on commissary stores to supplement government rations. A closer look reveals, however, that the current system of large on-base communities with their own housing, retail activities, family-oriented

---

ture benefits. The accrual estimates, derived by the Office of Management and Budget (OMB) and the Congressional Budget Office (CBO), take into account both the projected earnings that the set-aside funds might earn and the rise in health-care costs over time. See Congressional Budget Office, *Growth in Medical Spending by the Department of Defense*, September 2003, for a discussion of DoD medical benefits.

9.   Although the U.S. income tax system provides some exceptions to this in the form of child-care credits and deductions for dependents, the contrast in treatment between military and civilian families remains striking.

health-care clinics, and schools did not emerge until the 1950s and 1960s. These were the early years of the Cold War, in which the United States first took on the job of maintaining a large peacetime military. That peacetime force comprised more enlisted personnel with families than before: prior to this, the military services had actively discouraged married enlisted personnel from serving during peacetime. The un-stated policy was that, "if the military had wanted you to have a wife, it would have issued you one."

The on-base communities in the United States and overseas grew rapidly. From the early 1950s though the mid-1960s, the number of on-base family housing units increased from 200,000 to over 400,000.[10] Annual sales at commissaries during this same period rose from less than $1 billion to over $7 billion, in constant dollars.[11] Housing and commis-saries were built at all large military installations, even those that were not in isolated rural locations. Congressional hearings in the 1950s indicated that the development of the military communities was in large part a response to acute postwar housing shortages in both the United States and Europe. Military leaders felt that assured access to adequate housing was essential to support the frequent rotation of soldiers and their families to and from Europe.

Conscription, which allowed the military to pay first-term personnel low wages, also favored the expansion of family-friendly in-kind benefits. Although most young conscripts were single, it was impractical to release conscripts who married while on active duty, or to defer all married men from conscription during times of conflict. Yet DoD did not pay all conscripts enough to support families, and it would have been costly—at least in terms of the military budget—for it to do so.[12] To avoid the prospect of having military families living in poverty, DoD could either send cash allowances to the families of young conscripts, as it did during World War II, or offer in-kind benefits to those families.

---

10. Congressional Budget Office, *Military Family Housing in the United States*, September 1993.

11. CBO, *The Costs and Benefits of Retail Activities at Military Bases*, p. 8.

12. Under conscription, much of the cost of military personnel is borne by the individual conscripts and is not seen in any government budget. The full economic cost of a conscripted force, budgetary and non-budgetary, is none-theless greater than that of a similar volunteer force.

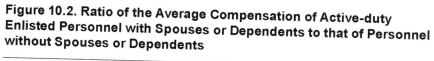

Figure 10.2. Ratio of the Average Compensation of Active-duty Enlisted Personnel with Spouses or Dependents to that of Personnel without Spouses or Dependents

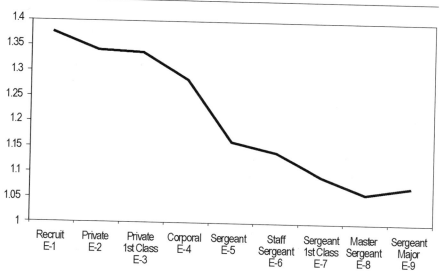

Note: These estimates take into account Regular Military Compensation (RMC), DoD data on the average number of dependents by pay-grade, CBO estimates of the immediate cost to DoD of medical benefits for active-duty personnel and their family members, and the cost to DoD of providing commissary benefits to active-duty families. Estimates do not include the value of veterans' benefits, retiree pay or benefits, or active-duty compensation other than RMC, current medical care, and commissaries. The pay-grades E-1 to E-9 apply to enlisted personnel in every service; the titles for the corresponding ranks (recruit through sergeant major) are drawn from the Army.

One advantage of in-kind benefits over cash allowances was that the extent to which they raised the compensation of servicemembers with families relative to single personnel without dependents was less obvious, and thus less likely to raise questions of fairness.

Even today, non-cash benefits raise the cost of compensating junior enlisted personnel with dependents relative to single personnel at the same rank. The prominence of the family benefits declines with rank, as in-kind benefits, including health care and subsidized shopping, become a smaller share of total compensation (see Figure 10.2).

The introduction of the all-volunteer force in the early 1970s could have provided an opportunity for DoD and Congress to equalize the compensation packages for married and single personnel. The end of conscription required an increase in the pay of junior enlisted personnel, making it easier for those who were married to support families. More important, it ensured that junior personnel with dependents who took on the rigors of military service were those who chose to do so: no one was forcing them to enlist. Instead, however, the United States enhanced the existing structure of family benefits for enlisted personnel as it moved to a volunteer force. Military leaders gave up conscription reluctantly, and thus it may not have been the ideal time to challenge other practices, particularly those that—for the most senior officers who were the decision-makers—had long traditions. Moreover, the on-base communities were already built, and were still relatively new.

Impact of the AVF on Deferred Compensation and Family Benefits

During the 1980s and 1990s, as the first cohorts to enter under the AVF progressed through their military careers, demographic changes within the military increased the costs associated with family benefits and deferred compensation, as well as the size of the interest groups supporting those elements of compensation. Some of the demographic changes were logical outcomes of the shift to a volunteer force; some were a matter of policy reflecting broader trends in U.S. society; and some were the unintended consequences of a military that pays young workers with family responsibilities more than they could earn in the civilian sector.

One change is that the force became more experienced and older. Unless deliberate efforts are made to hold down reenlistments, a force consisting of individuals who chose military service will be more experienced than a force of conscripts and, relative to a conscript force of the same size, is likely to produce more military retirees. In 1969, near the height of the draft, the U.S. military had an active-duty force of almost 3.5 million and a military retiree population of 700,000. Today, there are more military retirees than servicemembers on active duty; the active-duty force is 1.4 million and the retiree population is 1.7 million. The growth in the number of retired military personnel and their beneficiaries has increased both the cost of deferred benefits and the political support for efforts to protect such benefits and further increase them. Although today's smaller force will eventually lead to a smaller retiree population, current retention rates and life spans suggest that even in the long term there will still be one retiree for every two or three active-duty servicemembers.

Figure 10.3. Percent of Civilian and Military Personnel Married, by Age

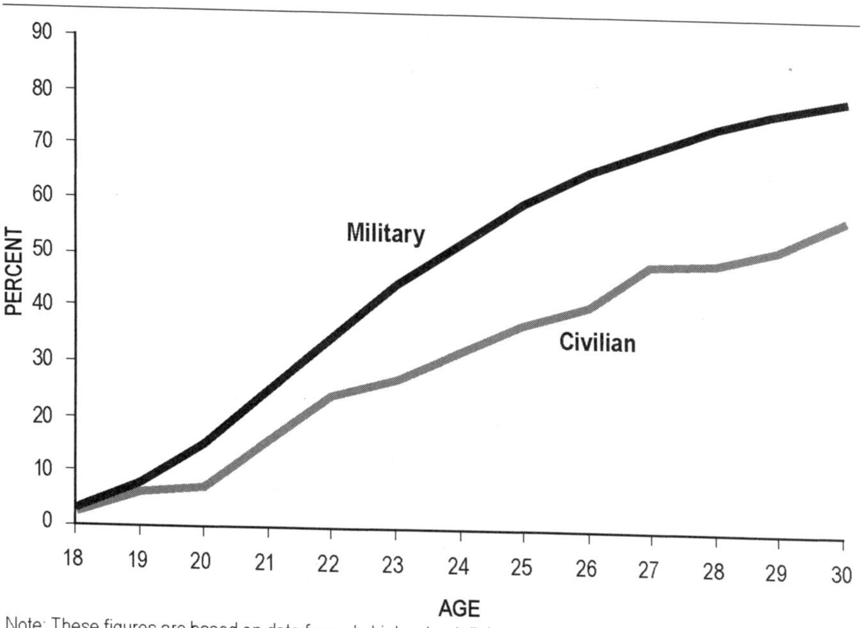

Note: These figures are based on data for male high school diploma graduates working full time in the military or in the civilian sectors. They are averages for the years 1995 to 1999.

Source: Congressional Budget Office, "Family Status of Enlisted Personnel," CBO Technical Paper (by John Cadigan), August 2000.

A more experienced force is also likely to include a higher proportion of married personnel with family responsibilities. With the advent of the all-volunteer force, the percentage of married servicemembers, which had fallen to a Cold War low of 45 percent during the heavy draft calls of the 1960s, quickly rose toward 60 percent. Although this increased the cost of family benefits, it also made family support an important aspect of military readiness.

In addition, the need of a volunteer force to draw high-quality volunteers from a broad population of youth interacted with changes in the role of women in U.S. society as a whole. In 1973, women accounted for only 2 percent of non-prior-service recruits. Today, women play a much broader role in the armed forces, accounting for 15 percent of the active-duty force. One result has been an increase in the number of servicemembers who are married to other servicemembers. Currently, about 47 percent of married women in the military have spouses who are also in the military. This trend, in conjunction with increases in the proportion of the civilian

Figure 10.4. Percent of Civilian and Military Personnel with Children, by Age

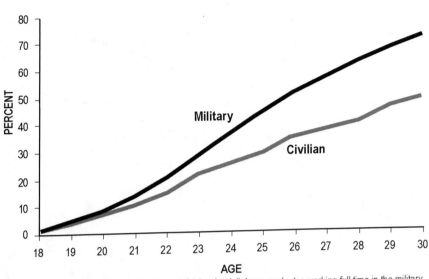

Note: These figures are based on data for male high school diploma graduates working full time in the military or in the civilian sectors. They are averages for the years 1995 to 1999.

Source: Congressional Budget Office, "Family Status of Enlisted Personnel," CBO Technical Paper (by John Cadigan), August 2000.

spouses of servicemembers who work outside the home, increases the demand for services such as child care while reducing the availability of traditional volunteer sources of family support.

Today, higher first-term pay combined with the increased availability of family benefits appears to have affected the makeup of the U.S. military. At least in peacetime, the military is now an exceptionally attractive employer for young high school graduates with family responsibilities. Even after controlling for age, education, employment status, and sex, studies find that military personnel marry and have children earlier than their civilian counterparts. (See Figures 10.3 and 10.4.) About 10 percent of incoming recruits have at least one dependent, and over five percent have more than one. By the end of their first term of service (which is typically about four years), 40 percent of servicemembers are married. This pattern could result either because the military attracts recruits interested in marriage, or because it encourages early marriage, or both. Anecdotal evidence of first-term servicemembers marrying so that they can qualify for housing allowances and move out of on-base dormitories suggests that, at least in some cases, family benefits do encourage early marriage.

The increase in the family responsibilities of young enlisted personnel is a sensitive subject in the United States. Sociologists characterize both the military and the family as "greedy" institutions—institutions that demand an extraordinary amount of time and commitment. Young servicemembers and their spouses, many of whom are even younger, often have difficulty balancing those demands. Studies show that married servicemembers and single members with children are less able to respond to no-notice deployments and are less likely to complete their first term of service than single members without children (although if they do complete it, they are more likely to reenlist).[13] Young married personnel have fewer instances of behavioral problems than do single personnel, but according to commanders, the problems they do have are often more complex and difficult to resolve. Although married senior personnel have faster promotion rates than those who are single, it is not clear that they are any more productive, and thus worth more to the military, than those single personnel who are also promoted rapidly, and who are, in effect, less expensive.

Despite these issues, it may not be politically feasible to reduce the number of very young servicemembers with dependents by cutting family benefits. The availability of low-cost but high-quality health care, housing, groceries, and child care for young military families is not necessarily an issue of cost-effective recruiting and retention. In the eyes of many, it is a matter of national honor. The fact that even a few junior enlisted personnel with large families have qualified for food stamps—a federally supported welfare program—is viewed by many in the military and the Congress as a national scandal. Stories of homeless veterans generate a similar reaction. Given the limited government benefits for families available to the U.S. civilian population, it is difficult for the military to ensure that families in the military do not suffer hardship, while at the same time not attracting or retaining those young families who are least equipped to deal with the stresses of military life.

---

13. Audrey Burman, et al., *Army Families and Soldier Readiness*, R-3884-A (Santa Monica, Calif.: RAND, 2002), p. vii.

The tension between these goals is particularly acute within the U.S. Marine Corps, a service that combines a need for youth, vigor, and frequent unaccompanied deployments with a strong tradition of taking care of its own. In 1993, Marine Commandant Carl Mundy directed the Marines to restrict enlistments to single personnel. That policy, interpreted by some in the media as an attack on families, provoked a public outcry and was immediately rescinded. It has been replaced by a policy that has brought marriage rates down somewhat by requiring counseling for first-term personnel who plan to marry. Benefits for young families who are in the military, however, have never been greater. For example, on-base family housing, which was once a privilege of rank, is now more available to the families of first-term personnel, as they are considered the least able to manage off-base.

Potential Advantages of Deferred and In-kind Benefits Over Cash Pay

Supporters of the current U.S. military compensation system emphasize the potential advantages of offering family-friendly in-kind benefits as well as deferred benefits and pays to veterans and retirees. The question raised by the U.S. compensation system is not whether there should be such benefits, but rather how to achieve a cost-effective mix of cash, deferred, and in-kind compensation.

For example, deferred benefits that protect disabled military veterans from destitution and that provide them with health care may be a cost-effective way to protect national honor. Military retirement pay may prove more effective than immediate cash pays in encouraging both the retention of mid-career personnel and the departure of senior personnel whose services are no longer required by the military

Subsidized goods and service can also be cost-effective in some circumstances. One argument for providing servicemembers with some free or low-cost goods and services, rather than providing cash pay that the member could spend as he or she desired, is that the consumption of those goods and services contributes to military readiness. For example, free or subsidized gyms may encourage servicemembers to remain fit. High-quality child care, family medical care, and housing may also enhance readiness if, in the absence of such benefits, family concerns would distract deployed servicemembers from their jobs. Some argue that encouraging servicemembers to live together in military communities enhances military cohesion.

In-kind benefits might also be cost-effective if the military can provide them for less than it would cost members to purchase them independently. The ability to pool risk allows DoD, like private employers in the United States, to provide health insurance for less than it would cost individual workers on their own. In theory, it could also be less costly for DoD to provide on-base communities than to require servicemembers who are assigned to new duty locations to search within unfamiliar civilian communities for housing, schools, and child care.

Still other family-oriented benefits, such as DoD's efforts to make deployments more predictable, are not market goods that could be purchased by individual servicemembers at any price. Where the military can identify and ease conflicts between family life and military service at little cost, such an approach to retaining servicemembers can be very cost-effective, given that a volunteer force will be mostly a married force.

These are explanations of why some elements of deferred compensation and in-kind benefits could make a cost-effective contribution to the military compensation package. However, these justifications cannot explain the full extent of the deferred compensation that the U.S. military provides, the kinds of goods and services it offers servicemembers and their families, the subsidized prices it charges for those goods and services, or the use of government employees to produce some of the services.

In the case of deferred benefits, many studies indicate that servicemembers and their families heavily discount future benefits and are, as a result, likely to value deferred compensation at less than its cost to the federal government. Thus, as an incentive, it is not generally cost-effective.[14] Attitudes toward risk also reduce the value of retirement benefits to servicemembers. Only about 15 percent of each incoming cohort will remain on active duty for the twenty years necessary to qualify for retirement benefits, and even servicemembers who plan to stay in the military for twenty years know that they may have to leave earlier for health or other reasons. Although in 2001 the military sought and gained increases in health-care benefits for retirees, military compensation experts both within and outside of the Department of Defense

---

14. See John Warner and Saul Pleeter, "The Personal Discount Rate: Evidence from Military Downsizing Programs," *American Economic Review*, Vol. 91, No. 1 (March 2001), pp. 33-53.

argued that such benefits, viewed as a tool for retention, were much less cost-effective than increases in cash.

In many cases, military readiness does not seem to explain the types of goods and services that DoD chooses to provide. For example, it is hard to argue that DoD-operated slot machines or sales of alcohol and tobacco at attractive prices promote military readiness. DoD's role in offering easy access to credit cards for junior personnel may, in some cases, create financial problems that actually reduce readiness.

In other cases, the disconnect between justification and practice is more subtle. Health care is an area in which some DoD involvement is cost-effective, given the contribution of servicemembers' health to readiness and DoD's ability to lower costs by pooling risk. Those arguments, however, do not easily explain increases made in recent years to the health-care benefit provided to military retirees and their dependents. The issue is not whether DoD should offer health insurance, but how much it should be subsidized by DoD and to what extent it should be provided through hospitals and clinics operated directly by the military.

Health plans offered by private U.S. firms typically require employees to share the cost of premiums and to pay deductibles and co-payments. Premiums are often higher for families than for individuals. In addition, fewer and fewer private employers are offering health-care benefits to retirees. The cost of health care for large private employers is roughly 8 cents for each dollar of salaries and wages they pay.[15] Although employers could offer more generous health insurance, they have found that their workers are unwilling to pay for it through lower cash wages.

DoD, in contrast, offers virtually free, unlimited health care to most military beneficiaries, including the dependents of active-duty personnel and retirees and their dependents. As a result, DoD beneficiaries use medical services at a higher rate than do comparable civilian employees and their dependents. In some cases, DoD may also attract or retain individuals in need of generous health-care benefits. For example, despite the hardships associated with deployments and frequent moves, more than 100,000 military families have members with disabilities.[16]

---

15. CBO, *Growth in Medical Spending*, p. 9.
16. From *Special Needs*, a fact sheet provided by the Department of Defense, at <www.militaryhomefront.dod>, January 2005.

In 2003, DoD spent 50 cents in health care for each dollar of cash it paid to active-duty personnel. Under current policies this is projected to rise to 80 cents by 2020.[17] Given the choice, as in a cafeteria plan for benefits, many active-duty members might choose to accept more modest lifetime health-care coverage in exchange for higher current cash compensation.

Similarly, the argument that DoD can provide on-base housing, stores, and child care at lower cost than if servicemembers had to search individually in unfamiliar civilian communities might explain why DoD would offer access to such services. But by itself it does not explain why DoD provides them at less than their cost to DoD. If it chose, DoD could sell the goods and services to members at cost. Members could use their cash salaries to choose the mix of goods and services they preferred, and would thus get the greatest benefit per dollar spent by DoD. If servicemembers were not willing to purchase goods and services from DoD at prices that would allow DoD to recoup its costs, the department would have a clear signal that the cost of access to goods and services on-base exceeded its value to servicemembers. The use of cash could also equalize the cost of the compensation offered to married and single personnel. By linking pay more closely to skill and experience, rather than family status, this could reduce the cost to DoD of maintaining a high-quality force.

Even if one were to accept the tenuous argument that heavy subsidies for family-oriented benefits are cost-effective because of their impact on military readiness, this would not explain why the federal government produces many of the subsidized services itself, instead of relying on the private sector. If DoD wished to provide goods and services at subsidized prices to enhance military readiness, it could contract with private firms instead of operating its own retail activities and child-care centers using special government employees.

In the United States, it is difficult to argue that government-sponsored monopolies can operate grocery and general retail stores more cheaply and efficiently than stores in the competitive private sector. DoD does argue that it can provide some peacetime health care at lower cost than the private sector because its own system of military doctors and hospitals, designed to meet wartime requirements, would otherwise be underutilized. Many, however, would question whether

---

17. CBO, *Growth in Medical Spending*, p. 16.

this argument, based on DoD's wartime needs, applies to its military hospitals in the United States in which, during peacetime, normal childbirth is the most common reason for admission.

In addition, many military benefits, including DoD-operated and subsidized on-base family housing and stores, make less sense today than they did in the past. As the United States moves to a more expeditionary military, and families stay behind at installations in the United States, the argument that it is less costly for DoD to provide on-base communities that are separate from civilian society is weakened. Military families that "homestead," rather than rotate overseas, are better able to search out housing, child care, and schools in civilian communities near military bases. Internet-based tools also reduce the costs of such searches. Recent improvements in cost-of-living and housing allowances that vary across geographic areas ensure that private-sector goods and services are affordable in all but a very few isolated locations.

Other social changes have also reduced the benefits of separate military communities. As the size of the active-duty military declines relative to the civilian population, and fewer citizens have contact with the active-duty force, integrating the small professional military into civilian communities could help ensure that each would be exposed to the values and beliefs of the other. Otherwise, for example, military families who benefit from free health care and heavily subsidized child care might be increasingly isolated from the day-to-day concerns that face civilian families in the United States. One of the risks of a professional, career-oriented military is that, unless its members are integrated into civilian society, their norms may diverge from that of the broader society. For example, despite increasing acceptance of homosexuals in U.S. society as a whole, acknowledged homosexuals are not allowed in the military because of concerns that their presence might disrupt fellow servicemembers.

To a large degree, therefore, the view that on-base communities are an effective way to support the families of deployed troops appears out of date. More and more reliance is being placed on reservists, who almost all live in civilian communities. Yet a deployed reservist who is a single parent is much less likely to have access to DoD child care than the two-earner family of a non-deployed active-duty member. This raises equity issues in a system that relies on military bases to provide support to the families of deployed personnel.

Alternatives to the Current System

Questions about the cost-effectiveness of benefits that are focused primarily on families and are DoD-subsidized or even produced by DoD are not new. Any number of proposals have been advanced that would make military compensation more marriage-neutral and leave DoD leaders free to concentrate on their core warfighting missions rather than on running small cities on-base.

For example, housing might be dealt with by gradually raising the allowances of single members until they match those of married personnel, and then allowing members to rent housing—on or off base—at a market-clearing rent. The price of goods and services from DoD-controlled retail activities could be set equal to their cost to the federal government. More generally, the military might move in the direction taken by some civilian employers, who offer "cafeteria-style" benefit plans in which employees are given a budget constraint within which to construct their own preferred package of benefits from a menu of options. The cafeteria approach ensures that workers do not consume benefits that they do not value; at the same time it equalizes the total value of benefits received by different employees.

Changes in family-oriented in-kind benefits would need to address the issue of junior enlisted personnel. Although junior personnel with large families are a small percent of the force, they cannot be neglected. At least in the United States, restricting the enlistment of all individuals with dependents is not politically feasible. The Marine Corps model might be used, however: recruits with dependents, and first-term personnel planning on marriage or about to have children, might be required to undergo extensive counseling. Those who did marry or have children and then found themselves in financial or stressful marital difficulties might apply to DoD for low-cost counseling as well as aid in paying for child care, groceries, and housing. Mandatory financial counseling and the development of a plan to reduce the need for future aid could be required, and failure to follow an agreed plan and achieve financial stability could be a bar to reenlistment or a cause for dismissal. To the degree that marital and financial stress is truly an impediment to readiness, this could be viewed not as a civilian welfare program or an intrusion on servicemembers' personal lives, but as another aspect of military training and discipline.

Support for the families of deployed troops is another area in which DoD, with its special knowledge and its familiarity with the military mission, must play an ongoing role. This role might be met through Internet-based or regional networks of family support programs that would work with all active and reserve families affected by a deployment, regardless of whether they live on or off base and regardless of which service—Army, Navy, Marine Corps, or Air Force—they are associated with. Emphasis would be on providing information about the deployments and about local community support services.

Why Does DoD Continue to Rely Heavily on Deferred and In-Kind Benefits?

Why continue current policies? Why doesn't the United States make its policies marriage-neutral, provide cash payments, and then recruit and retain soldiers in the fair expectation that—given a volunteer force—many of those it retains will be married personnel with a preference for military service and a spouse who is able and willing to accommodate the demands that service will place on the family?

One reason for the persistence of deferred pay and benefits and of family-oriented in-kind benefits is that these were a tradition among the senior leaders who helped to shape the all-volunteer force. Later, as the volunteer force matured, the growing career force and the growing number of retirees and military dependents provided additional support for in-kind benefits for both active-duty and retired servicemembers.

On the whole, most compensation experts believe that servicemembers would be better off if DoD increased cash pay while reducing deferred pay and in-kind benefits. But one source of resistance to such a move is that many advocates for military personnel believe, perhaps correctly, that deferred pay and in-kind benefits tend to be more permanent than cash pays: if servicemembers were to give them up in exchange for more cash, the higher cash pay might be subject to erosion. In the end, DoD would have a more cost-effective force, but servicemembers might not have an equally generous compensation package.

Another concern relates to the distribution of benefits. Only about 15 percent of servicemembers remain in the military until retirement, and not all servicemembers and military retirees who are eligible for in-kind benefits use them. As a result, if all current servicemembers were free to choose between cash and deferred or in-kind benefits, those who do not expect to receive deferred benefits and those who do not currently use their in-kind benefits would choose cash and thus raise DoD's costs. Alternatively, in the unlikely event that the Congress were to require the military to quit offering deferred and in-kind benefits and use the savings to increase cash pay, at least some members of the military would be worse off. Among the greatest losers would be future retirees and those families that rely the most on in-kind benefits.

An important but often overlooked factor behind the persistence of in-kind benefits is that DoD does not pay the full economic costs of its activities when it produces goods and services in-house. This can make it appear less costly, from DoD's budgetary perspective, to produce services in-house rather than to pay servicemembers in cash or to subsidize purchases of goods and services from private providers. One of the economic costs of production that does not show up in the DoD budget— but is nonetheless a real cost to the U.S. economy—is the forgone return on capital invested in DoD child-care centers, housing, and stores. In addition, retail sales are a particularly attractive activity for the military because DoD-operated stores are exempt from state and local sales taxes as well as from state and local excise taxes on alcohol and cigarettes. These tax exemptions give DoD a significant advantage over private-sector providers who operate on very narrow margins. According to one estimate, less than one-third of the subsidies enjoyed by on-base retail activities actually appear in DoD's budget.[18] Because DoD does not bear the full cost of its retail activities, receipts from the activities exceed recorded costs, giving the department funds that do not need to be appropriated by the Congress.

Those who operate DoD activities or provide supplies to them also have a vested interest in continuing the current system. Military doctors and hospitals are proud of their role and fight to preserve it. The federal employees who work in VA hospitals and DoD-operated stores can be protective of their jobs. In addition, private industry has adapted to meet the unique needs of DoD's retail activities, so that there is now an organized association of brokers and suppliers whose livelihood depends on DoD maintaining its on-base communities.

---

18. CBO, *The Costs and Benefits of Retail Activities at Military Bases.*

The U.S. public supports the U.S. military, particularly in times of war, and those who would change the current system risk being publicly characterized by critics as opponents of the military. If anything, the trend in recent years has been to provide new benefits, including new health-care benefits to retirees and reservists, and to build new housing and child-care centers for active-duty personnel.

It is difficult to imagine a scenario in which DoD would actively seek a major shift toward cash compensation. However, the creation of a budget display that showed the total cost of military personnel might at least help forestall further growth in deferred and in-kind benefits. This would allow the public, Congress, and DoD leadership to track what is happening to total military compensation and compare it with trends in the civilian sector. Currently, the costs of veterans' benefits, housing, child care, commissaries, and some health care are not integrated into the same account used to make cash payments to military personnel. Displays that would show costs by rank for married and single personnel might help foster a debate about marriage-neutrality.

Meanwhile, the continuation of current compensation policies has broad implications for the military. If the average compensation cost for an active-duty servicemember is about $99,000, and if the servicemember can only be deployed one year in three, the average compensation cost for maintaining the capability to deploy an active-duty soldier is almost $300,000 a year.[19] That rough estimate omits some deployment-related compensation, such as family separation pay, hazardous-duty pay, and the federal income tax exemption tied to deployments. Moreover, it reflects only compensation costs. Thus it does not include personnel costs that are not part of the compensation package, such as the costs of training military personnel over their careers or the costs of transporting and supporting them in-theater during deployments.

That $300,000 price tag may encourage the U.S. to rely more on contractors and labor-saving technologies, even when military boots on the ground might be the most effective solution. In addition, to the extent that DoD is responsible for providing and overseeing non-cash benefits for military families, the attention of its leaders is not on the military's

---

19. See the Congressional Budget Office, *Logistics Support for Deployed Military Forces*, October 2005, p. 30, for a discussion of rotation base requirements.

primary mission. The U.S. system of relying on in-kind benefits to retain families, rather than cash pays to retain servicemembers, raises issues of fairness between single and married personnel and may reduce the level of military capability that the United States can achieve with a given budget.

Because it has proven so difficult to change the U.S. system, solutions to the high cost of military personnel may ultimately lead to the creation of new categories of military personnel rather than changes in the benefits to which military families currently feel entitled. One option would be a system that allowed contractors or DoD civilians with particularly desirable skills to become members of a military auxiliary in wartime, temporarily entering the military as specialists at an appropriate paygrade. That approach might provide cost-effective military manpower—under the direct command of the military and subject to the Uniform Code of Military Justice that applies to all U.S. military personnel—without directly challenging the current system of subsidized, in-kind benefits for the permanent active-duty force.

Conclusion

Some NATO members are seeking to improve the quality of life for military families and to expand the array of benefits they provide to such families. In some instances, the benefits provided by European governments to military families are already more generous than in the United States. For example, several Western European governments provide cash supplements to servicemembers with families. In general, however, family benefits are not as extensive in Europe's militaries as they are in the U.S. military, and some European leaders are examining the U.S. model for ideas. However, the U.S. system of compensation that focuses on retaining families, rather than retaining soldiers who may have families, has had some unintended consequences. Whether other nations would face similar consequences from such policies would depend on the specific economic, social, and military circumstances in those nations. Nonetheless, the U.S. experience points to five broad lessons that may apply, in part or in whole, to at least some other nations.

First, a country should proceed cautiously when introducing policies such as across-the-board pay raises or in-kind family benefits that servicemembers might come to view as an entitlement. A nation that is in the process of implementing a new system for paying volunteer personnel may have many options, but once a system is in place, it may be difficult to change.

Second, it is necessary to proceed with even greater caution in the case of benefits likely to create broad constituencies outside of the active-duty military, such as a benefit that serves former military personnel and their dependents, or one whose provision involves government employees or specialized government contractors.

Third, in making changes to military compensation, a country must be alert to possible unintended consequences. Will alleviating the hardships faced by one group create inequities from the perspective of other servicemembers? What incentives—desirable or otherwise—does a policy create for servicemembers or decision-makers?

Fourth, it may be a good idea to make all costs of military compensation visible within the budget for military personnel. This might involve the use of accrual accounting so that the cost of deferred benefits for retirees, veterans, or their dependents appears in the budget as part of the cost of today's military personnel.

Finally, the balance among cash pays, deferred compensation, and in-kind benefits should be monitored, and it should be recognized that, while there are exceptions, cash pay is generally most cost-effective. Choices about how compensation is provided can make a big difference in its cost-effectiveness. Because benefits provided in kind restrict individual choice, they are generally—although not always—less efficient than cash payments. Deferred benefits may also be inefficient if military members have a strong preference for benefits today over benefits later.

As the U.S. experience illustrates, it can be difficult to change an existing system that relies on deferred pays and in-kind, family-friendly benefits instead of cash. Countries that are starting from a relatively clean slate, and are just now developing compensation policies for a volunteer force, may have a better opportunity to develop a balanced, cost-effective, and transparent system combining cash, in-kind, and deferred compensation.

Chapter 11

The British Experience with an All-Volunteer Force

Keith Hartley

The UK introduced an all-volunteer force (AVF) in 1963. This chapter describes the background to that shift, from a mixed conscript-volunteer force to an all-volunteer force. It then reviews and analyzes the current state of the UK's AVF. It describes how the UK armed forces have adjusted to the "defense economics problem" presented by budget constraints and rising input costs for both equipment and personnel. These economic pressures have required defense policy-makers to make difficult choices, especially in relation to the UK's continued desire to remain a world military power. For the future, there are challenges both for the UK's armed forces and for its military personnel in adjusting to new threats and a different security environment. The British experience has potential lessons for other nations that have chosen an AVF, as they too will be unable to ignore the defense economics problem. They will have to consider substitution opportunities, radically reviewing their defense commitments, seeking further efficiency improvements, and allocating more money for higher military salaries.

The UK's Shift to an AVF

By the mid-1950s, the UK's Conservative government was concerned about the economic burdens of defense. The costs of defense in terms of "manpower, materials and money" were overloading the economy. There was a desire to release resources, especially military personnel, for the improvement of UK industrial production. Continued concern about the increasing costs of defense in relation to the UK's internal and external performance (exports and the balance of payments), together with advances in military technology, led to the 1957 Defence Review.[1] This followed a period during and after the Korean War when defense spending had absorbed some 10 percent of GDP, which the 1957 Defence Review declared "too high."[2] Manpower being used in both the armed forces and defense industries had alternative uses in civil industry; defense was thus absorbing an "undue" proportion of scarce scientists and engineers (the "crowding-out" hypothesis).[3] Defense was consuming one-eighth of the output of the metal-using industries, which were important to Britain's export trade.[4] It affected the general level of taxation. The large numbers of UK military personnel based overseas had direct and adverse balance-of-payments impacts. International equity comparisons provided support for the view that the UK was bearing a disproportionately large share of the total NATO European defense burden. Figure 11.1 shows the UK's relative defense burden during the 1950s compared with its major European allies, which were also its rivals in world export markets.

The 1957 Defence Review was the first significant review of UK defense spending since 1950. There was a need for a new approach that would reflect major changes in military technology and strategy (nuclear weapons, rockets, missiles); a change in the nature of the threat facing the UK; the need to adjust the shape of UK armed forces from that set in 1950 at the time of the Korean War; and recognition of the increasing demands of defense on the nation's economic resources. The 1957 Defence Review announced the substitution of nuclear forces for large-scale conventional forces, based on the UK's independent nuclear deterrent.[5]

---

1. Ministry of Defence, "Defence White Paper: Outline of Future Policy," Cmnd 124 (London: Her Majesty's Stationery Office [HMSO], 1957); hereafter referred to as *1957 Defence White Paper*. ("Cmnd" is a Government Command Paper.)
2. *1957 Defence White Paper*. In 1952, the defense share of GDP was 9.8 percent, in 1953 it was 9.7 percent, and in 1954 it was 9.2 percent.
3. The crowding-out hypothesis states that defense spending adversely affects economic performance by diverting research and development (R&D) and production resources, especially scientists and skilled labor, from civilian to military purposes.
4. *1957 Defence White Paper*.
5. The 1957 Defence Review also called for an end to manned combat air-

Figure 11.1. NATO Europe Defense Burdens (Defense Share of GDP), 1953–63

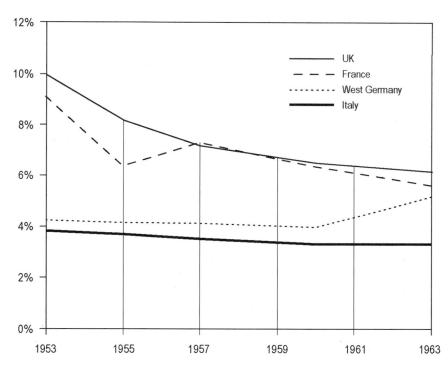

Source: *SIPRI Yearbook 1975* (Stockholm: Stockholm International Peace Research Institute [SIPRI], 1975).

THE END OF CONSCRIPTION AND THE TRANSITION TO AN AVF

In the UK, compulsory service in the armed forces was a feature of the two World Wars and was continued on a fixed-term basis by the Labour government after 1945. In 1957, the UK's armed forces comprised a mix of regulars and conscripts, with conscripts accounting for 35 percent of total military personnel, but more realistically the conscript share was over 50 percent (see Table 11.1).[6] In peacetime, UK conscription (known

craft. However, as late as 2003, the UK was receiving first deliveries of its Typhoon combat aircraft; it plans to purchase the U.S. Joint Strike Fighter with deliveries originally planned around 2012. Thus the 1957 forecast of the end of manned combat aircraft had not been achieved some fifty years later.
6.   The calculation leading to the 35 percent conscript share is misleading, since it considers as regulars many members who chose to join the Army for

Table 11.1. UK Armed Forces: 1956–57 (Thousands)

Type	1956				1957			
	Royal Navy	Army	RAF	Total	Royal Navy	Army	RAF	Total
Regulars	106,600	198,900	161,700	467,200	102,200	194,800	155,100	451,900
National Service	11,600	202,600	74,800	289,000	9,800	172,300	69,600	251,700
Women	3,900	6,500	6,100	16,500	3,700	6,200	5,300	15,200
Total	122,100	408,000	242,600	772,700	115,700	373,300	230,000	718,800

Note: In 1957, Army regulars included over 115,000 personnel who were on three-year engagements only. Data for 1957 are shown since this was the year of the Defence White Paper; but the 1957 numbers were presented as estimates. Regulars and National Service personnel are all males.

Source: *Defence Statistics 1957–58*, Cmnd 130 (London: HMSO, April 1957).

as National Service) achieved equity through a universal service obligation, requiring all fit males 18 years of age and over to serve in the armed forces for two years. Deferment was allowed for attendance at university or a similar educational institution.

The 1957 Defence Review announced that conscription and certain reserve forces were to be abolished and replaced by a relatively small AVF, initially planned at 375,000 personnel, to be achieved by the end of 1962. This planned AVF would replace a UK force that had some 700,000 military personnel in 1957, releasing over 300,000 men from the armed forces (see Figure 11.2). The target AVF of some 375,000 personnel was expected to comprise 20 percent for the Royal Navy (75,000 personnel), over 40 percent for the Army (over 150,000), and almost 40 percent for the RAF (under 150,000). The basis of the targets was the government belief that a force of 375,000 was about the limit of what the nation could sustain with volunteers.[7]

---

three years for officer training rather than be conscripted. In fact, in 1957, fewer than 80,000 Army personnel were on engagements of more than three years. Adjusting accordingly for Army personnel gives a conscript share of 51 percent; further adjustments for the other services would be needed to arrive at a more accurate figure. Prior to 1914, the UK historically had a tradition and preference for all-volunteer forces.

7. Hansard, *Debate on 1957 Defence White Paper*, D. Sandys, vol. 568 (1957), p. 1782; see also Ministry of Defence, *Progress of Five Year Plan* (London: HMSO, 1959); Ministry of Defence, *Defence Statistics 1957-58*, Cmnd 130 (London: HMSO).

Figure 11.2. UK Military Personnel, 1950–2005

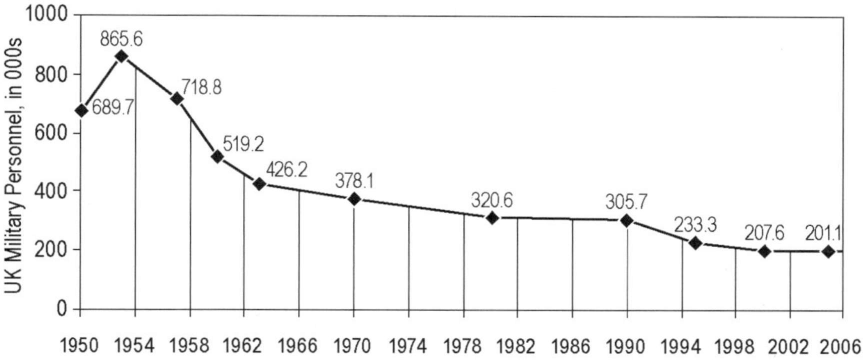

Source: MoD/DASA, *UK Defence Statistics 1997* (London: The Stationery Office, 1997); MoD/DASA, *UK Defence Statistics 2002* (London: The Stationery Office, 2002); MoD/DASA, *UK Defence Statistics 2003* (London: The Stationery Office, 2003); MoD/DASA, *UK Defence Statistics 2005* (London: The Stationery Office, 2005).

Note: Selected years are shown in which significant events affected the numbers: 1953 was peak of Korean War; 1957 was the Defence Review; 1963 was change to an AVF; 1990 was the end of the Cold War and a Defence Review; 1995 was the year of a defense efficiency review known as "Front Line First"; 2000 and 2005 show recent years.

The transition from conscription to an AVF required an adjustment period. The 1957 Defence White Paper announced that the last call-up would be in 1960 and that National Service would end in 1962. During the transition, the numbers available for National Service exceeded the numbers needed by the armed forces. The government rejected a ballot (a lottery) as a solution for the adjustment and decided to make the adjustment by raising the age of call-up. Men born before October 1938 (age 18 and older in 1956, including those whose service had been deferred) were called up for National Service. It was decided not to call up those born in 1940, although they were legally liable for National Service starting in 1958. Adjustment was not restricted to conscription. The 1957 plans to reshape the UK's armed forces also involved adjustment issues and costs for regular personnel. There were special lump-sum payments to entice redundant military personnel to leave the force; the rules for retirement pay for premature (early) retirements were relaxed.

In its 1957 Defence White Paper, the government recognized the potential recruitment problems for an AVF. It announced that if the UK failed to recruit sufficient numbers for an AVF, it would consider re-introducing a limited form of conscription.[8] It acknowledged that the task of recruiting an AVF would not be easy, and that the problems would not be the same for all three services.[9] The Royal Navy was already a mainly regular force. The RAF had a 66 percent regular strength, so it, too, was expected to cope with the AVF. The Army, most dependent on National Service, was expected to have the greatest difficulty. To encourage recruiting, the government declared its intention of making service life more attractive. To do so, it introduced various measures, including across-the-board pay increases; the provision of a career structure; and after 1969, the introduction of a military salary based on the principle of comparability with the civil sector.

In the event, over the period 1963–75, the armed forces rarely exceeded 90 percent of their target, only achieving it in 1971–72.[10] Similarly, over the period 1980 to 2005, there was typically a net outflow of military personnel, especially officers. However, in the late 1990s through 2002, the net flow for other ranks was in balance, and a small net inflow was achieved in 2002–04, but there remained a net outflow for officers.[11]

THE CASE FOR ABOLISHING CONSCRIPTION

The government's case for abolishing conscription was that it was extremely wasteful in its use of manpower, especially in the training organization. For example, in 1957, there were 150,000 men training or being trained, which reflected the continuous turnover that was inevitable with National Service.[12] The increasing costs, complexity, and skill requirements of modern weapons contributed to the end of conscription in the UK by requiring costly training for the necessary skilled labor.

---

8.   *1957 Defence White Paper*, para. 48.

9.   Ibid., para. 50.

10. G. Harries-Jenkins, "The British Experience with the All-Volunteer Force," in J.B. Keeley, ed., *The All-Volunteer Force and American Society* (Charlottesville: University Press of Virginia, 1978).

11. Ministry of Defence, Defence Analytical Services Agency (DASA), *UK Defence Statistics 2003* (London: The Stationery Office, 2003); DASA, *UK Defence Statistics 2005* (London: The Stationery Office, 2005).

12. *1957 Defence White Paper*, para. 43; Hansard, *Debate on 1957 Defence White Paper*, p. 1770.

Government policy-makers and politicians believed that a more efficient solution would involve skilled, experienced, and hence longer-service regulars. People able to use and to maintain modern weapons effectively would give the armed forces a worthwhile return on their substantial and rising training costs and investments in personnel. For example, by 1966, training outlays were almost 10 percent of the UK defense budget; in the 1980s, the RAF required three years to train a combat-jet pilot at a cost of £3 million (1987 prices); a minimum of six years of productive service was needed to justify such training costs. By 1998, this training period was 5.5 years at a cost of £5.8 million (1998 prices).[13] Such high training expenditures meant that the armed forces could not afford to ignore the relative efficiency of varying the length of service in its employment contracts in order to obtain an adequate return on their increasingly costly human capital investments.

It was widely recognized in government, the military, and Parliament that conscription was an inefficient method of acquiring military personnel.[14] Labor may appear to be relatively "cheap" in budgetary terms, but budgets fail to reflect the true opportunity cost of labor in terms of its alternative use and value elsewhere in the economy. (See Chapter 5 by John Warner and Sebastian Negrusa in this volume.) As labor was relatively cheap, military commanders were encouraged to substitute labor for capital (weapons) and to adopt labor-intensive forces. Conscription also required substantial training, but the armed forces often lost their valuable investments in human capital after the two years of conscript service, resulting in high labor turnover costs. Furthermore, there were adverse motivational aspects of conscription which could not be ignored. It was "involuntary servitude," as young males in the population provided "payments in kind" to finance UK defense spending and policy. Such an employment contract does not

---

13. K. Hartley, "The All-Volunteer Force: An Economics Perspective," in G. Harries-Jenkins, ed., *Recruitment to the All-Volunteer Force*, Report for U.S. Army Research Institute for Behavioral and Social Sciences (Hull: University of Hull, 2001).

14. In the Parliamentary debate on the *1957 Defence White Paper*, the government stated that, "National Service is extremely wasteful in its use of manpower." The Opposition agreed that the "end of National Service will lead to smaller, more efficient, highly mobile and less costly forces." Hansard, *Debate on 1957 Defence White Paper*, pp. 1770, 1778.

encourage efficient behavior by conscript personnel. In fact, the opposite result emerged: the armed forces were characterized by major inefficiencies as conscript personnel consumed "on-the-job leisure." The result was "organizational slack" and inefficiency. In addition, resources were devoted to avoiding or deferring the draft, and therefore further resources had to be devoted to policing and enforcing the system. The abolition of conscription was also a potential vote-winner for vote-maximizing governments and political parties, giving all of the major UK political parties an incentive to adopt policies favoring an AVF.

Economic theory predicts that the abolition of conscription and the introduction of an AVF would make military personnel relatively more expensive from a budgetary point of view, leading to reduced numbers and encouraging extensive substitution effects.[15] It would predict substitutions between equipment (capital or weapons) and labor, between skilled and unskilled labor, between reserves and regulars, between service personnel and civilians, and between men and women.[16] As an example of reduced numbers, it was expected that the end of UK National Service would release over 100,000 soldiers employed on non-operational duties.[17]

The impact of introducing an AVF on total defense budgets and labor costs would depend on the magnitude of the changes in relative factor prices (the prices of labor and of capital) and on the possibilities of substitution. In 1957, the government's view was that its new defense policy would save taxpayers quite a lot of money and would also lead to manpower savings.[18] However, no forecasts were provided of the level of future UK defense expenditure, apart from an expectation that it would not decline "in any way comparable [to] the manpower strengths

---

15. Interestingly, in contrast to the United States, economists in the UK did not contribute much to the debate about the relative merits of the draft versus an AVF. See K. Hartley and T. Sandler, eds., *The Economics of Defence*, The International Library of Critical Writings in Economics, No. 128 (Cheltenham, UK: Elgar, 2001), Vol. II.

16. The principle of substitution was acknowledged when the UK government linked the nuclear deterrent to conscription: "If we refuse to rely upon the deterrent we cannot urge the abolition of National Service." Hansard, *Debate on 1957 Defence White Paper*, p. 1958.

17. *1957 Defence White Paper*, p. 6.

18. Hansard, *Debate on 1957 Defence White Paper*, p. 1774.

of the Forces."[19] In the event, real UK defense spending rose by some 11 percent between 1963 and 1968, followed by fluctuations, leaving defense spending by 1977 some 3 percent higher (in real terms) than the 1963 level.[20] However, since the introduction of an AVF, defense as a share of GDP has shown a long-run downward trend, from some 6 percent of GDP in 1963 to just 2.3 percent in 2004.[21] There has been a more substantial long-run downward trend in the number of UK military personnel. From the 375,000 troops initially envisioned for the AVF, numbers have fallen by another 46 percent, to 201,100 in 2005, as shown in Figure 11.2.

The Evolution of the UK's All-Volunteer Force

The record of UK defense policy since the introduction of the AVF has been one of continued need to adapt the UK's commitments and its desire to be a world power to its budget constraints. Thus, major defense reviews were undertaken at frequent intervals.[22] The Reviews resulted in the cancellation of major defense programs, the withdrawal of UK forces from overseas bases, a narrowing of global focus to a concentration on Europe, and reductions of military personnel in support areas and in front-line forces.[23]

THE DEFENSE ECONOMICS PROBLEM

The defense economics problem has compelled the UK to make difficult defense choices. The defense economics problem—a standard economic problem of the need for choices in a world of uncertainty—results from constant or falling defense budgets (in real terms) and rising input costs

---

19. *1957 Defence White Paper*, para. 72.

20. K. Hartley, "The Cold War, Great Power Traditions and Military Posture: Determinants of British Defence Expenditure after 1945," *Defence and Peace Economics*, Vol. 8, No. 1 (1997), pp. 17–35.

21. Ministry of Defence, DASA, *UK Defence Statistics 2004* (London: The Stationery Office, 2004).

22. Major defense reviews were undertaken in 1965–68 by the Labour Government, in 1975 by the Labour Government, in 1981 by the Conservative Government, in 1990–91 by the Conservative Government, in 1994–95 by the Conservative Government ("Front Line First"), and in 1998 and 2003–04 by the Labour Government.

23. Hartley, "The Cold War, Great Power Traditions and Military Posture."

of both equipment and personnel. UK equipment unit costs have typically been rising at some 10 percent per annum in real terms, reflecting the increasing technological complexity of modern weapons. As a result, smaller numbers have been purchased and weapons are no longer replaced on a one-for-one basis.

Moreover, military personnel costs in the form of pay for an AVF must be higher or must rise faster than wage increases in the civilian sector in order to attract and retain personnel. Individuals choose to serve in the forces for a variety of reasons, including patriotism and a commitment to public service, while some have a positive preference for military life, its status, and its associated dangers. But when the dangers and rigors of military life—such as military discipline, unsocial hours and conditions, overseas service, use of lethal force, and the possibility of death or injury on active service—are weighed against the benefits, many perceive a net negative. As a result, differential wage increases compared with the civilian sector are needed to compensate personnel for the net disadvantages of military service reflected in the unique nature of the military employment contract. In the UK, the net disadvantages of military life are compensated in a pay increment dubbed the "X-factor" by the UK MoD.

The defense economics problem applies to all nations. Difficult choices cannot be avoided: something has to go and the question is what. In making its choices, the UK has usually selected from four basic policy options. First, "equal misery" involves cuts across all the services, reflected in less training, the cancellation of some equipment programs, delays in the development and delivery of new equipment, and fewer replacement buys. Second, a major defense review is sometimes undertaken in which the UK reassesses its defense commitments, the size of the defense budget, and the size of its armed forces, and then rebalances among services or programs based on new strategic priorities. Third, efficiency improvements involve more competitive procurement for defense equipment, more outsourcing, and a continued search for economies. Fourth, the need for difficult choices can sometimes be reduced through increased defense spending, but this option shifts the burden from defense to social welfare spending for schools, hospitals, roads, pensions, and the like. Since the end of the Cold War, UK voters have generally preferred social welfare spending over defense spending.

Between 1990 and 2005, UK defense policy was subject to major defense reviews, efficiency drives, and the need to respond to new threats from international terrorism. The UK was also involved in conflicts in the Persian Gulf War of 1991, Bosnia, Kosovo, Afghanistan, and Iraq, as well as the continued commitment in Northern Ireland. During the 1990s, and with the military downsizing following the end of the Cold War, UK defense spending in real terms declined by over 20 percent, from £30.4 billion in 1990–1991 to £23.6 billion in 1999–2000.[24] Most of this reduction occurred over the five years from 1990 to 1995, as the UK's defense policy and its armed forces adjusted to the new post–Cold War security environment.

In 1991, UK defense policy outlined a major restructuring of its armed forces to provide forces that were "smaller but well-equipped, with flexibility and mobility."[25] There were major reductions in military and civilian personnel employed by the UK Ministry of Defence (MoD); withdrawals from overseas bases, especially in Germany; base closures; and the disbanding and amalgamation of Army units. The reductions involved both front-line units and support activities such as administration, management, and organization; recruiting, manning, and training; equipment and logistic support; and bases, repair, and storage facilities. Military personnel numbers were reduced by some 20 percent, and there were similar cuts for support areas (that is, cuts in numbers of military personnel were similar, in percentage terms, to the budget cuts). The Army bore the greatest cuts in personnel at some 25 percent; reductions in the Navy and RAF were 13–16 percent (See Figure 11.3).

Further emphasis on efficiency improvements occurred in 1995 in the form of "Front Line First," a defense study that identified ways to save on support costs without any apparent reduction in front-line capability.[26] The "New Management Strategy (NMS)" and other efficiency-improving measures were reinforced with a further commitment to extend military outsourcing with an emphasis on competing for quality

---

24. Prices for 2001–02 from Ministry of Defence, DASA, *UK Defence Statistics 2002* (London: The Stationery Office, 2002).

25. Ministry of Defence, *Statement on the Defence Estimates: Britain's Defence for the 90s*, vol. 1, Cmnd 1559-I (London: HMSO, 1991), p. 6.

26. Ministry of Defence, *Statement on the Defence Estimates: Stable Forces in a Strong Britain*, Cmnd 2800 (London: HMSO, 1995), p. 8.

Figure 11.3. Military Personnel Cuts Following the End of the Cold War

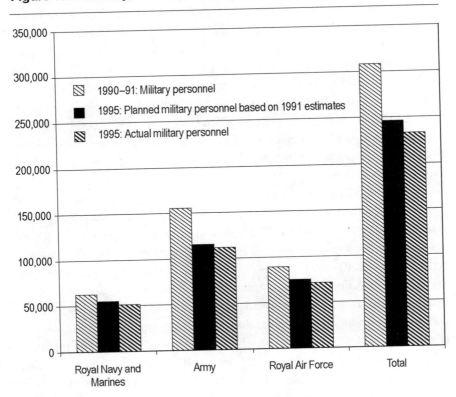

Note: Numbers include trainees. Planned strengths are approximate.

Source: Ministry of Defence, *Statement on the Defence Estimates: Britain's Defence for the 90s*, Cmnd 1559-I (London: HMSO, 1991); Ministry of Defence/DASA, *UK Defence Statistics 1997* (London: The Stationery Office, 1997).

and use of the Private Finance Initiative (PFI), in which private firms financed capital projects and service provision in return for annual rental payments from MoD.

In 1995, there was also an independent review of service career and manpower structures and the terms and conditions of service (the Bett Report).[27] Amongst its recommendations to MoD, the Bett Report suggested a review of rank structures and possible reductions in the num-

27. M. Bett, chair, *Independent Review of the Armed Forces' Manpower Career and Remuneration Structures: Report to the Secretary of State* (London: HMSO, 1995); Ministry of Defence, *Statement on the Defence Estimates* (1995), p. 84.

ber of ranks; measures to improve the employability of service personnel when they leave the forces; a new pension scheme; new and more flexible pay structures; closer alignment of service housing charges with costs of civilian accommodation; and "pay-as-you-dine" arrangements. Some of the recommendations were accepted within the year, such as proposals for a more flexible pay system and the creation of a Service Personnel Board with the responsibility for developing a strategic personnel policy and providing a focus for considering personnel matters at the highest levels. Others were modified by MoD: for example, MoD decided not to implement the full package of changes to the rank structure proposed in the Bett Report (it was, however, decided to end officer promotion to five-star rank in peacetime). Some recommendations were made subject to further studies.[28] Following the Bett Report, MoD embarked on a program of pay modernization for the armed forces which was developed further as part of the 1998 Strategic Defence Review (SDR, discussed further below). Following SDR, with its focus on "overstretch and under-manning," a new pay system was introduced in April 2001, known as "Pay 2000." This system allows the majority of personnel the potential for higher pay and higher career earnings compared with the old system; it rewards exceptional performance with incremental pay that is suspended for poor performance; and it provides a new pay structure that varies pay by occupation. A Joint Personnel Administration (JPA) organization has replaced the various personnel systems operated by the three services. The implementation of JPA will enable the services to target bonuses for individual trades or ranks to achieve specific manning goals.[29]

THE 1998 STRATEGIC DEFENCE REVIEW

After 1998, UK defense policy was based on another major review under the new Labour Government. The Strategic Defence Review (SDR) was aimed at providing the UK with "modern forces for the modern world." It involved a further "fundamental reshaping of our forces," in accordance with a continued commitment to a world role, that is, an

---

28. Ministry of Defence, *Statement on the Defence Estimates*, Cmnd 3223 (London: HMSO, 1996), pp 74–75.
29. *Armed Forces Pay Review Body* (AFPRB), 33rd Report, 2004 (London: The Stationery Office, 2004), Chapter 2.

expeditionary strategy.[30] Where previous defense reviews had focused on inputs (such as the numbers of warships, aircraft squadrons, and infantry regiments), this Review specified for the first time the UK's desired defense capabilities. It called for the capability to respond to a major international crisis like the Gulf War, or to be involved in up to two lesser-scale overseas deployments like Bosnia.[31]

The UK's world role was also confirmed with the commitment to acquire two new aircraft carriers for the Navy (deliveries originally planned for around 2012 and 2015). The SDR aimed at "strong, modern and cost-effective defence, now and for the longer term," with plans out to 2015.[32] There were cuts in some front-line forces, especially those with a Cold War role such as anti-submarine forces, tanks, and fighter aircraft. The SDR placed a new emphasis on joint forces including joint rapid reaction forces, a joint helicopter command, and a joint Harrier force.

The 1998 Strategic Defence Review placed particular emphasis on personnel, with a "policy for people." It aimed to solve problems of "over-stretch and under-manning," to achieve "full manning" of units, and to improve recruiting, especially of women and ethnic minorities. Other personnel issues were addressed, including the failure of some enlistees to complete their training (wastage), achieving a better return on training investments, and making the services a more attractive career by providing transferable skill qualifications for a return to civilian society. The introduction of a new pay system was announced, together with improved welfare arrangements, including improvements in single living accommodation and a common annual leave entitlement by which personnel at similar ranks in different services receive similar amounts of annual leave.[33]

NEW THREATS FROM INTERNATIONAL TERRORISM

Following the events of September 11, 2001, and the increased threat from international terrorism, the 1998 Review was modified in 2002 and again

---

30. Ministry of Defence, *The Strategic Defence Review*, Cmnd 3999 (London: The Stationery Office, 1998) (and Supporting Essays), pp. 1–2, 4.
31. Ibid., p. 23.
32. Ibid., p. 53.
33. Ibid., Chapter 6.

in 2003–04.[34] In 2002, a "New Chapter" of the Strategic Defence Review emphasized rapidly deployable UK forces able to operate further afield than Europe, the Persian Gulf, and the Mediterranean (the sphere of interest originally identified by SDR), and the need to introduce a range of new technologies such as precision guided weapons and electronic warfare.[35] As a result, UK defense spending was increased between 2002–03 and 2005–06 by £3.5 billion, representing an annual average real growth of 1.2 percent over a three-year period (claimed to be the "largest sustained increase for twenty years").[36] However, it was recognized that recruitment, retention, and full manning of units were continuing problems: "high operational tempo, high levels of separation and repeated deployments to the same location have a cumulative effect on morale and are ultimately retention-negative for many service personnel, especially those with young families."[37]

Further modifications to the policies announced in the 1998 SDR were announced in 2003 and implemented in 2004. The new policies acknowledged the trans-national threats from international terrorism, the proliferation of weapons of mass destruction, and the destabilizing effects of failed and failing states. The 2003 Defence White Paper, *Delivering Security in a Changing World,* was a fundamental policy statement guiding the formulation of future UK defense policies and outlining its future strategic priorities.[38] In a change from the SDR, the new policy was intended to support three small to medium-scale operations (Macedonia would be an example of a small-scale operation; Afghanistan a medium-scale operation; and Iraq a large-scale operation). This required

---

34. Ministry of Defence, *The Strategic Defence Review: A New Chapter,* Cmnd 5566, vol. 1 (London: The Stationery Office, 2002); Ministry of Defence, *Delivering Security in a Changing World,* Cmnd 6041-1 (London: The Stationery Office, 2003).

35. Ministry of Defence, *The Strategic Defence Review: A New Chapter.*

36. Ministry of Defence, *The Cost of UK Military Operations in Iraq* (London: Ministry of Defence, 2005), <www.operations.mod.uk/telic/key>. The UK-Iraq conflict was an additional cost, borne by the Treasury's Special Reserve and estimated at some £3.7 billion over the period 2002 to the end of March 2006.

37. Ministry of Defence, *Delivering Security in a Changing World,* Defence White Paper, Cmnd 6041 (London: The Stationery Office, 2003) (and Supporting Essays), p. 20.

38. Ministry of Defence, *Delivering Security in a Changing World,* p. 1.

the "rebalancing" of the UK's armed forces. For the most demanding expeditionary operations, it was expected that the UK would be involved in a coalition with the United States or NATO. Further cuts were announced in those forces that were unsuitable for the new emphasis on rapid deployment and on expeditionary forces operating at a greater range from the UK. Cuts were announced in armored forces, warships, and combat aircraft, while there was an increased emphasis on transport, by sea and air, for rapid deployment of UK forces. There was a further small increase (in real terms) in UK defense spending of 1.4 percent per year over the period 2004–05 to 2007–08. However, it was recognized that an expeditionary capability with a high operational tempo and operations at greater distances from the UK would require improved ability to recruit, retain, and motivate the required numbers of military personnel.

Challenges for the UK's AVF

The efficient management of the UK's military is a major and continuing challenge. Producing "defense output" requires various combinations of military "inputs," including technology and capital in the form of equipment, bases, facilities, and land, together with labor inputs comprising military and civilian personnel. Defense output is difficult to measure, but it embraces notions such as peace, security, protection, and threat reduction. The UK now expresses these in terms of defense capabilities, that is, the ability to be involved in up to three small to medium-scale operations at one time.

Changing technology changes the inputs of capital and labor. For example, cruise missiles operated by the Royal Navy have mostly replaced RAF manned combat aircraft for striking fixed targets; unmanned air vehicles (UAVs) operated by the Army are replacing RAF manned aircraft for some missions such as surveillance. Technical change also has impacts on traditional roles and on labor and training requirements. For example, the Army's use of UAVs encroaches on the RAF's traditional monopoly over air warfare. Newer equipment often requires fewer military personnel for its operation and maintenance, and some of these tasks can be outsourced to civilian firms. Technology is not the only driver of change: other influences may include the emergence of new threats such as international terrorism, major cuts in defense budgets, defeat in conflict indicating that the military was not as effective as its leaders had thought, and occasionally the appointment of a new and innovative government defense minister.

The challenge for the armed forces of the UK and other nations is to adjust to change. Like other interest groups, they will tend to oppose change, especially where change makes some units and personnel worse off. And yet the private sector is able to respond to continuous change due to changing consumer demands, new technology, or the emergence of lower-cost rivals in the UK or overseas. For the private sector, the result of change is reflected in declining industries (for example, UK steel, textiles, motorcycles, and automobiles) and in the emergence of new industries such as aerospace, electronics, and pharmaceuticals. Similar adjustments to change by the armed forces will require some radical solutions and departures from their traditional ways of doing business.

For the UK armed forces, radical solutions will require recognition of the substitution principle. Examples include substitutions between equipment and personnel, such as combat aircraft replacing some land forces; between reserves and regulars; between military and civilian personnel (military outsourcing); between men and women and between white and other ethnic personnel; and between older and younger personnel with a willingness to recruit people from higher age groups and to retain experienced, highly-motivated personnel to the age of, say, 65. There are further possible substitutions between one branch of the armed forces and another, or between UK and foreign equipment, which would mean ending the "buy British" policy for warships, including nuclear-powered submarines. But such changes need to be achieved efficiently. Here, the private sector has incentives and markets to ensure that change is undertaken efficiently. In private markets, there is competition and rivalry: the profit motive and capital markets constitute a policing and monitoring system through take-overs and the threat of bankruptcy. Such efficiency mechanisms and incentives are absent from the armed forces. As a result, armed forces have to simulate private markets through competition for equipment and military outsourcing, through incentive systems for military personnel, and through defense budget constraints.

Figure 11.4. Defense Burden, Share of GDP

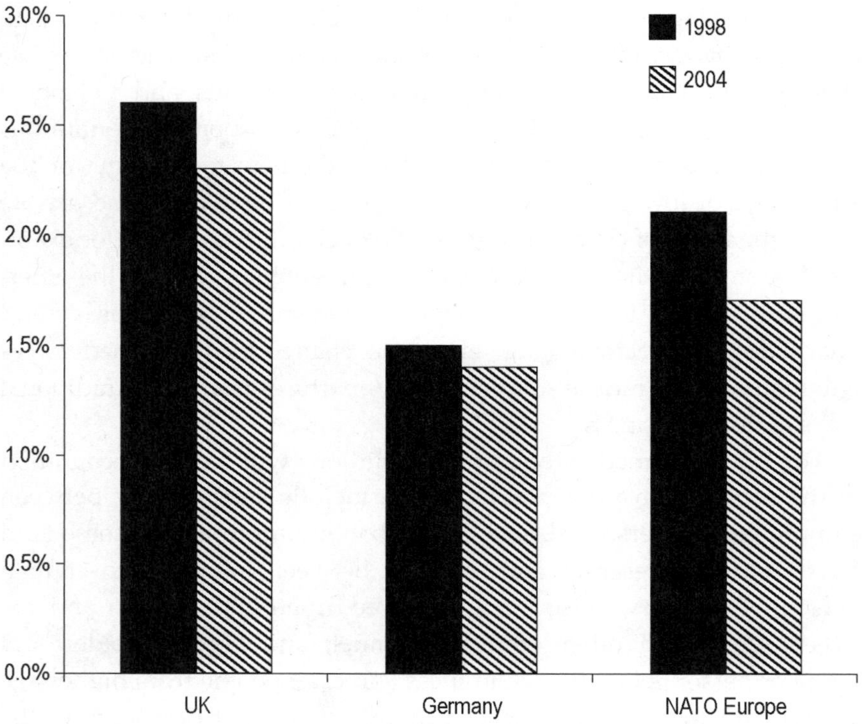

Source: Ministry of Defence/DASA, *UK Defence Statistics 2005* (London: The Stationery Office, 2005).

THE UK'S WORLD ROLE

The UK's commitment to a world role is costly. Achieving it requires a modern and balanced Army, Navy, and Air Force, each operating new and costly equipment with power-projection capability such as aircraft carriers, amphibious ships, air tankers, and sea and air transport. The costs of this world role can be indicated by comparing the UK's defense burden with that of other NATO European nations who do not have such a global power-projection role. Such a comparison suggests that its global role might be costing the UK an extra 0.5 percent to 1 percent of GDP, compared with NATO Europe and with Germany (see Figure 11.4).

The UK's world role also has a challenging personnel dimension. The UK's military commitments have changed from mostly static forces (based, for example, in Germany), with a fairly predictable pattern of time spent away from base on planned exercises and rotation of accompanied postings (those where service personnel are accompanied by their families). The new requirement is for UK expeditionary forces to undertake rapid deployment to trouble spots around the world, usually at short notice, on active service and unaccompanied deployments and operations. The Army has experienced the greatest shift because it is mostly Army personnel who are deployed on expeditionary missions in such places as Bosnia, Kosovo, Sierra Leone, Afghanistan, and Iraq. Within the Army, the infantry is the most overburdened. However, personnel in all three services have been affected.

Today's commitments have taken a toll on recruiting and retention. Fluctuating levels of operational commitments, including major commitments in Afghanistan and Iraq, make service life unpredictable. The result is shorter intervals between overseas tours leading to frequent and prolonged separation from families, difficulties in taking leave, long working hours, and reduced quality of life. If recruitment and retention are to be improved, then service personnel and those considering service life need to believe that efforts are being made to remedy the sense that those who volunteer for their country are overburdened. Possible solutions include reducing UK overseas commitments, or else increasing the size of the Army, either by re-allocating personnel from the other services or by a net increase in the numbers of UK military personnel, which would require a larger defense budget.[39]

PERSONNEL IN THE DEFENSE BUDGET

During the 1990s, the share of personnel costs in the UK defense budget showed a small decline and typically accounted for under 40 percent of the budget, with civilian staff bearing most of the cuts. The corresponding equipment share was about 40 percent or more, with "other expenditures" such as works, buildings, land, and miscellaneous stores and services accounting for the residual (see Table 11.2). The personnel share for the 1990s differed markedly from the share in the 1960s and 1970s. Over the period 1966 to 1975, for example, personnel costs varied between 38 percent of the defense budget in 1966 and 52 percent in 1971–

---

39. In the short term, the UK has eased the Army's personnel problems by reducing its commitments in Northern Ireland; 6,410 Army personnel were based in Northern Ireland in 2005. Ministry of Defence, DASA, *UK Defence Statistics 2003* (London: The Stationery Office, 2005).

Table 11.2. UK Personnel and Equipment Shares of Defense Budget, Selected Years 1975–2001

Expenditure	1975–76	1990–91	1995–96	1999–2000	2000–01
Personnel:	47.3%	39.5%	39.6%	37.8%	37.2%
Armed Forces	24.4%	21.6%	28.6%	27.7%	27.6%
Civilian staff	18.1%	11.6%	11.0%	10.1%	9.6%
Equipment	33.5%	39.6%	39.7%	43.0%	42.4%
Other expenditure	19.2%	20.9%	20.7%	19.2%	20.3%

Notes: 1975–76 and 1990–91 total personnel data includes retired armed forces expenditure at 4.8 percent and 6.3 percent, respectively; no such similar data are shown for later years, and thus the total personnel expenditures are not comparable pre- and post-1990. Personnel expenditures comprise pay and allowances and include all of the military's front-line and support units (e.g., training).

Sources: Ministry of Defence, *Statement on the Defence Estimates, 1980*, Vol. II: *Defence Statistics,* Cmnd 7826-II (London: HMSO, 1980); Ministry of Defence/DASA, *UK Defence Statistics 2002* (London: The Stationery Office, 2002).

72.[40] The decline in the personnel share between 1971–72 and the 1990s reflects the move to a more equipment-intensive force structure.[41] The Army remains the UK's most labor-intensive force. Indeed, between 1990 and 2005, the Army increased its share of total service personnel from 50 percent to 54 percent, mostly at the expense of a decline in the RAF share.

After 2002, the UK changed the basis of its financial statistics when it moved from cash accounting to resource accounting and budgeting (RAB, also known as accruals accounting); thus financial data after 2002 are not comparable to earlier figures. Resource accounting and budgeting aims to make the armed forces more aware of their costs of assets (capital), such as equipment, land, and buildings, as a private firm's balance sheet would do. But to achieve efficiency improvements, RAB needs defense output

---

40. Harries-Jenkins, "The British Experience with the All-Volunteer Force," p. 107.
41. The declining share of personnel suggests that the elasticity of substitution of capital for labor is not unity but is probably greater than one, reflected in a falling personnel share. Unit elasticity would mean that over time, the personnel share would remain constant: a 10 percent wage increase relative to equipment costs (capital) would mean a 10 percent reduction in military personnel.

indicators, together with opportunities and incentives to economize on physical capital inputs. In view of the unique nature of the military employment contract, which in effect gives the armed forces "ownership rights" in military personnel, it might also be useful to include the value of human capital in the military balance sheet.

Substitutions between various types of personnel over the period 1990 to 2005 are suggested by the data shown in Table 11.3. During this period, the ratio of civilian to military personnel does not suggest major substitutions of civilians for military numbers, but the civilians counted are only those employed by MoD. Elsewhere, civilians have replaced military staff through substantial military outsourcing; in Northern Ireland, for example, the police force has replaced Army units. There is no evidence of reserves being substituted for regulars over the years 1990 to 2005, although there is evidence of an increasing proportions of females and ethnic minorities amongst UK military personnel.[42]

THE UK MILITARY LABOR MARKET

The UK military labor market is like any other labor market in its focus on pay, recruitment, retention, training, and conditions of service, which offer further challenges for the UK's future AVF. However, the change of the UK's armed forces role to that of an expeditionary force is occurring alongside rapid changes in society, such that the perceived benefits of life in the services may no longer be enough to outweigh the attractions of civilian life. Typically, the UK armed forces need to recruit some 25,000 people annually. Unemployment levels are currently low and forecast to remain so; the number of young people in further and higher education has doubled and is rising; numbers in the target age group will decline after 2009; society's values are changing; and the role of women in society has changed.[43] All of these mean that the labor market is increasingly less favorable to the services.

---

42. I. Bellany, "Accounting for Army Recruitment: White and Non-White Soldiers in the British Army," *Defence and Peace Economics*, Vol. 14, No. 4 (2003), pp. 281–292.

43. House of Commons Defense Committee (HCDC), *Strategic Defence Review: Policy for People*, HCDC Report, Evidence and Appendices, HCP (House of Commons Paper) 29-I and 29-II (London: The Stationery Office, 2001); Ministry of Defence, *Delivering Security in a Changing World*, Vol. II.

Table 11.3. UK Personnel Trends

Personnel type	1990	2005
Numbers of civilian staff[a]	141,400	82,000
Ratio of MoD civilians to military personnel	1: 2.2	1: 2.5
Numbers of volunteer reserves	90,600	42,400
Ratio of reserves to regulars	1: 3.4	1: 4.7
Female officers	5.9%	10.9%
Female other ranks	5.6%	8.7%
Ethnic minorities in services[b]	1.4% (1996)	5.3%
Numbers of military personnel in:		
Army	152,800 (50%)	109,300 (54%)
Navy	63,300 (21%)	39,900 (20%)
RAF	89,700 (29%)	51,900 (26%)
Total: All Services[c]	305,800 (100%)	201,100 (100%)

Note: a. Over this period there were major changes in the definitions of MoD civilian staff so that the figures are not comparable. b. Data on ethnic minorities were available only from 1996 onward. c. Service totals include trained and untrained (trainee) personnel at April 1 each year.

Source: Ministry of Defence/DASA, *UK Defence Statistics* (various years).

Before 1970, the pay of UK military personnel was adjusted biannually for increases in the cost of living; food and accommodation for single personnel were free; and married servicemen were given a special allowance for household expenses and a daily ration allowance. Changes occurred in the late 1960s and early 1970s: in 1969, the National Board for Prices and Incomes recommended the introduction of a military salary that was based on a principle of comparability between earnings in the civilian sector and earnings in the armed forces. The Board's recommendation also incorporated and consolidated a number of allowances within the military salary. The comparability principle also required a judgment on the relative advantages and disadvantages of military life. In the UK, the net balance was judged to be adverse and therefore the net disadvantages of service life were reflected in the compensatory payment known as the X-factor: initially this was fixed at 5 percent but was raised to 10 percent in 1974, increasing military salaries.[44]

UK armed forces pay and conditions are now evaluated annually by the Armed Forces Pay Review Body (AFPRB), an independent body established in 1971 to provide independent advice to the UK government on remuneration and allowances for military personnel. Its recommendations are based on the need for the pay of the armed forces to be broadly comparable with civilian pay, together with the need to recruit, retain, and motivate suitably able and qualified people for service life. It seeks to compensate for the net disadvantages of service life, compared with the civilian sector, through the X-factor, which the AFPRB set at 13 percent in 2001. With the UK's increasing involvement in expeditionary operations, the X-factor might have to be increased substantially in the future.

In its 2005 Report, the AFPRB recommended a 3 percent increase in military salaries for 2005–06 to ensure adequate retention and motivation. This was considered especially necessary given uncertainties due to the force restructuring over the transitional period to 2008 that had been set in motion by the 2003 White Paper.[45] Overall, for the period 1990 to 2004, military pay increases exceeded both the average wage hikes in the private sector and the rise in consumer prices across the UK.

Concern was also expressed by the Board about hours worked by service personnel: average working hours rose to 47.7 hours per week in 2003–04, well in excess of comparable civilian figures. For military personnel on operations, the average was even higher, at 63.5 hours per week.[46] There were recommendations for increases in the rates of Specialist Pay for skills in short supply, such as flying pay, submarine pay, and diving pay. Furthermore, the AFPRB recognized the impact of the high tempo of overseas operations by recommending an increase in the daily separation allowance plus a higher bonus. These recommendations were accepted by the government, and were implemented in April 2005.

---

44. Harries-Jenkins, "The British Experience with the All-Volunteer Force," p. 116.
45. AFPRB, *Armed Forces Pay Review Body*, 34th Report, 2005 (London: The Stationery Office, 2005).
46. Ibid., p. 17.

Retention continues to be an issue. The AFPRB Report of 2005 found that the overall outflow or net loss of trained regulars was reduced between 2002 and 2004. Because the services could, therefore, reduce their recruitment targets, those targets were met. More significantly, however, the 2005 AFPRB Report found that the "imbalance ... between resources and commitments" was likely to be "exacerbated during the period of force restructuring" set in motion by the 2003 Defence White Paper.[47] Thus, the challenge will continue.

Training also continues to be an issue. The UK's armed forces are a major provider of training and education; every year almost 20,000 trained and experienced personnel leave the services, providing additional human capital for the civilian economy. This training role of the services is not without cost, especially with regard to general training and transferable skills. The problem is that if the forces provide and finance such training, they need to ensure that the trained personnel remain with the forces for a sufficient period of time, on average, to give the forces an acceptable return on their training investments. This is not such a problem where training is highly specific to the armed forces (for example, tank driving or missile operation), because the resulting skills are not transferable to the civilian economy.

Among the other elements of the total monetary and non-monetary package offered to both single and family personnel is accommodation. The UK armed forces offer a variety of housing types and have launched a Single Living Accommodation Modernisation program. However, the AFPRB recognizes a need to set accommodation charges below the market rates for comparable accommodation in order to compensate for the inherent disadvantages of living in service accommodation.[48]

A new pension scheme was introduced in April 2005 to replace the previous scheme established in 1960 and modified over succeeding years. The Bett Report of 1995 had recommended significant changes to the Armed Forces Pension Scheme. These changes were not introduced immediately, because the government decided that the Bett proposals on career structures should be developed first. The government initiated

---

47. Ibid., p. 10.
48. *Armed Forces Pay Review Body*, 33rd Report, 2004, p. 31.

a new review of pensions in 1998 with the aim of establishing pension arrangements for new entrants to the armed forces that would meet the service's future needs for recruitment, retention, and motivation. The new pension scheme retains the normal retirement age of 55, and provides benefits based on final pensionable pay received for the best 365 consecutive days over the last three years of service (including the X factor, but excluding allowances and specialist pay). The government claims that the new scheme reflects modern practice; it is fair, transparent, and simple to understand; it offers consistent outcomes with more benefits for the severely disabled and a new injury compensation scheme; and there are major improvements to dependents' benefits, including an extension of dependents' benefits to unmarried partners in a substantial relationship (including same sex). Under the new system, officers and other ranks are treated similarly: each group must serve for thirty-five years to earn a pension income worth 50 percent of pensionable pay plus a tax-free lump sum worth three times the annual pension. A new system of Early Departure Payments (EDP) was introduced for personnel who leave the services before age 55 provided they have a minimum of 18 years' service and are at least age 40. The EDP recognized that the armed forces need to shed a substantial proportion of people who reach about age 40, and that an incentive was required to retain people to this age. It is expected that the new pension values will be taken into account when the AFPRB recommends service pay increases.[49]

Conclusion

UK defense policy will continue to reflect the pressures of the defense economics problem and the need for difficult choices in a world of uncertainty. Issues of military personnel in an AVF present such choices and the need for change and radical solutions. The substitution principle is a starting point for policy options. Possibilities described above, some of which are already being implemented, include the substitution of equipment and new technology for personnel; imports of foreign equipment replacing nationally produced equipment; substitutions of

---

49. Armed Forces Pension Scheme, *Key Features of the Armed Forces Pension Scheme 2005*, April 2005, <www.mod.uk/issues/pensions/key_features_afps05>.

reserves for regulars and of civilians for military personnel via military outsourcing; and substitutions involving a greater use of women and ethnic minorities in the AVF. Further options include older people replacing younger military personnel. This would mean recruiting people from older age groups and retaining experienced, highly motivated personnel to the age of 65. Ultimately, the armed forces create a personnel recruiting problem by restricting entry to younger age groups.

Other policy options would include a reappraisal of the UK's desire to be a world power with a global role and the resulting requirement for expeditionary forces. Such a world military role is costly. More radical efficiency improvements might include a review of the Armed Force's organizational structure, including the Army's traditional regimental size and structure, the possible extension of joint forces (comparable to mergers in private industry), and the UK's acceptance of role specialization within NATO. Alternately, the UK could support the creation of a European army, navy, and air force in which it would also specialize in a limited range of roles, such as special forces, combat aircraft, nuclear submarines, and aircraft carriers. Another option, of course, is the standard solution to recruitment and retention problems, namely, higher salaries, but higher salaries require either sacrifices of equipment spending or a higher defense budget.

For the UK and other nations, the lessons of an AVF are that defense budget constraints and rising input costs of personnel and equipment mean that difficult defense policy choices cannot be avoided. Nations might adopt different solutions to the defense economics problem. Some might increase their defense budgets, sacrificing social welfare spending or lower taxes; some might prefer "equal misery" for their armed forces with a series of modest across-the-board budget cuts; some might pursue efficiency-improving programs; some might opt for a major defense review; and some might choose to continue bearing the costs and inefficiencies of a conscript force. The UK experience shows that an AVF is not cheap, nor does it solve a nation's defense problems or eliminate the continued need for difficult choices in a world of massive uncertainties.

Chapter 12

Transition to an All-Volunteer Force

The French Experience

Sylvain Daffix, Vincent Medina, and Cyr-Denis Nidier

In France as all over the world, the perception of threats and the type of potential conflicts changed dramatically at the end of the 1980s. The Cold War ended, but other types of possible conflict emerged. Conscription was called into question by public opinion. The requirement for conscripts declined, especially in key areas of national defense. For example, conscripts are not appropriate for nuclear deterrence, which requires highly specialized skills, nor should conscripts be asked to participate in foreign interventions. The need for a more effective and more efficient defense organization meant a need for more advanced technology and, consequently, a need for people with special qualifications and experience. International interventions by NATO, the United Nations, and the European Union and new readiness requirements established by multilateral agreements, as well as the development of a common European Security and Defense Policy, brought with them the need for a high level of preparedness and professionalism for the French forces.

France is presently a significant contributor to peacekeeping missions and other international interventions, as in Bosnia, Kosovo, the Ivory Coast, and Afghanistan. As of 2005, there were more than 30,000 military personnel outside Metropolitan France, including pre-positioned forces in

Any views or opinions presented are solely those of the authors and do not represent those of the French Ministry of Defense.

foreign countries and sovereignty forces in French territories overseas as well as forces involved in international interventions. France also has a major global role in terms of defense research, technology, and production. The French defense industrial base is internationally competitive and plays a central role in the building of a European defense industrial base.

The most crucial change of the last decade has concerned France's military personnel and the transition to an all-volunteer force (AVF). Such a transition would be challenging in any case, but it was even more demanding because it came at a time of increasing operational missions and decreasing budgets.[1]

In France, unlike the United States, little has been written by economists about military personnel.[2] This chapter seeks to provide some clarification of the economic background of the end of conscription in France. The chapter is presented in three parts: first, a look at the process of transition to an AVF, which was a success but faced some difficulties; second, the incentive scheme for military personnel, which has both monetary and non-monetary elements; and third, an analysis of the trade-offs between spending for personnel and spending for equipment.

The French experience shows that the overall economic situation in France was a key factor in the success and in the final cost of the transition to an AVF, even if the decision to enlist is not solely an economic question. To facilitate such a transition elsewhere, researchers should examine such questions as the optimal timing of military reform, paying attention to factors such as the civilian job market. In the conclusion to this chapter, we suggest a starting point for such a research program.

---

1.   From 2002 onwards, however, the budget began to increase in response to new threats and the demand for engagement of France's armed forces in both peacekeeping operations and homeland security.
2.   See, for example, J. Warner and B. Asch, "The Economics of Military Personnel," in Keith Hartley and Todd Sandler, eds., *Handbook of Defense Economics*, Vol. 1 (Amsterdam: North Holland, 1995).

Figure 12.1. Defense Manpower during the Transition Process

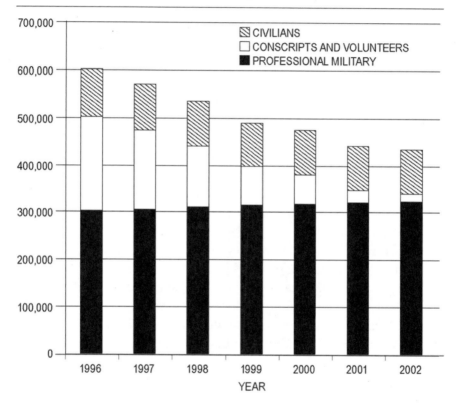

NOTE: Figures are annual averages. Since 2000, the personnel of the undersecretary for veterans (civilian employees) began to be included, and since 2003, shipyard personnel began to be excluded, making overall figures difficult to compare over time.

Source: *Bilan social de la Défense* (Social balance sheet for defense), Ministère de la Défense, Paris, 2004 (de la Defense, Paris, 2004.)

The French Transition to an AVF

After a six-year transition, the French military became entirely professionalized during 2002. Despite initial success in the recruitment of professional soldiers, the transition required significant efforts in human resources management, especially to generate enough candidates each year to ensure a reasonable selection rate and to maintain the quality of recruits. The formal decision to suspend conscription was taken in 1996;

the process of transition was organized by the military programming law that covered the period from 1997 to 2002.[3] The total number of military units was reduced, and the military was reorganized from a structure geared toward territorial defense to one that could more readily respond to new types of threats and engage in operations abroad. Military base closings, dissolution of some regiments, and reform of the defense industrial base had a large economic impact at the local level, and therefore economic planning was needed to accompany these changes.

Quantitatively speaking, the transition was undoubtedly a success.[4] The figures set by the military programming law for 1997–2002 were 95 percent realized: the number of defense personnel fell from 571,000 civilians and personnel in uniform in 1997 to 416,000 in 2002, a decrease of 155,000 individuals or 27 percent percent. At the same time, the ministry recruited 184,000 military personnel to take the place of conscripts. (See Figure 12.1.)

The distribution of defense personnel in 2003 is shown in Figure 12.2. Some elements are specific to France. The Gendarmerie—the French territorial police, equivalent to the Italian *Carabinieri*—holds a military status, although most Gendarmerie units are engaged within France as rural police or in other domestic security activities. A new type of enlistee, the one-year volunteer, was created to compensate for the end of the draft. A volunteer signs a one-year contract and may re-enlist up to four times, for a total of five years. Most of these volunteers occupy positions at the level of private, but some posts exist at the officer-cadet level. The services vary in their percentage of civilians, officers, and so on. Below we discuss how the distribution of personnel among the services evolved during the transition to an AVF.

---

3.   The main trends and evolutions of France's military are established by military programming laws fixed for six-year periods. This presentation focuses on the programming law for 2003–2008, and on its predecessor (1997–2002), which corresponded with the transition to the AVF.

4.   *Rapport au parlement sur l'exécution de la loi de programmation militaire 1997–2002* (Paris : Ministère de la défense, October 2002).

Figure 12.2. Rank and Service of Defense Personnel in 2003

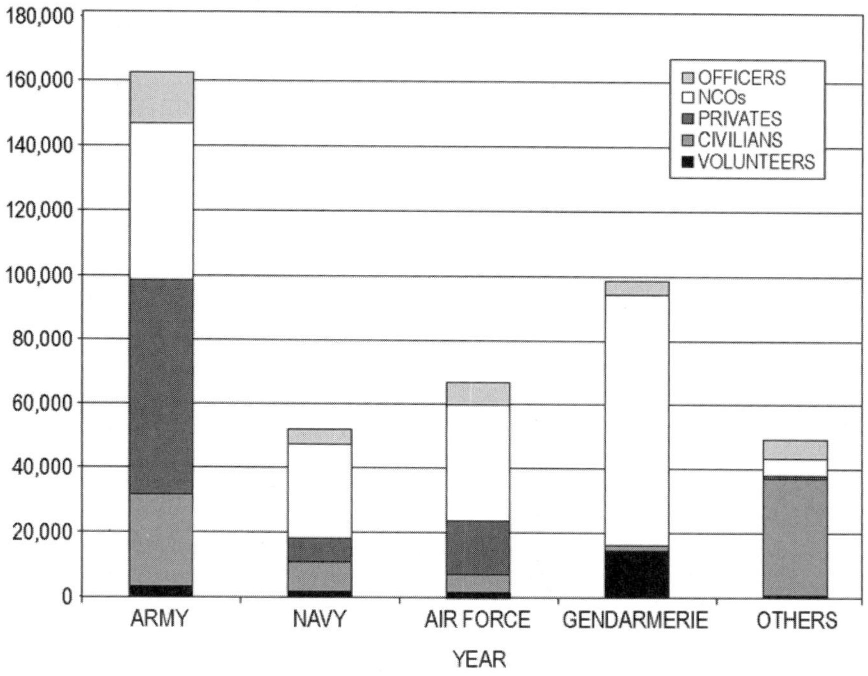

Source: *Bilan social de la Défense* (Social balance sheet for defense), Ministère de la Défense, Paris, 2004 (de la Defense, Paris, 2004.)

The "White Book" (Livre blanc) of 1994 defined four main operational functions for France's military: nuclear deterrence, crisis prevention, force projection, and territorial protection.[5] These missions are best performed by professionals, due to the need for experience and technical competence. The missions were defined before the decision to end conscription, indicating that the growing need for professionals was already recognized.

---

5.   "Livre blanc sur la Défense" (Paris: Ministère de la Défense, 1994).

Table 12.1. Manpower by Service and Category

1990 (during draft)	Army	Navy	Air Force	Gendarmerie	Others	Total
Conscripts	182,715	19,454	36,306	9,731	2,362	250,568
Civilians	38,276	7,148	5,401	969	77,585	129,379
Privates	31,390	10,692	7,880	248	28	50,238
NCOs	58,551	30,409	41,467	75,182	3,873	209,482
Officers	18,302	4,433	7,056	2,497	7,673	39,961
Total	329,234	72,136	98,110	88,627	91,521	679,628

1996 (end of conscription announced)	Army	Navy	Air Force	Gendarmerie	Others	Total
Conscripts	133,093	18,038	31,786	12,016	5,940	200,873
Civilians	31,128	6,383	4,721	1,232	55,761	99,225
Privates	30,229	8,100	5,656	95	378	44,458
NCOs	57,594	32,524	43,218	77,602	5,007	215,945
Officers	17,403	4,779	7,234	2,770	7,010	39,196
Total	269,447	69,824	92,615	93,715	74,096	599,697

2003 (first full year of AVF)	Army	Navy	Air Force	Gendarmerie	Others	Total
1-year volunteers	2,951	1,441	1,210	14,284	361	20,247
Civilians	28,477	9,060	5,575	1,812	36,305	81,229
Privates	66,989	7,477	16,581	3	1,047	92,097
NCOs	48,153	29,200	36,219	78,181	5,522	197,275
Officers	15,854	4,748	6,980	4,119	5,849	37,550
Total	162,424	51,926	66,565	98,399	49,084	428,398

Source: *Bilan social de la Défense*, Ministère de la Défense, Paris.

Table 12.1 shows the change in allocation of manpower between services and categories over time: the situation during the draft (1990), the year of the announcement of the transition (1996), and the first full year with a completely professional military (2003). As Table 12.1 shows, the main manpower reduction was in the Army, which had engaged more than half of the conscripts. Since 2003, the recruitment of privates and one-year volunteers has been far from adequate to compensate numerically for the end of the draft. However, because professional soldiers are more efficient and prepared than conscripts, the Army can achieve the same missions with fewer people. The navy and the air force were already more professionalized before the transition, so the reduction of their manpower was less drastic. The Gendarmerie has not been affected by this reduction effort at all, because its main missions, of rural police and homeland security, grew during the period.

Two major changes in the number of civilians employed by France's defense ministry occurred between 1996 and 2003. The personnel of the undersecretary for veterans, essentially administrative personnel, have been included in the statistics since 2000. In 2003, the personnel of the state-owned shipyard began to be excluded.[6] Due to both changes, it is not easy to see that there is, in fact, a growing need for civilians to occupy some jobs that were formerly filled by uniformed military people. Another evolution worth noting concerns the growing proportion of female military personnel: by 2003, they represented 12.5 percent of personnel in uniform, a rise from just 7.5 percent in 1994.

Conscripts previously occupied a variety of jobs in the military, from unskilled to highly skilled. As this relatively cheap and abundant resource had to be replaced by professional military personnel, some difficulties arose in recruitment, especially in the health and information technology (IT) sectors, where the civilian labor market was very tight. This required special efforts, first in communication to recruit candidates, then in compensation to retain the best ones. In addition, the process of professionalization had already started in some units before the 1996 announcement of the end of conscription. This was brought about by the need for professional units for interventions abroad. (The military is not permitted to order conscripts to participate in interventions abroad.) As Table 12.1 shows, the number of conscripts and civilians had already decreased between 1990 and 1996.

The cost of the transition was one of the major questions considered in a recent report of the *Cour des comptes*, the French government

---

6. Until 2002, the shipyard was an arsenal that legally belonged to the Defense Procurement Agency, but since 2003, it has been a publicly-owned company, legally independent from the Ministry of Defense.

accountability office.[7] It found, however, that it was too soon for a clear view of the costs and benefits. The report also pointed out that other recent reforms not directly related to the transition, such as reform of the procurement system, have also affected the Ministry of Defense (MoD), so that the specific budgetary effect of professionalization could not easily be isolated. The report of the Cour des comptes expressed the view that the overall operating budget appeared to be under control at that time. Nevertheless, the operating budget (including compensation) during the transition exceeded the amounts anticipated by the military programming law, due to unexpectedly high costs, and despite a decrease in non-compensation operating expenditures during the transition.[8]

The transformation of the military force structure has required a reduction in the number of commissioned and non-commissioned officers (NCOs) at higher ranks, while young people must still be recruited to the lower levels of the hierarchy. Even before 1996, it was possible for personnel to leave the military for civilian jobs in the public sector, but the number of jobs reserved for former military people was strictly limited. During the transition, a lump-sum payment was offered to commissioned and non-commissioned officers as an incentive to leave the military for the civilian sector. This was offered only to personnel who had already acquired rights to a military pension but were under the age limit for mandatory retirement of their rank. This incentive proved more successful than expected: between 1997 and 2002, 720 officers and 13,000 non-commissioned officers took advantage of this program for voluntary departure from the military. According to the Cour des comptes, this program cost an unexpectedly high 659.6 million Euros, or €48,000 per capita. The other unanticipated costs of the transition to AVF were mainly due to compensation enhancement and to the administrative cost of transformation.

---

7. Cour des comptes, *Rapport annuel public au président de la République* (Paris, 2003).
8. "Non-compensation operating expenditures" encompass operating costs attributable to food, clothing, petroleum products, and some maintenance.

The French Incentive Scheme for Military Personnel

The tangible rewards for military personnel include both monetary and non-monetary components, including immediate basic pay and bonuses, deferred incentives such as retirement benefits, and other rewards such as career and promotion possibilities.[9] In-kind benefits also play a significant role. The influences on recruitment and retention of the best performers are essential for every military force, because of the specific demands of military duty and of the lack of lateral entry.[10]

France's overall incentive scheme was, qualitatively, basically the same before and after the transition to AVF. The switch to an all-volunteer force did not imply a cultural revolution in French military personnel policy, but it did require some changes. Even after the end of the transition process, high levels of recruitment were still needed, and incentive problems still had to be addressed. In 2003, for example, 38,000 new personnel had to be recruited for the military.

Since the end of the draft, the military has had to recruit in many different domains and at different levels of skill. A recent advertising campaign pointed out that 400 different types of jobs are needed by the army. The military needs technicians with varied specializations and also new recruits with no particular skills who will receive specific training in the military. The challenge for the military is to attract people from the civilian labor markets. Often it must compete with the private sector, especially to recruit IT and health-care specialists. Due to the pay gap between the private sector and the military, the Ministry of Defense must rely on non-monetary motivations such as patriotism. It must also identify other incentives that it can increase where specific skills are scarce and in high demand.

The various civilian labor markets may have different un-employment rates, and thus the number of applicants for jobs offered by the military might vary greatly. For example, in 1995, the un-

---

9. Cindy Williams, Vincent Medina, and Sylvain Daffix, "La gestion des resources humaines militaires: l'apport de la théorie des incitations," *Ecodef*, No. 28 (July 2003).
10. The analysis in this section is largely based on recent work in the field of personnel economics. See, for example, Edward P. Lazear, *Personnel Economics* (Cambridge, Mass.: MIT Press, 1995).

employment rate for people having a bachelors degree or greater was 6.9 percent, while it was 16.4 percent for people having no diploma; in 2003, the comparable figures were 7.6 percent and 14.3 percent. Unemployment rates had a significant effect on recruitment during the period of transition, so recruitment advertising emphasized the military as a first employment experience and as an opportunity to acquire professional skills. But as unemployment figures vary significantly for different levels of education, the incentive scheme must be adapted to each specific labor market in order to meet recruiting goals.

There are, of course, many intangible incentives, such as honor, patriotism, and the spirit of sacrifice, but the discussion here is centered on the economic incentives that influence the decision to enlist. The first element of the economic incentive scheme to attract and retain professional military personnel is basic pay. This is a direct and immediate incentive, especially for the less-skilled positions. Basic pay must be high enough to attract enough candidates to fill the number of positions offered. After the choice to abandon conscription made it necessary to recruit a considerable cohort of privates, one of the first decisions was to enhance their pay significantly. In more competitive labor markets, where the applicants are scarce and wages in the civilian sector are higher, additional incentives are needed.

A second set of monetary incentives includes bonuses and special wages. In the French military pay system, these account for a large share of total pay for some personnel. They compensate for certain drawbacks and reward specific competencies. For example, a general bonus is meant to compensate for the shortcomings of military life; it is similar to the "X-factor" pay increment in the United Kingdom. Some bonuses are available if one is married or has children; another type depends on the location of one's residence. Bonuses that are rewards for special skills are used to compensate pilots, parachutists, submarine crew, and other specialists. The military invests a great deal in developing the competencies of these people. Because their skills are very specific and their training sometimes takes several years, replacing them frequently is expensive, so special salaries are aimed at retention. For medical staff and IT specialists, in particular, the bonus serves to make up the pay gap compared with the private sector.

Another bonus is related to interventions abroad (known as "OPEX"). As OPEXes have increased in frequency, this bonus has increased as a share of the French military paycheck. Unlike the UK or the United States, the bonuses that France offers its service members for foreign interventions are quite substantial compared to the basic pay.

However, even with such bonuses and special pay, the present compensation package is not always sufficient to attract, motivate, and retain people with the needed skills and experience. Candidates for military service also take into account the expected rate of increase of their pay and the possibilities of career training and return to civilian life.

Among the non-monetary incentives, career paths and promotion schemes play a major role in attraction and retention. Career officers, for example, may accept lower wages at the beginning of their careers because they know that if they stay in the military, they may progress through the hierarchy and gain better compensation. Thus, deferred benefits give many an incentive to stay in the military. The same mechanisms apply to military people under contract, too, giving them incentives to demonstrate their value as a condition of being allowed to renew their contracts or to be accepted as career members of the military rather than remaining on contract. The succession of contracts, which allows the military to control the numerical strength at each rank, also allows for the selection of the more able by offering such opportunities as incentives. (In 2002, half of France's military personnel were under contract; of these, most were privates and young NCOs.)

After losing too many skilled conscripts in administrative and technical fields, the Minister of Defense created a new category of contract officers called "specialists," for people who have acquired specific skills in the civilian sector. They do not have to take command positions, but are assigned to military units in such roles as communications officers, budget officers, or legal advisers. Candidates generally must have the French equivalent of a bachelor of science degree, but most have a master's or other post-graduate degree. It is much cheaper for the military to acquire such "ready-made" skills than to finance general training programs. Such specialists can renew their contracts for two to eight years at a time, up to twenty years of service; at that point there is mandatory retirement with an immediate pension benefit, or they may become career officers. Issues relating to the retirement system are very specific to military careers and are generally not sufficiently taken into account in the analysis of the French case.

The military needs youth and strength in the lower ranks, so it has to ensure a relatively high turnover at those levels. Older personnel must leave to make room for younger ones, but not so quickly as to prevent the military from capitalizing on their experience, or to waste the costs of their training. To address this, the MoD offers an immediate retirement benefit after fifteen years of service for an NCO, twenty years for contract officers, or twenty-five years for career officers.[11] (This instrument pre-dates the transition to an AVF.) Together, the promotion scheme and the retirement system ensure a relatively stable age pyramid and hierarchy.[12]

Among the non-monetary aspects of the management of military human resources are living conditions. Housing is often offered or substantially subsidized. This is a logical compensation component, given the high mobility required by military duty. As part of the transition to an AVF, the Army's "Plan Vivien" of 1997 aimed to improve housing for enlisted personnel. By the end of 2002, it had already spent €568 million toward this end; the Plan will continue to 2010. In some cases, a housing bonus is offered which depends on the location of the job; for example, it is indexed to the cost of living for expensive locations such as Paris. Food in military locations is also largely subsidized. Traditionally in France, health care is offered to military personnel and their families in military hospitals. There are also other tangible benefits such as subsidized public transportation—75 percent discount on railway tickets for military personnel, half-price tickets for their families—and entertainment. Attention is focused on families because interventions abroad, mandatory transfers, and military duty in general affect the whole family. In-kind benefits and assistance with regard to general living conditions constitute indirect, tax-free compensation; they comprise a significant incentive for retention of military personnel.

According to the Cour des comptes, the major challenge for the military in the future will be the continuing renewal of its workforce

---

11. There is a maximum mandatory retirement age that is different for each rank, service, and military specialty. For example, at the rank of colonel, the maximum age limit ranges from a low of 54 for Air Force officers to a high of 60 for those in the technical and administrative corps.

12. The base rule for calculating the military pension is the same as for civil servants in the public sector: 2 percent of the last pay times number of years of service, up to an amount equal to 75 percent of final pay (that is, a maximum of 37.5 years of service can be credited). Some exceptions exist for specific cases.

due to demographic trends and size of the military.[13] This will represent, in the coming years, a need for more than 30,000 recruits each year. The impacts of demography and the economy must be taken into account in personnel policies. The incentive scheme described above can help, but general incentives must be specifically adapted to each of many specific labor markets.

Tradeoffs between Personnel Costs and Other Expenditure Categories

Military personnel and their equipment are complementary in many respects; a policy enhancing one that harms the other cannot produce better defense. This rough analogy to the concept of a "production function" with complementary factors (labor and capital), as used by economists, points to a budgetary dilemma, in the short term at least. Even if labor and capital can be substituted for one another in the long term, new equipment and new doctrines generally take a long time to be developed and integrated into the combat forces. As a first step, therefore, it is more useful to take today's state of technology as an exogenous factor and to devise a complementary relationship to manage military personnel that emphasizes both technical and military training. But there are additional relationships among the motivation and readiness of military personnel, the availability of current equipment, and the future development of next-generation equipment.

Closely linked to the promotion system is the training of military personnel, which has two aspects, academic or technical, and military. First, academic and technical training is needed in the skills that ensure the autonomy of military units, such as mechanics, electronics, accounting, logistics, and management. The Ministry of Defense could acquire these technical skills from the civilian labor markets. Personnel who have already acquired skills in these fields would require some additional training to adapt their knowledge to the specifics of the military. Alternately, the ministry can organize on-the-job technical training for its existing personnel. Second, training in military skills is essential to a professional military, which benefits from more

---

13. Cour des comptes, *Rapport annuel public au président de la République* (Paris, 2003). The military employed 1.31 percent of the population of working age in 2003, according to NATO statistics.

Figure 12.3. France's Annual Defense Operating and Personnel Budget, 1995–2005 (millions of Euros in current prices)

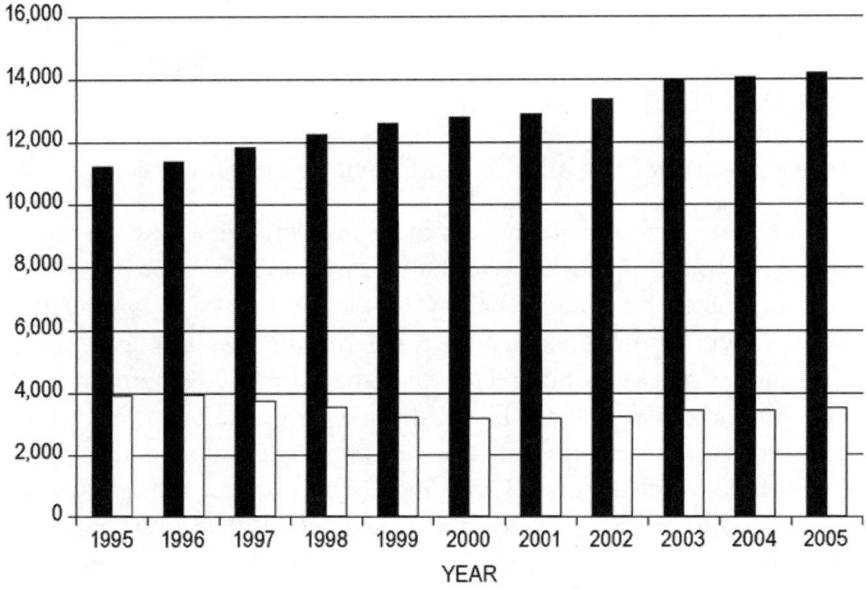

Note: Black bar: Personnel budget (compensation); white bar: operating budget (excluding compensation).
Source: *Annuaire économique de la Défense*, Ministère de la Défense, Paris, 2006.

experienced and better-trained personnel. Thus a significant effort to provide both individual training and collective drill or maneuvers in military units is worthwhile to prepare individuals and units and to keep readiness and motivation at a high level.

Defense operating costs other than compensation declined between 1995 and 2005, as shown in Figure 12.3, mostly as a result of the decrease in number of personnel. These operating costs, attributable to food, clothing, petroleum products, and some maintenance, dropped from €3.9 billion in 1995 to €3.2 billion in 2001. A non-compensation operating budget that is too severely constrained is likely to have a negative impact on the armed forces. The military programming law for 2003–2008 aims at providing sufficient resources to sustain an appropriate level of readiness. In 2005, this budget was approximately €3.6 billion.

The discussion above focuses on spending that affects individuals, but efficiency is also affected by equipment and other components of defense spending. A well-trained and highly qualified professional military would be useless without its armament and other supporting equipment, while even the latest technological equipment is of little value to an unskilled, untrained military staff. The defense "production function" requires some factors of production that are not substitutable. Thus, proportionality should be maintained between personnel and equipment; operating costs associated with both factors may also be proportionally linked. Some potential innovations in strategy or technology might affect the respective needs in terms of personnel and equipment to achieve the same mission. Even so, this balance should be taken into account when addressing personnel policy reforms. The crucial point is that defense efficiency will be constrained by the less available factor. This means that the maintenance of equipment also contributes to readiness. A professional military must have modern, functioning, and effective arms and equipment. Both personnel and equipment are essential to ensure national security and defense capabilities.

From the public finance point of view, implementing an AVF under severe budget constraints may have a negative effect on overall efficiency because the transition costs may force an under-investment in equipment. Consequently, a counterbalancing effort would have to be made after an AVF has been implemented. During such a period, defense missions outside a country's borders could be exceptionally challenging.

French budgetary norms distinguish operating expenditures (compensation and other operating costs) from capital expenditures (R&D, acquisition, and maintenance). The budgetary impact on personnel and equipment of the transition of the French military to an AVF are shown in Figure 12.4. Due to budget constraints at the governmental level and the end of the immediate threats of the Cold War, capital spending was reduced under the military programming law of 1997–2002. The president thereafter sought to recover from the impact of the transition to an AVF and the global budget increases since 2002. The military programming law of 2003–2008, therefore, made equipment a top priority in order to keep efficiency at the highest level.[14]

---

14. *Projet de loi de programmation militaire 2003–2008* (Paris: Ministère de la Défense, 2003).

Figure 12.4. France's Military Budget, 1995–2005 (millions of euros in current prices)

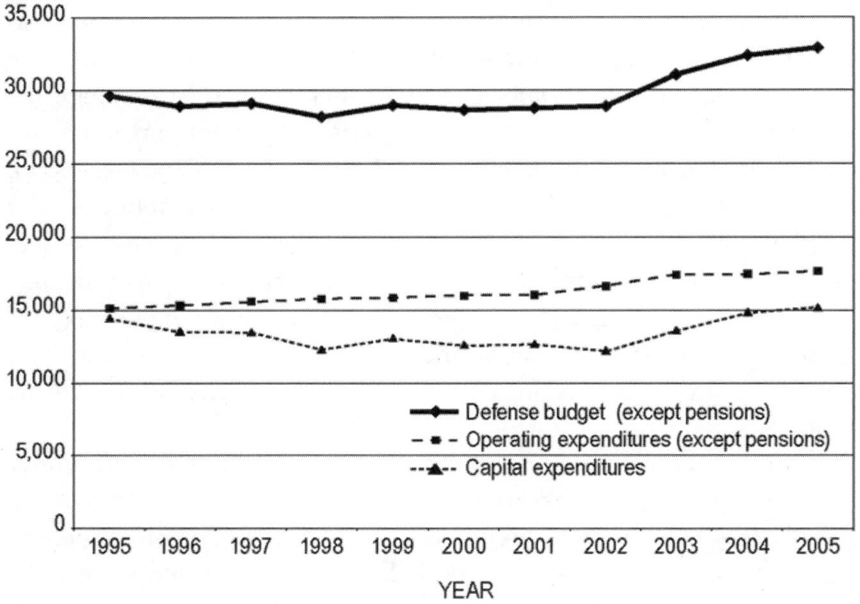

Source: *Annuaire économique de la Défense*, Ministère de la Défense, Paris, 2006.

Conclusion

France's transition to an AVF has now been achieved, but the military must continue to attract enough candidates each year to ensure the necessary quantity as well as quality of France's future military personnel. The lessons of the French experience show that distinctions must be made among different labor markets in setting compensation and other incentives related to recruitment and retention.[15] Economic considerations are also key to the organization of a professional military. An economic dilemma arises when the defense budget is

15. Christian Schmidt, *Marché du travail et recrutement des forces armées*, rapport pour le C2SD (Paris, 2001). In this chapter, we distinguish different levels of skill and different technical domains, but we could also have differentiated labor markets geographically; this element is of major importance in France, especially at lower levels of skill.

constrained: the readiness of the military and the motivation of professional military personnel require both up-to-date equipment and adequate training. These aspects also have an influence on the public image of the military in the population, which in turn will influence future candidates for enlistment.

The cost of transition to an AVF as well as its success depends on its economic and strategic environment. When labor markets are tight, it will be difficult to attract a sufficient number of candidates without incurring higher expenses. However, recruitment efforts must not be so high as to harm equipment spending. So there is a tradeoff between choosing to make the transition when there are numerous candidates on the labor market but the budget is restricted, and doing so when the budgetary situation is better but labor markets may be tighter. Finally, it must be remembered that military pay is not the only incentive for recruitment and retention. An effective military personnel policy must take into account all incentives contributing to readiness.

The choice of an all-volunteer force has to be viewed in the broader perspective of the proposed European Security and Defense Policy. Missions will be more diversified and more complex, including peacekeeping and asymmetric warfare. The objectives assigned by Europe's citizens will require its forces to work together, to develop a common culture, and to be able to intervene outside Europe for peacekeeping and peace enforcement, both within NATO and UN frameworks and outside them. The question of personnel policy is one part of the answer to this larger challenge.

Chapter 13

The All-Volunteer Spanish Armed Forces

Juan Lopez Diaz

The international security environment has changed dramatically over the last two decades, and Spanish security and defense policy has changed to keep pace with those developments. Ethnic conflict, state failure, and terrorism have replaced major state-on-state conflict as the primary security issues in Europe. Part of Spain's adaptation to this new strategic environment is the development of an all-volunteer military that will be smaller, more deployable, and more capable of meeting emerging security challenges.

The first chapters in this volume describe the changing security landscape and how it has affected military strategies, management, and alliances in countries throughout Europe and North America. Like Spain, many of these countries have responded to the changing security environment by downsizing their militaries and moving to highly trained, all-volunteer forces (AVFs). Domestic realities have also influenced these transformations, as countries face changing demographics and shifting public opinion.

Changes in technology have also affected military operations, and have repercussions for the size and makeup of armed forces in Spain and elsewhere. Innovations in areas such as precision weaponry can reduce the need for "boots on the ground," but these systems may also require highly skilled servicemembers to operate them.

Succeeding in this new environment requires high-quality, well-trained, and motivated personnel. Attracting and retaining these people will require effective personnel policies. An integral part of Spain's transformation effort has been ensuring that the military's personnel policies are designed to recruit, train, motivate, and retain the very best men and women.

This chapter chronicles the transformation of the Spanish military's personnel policies and how that transformation positions Spain for the future. Spain's approach to transformation has been shaped by a unique set of security challenges, domestic issues, and international commitments and opportunities. Yet Spain also has much in common with other European and North American countries making the transition to smaller, more highly trained, professional armed forces. Thus the Spanish experience may help others understand which personnel strategies are effective, which are not, and how specific political, demographic, and other factors affected the effort in Spain.

The chapter begins with a brief overview of Spain's new strategic circumstances and its aspirations for a more global role in the future. It describes the post–Cold War decisions that led to Spain's adoption of a volunteer force, the reasons behind those decisions, and the changes Spain has instituted in other aspects of military capability. The chapter then explains in detail the new all-volunteer model and how it will work. The chapter ends with a look at Spain's initial successes as well as mistakes, and the challenges that remain for Spain to get the most out of the new all-volunteer system.

A New Role for Spain

As outlined in the 2003 Strategic Review, Spain's ongoing military transformation is not simply an adaptation to changing strategic circumstances. It is also designed to support the increasing role that Spain wants to play on the international stage, and the weight that its defense policy and armed forces carry in fulfilling this role.

Spain, which has been a member of NATO since 1982, has been firmly anchored in the institutional framework of the Atlantic Alliance since its full incorporation into the newly renovated NATO command structure in January 1999. Spain is also actively committed to upgrading its military capability for autonomous action within the European Union (EU), in an effort to consolidate its role as a full-fledged global actor. One such change is a significant transformation in personnel policy. In 2001 Spain replaced its "mixed model" of conscripts and volunteers with an all-volunteer force. Women were also fully integrated into all jobs and assignments.

More recently, the National Defense Directive of January 2004 stated that the Spanish armed forces will collaborate in Spain's civil protection system and will thus, together with other state institutions, help protect citizens' security and welfare. In the multi-national framework, Spain will actively participate in the initiatives of an expanded and transformed NATO, particularly the Prague Capabilities Commitment and the Response Force, to contribute to effective conflict prevention and crisis management. Spain seeks to promote its relationships with the European Union and NATO, from the conviction that a solid, balanced and robust trans-Atlantic link is a vital element of peace and stability.

The January 2004 directive also establishes, as a key tenet of Spain's defense policy, the development of a new all-volunteer armed forces model. This model, based on quality and specialization, should be able to answer the needs of new technology and the organization of a modern military. The success of a professional armed forces model depends largely on the quantity and quality of personnel. Thus, personnel comprise its most important element and critical asset. Spain must therefore recruit and retain the highest quality personnel from a diverse, open, and competitive society; adequately train, motivate, and equip them; manage them carefully, ensuring that their needs and the needs of their families are addressed, recognizing the sacrifices that military service requires of them, and attempting to match service needs with personal preferences; and develop careers that motivate personnel and integrate them into the armed forces, fostering a sense of significance and the internalization of service objectives and interests. In December 2005, additional important reforms addressed some problems with the 1999 model for Spain's AVF.

Background for Recent Decisions

Since 1812, the Spanish military has been characterized by compulsory service. Although most servicemembers were conscripts, there were some professional units of volunteers, such as the Spanish Legion. Over the years Spanish forces were deployed in Cuba, the Philippines, Vietnam, Morocco, the Sahara desert, and Equatorial Guinea.

In 1991, a mixed armed forces model, known as Armed Forces 2000, was approved by Spain's Parliament. Under this model, Spain planned a force of 130,000 troops comprising 60 percent conscripts and 40 percent professional volunteer soldiers. At that time, of the nine Western

Figure 13.1. Number of Troops in Spanish Forces (Selected Years)

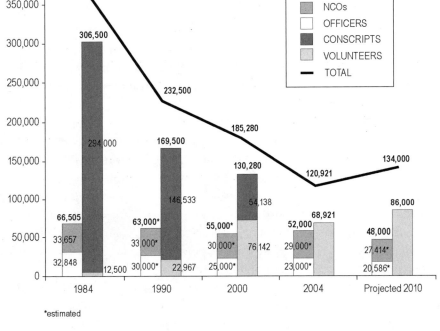

*estimated

European Union (WEU) countries, only the United Kingdom and Luxembourg had fully professional military forces. Ten years later, however, most WEU member countries had begun transitions to fully volunteer armed forces.

In June 1996, with the accession to power of the Popular Party, a joint Senate-Congress Commission was established to develop a fully professional model for the Spanish armed forces. Two years later, in 1998, the Spanish Parliament approved the commission's report and implementation was begun. In May 1999, Law 17/99 established regulations detailing how the fully professional armed forces model would work.[1] The law also established a maximum force strength between 150,000 and 170,000, to include 102,000–120,000 enlisted soldiers and sailors and 48,000 officers and noncommissioned officers (NCOs).

1.   Law 17/99, State Official Bulletin no. 119, May 19, 1999.

The law established a two-year transition period. However, in December 2001, one year before the volunteer force was to take effect, the government suddenly terminated nearly two centuries of compulsory service in Spain and launched its fully professional armed force. This decision arose, in part, in response to public demands not to employ conscripts in actions abroad.

Spain had also been drawing down its force since the mid-1990s. Figure 13.1 depicts the decline in Spanish armed forces personnel since 1984. Between 1984 and 2004, the size of the armed forces decreased by over 250,000. The number of conscripts dropped precipitously, while the number of volunteer troops and sailors rose from 12,500 in 1984, to about 50,000 in 2000, and 73,000 in 2005. The number of volunteers is targeted at 80,000–90,000 by 2010; about 27,400 NCOs and nearly 20,600 officers would round out the force, bringing the total strength of the entire armed forces to 128,000–138,000 troops.

Reasons for Change

Several factors contributed to Spain's decision to transition to a downsized and fully professional volunteer force. As Cindy Williams describes in the introduction to this volume, the security and defense environment changed significantly in 1990 when, after more than forty years, the threat of a major war disappeared with the fall of the Berlin wall and the dissolution of the Soviet Union.

However, new challenges emerged which required not only a different kind of force, but also new ways to employ military forces. Peace enforcement and support operations, humanitarian relief, and non-combatant evacuation operations became more critical. Spanish forces in the last twenty years have deployed forces, humanitarian relief, and observers in many places around the globe.[2]

---

2. Spain has participated in humanitarian and other missions in Albania, Afghanistan, Angola, Bosnia, Central and South America and the Caribbean, Chechnya, Congo, Eritrea, Ethiopia, Haiti, Iraq, Kyrgyzstan, Kosovo, Macedonia, Mozambique, Nagorno-Karabakh, Sudan, and elsewhere. Spain has deployed ships, aircraft, and land forces in support of many NATO operations, including "Joint Guardian," "Joint Forge," "Allied Harmony," "Deny Flight," "Eagle Assist," "Enduring Freedom," "Combined Endeavor," and "Allied Harbor." As of 2006, Spain's military maintained contingents in the

Concurrent with these changes, technological innovations began to allow Spanish forces to accomplish more with fewer members. Growing international cooperation on security matters let Spain and other countries share the security burden and thus meet their military obligations with smaller forces.

Domestically, changes in social and economic priorities also pressed Spain to downsize and professionalize its force. From a purely pragmatic viewpoint, the decline in the birthrate was another important reason why conscription was no longer a viable model for Spain. The population of men aged 18 to 27 will continue to fall, from about 2.85 million in 2004 to 2.15 million in 2016, a decline of about 25 percent. (See Figure 13.2.) The population of women in that age group will decline by one quarter as well.

Changing attitudes at home also contributed to Spain's decision to hasten the transition from conscription to a volunteer force. For example, with the decline in the size of the military in the post–Cold War period, and fewer conscripts needed to fill the shrinking ranks, people found it unacceptable that military service should be required of only a small percentage of the population, while most could avoid serving. Conscription was increasingly seen as inequitable, and society was calling for its elimination. Spain's growing role in multi-national operations also made compulsory service less popular, as the public resisted sending conscripts on missions far from home.

All of these factors contributed to Spain's decision to replace the mixed model of volunteers and draftees with a smaller, all-volunteer force. But in order for a smaller force to be successful in the new security environment, it would also have to be a more selective and highly trained force, committed and motivated as only true volunteers can be. The Defense Capabilities Initiative (DCI), approved by the Heads of State and Government at the Washington Summit in April 1999, established the premise—generally applied by Western armed forces—of compensating for smaller numbers with greater effectiveness. Countries must not only recruit, retain, and train high-quality forces; they must also supply their forces with advanced weaponry to make them strate-

---

Balkans (since 1992), and in Haiti and Afghanistan, and was performing humanitarian relief in Pakistan.

Figure 13.2. Spanish Population Between 18 and 27 Years of Age, 2004 to 2020

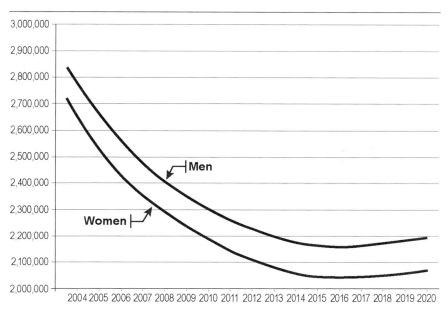

gically and technologically superior. Advanced technology can only compensate for smaller numbers if servicemembers know how to use it.

Budget Trends and System Efficiencies

During the first half of the 1990s, changes in the strategic landscape led to adjustments in the defense budgets of Western countries, as they pursued what has been called the "peace dividend." Spain was no exception to this trend. Spanish defense budgets increased only modestly during that time, hampering military modernization efforts.

This slow budget growth was reversed following the decision to move to a volunteer military. As Figure 13.3 shows, Spain's defense budgets grew substantially after 1997 in order to support government objectives to boost the number of volunteers in the armed forces.

There are several other components of defense spending besides the defense budget, and they should be included in any comprehensive picture of total defense spending. The Ministry of Industry, for example, finances military modernization through the development of three main armament programs: the EF-2000 aircraft, the F-100 frigate, and the

Figure 13.3. Spanish Defense Budget 1995–2006 (in million Euros)

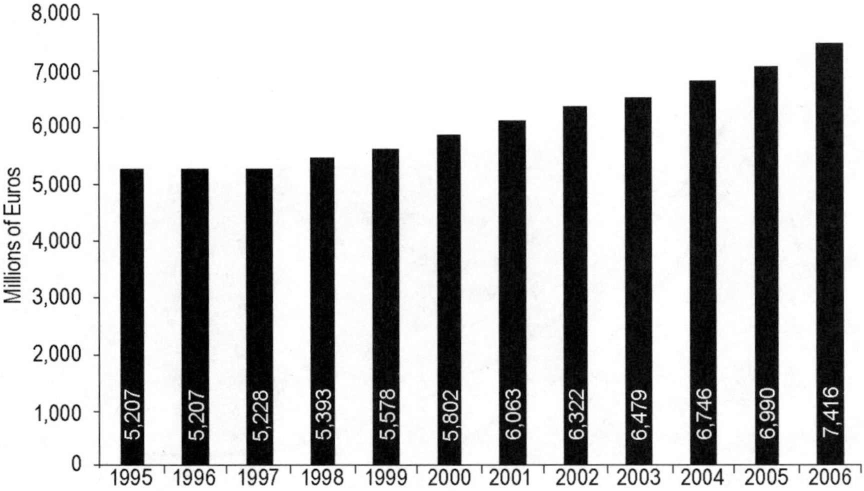

Leopard tank. This program supplies industry with repayable zero-interest loans, worth about 841.4 billion Euros in 2000.

International peace operations are also funded separately: because most such operations arise unexpectedly, their costs cannot be predicted and included in the defense budget. Salaries, living expenses, and other costs of these overseas deployments increase total defense spending by an additional 120 million Euros annually. The sale of military facilities, on the other hand, has generated surpluses which can be used to finance the modernization and professionalization of the armed forces.

In response to the changing security environment, the shift to an all-volunteer force, and technological innovations, Spain has instituted other changes, described in the remainder of this section, to enhance efficiency in military systems, structures, and programs.

DEFENSE STRUCTURES

The organization of the Ministry of Defense (MOD) has been centralized since 1978 to improve coordination of management and joint activities of the armed forces, while also supporting decentralized implementation of decisions by the three services. The Army, Navy, and Air Force headquarters may also be brought together in a single building under the administrative arm of the MOD, whose structure has been streamlined to facilitate efficiency by eliminating unnecessary elements. Several barracks and air and naval bases have been closed, consistent with the military's new focus on projecting military capabilities rather than defending geographical areas.

EDUCATION AND TRAINING

Both the quantity and quality of military education has been changed to meet the needs of volunteer professional men and women. A concerted effort has been made to minimize the size and complexity of the training organization, decreasing the number of schools and training centers and tailoring remaining facilities to the needs of a volunteer force. One of the new guiding principles of military training is to apply similar criteria to education in fields that are similar enough to be unified, while pursuing complementarity between different armed forces centers. Since Spain's armed forces will fight in a joint environment, they should be trained and educated in a joint environment. One example of this coordination is the establishment of the Armed Forces College for Higher Studies, which awards General Staff Diplomas to Army, Navy, and Air Force officers, as well as providing specialized advanced military studies.

ARMAMENT AND MATÉRIEL

The effectiveness of the armed forces largely depends on the availability of an integrated logistic support system that gets the appropriate matériel to the right place in a timely manner. Two key objectives in this area are to standardize the procurement of common elements in order to maximize market possibilities, and to achieve interoperability with Spain's allies.

HEALTH

The increased number of multi-national operations in locations far from home has compelled Spain to change the way it delivers health services to its military personnel. The military's health-care system now depends on medical facilities and equipment that can be moved to different theaters quickly, and can operate there for the entire deployment period.

Consistent with the trend in other European countries (principally those in NATO and the WEU), Spain will reduce the number of its military hospitals to a level that is sufficient to meet force needs in both normal and crisis situations. The integration of military hospitals within

Table 13.1. New Spanish Volunteer Armed Forces Model (2005)

	Officers	NCOs	Temporary officers and NCOs	Total officers and NCOs	Enlisted volunteers	Total
Army	8,804	15,173	1,797	25,774	52,978	78,752
Navy including Marines	2,942	5,088	471	8,501	14,755	23,256
Air Force	2,629	6,530	710	9,869	12,267	22,136
Medical, law, and other specialists	2,411	623	822	3,856		3,856
Total	16,786	27,414	3,800	48,000	80,000	128,000

Spain's national healthcare system will allow health-care support to the military to be coordinated more cost-effectively. It will also ensure that military health professionals maintain an appropriate level of medical proficiency.

The New Spanish Armed Forces Model

The ultimate objective is a fully professional force that integrates human resources in an effective and efficient joint organization; is flexible and thus capable of adapting rapidly to changing environments; and is capable of carrying out Spain's role in international commitments and of meeting the performance standards expected by Spanish society.

As shown in Table 13.1, the size of the force is meant to be 128,000 when the professional model is fully implemented (or, given the 2005 recruiting results, as much as 138,000). Officers (including NCOs) will account for about 37 percent of the force, while the remaining 63 percent will be made up of 80,000 volunteer enlisted soldiers and sailors. The army is the largest force, accounting for three out of every five members of the military. The Navy (including Marines) and Air Force each have shares of about 17 to 18 percent, with the remaining 3 percent made up of physicians, lawyers, and other specialists and professionals who are part of a separate service called the Common Corps.

Aside from being wholly voluntary, this model is different from the prior mixed model in three critical ways: it permits individuals to become either temporary or permanent members of the Spanish armed forces; it provides for the complete integration of women into the military; and it establishes a reserve component to supplement the active-duty force.

TEMPORARY AND PERMANENT TROOPS

In December 2005, Spain's new government changed the law on enlistment.[3] Under the previous system established by Law 17/99, individuals could sign up for a temporary enlistment term of twelve or eighteen months, or two or three years. After three years, the soldier or sailor could reenlist up to a maximum of twelve years of service or 35 years of age, whichever came first. After a certain number of years, the individual might have the opportunity to advance, based on examinations and favorable recommendations, to the rank of corporal, first corporal, or corporal major, the highest troop rank. After serving eight years in the military, individuals might make the transition to permanent status and serve until the mandatory retirement age of 58. This system was expected to produce an enlisted force comprising 70 percent temporary and 30 percent permanent members.

This model had two problems: excessive turnover (the average term was about three years), and lack of stability, because servicemembers were forced to leave the armed forces after twelve years if they were not accepted for permanent or career service. These problems prevented Spain from reaching its target figures.

For these reasons, in December 2005, the government established a new model, aimed at achieving a more balanced relationship between temporary and permanent servicemembers: about 35 percent on three-year terms (temporary), 45 percent in long-term (temporary) enlistment (up to age 45), and 20 percent of the force on a permanent or career basis (allowed to serve to age 58). The December 2005 reform established a total strength of 80,000–90,000 servicemembers.

Other changes, compared to the 1999 model, included establishing short-term contracts of two or three years, to a maximum of six years of service; and a longer-term contract which, with a favorable review, can be renewed after five years of service, up to the age of 45. At 45 years

---

3.   Official Bulletin of the Cortes (Congress), December 28, 2005.

Table 13.2. Women Military Personnel in the Spanish Armed Forces

	Officers and NCOs			Enlisted soldiers and sailors	Women as % of services 2006	Total
	Officers	NCOs	Training Center			
Army	124	71	94	7,203	16.83%	7,492
Navy/Marines	31	9	9	1,907	16.63%	1,956
Air Force	87	44	64	2,055	20.36%	2,250
Medical, law and other specialists	509	8	48	—		565
Total	751	132	215	11,165	17.34%	12,263

old, those not accepted as permanent or career servicemembers could leave the armed forces and become "special reservists"; in this status, they would be entitled to an annual stipend (7200 Euros), and could work at a civilian job, but could be recalled to service in case of an emergency. The reform also allowed for bonuses to servicemembers who left the service before the age of 45. To become a permanent servicemember under the new model requires a long-term contract, credentials from Spain's General Education System (at least a technician's degree), and at least fourteen years of service.

THE ROLE OF WOMEN

Full participation of women in the new volunteer military is a milestone for the Spanish armed forces. Initially, there were limitations on their participation: for example, women were not permitted to serve in some marine units, on submarines, or as parachutists. Today, however, women can fill any post within the armed forces, and they currently account for about 17.3 percent of the force (see Table 13.2). Women must meet the same physical standards and other qualifications for occupational assignments and deployments that are required of men. Typically, women choose administrative and logistical units rather than operational units. The physical requirements of some occupations, such as rifle companies, artillery, and special operations, can be more challenging, but as long as they are qualified, women are free to volunteer for any occupational specialty or deployment.

The rising number of women in Spain's armed forces has made family issues an increasingly important part of personnel policy. For example, women are now granted maternity leave for up to sixteen weeks; Spain is exploring the option of offering paternity leave as well. In addition, many of the large Army, Naval, and Air bases now provide child-care.

Spain has found that women can be a very positive influence on their units, often providing a perspective different from that of their male peers. On missions abroad, local women, children, and the elderly often interact more easily with female servicemembers where there are cultural or religious challenges. Because they are often viewed as less threatening, women may improve force protection by more easily gaining acceptance among the civilian population. They may also be able to facilitate negotiations and other interactions with the local citizenry. In addition, there are certain duties that only women may perform, such as body searches of women and, in some countries, administration of medical care.

Spain's recruitment advertising campaigns highlight the achievements of successful women in uniform, demonstrate the full spectrum of roles that women can assume, and show servicewomen working in teams with their male counterparts. Spain also includes young servicewomen on recruiting teams to relate better to prospective female recruits.

THE RESERVE COMPONENT

Spain has modified its reserve system so that it better complements the smaller, all-volunteer force structure. Until recently, the reserve force was made up of temporary reservists: soldiers or sailors serving as reservists for one to five years after leaving active duty. Such temporary reservists currently total approximately 28,000. Young people aged 19–25 could also be called upon to serve as compulsory reservists, but only if authorized by Congress during times of emergency, something that has never occurred.

In 2004, Spain added a volunteer component to its reserve force. The volunteer reserve is made up of civilians. They can join any of the three services for two or three years, and thereafter sign a temporary agreement to serve up to fifteen additional years. Upon enlistment, volunteer reservists receive basic, short-term military training as well as specialized training related to their job responsibilities in the reserve. Annual retraining is also required to maintain and update skills. While application to the voluntary reserve is open to the general public, to date most applicants have been former military personnel who were previously under temporary contracts with the armed forces.

Recruitment goals for the reserves are included in the annual plan for the recruitment of armed forces personnel. As of mid-2005, the Ministry of Defense had held two recruitment drives for 2,214 volunteer reserve positions, and had enrolled nearly 1,500 reservists. The goal is to increase volunteer reserve totals to 3,000, and to begin activating volunteer reservists in the near future.

The volunteer reserve will serve as an important complement to the downsized professional active-duty force. At this time there are no plans to replace any permanent forces with reservists. Instead, reservists will supplement and reinforce active-duty personnel, and allow for expansion of capability during times of conflict or crisis. When activated, volunteer reservists will be integrated into existing military units based on their specific skills rather than organized into separate reserve units.

Volunteer reservists' dual roles in the military and civilian sectors present opportunities and challenges. Because reservists will operate in both sectors, they will provide a critical link between the armed forces and civilian society, a connection that might otherwise become more tenuous following Spain's move from a conscription-based military to an all-volunteer professional force. Their civilian training and work experience will also provide the reserves with particular skills, such as foreign language proficiency or computer expertise, that could be valuable in fulfilling Spain's current military missions.

At the same time, Spain must develop strategies that protect reservists' dual roles so as to enable volunteer reservists to meet their military obligations while continuing to succeed in their civilian careers. To that end, the Royal Decree that created the volunteer reserve force calls for agreements between the Ministry of Defense, employer organizations, public administrations, and social agencies to coordinate reservists' military and civilian responsibilities and minimize workplace disruptions due to reservists' military service.[4]

A viable reserve force needs the support of civilian employees and employers. Employees must believe that volunteering for the reserves will not hurt their civilian careers, and employers must be assured that employing a reservist will not disrupt workplace operations.

---

4. Royal Decree 1691/2003, December 13, 2003.

Essential Personnel Processes

The Joint Parliamentary House-Senate Committee Report enacted in 1998 may be considered the seminal document for Spain's professional armed forces model.[5] It established:

- a force size defined by the missions of the new Spanish armed forces, numbering between 150,000 and 170,000 military personnel (officers, NCOs, and enlisted soldiers and sailors);

- a reserve and mobilization system that allows progressive and selective filling of ranks for the services, and for generation of extra forces when necessary to meet security and defense needs;

- full and meaningful integration of civilian personnel serving in the Ministry of Defense.

The successful implementation of an all-volunteer professional armed force requires smooth functioning of six fundamental personnel processes: personnel planning; recruiting; integration; personnel management; training; and return to civilian life. These processes are closely related, since decisions and actions in one area may have profound repercussions elsewhere in the system. The Spanish armed services are working aggressively to ensure that these personnel processes are operating as effectively as possible to support Spain's all-volunteer force.

PERSONNEL PLANNING

The personnel planning process is the set of activities that determine the size of the force. Specifically, it includes plans that determine annual numerical requirements for officers, soldiers, sailors, marines, and civilian personnel; analyze manpower requirements for occupational specialties as well as training capacity; establish a procedure for evaluating, selecting, and classifying personnel for optimal job assignment; and determine the number of reservists needed, matching skills and training of personnel with particular job requirements.

---

5. 1998 Joint Parliamentary House-Senate Committee Report, approved by the Congress May 28, 1998, and by the Senate June 9, 1998.

RECRUITING

Recruitment activities are critical to the viability of the all-volunteer force. The recruiting process involves activities designed to obtain a sufficient number and quality of young men and women to sustain the force. These activities include establishment of recruiting facilities and the fielding of a cadre of professionally trained recruiting teams; determining specific enlistment incentives; developing an aggressive mass-media advertising campaign; and establishing a selection plan to avoid losses of new recruits.[6]

Figure 13.4 shows the growth in the number of enlisted volunteers (excluding officers and NCOs) by service since 1987. As the figure illustrates, the number of volunteers in the Spanish armed forces increased dramatically during the mid-1990s, growing from just over 28,000 in 1994 to a high of over 76,000 in 2000. The most rapid growth during this period occurred from 1998–2000, and coincided with the introduction of the all-volunteer force. Since then, however, volunteer force totals have fallen off, dropping to under 71,000 in 2003, more than 10 percent below the 80,000 target. The total force size had only reached 73,641 by December 2005.

To address the shortfall, Spain took steps in December 2005 to strengthen recruiting, including offering a joining bonus of 564 Euros and a 7 percent salary increase. Other aspects of the new reforms also provide recruitment incentives, such as the changes allowing someone to remain in the service until age 45, and to receive a stipend after this period.

While Spain is working aggressively to increase recruitment and total force levels, it still must ensure that the individuals it recruits meet standards for high quality. Despite the recruitment shortfall in 2004, many applicants were not accepted because they did not meet the quality standards that are necessary for success in today's armed forces. Spain prefers to take additional time to meet recruitment goals with high-quality servicemen and women, even if this delays meeting those recruitment targets. As the Defense Capabilities Initiative emphasized, to respond

---

6. These losses, known as "initial wastage" or attrition, total about 30 percent; they can be lessened by, for example, reducing the period between the initial selection of new recruits and the date on which they actually enter the military.

Figure 13.4. Number of Enlisted Volunteers in Spanish Armed Forces, 1987–2003

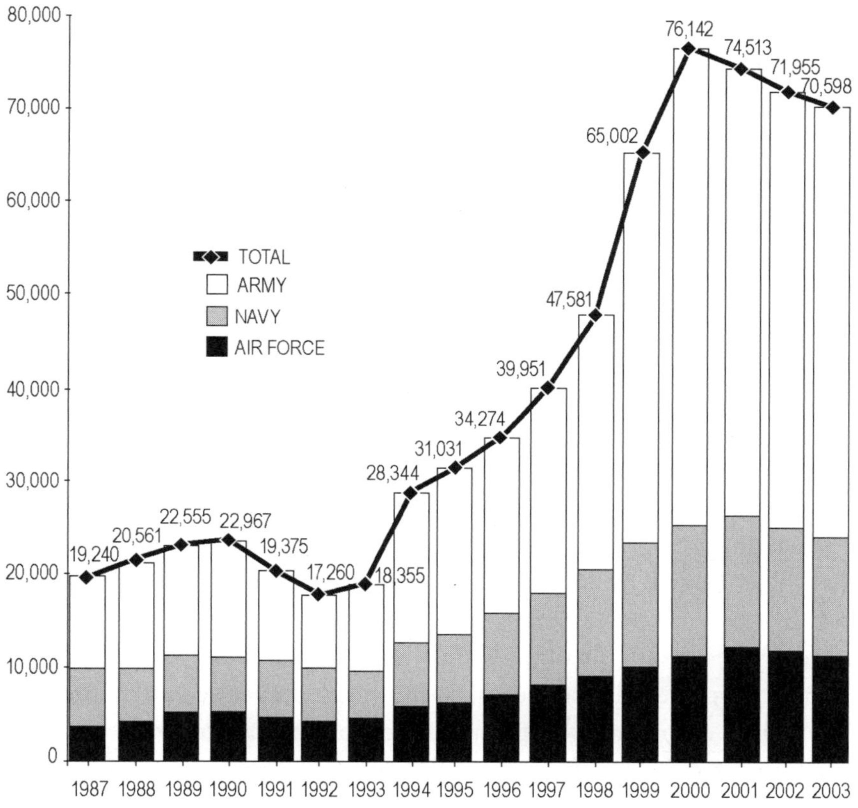

Note: Figures are as of December 3 for each year.

successfully to today's diverse security challenges, a smaller armed force must be sufficiently talented, trained, motivated, and equipped.

Recruitment results are also affected by public opinion and societal expectations. In Spain and around the globe, societies are increasingly influenced by a materialist perspective emphasizing the pursuit of individual well-being and personal success with minimum effort. The result is a decreasing acceptance of personal sacrifice. These values have led to increasing public protests, often prompted by "friendly fire" and casualties among armed forces personnel. With Spanish armed forces active in missions at home and abroad, these public expectations can make recruitment more challenging.

Meeting recruiting goals will become even more difficult over the next fifteen years as the target population of 18-to-27-year-olds drops by 25 percent. To improve the supply of potential recruits, the government has expanded eligibility so that immigrants from South America and Equatorial Guinea can join the Spanish armed forces, up to a maximum of 7 percent of the total force (roughly equivalent to the immigrant proportion of Spain's population).

Spain must also look for other, more creative ways for people to serve. For example, people who are not interested in full-time military careers may be willing to enlist in the reserves. The size and role of the reserve forces could be expanded to maximize the contribution such individuals could make to the total force.

INTEGRATION: RETENTION AND QUALITY OF LIFE

Personnel integration policies are designed to align the objectives of the organization with those of its servicemembers. The aim is for members to internalize the organization's goals while the organization promotes individual participation and development, along with order and discipline. The Spanish military is developing policies to enhance motivation and, in turn, the performance and productivity of the force; facilitate retention and ensure a high-quality force by selecting and promoting the best people; establish lines of communication between the organization and its members, permitting a free flow of information consistent with respect for and efficiency of the chain of command; and provide assistance and support to military members regarding their personal and family life.

Prior to the December 2005 reform, the policies to enhance retention were primarily focused on retaining troops for twelve years. A bonus equivalent to three months' pay (approximately 3,000 Euros) was generally offered after four years and again after six years of service, with another 1,000 Euros after eight years of service.

This bonus structure was changed by the December 2005 reforms. The bonuses at four and six years remain, but the bonus at eight years has been eliminated. New incentives in the same amount are now given after three, five, and seven years in service to servicemembers who have been posted in specified units for a minimum period of time (at least twelve months, for the three-year bonus, and 18 months for the five-year and seven-year bonuses).

Other benefits also support retention:

- a clothing allowance is given after two years of service;

- food and accommodation on board ships and in barracks is provided free of charge;

- a bonus is given to enable a servicemember to buy a house after five years of service; after three years in service one can apply for military housing; after three years, a special bonus for housing is offered to those who have been posted abroad during this period; and housing loans can be requested in certain circumstances;

- insurance is offered in case of death or injury at home or abroad;

- free health care is provided for servicemembers and their families;

- a retirement pension is offered to permanent servicemembers with at least twenty-three years of service (eight years as temporary servicemembers and fifteen years as permanent members);

- those who have served at least fifteen years become entitled to receive a pension beginning at age 65; the amount of the pension depends on how many years were served.

PERSONNEL MANAGEMENT

The personnel management process is designed to ensure that all military jobs are filled with the right people. Personnel policies and incentive programs are formulated to ensure that actual personnel inventory by rank and years of service matches the desired personnel planning requirements; to optimize the personnel assignment system so that sufficiently qualified military members are in the right jobs at the right time; and to improve promotion prospects of all military personnel and ensure that the promotion process is perceived as fair and equitable by all.

TRAINING

Personnel training involves programs and policies that prepare military personnel to perform well on their jobs at all levels. Training programs are designed to balance classroom and on-the-job training, as well as service-specific and joint training; to permit access to various courses according to service needs; and to ensure coordination and updating of study plans. For soldiers and sailors, as well as officers and NCOs, a progression of courses and exams is offered by which they can be evaluated and promoted. There are also provisions for courses by which soldiers have access to Spain's General Education System and can obtain degrees and credentials that are essential to advancement (for example to become a permanent soldier or sailor) within Spain's military.

Promotion and Professional Activities

Promotion is a critical factor in personnel management: the military system is basically a hierarchical organization in which individuals enter the system early in their careers and advance in rank over time. Under the new model, only 80 percent of NCO posts are reserved for soldiers and sailors with at least three years of service (prior to December 2005 it was 100 percent); the idea is to permit lateral entry at the NCO level by people who have not already served as soldiers or sailors.

Under the December 2005 reforms, those who have served in a temporary status can apply to become permanent members of the Spanish armed forces; up to 1,500 may be accepted into the permanent force each year. To become a permanent servicemember, an individual must agree to a long-term contract; must have education credentials under Spain's General Education System (a technician's degree); and must have served at least fourteen years. Soldiers and sailors can also apply for acceptance to the Officer Academies of the three services.

Several December 2005 reforms focus on servicemembers' transition to the civilian job market after leaving the armed forces. For example:

- time of service may be credited toward jobs with the State Administration;

- the Ministry of Defense will negotiate agreements with local administrations to reserve posts for former servicemembers;

- at least 50 percent of civilian posts in the Ministry of Defense and Civil Guard, and at least 10 percent of posts with the National Police, will be reserved for those with at least five years in the armed services;[7]

---

7. Posts in the Civil Guard were reserved for former servicemembers under Law 17/99, but the prerequisite was only three years of military service; the December 2005 reform changed that to five years.

- more time in military service may be credited toward a retirement pension; and

- people leaving the armed forces may receive a stipend until finding a civilian job.

In addition, an Employment Bureau maintains a computerized database to match job preferences and skills with current job openings in the private sector, and former soldiers and sailors who want to start their own businesses can apply for very-low-interest loans.

The education and training provided to servicemembers can also help facilitate the transition to the civilian labor market. Currently, there are forty-nine military occupational specialties in Spain's armed forces, requiring different types and levels of educational and training. Most of these specialties have an equivalent in Spain's national education system, providing a convenient transition of servicemembers' training and credentials to the civilian sector. The Ministry of Defense has made agreements with many private-sector Spanish enterprises and with other government agencies to facilitate the transition of departing military members to civilian life. The possibility of a smooth transition to the civilian sector, aided by training and job experience gained in the military, is a powerful incentive for recruiting.

Initial Success and Future Challenges

Three years after the transition to an all-volunteer military, its positive effects were already evident in Spain. Yet there is still much to do, even with the reforms of December 2005. After all, even after ten years, there were still those in the United States who were skeptical that a volunteer force would work there. Indeed, it took twenty years for the United States to consider its volunteer force a complete success.[8]

Spain's transition can be considered an initial success for several reasons. First, the Ministry of Defense has been able to work within the Spanish socio-cultural milieu to make the fully professional armed forces model acceptable to many of those in both public and private sectors who had serious doubts about its viability and effectiveness. Sec-

---

8. See Chapter 9 by Bernard Rostker and Curtis Gilroy in this volume.

ond, during a very short period of time, Spain has been able to recruit and retain enough professional soldiers and sailors—about 73,000 as of December 2005—to make the volunteer force viable.

Third, Spain has made this transition during a time when the Spanish armed forces have been active in missions at home and abroad. Fourth, the military itself has supported the notion of a volunteer force, which represents a significant departure from the previous mixed model of conscripts and volunteers. Finally, Spain has fully integrated women and immigrants into the armed forces, a significant social and demographic advance for both Spanish society and the Spanish military.

With the December 2005 reform, the Spanish government has addressed some of the issues that arose during Spain's transition to an all-volunteer force, most notably lower-than-anticipated recruitment and total force levels. Important steps included increasing from 35 years to 45 years the maximum age by which non-career servicemembers must leave the force; eliminating the twelve-year service limit for temporary soldiers and sailors; reducing the maximum force strength for enlisted soldiers and sailors to 80,000 or 90,000; allowing immigrants to join; annually reserving 10 percent of national police positions for soldiers and sailors; adding a permanent monthly stipend of approximately 500 Euros for members who leave the military after 45 years of age; creating a new "special reservist" category for former servicemembers who would receive reserve pay and be available for recall; and creating new training and job placement initiatives to assist separating servicemembers in their transitions to civilian life and employment.

For recruitment, retention, and equity reasons, Spain has ensured that salaries of military members at all ranks are commensurate with salaries they could earn in the private sector. From November 2005, salaries were updated with raises of 6.7 percent for soldiers and sailors, 9.4 percent for NCOs, and 6.2 percent for officers (2.7 percent for generals). Spain must take further steps to compensate servicemembers for the substantial differences in working conditions among units and across the services. For example, recruiting for the Navy is more of a challenge than recruiting for the Air Force, because sailors spend more days away from home base and family and work under less desirable conditions. Pay reforms could address this.

With the new reforms, Spain has achieved a new balance between temporary and permanent military status. The former policy of requiring eight years of service in the armed forces before becoming eligible for permanent status has been abolished because there was evidence that it caused significant attrition. Under the new reforms, Spain will increase the number and proportion of permanent soldiers and sailors in its armed forces.

Spain needs to work more with industry, employers, and organizations on collaborative agreements to facilitate the transition of separating military members to civilian status. Similarly, Spain should speed up the process for recognition of military education and qualifications by the General Education System. As part of this process, in the last two years 47 military technician degrees have been created which are equivalent to the corresponding credentials in Spain's General Education System.

Spain must watch its recruiting process, emphasizing quality recruits, the lifeblood of a volunteer military. Advertising must be designed to highlight the prestige of the armed forces. Publicity campaigns should raise awareness among youth that the military is a good career choice, offers valuable education and training that can be transferred to the civilian sector, is a noble calling, and is selective. Military advertisements have abandoned the slogan "In the armed forces you can find a job" for new mottos that emphasize military values: "be ready," "work like a team," "no routine."

Finally, Spain must be ever mindful of retention and quality-of-life issues. Although retention—at about 80 percent today—is impressive, this could deteriorate if Spain does not provide servicemembers and their families, particularly those working under harsh conditions far from home, with the support they need.

Spain's new armed forces model requires the right number of high-quality, well trained, and highly motivated military and civilian personnel, along with leaders at all organizational levels who ensure discipline and success within the ranks. But while its personnel must be capable of operating the most advanced modern weapons systems and managing a complex organization, they also are part of an enduring and glorious military tradition, with high standards of courage, discipline, moral values, comradeship, loyalty, and a spirit of sacrifice.

Chapter 14

Romania's Transition to an All-Volunteer Force

Managerial Challenges and Opportunities

Mihaela Matei

Starting in the early 1990s, the reform of Central and Eastern European armed forces presented difficult challenges, as it had to deal with the same transformation in missions and roles as in Western Europe—from territorial defense to tasks of crisis management, stabilization, and re-construction—but starting from a historically different foundation. The post-communist legacy in most of the former Warsaw Pact countries meant large forces, mass-intervention doctrines, obsolete equipment, and in many cases a politicized officer corps.[1]

Personnel can be one of the most difficult arenas in which to accom-plish transformation. Conceptual and managerial inertia present much bigger obstacles where people and traditions are involved rather than, for example, the acquisition of new equipment. It is also complicated because it requires not only new administrative policies, but also a new infrastructure for recruitment, training, pay, and other functions.

New members of NATO, furthermore, had at the same time to man-age the overall transition to market economies, democratic institutions, and patterns of good governance. During the past decade, Romania has made substantial progress in all these areas. Romanian forces have been

---

1. Some analysts speak of "dual-track" military reform, based both on catching up with Western systems procedures and defense strategies and on keeping up with the current transformations in NATO. Others have also in-cluded economic reform in this pattern of development, identifying a triple transition in the defense planning processes of the Central and Eastern coun-tries. See Daniel N. Nelson, "Democracy, Market, Security," *Survival*, Vol. 35, No. 2 (Summer 1993), pp. 156–171.

actively involved in NATO missions in the Balkans, Afghanistan, and more recently Iraq. In addition, Romania has begun to define a path toward all-volunteer forces. Nevertheless, there is still much to be done in order to adapt personnel policies and personnel management to the challenges of today's military engagements.

The analysis of the transition to all-volunteer militaries in Central and Eastern Europe must take into account a number of complex variables. First, the transition to Western-type democratic management of the military profession was in a metaphorical sense like jumping from "pre-modern" thinking, in which soldiers were called upon for agricultural labors, as in Romania before 1989, right into the middle of postmodernity, when they found themselves training for new constabulary missions in complex foreign environments. Communist military practices have had a much more lingering effect than one might have expected at the beginning of the 1990s. Second, the ways in which the various Eastern European countries managed reform in previous years affects their current options for professionalization of the armed forces, whether through an all-volunteer system or a hybrid system that preserves the draft.

Finally, another variable is the transformation of management processes within the military. The relationship between the system of management and the individual expectations—the tension between the general requirements for force deployability and usability in operations, and the specific demands of people working in the military—also affects the creation of a professional military. This factor is even more important in a society facing its own transition to a market economy and the free movement of people and goods.

The chapter starts with a general overview of the main factors that drove Romania's military reforms and especially its moves toward professionalization of its army: the changes in the international security picture after September 11, 2001; public opinion in Romania; economic constraints; and Romania's preparation for NATO membership. That section is followed by a more detailed review of the context in which reform took place. Then the first phase of reforms, involving new legislation, downsizing, and restructuring, is discussed, followed by a review of the second phase, which focused specifically on personnel policies. The "first" and "second generation" of reforms are differentiated based on Cottey's study of civil and democratic control in post-communist countries.[2] He distinguishes between the initial steps in military reform, which mostly involve the development of a new legislative and structural framework, and the next stages, which actually tackle the tangible transformation of the armed forces and concrete measures for reshaping post-communist military establishments. These phases may overlap chronologically, but it is useful to distinguish them in order to highlight the differences between the first generation of early reforms aimed at establishing the rule of law, civilian oversight of the military, and the basic requirements for force restructuring, and the later or second-generation stages involving changes in the defense establishment. The economic and political context is also discussed, as well as the role of NATO accession in furthering the option for all-volunteer armed forces in Romania. The future challenges of professionalization for Romania—what could be called a third generation of military reforms—are then outlined. The chapter concludes by pointing out some of the lessons of Romania's experiences, as well as the way ahead in military transformation.

Professionalization of the Romanian Armed Forces

The main change in personnel policies for the Romanian Armed Forces occurred in 2003 when the decision was taken to switch from a universal conscription system to an all-volunteer force. This choice was the result of a long and sinuous process of reform that started in 1990 after Romania's revolution as well as of major external changes in international security and in Romania's economic and social conditions. Furthermore, this decision deeply affects the way military reform can develop in future years.

Four main factors led Romania to choose an all-volunteer force: new political and strategic requirements, public demands, economic appraisals, and the desire to become a reliable member of NATO. First, the changes in the international environment after September 11, 2001, led

---

2. Andrew Cottey, Timothy Edmunds, and Anthony Forster, "The Second Generation Problematic: Rethinking Democracy and Civil-Military Relations," *Armed Forces and Society*, Vol. 29, No. 1 (Fall 2002), pp. 31–56.

to a revision of domestic priorities for the reform of the overall security sector. They created the demand for an enhanced inter-agency approach to homeland defense, and accelerated change in views of the role and tasks of the military. The defense of Romania's interests and objectives and those of its allies went beyond the classic territorial approach, and the focus of the ensuing military reforms was towards new types of responses to new risks and threats. Since any conventional military attack against NATO members seems highly unlikely to occur in the next ten to fifteen years, the most probable missions for the Romanian armed forces were identified in national planning documents as out-of-area crisis response operations, counter-terrorism, and stabilization tasks.

The switch to an all-volunteer force was also based on previous operational experiences that indicated the shape the military forces should have to be successful in such new missions. From the mid-1990s, when Romania participated in the first NATO–Partnership for Peace (PfP) peace-support mission in Bosnia, the practice in Romania has been to rely for such operations only on enlisted (volunteer) personnel, because their training and skills correspond to the interoperability requirements of these missions.[3] Later it was recognized that the old mission concepts—of a long mobilization of forces for a territorial defense—no longer made sense, and that rapid-reaction capabilities should become the core of the military. The conscript component was deemed unsuitable to these new roles.

Second, public opinion also played an important part in the decision to give up conscription. Surveys in 2001 showed that 60 percent of the population favored a smaller, professional military, whereas only 34 percent supported a "larger army composed by the majority of men able to do service," that is, a nearly universal conscription-based system.[4]

---

3. Before Bosnia, Romanian forces were involved in a number of other operations, mostly under the UN flag, in Kuwait, Somalia, Angola, Albania, and elsewhere, but the requirements for interoperability were not as important during such missions as they would become in Bosnia. This is why the official decision to employ only enlisted personnel was made, starting with Bosnia SFOR mission.

4. Metro Media Transylvania, "Population's Attitudes Concerning the Military," February 2001. During the communist period, conscription was compulsory for women as well; this system of draft for women was eliminated at the beginning of the 1990s.

Conscription was increasingly perceived as an obstacle to young people seeking jobs in a fluid market environment, as their term of duty would interfere with their civilian careers.

During the last few years, the number of conscripts has been reduced; enlisted personnel as of 2005 made up more than 70 percent of Romania's troops. At the beginning of 2006, the Marines and Air Force were already fully based on volunteers.[5] These reductions have not been followed by a decline in public support for the armed forces, as some officials feared in the mid-1990s. On the contrary, the end of conscription was a major reason for public support when the new Romanian Constitution was approved by referendum in 2003.[6]

Third, professionalizing the military also reflected the growing influence of economic analysis on defense resources planning. Conscripts' terms of duty have been reduced from a year and a half (in 1990) to 12 months for high school graduates, and from 9 months to 6 months for university graduates. Due to the lack of funding, the quality of their training and equipment decreased dramatically during the first decade after 1989. The system of reserve training (based on periodic call-ups of former conscripts for limited training) also suffered from the lack of financial resources. Many conscripts did not receive refresher training after completion of their duty, and this diminished the opportunities for employing them in the reserve component. It became obvious that the conscript system did not offer the best value for money: conscripts' operational value was low, compared to the costs borne by the military establishment for their accommodation and training. Perhaps the sole benefit was to maintain a recruitment base of potential enlisted personnel.

There were other economic costs to society as well. One analyst described conscription as a "regressive tax" on citizens: conscripts receive

---

5. Romania's Minister of Defense Teodor Atanasiu outlined at the beginning of 2005 that, "We have a few more steps until the finalization of the process of professionalizing the army—an important part of modernization of this institution. The Naval Forces have concluded this process. The Air Forces are following, being set to complete this request by the end of 2005, and the Land Forces by 2007." *Nine O'Clock* (Bucharest), February 1, 2005.
6. Many headlines in Romanian newspapers covering the summer 2003 referendum on the new Constitution referred to the end of mandatory conscription as one of the provisions of the new Fundamental Law most "attractive" to citizens.

low incomes and serve in the military at low cost for a defined period of time.[7] But the results of such indirect taxation did not provide Romania with an increased military capability—a direct benefit for the armed forces—but rather a cheaper supply of labor for base maintenance, logistics, and guard functions.[8] Transition to an all-volunteer force should therefore improve the operational quality of forces, with higher costs in the short term, but lower costs in the long run. It will also require outsourcing some of the functions currently handled by conscript personnel for which a volunteer solution would be more costly than outsourcing.

Fourth, Romania's new security and defense policy objectives, as defined in the 2001 "National Security Strategy" and the 2004 "White Paper on National Security and Defense," called for the development of a new type of armed forces, rapidly deployable and interoperable, with adequate force-projection capabilities and the capacity to sustain themselves in distant and demanding out-of-area theaters.[9] This "Level of Ambition" was based upon the NATO Ministerial Guidance after Romania was officially invited, in November 2002 at the Prague Summit, to join the North Atlantic Alliance.[10]

---

7.   Zachary Selden, "Changing Patterns of Military Service in Europe," paper presented to Transatlantic Roundtable, "Filling NATO's Ranks: Military Personnel Policies in Transition," at the Transatlantic Center of the German Marshall Fund of the United States, Brussels, Belgium, September 8–9, 2003. See also Chapter 5 by John Warner and Sebastian Negrusa in this volume.
8.   It should be underlined that the changes in this area remain among the most difficult, since the reliance on military personnel to perform even non-military tasks was one of the main legacies—in practices and in mentality—of the communist regime. At some points during the late 1980s, most of the autumn harvest was brought in by conscripts, enlisted personnel, and students.
9.   According to Law 63 (2000), modified by Law 473 (2000), the president of Romania is responsible for the development of the "National Security Strategy." It is then adopted by the Parliament, and the Government issues a "White Paper on National Security and Defense" to guide security sector reform. On the basis of the White Paper, the MoD develops the "National Military Strategy." These three documents form the foundation of a planning cycle and are reviewed every four years, corresponding with the election of a new president and a new Parliament. See "National Security Strategy of Romania," December 2001, *Official Gazette*, Bucharest; "White Paper for National Security and Defense," 2004, *Official Gazette*, Bucharest.
10.   Romania was invited to join NATO in 2002; it officially joined the Alli-

On the basis of these new requirements, the decision to develop an all-volunteer force was made by the Romanian government in mid-2003. The negotiations for the accession to NATO that took place in the spring of that year also played a significant part in opening the debate on how the structure of the armed forces should be shaped after Romania's entry into NATO.

In the summer of 2003, Romanian citizens adopted by referendum a new Constitution which removed the former requirement of compulsory military duty. In December 2005, the Romanian president promulgated the decree for the adoption of the Law on suspension of compulsory military duty during peacetime, and the switch to the volunteer military service.[11]

Full professionalization is expected to be reached by the end of 2007 through a gradual decrease in the number of conscripts.[12] Some will be replaced by enlisted personnel, and others made redundant as force levels are reduced.

The Beginnings of Reform in Romania

Although proposals for an all-volunteer military had been discussed since the mid-1990s, Romanians were at first reluctant to give up conscription, based on perceptions that breaking this strong national tradition could create a civil-military gap and diminish public support for the armed forces.[13] Most countries in Central and Eastern Europe faced similar situations, as conscription has been a powerful historical institu-

---

ance in March 2004. During this one-and-a-half year period, all seven invited countries participated in NATO activities and force planning procedures; their internal documents and planning mechanisms had to be adapted so that they would be consistent with NATO.

11. See <www.mapn.ro> for the complete text of Law 395 (2005), published in the *Official Monitor*, Part I, no. 1155, December 20, 2005.

12. As of the beginning of 2005, expected numbers of conscripts were: in 2004, 27,000; in 2005, 22,500; in 2006, 18,000; and in 2007, 13,500. Given that the lesser the number, the greater the difficulty in choosing whom to conscript, the process may move faster than planned. Proposals for a random lottery solution are being considered.

13. Metro Media Transylvania polls of November 1998 and May 2002 show a constant and fairly high level of support for the armed forces at 70 to 80 percent.

tion in the region, connected with the unification and liberation wars of modern times and with popular perceptions about the positive effects of military training for young people.

Military reform in Romania started after the 1989 revolution with successive reductions in force numbers throughout the first decade, following various force-structure plans; concurrently one of the main targets for defense reform was the development of civilian oversight within the Ministry of National Defense.[14] In the mid-1990s, the overall defense policy and the drafting of strategic requirements for military reform were entrusted to a new civilian central unit in the MoD, the Department for Defense Policy and International Relations, while the strategies for personnel management became the responsibility of a new central directorate, the Human Resources Management Directorate, reporting directly to the Minister of Defense (prior to this, all personnel policies were the responsibility of the J1 military unit in the General Staff). At the end of the 1990s, the first plans for reduction of the armed forces were developed with the creation of a "pyramid of ranks" and initial measures to reduce the number of high-ranking officers. Personnel policies and guidelines were developed by the Human Resources Management Directorate and implemented by the J1 (Personnel) Directorate within the General Staff, thus ensuring a centralized policy process under civilian oversight, and decentralized management and control in personnel matters, distributed down to the military units.

At the beginning of the 1990s, Romania had very little civilian expertise to draw upon in the management of military reform. Most of the civilians working in those departments had been employed right after graduation from university, so most of their expertise had been gained by on-the-job training. After Romania joined the Partnership for Peace in 1994, training offered by NATO members helped to build civil servants' skills and improve civilian oversight of military affairs. The development of civilian oversight mechanisms took almost the entire decade; even today, control and supervision of certain areas is still under development and there numerous legacies and lingering inertia remain to be overcome.

---

14. The Ministry of National Defense (MND) includes the General Staff and the Ministry of Defense, MoD.

Since the beginning of the 1990s, reform of the Romanian armed forces has enjoyed a high level of public and political support, connected as it was with the strategic objective of accession to the North Atlantic Alliance. However, resources allotted to this process fluctuated for most of the 1990s and were not enough to cover all of the personnel costs associated with the restructuring process. The reason lies in the difficult overall economic transition in Romania, which has been characterized as one of the toughest in Central and Eastern Europe. At the beginning of the 1990s, ambitious plans for structural transformation in various sectors of the economy and public administration were delayed by strict constraints on the state budget and the challenges of privatizing a large heavy industry sector that had been oriented toward self-reliance.[15] Only by the end of the 1990s and the beginning of 2000 did economic recovery and a gradual decline in the inflation rate permit an increase of investments in the security sector.

During the early 1990s, most European Commission (EC) assessments found fault with Romania's management of public administration, noting ineffective personnel policies, inadequate pay, cumbersome bureaucratic procedures, and corruption.[16] However, the EC's 2004 Report acknowledged improvement and the development of a new strategy for "civil service reform, decentralization and deconcentration, and policy coordination," which the report called "a good basis for future reform"; it urged that "priority should now be given to its implementation."[17] Steps taken since the mid-1990s in reform of the civil service show progress towards better management of public administration.

---

15. "The World Bank Group's Country Assistance Strategy for Romania," see executive summary at <siteresources.worldbank.org/ROMANIAIN ROMANIANEXTN/Resources/cas_summary.pdf>, in "Memorandum of the President of the International Bank for Reconstruction and Development and the International Finance Corporation to the Executive Directors on a Country Assistance Strategy of the World Bank Group for Romania," May 22, 2001.
16. EU Regular and Progress Reports for Romania, 1998–2000, at <www.europa.eu.int/comm/enlargement/romania/key_documents.htm>. The EC Report of 2000, for example, states that, "corruption continues to be a widespread and systemic problem" (p. 18), and that "administrative reform ... remains an area where considerable additional efforts will be needed"; ibid., p. 16.
17. The 2004 and 2005 EU Commission Reports provide considerable data

The gradual reduction of the inflation rate and the steady growth of Romania's GDP since 2000 have allowed the defense budget to increase.[18] In the national planning documents—the "National Security Strategy" and the "White Paper on Security and National Defense"—a political decision was made that defense would be granted a standing annual budget allotment of 2.38 percent of GDP. During 2002–2004, this decision has provided the necessary funding to support the costs of NATO integration. The resulting gradual increase in the defense budget also resulted in the improvement of salaries both for military personnel and for civil servants working in the MoD. It alleviated some of the pressure on the defense budget created by the costs of force reduction (such as aiding personnel in their "reconversion" to civilian life) and base closures. It has also allowed the development of more ambitious plans for equipment modernization and multi-year acquisition programs. Although it seems that the defense budget will not be maintained at a similar percentage of GDP in 2006, Romania's economic growth will ensure an improved capacity to invest in security and defense.

Force Restructuring and Personnel Reductions: The First Generation of Reforms

The first generation of reforms focused on force restructuring and personnel reductions, especially during the period from 1990 to 2001. New legislation aimed at establishing the rule of law, civilian oversight of the military, and the basic requirements for force restructuring.

Several factors influenced the reform of Romania's military and the 2003 decision to build an all-volunteer military by 2007. First, the Romanian armed forces were one of the largest military establishments in Eastern Europe, with a wartime strength that would be significantly increased by reservists to double its peacetime size. Second, it was a military whose strategy was designed to ensure an autarkic "circular defense" of Romania's territory against any potential military threat,

---

on political and economic reform in Romania and on positive changes in its economic growth, governmental reform, and respect for the rule of law. <www.europa.eu.int/comm/enlargement/romania/index.htm#Roadmap2002>.
18. Annual GDP growth increased from 2.1 percent in 2000 to 6.1 percent in 2004; EU Commission Report 2004.

including the Soviet one. Romania had to deal with a considerable military legacy, and particularly a tradition of mass participation in the wars of the nineteenth and twentieth centuries. Conscription was therefore considered a part of national history and tradition.

The first years of military reform brought a continuing overall reduction of personnel, with minimal attention, if any, to overall personnel management policy. "Officially numbering 320,000 at the time of the Revolution ... the Romanian armed forces were cut to 143,028 by the end of 2000."[19] These figures included conscripts. Wartime strength levels of more than half a million (on paper) were decreased to 230,000 in 2001. Military personnel on active duty were less than 96,000 in 2002 and this level has continued to decrease.

In order to accelerate the drawdown, incentives were offered to officers to leave the system voluntarily. This, however, led to significant imbalances among the various ranks and specialties. Initially the officers who left the system were among the youngest and most capable, who quickly found more attractive and lucrative careers in the emerging private sector. This evolution contributed by the mid-1990s to a process of "colonelization" in the military, which was particularly visible within the General Staff and the central departments of the MOD.[20] The term refers to expansion at higher ranks of people employed in staff and administrative functions, with marginal operational deployability. Unregulated promotions in ranks further distorted the armed forces' shape, resulting in a "reverse pyramid" structure, a growing bureaucracy, and reduced operational capability. Promotions during the first years of reform were also used by the military to compensate for lagging pay scales, as higher rank meant higher salary, but this, too, worsened the "reverse pyramid" structure.

A number of reform plans and strategies were developed to reshape the force structure and reduce the administrative burden. The 1997 "Strategy for the Armed Forces" for the period 2005–2010 proposed a

---

19. L. Watts, "The Crisis in Romanian Civil-military Relations," *Problems of Post-Communism*, Vol. 48, No. 4 (July/August 2001).

20. George Cristian Maior, "Force Professionalization and Personnel Management: Romania's Case and the Future Transatlantic Challenges," paper presented at the Transatlantic Roundtable, "Filling NATO's Ranks: Military Personnel Policies in Transition."

military organization of 112,000 military personnel and 28,000 civilians.[21] Its structure was based on active forces, a territorial component, and a reserve component that was still significant in size. The reservists would be designated exclusively for traditional mobilization and homeland defense, because at this time Romania was still seeking NATO membership and had no outside security guarantee. A second plan adopted in 1998, called "Program Force 2003," proposed to eliminate the reserve, leaving active and territorial forces, and building up components for surveillance, early warning, and rapid reaction.[22] It put into practice some of the main requirements for NATO membership, which Romania had begun seeking in the mid-1990s. This plan allowed for further reductions to be made. It also contributed to clearer modernization priorities, mainly related to the requirements of interoperability with the militaries of NATO member states in the fields of communications, infrastructure, airspace management, logistics sustainability, and deployability of forces in theaters of operations.

In the spring of 2002, a new force plan called "Objective Force" further decreased the targeted force structure to 75,000 military personnel, a figure to be reached by 2007.[23] The new concept would maintain a lower-readiness territorial component and focus on enhancing deployable high-readiness forces to be available to NATO. It targeted a force structure composed of 90 percent professional military personnel.

In the fall of 2002 and throughout 2003, there was discussion calling for a new revision of this project to address issues of affordability and adaptation to NATO requirements for readiness, sustainability, and deployability. Therefore, in 2002, a Ministry of Defense working group was tasked to produce a strategic vision that would better balance spending between equipment modernization and personnel. Based on the work of that group, a ministerial guidance in 2003 established four basic missions for the armed forces, namely peacetime security, collec-

---

21. "Strategy for the Armed Forces" 2005–2010 (known as "FARO 2005–2010, 1997" after the Romanian acronym for Romanian Armed Forces, FARO), mentioned in *Rebuilding the Armed Forces for XXI Century* (Bucharest: Editura Militara, 1999), pp. 70–85.
22. George Cristian Maior, "Personnel Management and Reconversion," in Larry Watts, ed., *Romanian Military Reform and NATO Integration* (Bucharest: Editura Militara, 1999), pp. 70–71.
23. Maior, "Personnel Management and Reconversion."

tive defense, support and preservation of peace through participation in crisis management and defense diplomacy, and support for other national agencies in civil emergencies.[24] On the basis of these missions, a new structure for the armed forces that might take military personnel levels below 75,000 is currently under development within the Ministry of National Defense for the period after 2007.[25]

At the beginning of 2005, a new internal MoD working group was established to define the structure of the armed forces further, joining together experts from the General Staff, the Department for Defense Policy, and other financial and human-resources directorates. Its new plans for reduction and transformation of the General Staff have been forwarded to the government and are intended to reduce the excessive levels of bureaucracy that impede rapid action in making decisions and planning forces.[26] It designates effective command and control and the reform of logistic and support structures as major priorities. It also provides for enhanced coordination among the various directorates in the General Staff, such as Operations (J3), Logistics (J4), and Communications (J6), especially with regard to better planning of Romania's participation in international operations abroad. This plan, when implemented, will also make it possible to cut the number of civilian and military personnel employed in the central structures of the Ministry of National Defense by one-third.[27]

---

24. The missions and ensuing guidelines for reform were incorporated in the 2004 "White Paper on National Security and Defense," approved by the Romanian Parliament in mid-May 2004.

25. Minister of National Defense Teodor Atanasiu has announced that another 10,000 people, both military and civilian, are expected to leave the armed forces between 2007 and 2015; plans under development envisage a total of about 80,000 personnel in Romania's military after 2015. *Rompres* (news agency), March 28, 2006.

26. A new Law on the organization of the Ministry of National Defense was discussed by the Supreme Council for the Country Defense at its meeting of February 13, 2006; a decision has been made to forward this project to the Romanian Government and then to the Parliament for adoption. See *Rompres* (news agency), February 13, 2006.

27. Public statements by the minister of national defense indicate that the administrative personnel of the Ministry of National Defense will be reduced from more than 2000 people to around 1500–1600. See *Romania Liberă*, March 2, 2005.

Second Generation of Reforms: Defining Personnel Policies and Managing the Change in Pyramidal Structure

In numerical terms, the Romanian military actually exceeded the reductions called for under the first generation of reforms. Unfortunately, the reductions were not managed in a way that would put the right people with the right ranks into the right jobs. Far too many senior officers remained.

Second-generation reforms, therefore, were aimed at restructuring the force to achieve an appropriate balance among officers, NCOs, and enlisted soldiers and provide a clear picture of how the armed forces will be shaped and what personnel policies will support their effectiveness and interoperability with the Alliance.[28] These second-generation reforms called for a target figure of 90,000 personnel (75,000 military and 15,000 civilian defense workers), as stated in the Objective Force. Although the 90,000 figure is still subject to internal debates, it seems a realistic target and one that will allow Romania to deliver on the division-equivalent it has promised to NATO by 2012.[29] However, experience with reform has shown that resource constraints and the difficulty of creating new military units will likely push the number lower. Therefore the target figure is to be achieved by 2007, but for the period after 2007, a new plan will probably call for further personnel cuts to compensate for the high costs of transition to the all-volunteer force.

The second-generation reform process had to reconsider two major inter-related objectives: the required increase in operational capability and the equally necessary development of a new strategy for personnel management. During the first generation of reforms, the Romanian military rapidly overcame its worry that smaller forces meant lost capability; by contrast, it took years for the direct connection between force effectiveness and career management to be recognized and acted upon.

---

28. The second generation, aimed at personnel policies and force restructuring, is distinct in theory from the first generation of reforms, aimed at giving the overall legal and structural framework for civilian control and reform, although these two generations may in practice overlap in chronological terms.

29. 2004 "White Paper of Security and National Defense," p. 14.

The first step in this direction was the adoption in 2001 of the *Military Career Guide*.[30] This guide established, for the first time, clear promotion criteria and set up special commissions for examination of candidates for promotion. It regulated each step of the professional military career up to the highest ranks. The main merit of the Guide has been to introduce transparency and equal opportunities to military careers and to eliminate the previous detrimental practices of arbitrary and "exceptional" promotions.

The *Guide* also called for a new rank pyramid, with a target of one officer for every three NCOs, and it has established a target share of service jobs at each rank. Based on the *Guide*, personnel managers have already begun to improve the distribution of people across ranks. For example, a process of "decolonelization," pursued within the MoD during 2001–2002, dramatically diminished the number of positions for senior officers. During the first ten months of 2001, 4,134 officers were made redundant, including 44 generals, 888 colonels, 1,442 lieutenant colonels, and 1,335 majors. In addition, age limits were established for mandatory retirement, thus ushering in the rejuvenation of the officer corps.[31]

The implementation of the new system has shown results in the revitalization of the senior officer corps. An emerging new generation of flag officers has been appointed to key positions on the Defense Staff. Between 2003 and 2005 the average age of military personnel on the MoD and Defense Staff dropped significantly.

---

30. Human Resources Management Directorate, *Military Career Guide* (Bucharest: Romanian Ministry of National Defense, 2001).

31. A mandatory retirement age has been set at 55 for every officer below flag officer. Those with the equivalent of 30 years of duty, even if younger than 55, may retire; those with 20 years of duty may retire with a partial pension. Age limits were also lowered for flag officers; for example, four-star generals are now required to retire at age 59 (previously the limit was 65, and often, even older generals were kept in the military for extended periods of time). However, Minister of National Defense Teodor Atanasiu recently announced his intention to make the mandatory retirement age for each rank five years later; for example, a four-star general would retire at 64 instead of 59. Because the age limits are quite low, even by NATO standards, he argued, and because many high-ranking officers have retired already, an increase in the age limits would not affect the restructuring process. This debate is still open. Reported by *Rompres* (news agency), March 28, 2006; and *Ziua* (Bucharest), March 28, 2006.

Another goal of the *Military Career Guide* was to provide increased career mobility by establishing a four-year limit for officer assignments. The system has been extensively applied in the military units, and initially to a more limited extent within the MoD. Within the Ministry of National Defense, the principle of rotation has been applied to senior officers unevenly; too many officers still stay for long periods of time in their positions. In some cases, senior officers were promoted merely to avoid mandatory retirement at the age specified for their former rank. Such cases have been publicly debated, and in March 2005 the Romanian president announced that no more flag officers would be promoted without a clear plan for the total number in each rank based on the new force structure.[32]

To coordinate operational requirements and personnel management, a MoD plan on further restructuring will require increasing the reductions in the number of territorial units, most of which lack sufficient manpower, training, and equipment. The plans that are under development focus on improving the readiness of operational units, with a special priority given to the forces earmarked for NATO operations.[33] Restructuring of the MoD will decrease administrative functions, freeing up resources for the deployable component of the armed forces.

In 2004 and 2005, considerable work has been dedicated to the development of new strategies for military career management, as a basis for regulations defining more focused career paths, increasing personnel mobility, and implementing specific regulations for career tracks in Romania's armed forces. Once these regulations are approved by the minister of defense, they are expected to define the application of the *Military Career Guide* within the MoD. Following the 2004 work, a new directorate for individual military career management was established in the General Staff; it started its work in 2005.[34]

---

32. By law, only the president, as commander in chief of the armed forces, can offer any promotion to the rank of general or offer an additional star to flag officers. For presidential declarations that no promotion to the rank of general will be approved before the overall force structure is defined, see the news agency "Mediafax," March 10, 2005.

33. See statements by minister of national defense, *Nine O'Clock*, February 1, 2005.

34. Work on a civilian career guide may be started in 2006 or later as part of proposed reform applying to all civil servants.

REFORM OF THE CIVIL SERVICE AND CIVILIAN CAREERS

The civil service component in Romania's armed forces has been significantly reformed in recent years. At the beginning of the 1990s, little attention was given to the role of civilians in the Ministry of Defense; existing civilian departments and agencies dealt mainly with public relations and cultural affairs. In 1994, the first Department for Defense Policy led by a civilian state secretary was created. Since then, new legislation has established the specific duties and responsibilities of civil servants in all public administration departments and agencies.[35] New regulations for the work of civil servants in the MoD have been developed.

The number of civilian defense employees in the central departments of the MoD was significantly decreased during the 1990s due to the overall reductions in force size. At the beginning of the 1990s, a large number of civilian employees were performing relatively routine low-level administrative tasks. The reforms led to new civilian roles and leadership in defense policy, acquisitions, budgetary planning, human resources, and international military cooperation. The new law on public servants served as a basis for implementing a new system for employment, training, and career development in the Ministry of National Defense. In 2003 and 2004, the MoD also embraced several new measures aimed at improving retention of civil servants. These include financial incentives similar to those offered military personnel, new opportunities for training and education, and the emerging possibility of filling positions in international organizations. With the accession to NATO, a number of civilians have applied for jobs in NATO Headquarters; in the future the same will happen with European Union vacancies in the security and defense sector.

A strategy for individual careers has yet to be developed to provide clear career tracks for civil servants, however. Currently civil servants might stay in the same position indefinitely, since there are no requirements for rotation as there are for military personnel. Flexibility in rota-

---

35. Law No. 188 (1999) on the status of civil servants, *Official Gazette*, December 18, 1999, dealt with the status of civil servants throughout the whole central and local public administration. A few years later, with the demilitarization of the Ministry of Interior, police functions became civilian as well; the police are included in the legislative provisions under Law 188, but they have a special status.

tion and promotion, and a clear career path for mid- to high-level defense managers, are needed in order to compete with the incentives offered by the private sector and retain professionals in the MoD.

RETENTION AND RECONVERSION POLICIES

Inevitably the negative effects of both the overall social and economic transitions of Romanian society and the military transition have affected the cohesiveness and effectiveness of the military. Economic conditions affect the armed forces through inadequate housing, lack of individual equipment, and servicemembers' inability to keep up with growing living expenses in Romania's underdeveloped market economy. Recruitment policies were successfully implemented to cover most force requirements during the early days of military reform. However, retention and reconversion (R&R) policies began to be coherently applied only after the first decade of restructuring ("reconversion" refers to return to civilian life). In 2001, responsibilities for public relations and information, relations with Romania's Parliament, and R&R policies were merged in a single new department.[36]

Financial assistance from the World Bank has helped with the transition of active-duty military personnel into the civilian sector, starting in 2001.[37] A significant number of military personnel (mostly officers and NCOs) received counseling and retraining. However, the resources were not adequate for all of the redundant personnel. As reductions in force structure continue, a further expansion of this program will proba-

---

36. Department for Relations with the Parliament, Public Relations and Legislative Harmonization. During the first R&R projects with the World Bank, the state secretary and head of this department also ensured coordination of these areas and was responsible for developing plans for building new housing for the military. The head of this department coordinated the overall plans as developed by the Human Resources Directorate (in the R&R field), the Infrastructure Directorate, and other departments with related functions. The concrete tasks remained under each responsible unit, while there was an effort to ensure coherence among them at the highest level.

37. See, e.g., "Reconversia profesionala a personalului military disponibilizat" (The professional reconversion of redundant military personnel), *Newsletter Militar Romanescu*, Vol. 1, No. 1 (May 22, 2001), pp. 3–4. From September 2000 to September 2001, 1,687 personnel received employment counseling, 850 applied for training courses, 143 were advised on starting new businesses, and 172 received training for civilian occupations.

bly be necessary. Additional programs have been developed. For example, the Ministry of Defense has made agreements with other state agencies, such as the Ministry of Education and the Ministry of Administration and Home Affairs, to hire former military personnel. However, in transitional economies, the strictures of an evolving labor market and the simultaneous outflow of people from other public-sector jobs tend to limit the outside opportunities for people made redundant by military downsizing.

The new R&R approach also emphasizes the retention of officers and enlisted personnel with needed skills. New family-oriented policies are being developed, including new programs for building houses on military property (which are also available to civilians working in the MoD); however, even with the acquisition by the MoD of apartments for servicemembers, this is far from adequate. Probably the most effective retention policies have been increases in salaries and allowances to offset the effects of inflation. Compared to other budgetary sectors, the military offers significant financial incentives through supplementary payments for working in difficult conditions, bonuses for specialists, and so on. Bonuses and additional payments now make up nearly half of the net income of the typical NCO or officer, which is thus much higher than the average Romanian's income.

The Ministry of National Defense is also working to explain and promote military reform objectives, both through public information strategies and through an increased number of joint visits by civilian and military leaders to military units. These visits aim at explaining the reform process, addressing needs the needs of military personnel, and listening to their requirements and their ideas. A public relations strategy for recruitment to the new all-volunteer force will be necessary in the near future.

Future Challenges of Professionalization

Adaptation of personnel policies is a continuous process. It must incorporate defense planning requirements for the force structure; keep pace with changes in society and labor markets; and maintain military cohesiveness and loyalty, as well as sound civilian control over the armed forces. It is also key to the integration of military developments into the overall public policies of a government. In the realm of personnel policy, there will always be tension between the need for efficiency and highly hierarchical and disciplined structures, on the one hand, and on the other, the demands of individuals and of the society that pays taxes to sustain the military establishment. The way professionalization is defined and developed should be responsive to such concerns within the specific context of each country.[38]

Under legislation proposed in March 2006, young people selected as volunteer soldiers would undergo special training prior to being sworn in, and then would receive advanced training prior to signing a contract for a four-year term of service. Subsequent contracts for terms of two or three years could be signed, up to the age limit for retirement.[39]

Challenges in the transition to an all-volunteer military fall into three main categories: new requirements for structural and managerial transformations; enhanced coordination with defense policy and planning through education, training, and selection; and the need for new types of military career policies.

STRUCTURAL AND MANAGERIAL TRANSFORMATIONS

The implementation of the *Military Career Guide* has demonstrated how personnel policies could be coordinated with structural changes. Personnel mobility and flexibility require more elasticity in planning and managing the units and organization of the armed forces; they need to be able to adapt rapidly to the flow of new personnel. Administrative management must adopt modern business techniques for use of human

---

38. In legislative debates, the point was raised that the end-of-conscription issue affects the overall security sector, not just the armed forces. Discussions of professionalization of interior forces such as the gendarmerie or fire corps (which are subordinated to the Ministry of Interior) as part of overall homeland security structures began after the 2003 change in the Constitution that ended compulsory conscription. It is expected that some security institutions would prefer to retain conscription, while for some others further professionalization measures will be developed. The debate has not concluded.

39. A major change of this proposed legislation, which would apply to the entire military starting in 2007, is that volunteer soldiers would participate unconditionally in international missions, without the necessity under previous law of each individual soldier agreeing to do so. A separate section of the bill applies to reserve forces; it establishes the conditions under which civilians may become part of the volunteer reserve forces. See *Nine O'Clock*, March 30, 2006.

resources: the organization should be able to provide appropriate training and posting for each step of an individual's career path.

During recent years, a number of additional steps have been taken to improve the evaluation of military performance and thus to increase the system's responsiveness to quality of performance. Romania's previous large conscript military created a bureaucratic burden in terms of administrative norms, and attention is currently being given to simplifying procedures for personnel testing and evaluation.

Structural flexibility is also a requirement for the integrated management of the entries and exits of enlisted personnel. Because payment in Romania's armed forces is above the average national income, there should be little problem, in the medium term, in recruiting the required number of qualified volunteers. According to current plans, which target an overall force structure of 75,000, the overall number of enlisted soldiers should reach about 30,000 at the end of 2007. Plans for annual recruitment are under development to ensure an appropriate balance of entries and exits from the military.

For the medium term, a similar situation applies to career officers. Many join the military because it currently offers more job stability than the private sector, as well as better opportunities for training and for international experience. In the last four years, since 2001, career officers benefited from an increase of approximately 25 percent in salaries which largely matched inflation and ensured that the military enjoyed one of the highest levels of pay in the public sector.[40] But with economic development, the private market may begin to offer better long-run career prospects. The military system should be prepared to respond to this, especially in retaining specialized personnel such as pilots and information technology (IT) experts.

The transition to a market economy created great disparities between the poorer rural communities and the richer urban population with its emerging middle class. Enlisted soldiers have been recruited mostly from the rural population, while the number of well-educated urban

---

40. A similar increase for civil servants has reduced the former differences in payments between the officer corps and civilian employees. In the first half of the 1990s, the gap was quite large: for a similar job, a civilian employee might receive only two-thirds as much as an officer's average salary.

"targets" for recruitment to the officer corps has somewhat diminished. The officer system began to be organized around specialties according to NATO classifications (J1 to J9) after Romania's accession to PfP; an analysis to predict the level of financial stimulus necessary to recruit people with certain desired areas of expertise needs to be developed on this basis. On the other hand, it has been determined that it is more cost-effective to contract out to civilian companies some projects requiring high-tech expertise, such as certain communication programs or computer and database management; this limits the number of specialists that will be needed within the Ministry to run and manage the civilian-built technology in such areas.

ENHANCED COORDINATION

Within the architecture of a future volunteer military, force structure requirements will have to be increasingly and rapidly coordinated with recruitment and assignment policies. The new military tasks undertaken by Romanian armed forces in Afghanistan and Iraq, for example, have involved complex stabilization and reconstruction activities in difficult and unpredictable environments. Consequently, the transformation of today's armed forces is more a matter of rapid adaptation to evolving security requirements than a question of temporary targets and limited reforms. In addition to the emphasis on new technological developments, experimentation, and new doctrines, adaptive personnel policies may be equally important.

A professional military can be more open to change, more adaptable to the requirements of defense transformation, and more able to keep up with new technological developments. However, an all-volunteer military will not necessarily be more professional in fulfilling its duties compared to a conscript-based armed force, unless its troops and units are effectively trained, properly motivated, and cohesive.

In the 1990s, countries in Central and Eastern Europe had limited experience in the integration of defense policies, resource planning, training, and personnel policies into a single comprehensive strategy. But with the demands of participation within NATO, personnel management will become an essential component of the new defense objectives. The assignment and education of enlisted personnel will be a key factor in the development of forces able to undertake complex crisis-response operations and to participate in "niche" military roles such as military police; nuclear, biological, and chemical (NBC) response; or military engineers.

These new and more demanding military missions will also require new abilities from NCOs; their importance will grow during the coming years. Appropriate training and improvements in administrative and managerial skills will be required, as well as additional focus on issues related to CIMIC (civil-military cooperation) and relations with local populations in areas of conflict. The success of Romanian NCOs as instructors for the new Afghan National Army has shown that this is an area with promise for the future.

Officer training for leading troops will likewise have to incorporate new areas of expertise, such as civil administration skills, ability to negotiate, and management and supervision of reconstruction and humanitarian efforts. Romanian officers will also need to enhance their ability to lead multi-national formations in operations, to advise on the reform and development of defense institutions in post-conflict environments such as in Iraq or Afghanistan, and to integrate their troops into multi-national environments, both in operations or in postings to international headquarters.

The training and education system must also be adapted to respond to new force requirements and to be efficient at promoting and advancing new options for transformation through its academic research component. One of the main challenges in the reform of personnel policies in Romania has been the development of a clear-cut strategy on military training and education, which had been one of the most stagnant components of the armed forces. Academic research and analysis in the field of strategy and defense policy, and especially on questions of operations and reforms, has been significantly weakened by the lack of well-trained and motivated researchers and analysts (most studies for the MoD on reform alternatives were done by outside contractors—foreign analysts or private companies—with no competing evaluations from inside MoD). Changing national security policies make the areas of education and research more critically important than ever.

NEW MILITARY PERSONNEL POLICIES

A third challenge lies in the development and implementation of individual career management policies. The transformation of personnel policies between 2001 and 2004 in Romania's armed forces was approached from a system perspective, with the creation of regulations and boards to deal with categories of personnel, not individuals. However, the transition to a professional military demonstrated that the "three R" plans—Recruitment, Retention, and Resettlement or Reconversion—also have to deal in real life with the individual expectations of people in uniform. Domestic transitions and international uncertainties can affect military cohesiveness; it can be a challenge for civil-military cooperation to foster a sense of mission and a sense of direction in the officer corps. Individual career management has been considered key to success in retaining and motivating young officers and in defining coherent career paths.

Beginning in 2004, committees for military personnel and for civil servants were established to prepare guidelines for individual career management. The military board has called for restructuring the Ministry of National Defense human resources departments to include a new career managers' division to advise on promotion, job assignments, and development of career tracks for military personnel (based on a simplified UK model). An area of further focus should also be the evaluation and development of lateral entry to the military by mid-career civilians (also called indirect accession or indirect path). This would have the advantage of increasing the connections between the officers corps and civilian society, and taking advantage of high-quality civilian academic training.

A new system for reserve training also needs to be defined. Evaluations of the role of the reserve component have looked at a range of possible plans, from the creation of a national guard–like function (to be used, for example, for specific military tasks in certain circumstances or for certain specialties needed from time to time) to the development of a reserve role for crisis situations such as domestic civil emergencies or natural disasters. The development of an all-volunteer system will have to include further analysis of the role of the reserve, including issues of military relations with civilian society. A new study, looking at affordable training and employment options for the reserve system, has yet to be completed, pending expected changes in national legislation.

Conclusion

A professional military depends on both the quality of its personnel and the quality of its leadership. Structural challenges in the transition from conscription to all-volunteer forces are affected by conceptual and psychological determinants. There are still many partly or fully volunteer military systems in Europe in which changes in concepts and strategies are not fully understood and in which, as a result, the military job is still perceived as a life-long career. Inherent aging problems will be difficult to address with such a conformist approach. Promotion of officers who are more transformation-oriented, open, and capable of catalyzing structural changes in the military establishment could be a major factor in developing professional and usable armed forces.

There are no universal solutions to personnel management. What works will depend on the circumstances in a given state and a given society at a given time, including public opinion, economic trends, budget, demographics, and administrative traditions and burdens. Assessing personnel management as a major component of defense policy and planning requires a clear determination of what role the military is to play, how much can be invested in it, and what relation is desired between the military, society, and the state. The common objective of any transformation in personnel policies is the creation of defense instruments that are able to respond to both governmental and societal demands for effectiveness in countering the risks and threats of the current security environment.

The Romanian armed forces have been extensively transformed during the last fifteen years from the former system of massive structures with strong reliance on conscription to a flexible, smaller, and more deployable military seeking to reach full interoperability with its allies' armed forces. The accession to NATO played a critical role in advancing the process of reform and establishing measurable targets and objectives for the restructuring of the armed forces. Romania entered NATO in a time of major transformations for all defense establishments and had to adapt quickly to new and very demanding defense tasks. Romanian soldiers benefited from their experience in multi-national operations, which led to the development of new ideas about missions, doctrines, and necessary changes in education and training.

Transformation to all-volunteer armed forces—a decision that many countries in a similar strategic position have made—will generate new pressures for further transformation in personnel policies, with a focus on maintaining quality and professional expertise. The transformation of individual attitudes, mindsets, and expertise will also play a significant role in reform of the military establishment in Romania. It will require military leaders to be ready to undertake new tasks and to think open-mindedly about today's security requirements.

As the burden of the former communist system has gradually lessened, defense reform has begun to focus more on adaptation to new challenges in military missions and further integration into the system of collective defense planning within the North Atlantic Alliance; these might be called "third generation" plans. The introduction of Western concepts of personnel management has already brought significant progress in the reform process. Their implementation has also generated concrete findings to help in adapting to the specifics of Romanian society and governance models as part of the process of full professionalization of the armed forces. There is still a long way to go, but the most difficult stages of defense reform have been achieved. The development of human resources management now has the advantage of a starting point much more similar to that of Western NATO allies that chose, during the 1990s, the all-volunteer option for their armed forces.

Chapter 15

Recruitment in a Period of Transformation

The Italian Experience

Domenico Villani

Italy's armed forces, like those in many NATO nations, are in the midst of a major transformation—perhaps the most challenging transformation that they have faced in the past fifty years. This transformation is occurring along several dimensions. First, the military is being cut nearly in half compared to the number of servicemembers at the end of the Cold War. Second, the mission of Italy's armed forces is being redefined, to focus more on international expeditionary operations rather than territorial defense; as a result, changes are required in equipment modernization, training, and skilled manpower. At the same time, the force is making the transition from a conscript-based force to an all-volunteer, professional force—a transition that is a challenge in its own right, as the experiences of the United States and other European nations demonstrate.

This chapter addresses the Italian experience and challenges during the course of this transformation, and in particular, one of the most important concerns: that of recruiting volunteers in sufficient quantity and quality to meet the needs of the armed forces. How this challenge is addressed depends on the expectations of the men and women who volunteer to serve. Those expectations serve as the basis for the current professional model discussed in this chapter.

This chapter starts with some introductory notes about the defense model of the Cold War period, which was based on a simple distribution of roles among the armed forces. The chapter then reviews the changes in the background brought about by the end of the Cold War, as the missions of the armed forces started to adapt to constantly changing politico-strategic requirements, to complex operational scenarios, and to the need for joint and combined operational effectiveness. The chapter explains how the new millennium has been a major turning point for Italian national defense policy in terms of changes, results, reforms and forward-looking initiatives.

Finally, the new professional military model is described, including Italy's 2004 decision to accelerate the move to an all-volunteer force.[1] Maintaining a mix of conscripts and volunteers would not have been cost-effective because operational employment in demanding missions is reserved for all-volunteer units. Conscripts could perform only increasingly marginal tasks, and only on Italy's national territory. Therefore, the Italian armed forces have been involved in an ongoing process of transformation to bring about an all-professional system. Recent legislative measures in Italy have not been limited to accelerating the date by which conscription was to be suspended. Recruitment flows and occupational incentives monitored in the period of application of the legislative measures adopted in 2000–2001 showed the need for further measures. Otherwise, once conscription was suspended, Italy could not be sure of an adequate number of volunteers, to the detriment of the new model.

Background

Historical requirements, derived from geopolitical circumstances, were the basis for Italy's past decisions regarding force structure and manpower policies for its armed forces. Prior to the mid-1980s, the bipolar world—characterized by the confrontation between NATO and the Warsaw Pact—presented a well-defined threat and alliances that were clearly drawn. This geopolitical environment led to a military strategy of deterrence and forward defense; these, in turn, called for large standing armies with a complete range of military capabilities to defend Western Europe against a possible Warsaw Pact invasion. In 1985, for example, the Italian armed forces comprised 385,100 servicemembers, about 258,000 of whom were conscripted soldiers.[2]

---

1. Law No. 226 of August 23, 2004, established early suspension of conscription.
2. Until January 1, 2005, Italy had mandatory military service for men between the ages of 18 and 45. The duration of the draft period was changed

In the early 1990s, with the end of the Cold War, this classic military concept became less appropriate. Instead of forces focused on territorial defense, the new strategic environment called for forces that could be rapidly deployed in support of international contingencies involving peacekeeping and low-intensity operations. As the demand to support international operations has grown, so too has Italy's involvement. Today, Italy has nearly 3,000 troops deployed in Iraq, and several thousand more in support of fifteen United Nations and other peacekeeping operations.

The new operational requirements for crisis-management and peacekeeping operations in the early 1990s prompted Italy's Ministry of Defense to consider a new approach to manning its armed forces. While universal conscription had produced a large number of general purpose forces, the needs of a more high-technology war-fighting environment can best be met with more highly trained and specialized units. These new missions placed new demands on manpower. In order to support a large number of military operations outside of Italy, it has become necessary to maintain an adequate rotation base, as well as logistic and administrative support at home. For every soldier deployed abroad, the military requires a rotation base of at least three soldiers, plus another two or three soldiers to guarantee effective logistics support. Thus, to deploy 10,000 soldiers in the operational theater, it is necessary to have some 60,000 volunteers available at home. Moreover, conscripts cannot be sent abroad.

---

several times: from 15 months for the Army and the Air Force and 24 months for the Navy in 1964, to 12 months for the three services in 1975, and 10 months from 1997 until conscription was suspended in 2005. Anyone objecting to military service for religious or ethical reasons could claim to be a conscientious objector, in which case community service (eight months longer than the military service) was usually authorized as an alternative to military service. A 1989 Constitutional Court decision established equality in the duration of military and civil service, which resulted in an increase in the number of conscientious objectors. Voluntary female military service was established by Law No. 380 of October 20, 1999. As part of the transformation of the Italian Armed Forces, an all-professional system was approved by Law No. 226 of August 23, 2004. Italy's armed forces have not conscripted anyone since January 1, 2005. All those drafted before that date finished their duty by July 2005.

Table 15.1. Italian Armed Forces, 1990–2004 (thousands)

	1990	1995	2000	2004
Army	251.5	207.2	170	121
Navy	53.8	42.9	40	37
Air Force	79.3	71	60	49.2
Total	**384.6**	**321.1**	**270.0**	**207.2**
Number of Conscripts	232.2	174.9	116	30
Conscripts as Share of Total	60.4%	54.5%	43.0%	14.5%
Carabinieri	108.4	114.4	112	112.6

Source: Italian Defense General Staff, "Serie Storiche."

Italy, like the United States and much of Europe, has begun to downsize its armed forces to support changing post–Cold War requirements. Throughout the 1990s, the size of both the active and reserve components has decreased. The largest changes have taken place in the Army, where the number of soldiers declined by more than 80,000 between 1990 and 2000. (See Table 15.1.) In the active force today, the three services have some 26,000 officers, 74,000 noncommissioned officers (NCOs), and 94,000 enlisted personnel. (See Table 15.2.)

Even as demand for forces is changing, Italy—like other European countries—has a declining pool of young people of draft age. This shrinking pool is the result of many factors including a decline in the youth population (a trend that is expected to continue, as discussed in Chapter 3 by Rickard Sandell), an increase in conscientious objection to military service, and other exemption provisions such as the option to complete national service in organizations other than the military.[3] Furthermore, these factors combined to produce a shift in public opinion away from conscription and toward a professional model for a military that is based on volunteers. The first steps toward diminished reliance

---

3. In 2001, new legislation (Law No. 64) created a National Civilian Service. It is open to conscientious objectors, young people who do not meet either the quality or the quantity requirements of the Armed Forces, and women (who were not then permitted to serve in the armed forces); it is still open to women who choose to join the civilian service.

Table 15.2. Italian Armed Forces, Officer and Enlisted, 2005

	Officers	Non-Commissioned Officers	Enlisted	Total
Army	14,208	26,400	73,400	114,008
Navy	5,000	16,900	13,100	35,000
Air Force	6,600	31,000	7,200	44,800
Total Active Force	25,808	74,300	93,700	193,808

Source: Italian Ministry of Defense, "Nota aggiuntiva allo stato di previsione per la difesa per l'anno 2004."

on conscripted soldiers occurred in 1995 when the Italian government and parliament, in debating whether Italy would support a joint operation in Bosnia, decided to end the use of conscripted soldiers in operations outside of Italy. Prior to that time, Italy had conducted numerous operations abroad with conscripts. In 1992–93, for example, the Italian armed forces participated in operations in Somalia and Mozambique with units comprised largely of conscripted personnel. However, in Bosnia, and in 1998, when Italy took part in operations in Kosovo, East Timor, and Albania, it did so with volunteer forces—a practice that has continued.

Also in 1995, Italy's parliament passed legislation in support of a new military model, still based on a mix of conscript and volunteer soldiers, but one whose foundation would be career soldiers and short-term enlisted volunteers.[4] Implementation of this new model began in 1998, with a force size targeted at 230,000 servicemembers, including 64,000 enlisted volunteers and 72,000 conscripts.

Changes in the Italian Armed Forces

In 1999, the Ministry of Defense began work on its plan to transform the military to an all-professional force. The plan envisaged transformation along multiple dimensions, based on a fundamental rethinking of the entire national defense model. In 2000, the plan was enacted into law.[5]

---

4. Law No. 196 of 1995.
5. Law No. 331 of 2000.

The 2000 "Professional Law" called for reshaping the personnel profile of the forces, including the redistribution of personnel among the three services and across ranks (officers, warrant and noncommissioned officers, sergeants, and enlisted troops). It also addressed equipment modernization, command and control structure, and personnel policies. The law specified a timetable for ending conscription and completing the transition to an all-volunteer force.[6] It set certain milestones: by January 1, 2007, the draft would be suspended and the size of the armed forces would be reduced to 190,000 servicemembers (112,000 in the Army, 34,000 in the Navy, and 44,000 in the Air Force). By January 1, 2021, Italy would complete the transition to the new steady-state volunteer force, including reductions in force size and redistribution of personnel across the services and ranks.[7]

The long period of transition to the planned personnel profile was established to allow sufficient time to put in place procedures to recruit new volunteers and to bring other categories of personnel into alignment with the proposed reduction to 190,000. For example, today there are more officers and noncommissioned officers on active service than are planned for. Thus, over the period of transition, recruitments and separations must be managed carefully to achieve the new targets for each personnel category.[8]

Following the passage of the 2000 legislation, recruiting proved more difficult than anticipated. In addition, the government grew concerned over the relatively slow pace of ending the draft. To address these concerns, the Italian Ministry of Defense conducted a series of studies

---

6. It is important to note that the 2000 law suspended conscription, rather than abolishing it. Under Italian law, military service is still considered a sacred duty of citizenship. The 2000 law permits a return to conscription if, in the event of a severe national or international crisis or declaration of war, the number of volunteers is insufficient to meet military requirements. (The Carabinieri are also considered a branch of the armed forces, for their military police functions, but they are not included in this discussion.)

7. By 2021, the 190,000 servicemembers were to be distributed among the ranks as follows: 22,250 officers; 25,400 warrant officers and noncommissioned officers; 38,500 sergeants; and 103,800 enlisted volunteers, including about 61,000 career soldiers and some 43,000 short-term volunteers.

8. To ease the impact of personnel reductions, the Italian government moved to employ some redundant career military personnel in other government agencies and to permit early retirement of others.

aimed at improving career prospects for individuals who join the military and thus ensuring an adequate flow of potential recruits.

The studies led to a package of legislative proposals that were enacted into law and passed overwhelmingly by parliament in August 2004.[9] The law accelerated the end of conscription from January 2007 to January 2005 and altered the selection processes and terms of service for volunteers. Thus, the 2000 Professional Law was superseded by the 2004 law. Nevertheless, it is instructive to examine the provisions of the earlier law because they illustrate the challenges of Italian military transformation and show the direction in which Italy began its military transformation.

Challenges of the Transition

The cornerstone of a professional military model is the ability to recruit sufficient volunteers. Between the decision in 2000 to shift to an all-volunteer force and the legislation in 2004 to accelerate the transition, the Italian government developed two successive models of recruitment and service. The first model saw the nation through the end of the draft, but did not produce sufficient numbers of volunteers to sustain a fully professional force. The second model, adopted in the August 2004 law, is expected to produce substantially better results.

Based on the 2000 legislation, the volunteer enlisted force was to comprise three categories of personnel. One-year enlistment volunteers (VFAs) would agree to serve for a twelve-month tour of duty and could participate in some operations outside Italy, such as conflict prevention, peacemaking, peace-building, or humanitarian operations, but they were not permitted to participate in operations such as peacekeeping or peace enforcement operations.[10] VFAs received better pay than the nation's ten-month conscripts and, unlike conscripts, were generally permitted to serve in the city and unit of their choice. Since the VFA system coexisted with conscription, it benefited from "draft-induced volun-

---

9. Law No. 226 of August 23, 2004.
10. High-intensity conflicts, as distinct from low-intensity conflicts (defined in a variety of ways in the military and strategy literature), are those that are aimed at the military destruction of concentrations of enemy forces or the invasion or defense of territory.

teers": young men who preferred to take the certainty of a desirable city and unit and better pay, rather than roll the dice with the draft, even though VFA service meant two more months with the military compared to conscription.

A second category was known as short-term enlistment volunteers, or VFBs. They would be drawn from the pool of applicants for positions in one of the Italian security departments, including the national police and fire departments as well as the armed forces. They would compete for selection through a process administered by the services and the national police and fire departments. They would be expected to serve for three years in the Army, Navy, or Air Force, and could participate in the full range of military operations.

Career soldiers, or VSPs, would be recruited exclusively from among VFB personnel who, during the initial interdepartmental competition, declared an interest in permanent military service and met appropriate standards. VSPs are career soldiers and may serve to age 60. During the course of their careers, these servicemembers may compete for promotion to become sergeants, noncommissioned officers, and officers.

Effective recruiting procedures combined with the threat of compulsory service translated into initial success in staffing the VFA category. As of June 2004, the armed forces were meeting recruiting targets for one-year volunteers, and VFAs were taking part in low-intensity operations abroad. VFAs were also performing logistics tasks at home alongside conscripts, and taking part in national disaster assistance and in counterterrorism-related operations alongside police forces. Despite those initial successes, however, military leaders feared a drop-off in VFA recruitment once the end of conscription decreased the attraction of VFA service for some volunteers.

The VFB were meant to be the heart of the volunteer force, and the ability to recruit them in sufficient numbers was critical. Yet two factors made VFB recruitment problematic from the beginning. First, the government could not guarantee a job after service for every VFB volunteer. In Italy's competitive economy, job security is extremely important to young workers. The VFB system recruited talented young people based on the joint-service and interdepartmental competitions.[11] Initial screen-

---

11. Initially, the competitions were conducted annually. The narrow win-

ing was carried out by the armed forces and Carabinieri, national police, financial police, national forestry corps, national fire department, and department for prison administration police. After their service, former VFBs would be eligible for a job with one of the three services as well as one of the federal security departments (fire, police, etc.); they could also seek assistance in finding another job through an agency within the Italian Ministry of Defense that maintains links with civilian organizations dealing with employment opportunities.

Under the 2000 law, however, not every member of the VFB could be guaranteed a permanent position with the armed forces or other federal departments upon separation from military service. As of June 2004, it was expected that only 3,000 of the 11,000 VFBs recruited each year would ultimately be invited to join the career military force of VSPs. No more than 1,300 could become members of the police forces. Thus, around 6,500 would likely be given the option of dismissal or the opportunity to re-enlist for a further two-year term. The uncertainty of future employment made it difficult to attract the needed number of high-quality recruits into the VFB pool, and VFB recruitment was lower than anticipated. Service leaders feared that if the nation could not offer secure career prospects to all of its multi-year volunteers, a recruiting crisis would result.

The problem was compounded by lengthy and costly bureaucratic procedures. Difficulties in coordinating within and across the services and police forces led to delays in selection decisions. Initially, it took some eight months between the time a recruit filled out an application and the actual enlistment. About half of those who submitted application forms lost interest and withdrew from the selection process before taking the qualification exams. Since not all of the remaining applicants could be expected to pass their exams, losing so many potential recruits early in the process jeopardized the armed forces' ability to meet their recruiting goals in an already difficult recruiting environment. That put the services in the difficult position of either accepting recruits who fell below established standards or facing manpower shortfalls.

In contrast, the recruitment of career soldiers into the VSP category got off to a good start, in part because only 3,000 new VSPs were needed

---

dow for applications was felt to be an obstacle to recruiting, and the centralized competitions were expanded to three times a year.

annually and, in part, because the promise of a secure career with the military was attractive to many of the VFBs from whom many of the VSPs are chosen.

As of mid-2004, Italy's defense leaders were deeply concerned about prospects for the future force. If VFB recruitment shortfalls continued, and if genuine volunteerism did not replace draft-induced volunteerism as conscription wound down, then the Italian armed forces might face staffing shortfalls in the tens of thousands. Accelerating the suspension of conscription to 2005 could exacerbate the gap.

The potential for crisis led the Italian Ministry of Defense to conduct the studies described above that led to formulation of the August 2004 law, which took effect on January 1, 2005.[12]

A New Defense Model for the Future

These experiences under the 2000 Professional Law led military leaders to focus on maintaining a flow of one-year volunteers, improving job security for multiple-year volunteers, and further streamlining recruitment and selection procedures. The August 2004 law accelerated the suspension of conscription from 2007 to January 1, 2005. To ensure the flow of one-year volunteers and improve job security for longer-term volunteers, the law introduced two new categories of voluntary service—VFP1 and VFP4—to replace the VFA and VFB categories of the system set up under the 2000 law. Every fresh entrant to the Italian armed forces or security forces must first serve as a VFP1, or one-year enlisted volunteer. Individuals who have volunteered for service in the VFP1 category may compete, after nine months of service, for a position in the VFP4 category, as a four-year enlisted volunteer. VFP4s serve a further term of four years and may reenlist for successive two-year terms for a total of nine years. Those who become VFP4s are ensured a career in either the armed forces or the police forces after completing at least five years of service.

Under the new system, a year of voluntary service in the armed forces is a precondition to entering either the armed forces or the police forces for permanent career positions. It is hoped that—as with conscripts in earlier

---

12. Law No. 226 of 2004.

years—a substantial fraction of the young men and women who join with the intention of serving for a single year will find that they have a taste for military life; thus the VFP1 pool will, it is hoped, become a good source of recruits for the VFP4 and VSP categories.

In addition to substituting the two new personnel categories for the VFA and VFB, the new system also improves pay for the one-year volunteers (approximately doubling the pay that was received by VFAs) as well as the four-year volunteers (VFP4s). At the beginning of the first two-year re-enlistment, VFP4 pay is the same as that of career soldiers (VSP) at the lowest rank. This is particularly important since, as studies have shown, there is a positive impact of adequate pay on military recruiting (as discussed in Chapter 5 by Warner and Negrusa and Chapter 9 by Rostker and Gilroy in this volume).

Young men and women who are interested in permanent service in the armed forces or the police forces must first apply for a year-long period of service as VFP1s in the armed forces. It is anticipated that about 100,000 applications would be received at this point in the process (based on the number received in recent public competitions for these forces). From those applications, one-year enlistees would be selected, based on recruiting goals for the armed forces and available financial resources. It is anticipated that about 24,000 to 36,000 VFP1s would be selected each year. During their period of service, the VFP1s may apply for entry into one of the annual competitions established by the armed forces and police forces.

The armed forces will then admit, as VFP4s, about 4,500 individuals who scored well on the exams. Individuals interested in careers in the police force could proceed along one of two tracks. One group of applicants (perhaps 900 each year) would directly enter initial careers in the police forces after having served a year as a VFP1. The remainder (about 1,300) would be admitted into the police forces after a four-year period of service in the armed forces. Thus, entry into initial careers in the police force would be tied to volunteer service in the armed forces, for one year as a VFP1, or for at least four years as a VFP4.

For this new system to work, the total number of VSPs—career soldiers—must increase from about 61,000 (the level set by the 2000 law for 2021) to about 73,300. At the same time, the number of VFP4s must be reduced from about 43,000 to 30,000. To validate whether or not this system could be effective—that is, whether the armed forces could reach a new steady state between 2005 and 2021—the Ministry of Defense conducted a series of simulations. These simulations suggested that, by 2021, the armed forces will be able to achieve a steady volume of enlisted volunteers (VFP1, VFP4, and VSP) totaling 103,800. Along with the planned number of officers and noncommissioned officers, this would result in the target force size of 190,000 servicemembers. The simulations also indicate that operational requirements can be met with a sufficient number of servicemembers under age 30, which would include VFP1, VFP4, and the youngest members of the VSP. Finally, they suggest that all enlisted personnel recruited as VFP4s could be assured a permanent career in either the armed forces or the police forces.

Thus, by establishing a permanent career path for all individuals enlisting for a four-year term, requiring all individuals interested in an initial career in the police force to serve at least a one-year enlistment term in the armed forces, and improving pay for one-year volunteers, it is anticipated that the Italian armed forces will be able to sustain its all-volunteer force.

Conclusion

Changing international requirements and shifting public opinion have together created an environment where conscription is no longer an option for Italy. Thus, the challenge of recruiting an all-volunteer force is one that the armed forces must address. The new defense model developed as part of the planning for the 2004 law will enable the armed forces to meet this challenge. By offering young people the option to begin their professional career as a volunteer in the armed forces, continuing to a longer enlistment, and then to permanent service in either the armed forces or the police forces, this approach ensures job security upon completion of military service, a factor that is essential for success of a volunteer military in today's culture. Moreover, during the period of transition, this model would allow the Ministry of Defense to continue to provide an effective force to respond to continuing demands in both national and international arenas.

This new plan should give more momentum to the transition to an all-volunteer armed force initiated in 2000 and accelerated to end conscription in 2005. It addresses the most fundamental concern in transitioning to a volunteer military, that of ensuring a sufficient quantity of high-quality volunteers to sustain the force.

That said, it is important to remember that professional armed forces differ from conscript forces in many ways beyond recruiting. For example, matters of pay, educational benefits, housing, health care, and family services (such as those discussed in Chapter 10 by Deborah Clay-Mendez in this volume), which under a conscript force were of concern primarily to officers and noncommissioned officers, will now affect all military personnel. Furthermore, as the transition to an all-volunteer force continues, the armed forces must continually evaluate their manpower requirements—for certain skills and training, for example—as well as structural and organizational issues. Thus, during the next decade and a half, policy-makers and legislators will have to debate and address these issues and to devote policies and resources to ensure success in Italy's transition to an all-volunteer, professional military.

Part IV
Transforming Reserve Policies

Chapter 16

Sustaining an Effective Reserve

Implications of the New Security Environment for Reserve Forces

Chris Donnelly

Within the context of restructuring armed forces for the new era, there is one area in particular which is often neglected—the issue of reserves. It is an issue not just of personnel, but of organization, training, and equipment too. It is in the area of personnel policies that the issue of reserves has most impact, and it is on its personnel policy rather than its equipment that a reserve system usually stands or fails.

Today, the process of force structuring and generating reserves is made increasingly complex because of the radical changes affecting the international security environment. The intensity, pace, and extent of these changes are forcing many nations to make profound reforms of their military systems. But when armed forces are closely integrated into their societies, such radical reforms cannot be accomplished without serious social impact. It is this that makes reform so difficult and which reflects particularly on the generation of reserves, as reserves by definition are always drawn from the heart of society. An understanding of the nature of the changes in the security environment is therefore crucial to improving a country's capacity to generate effective reserves, because these current changes are socio-political rather than just military-technical in nature.

The views expressed in this chapter are those of the author alone. They do not represent the views of the Defence Academy of the United Kingdom, of the UK Ministry of Defence, nor of any other body.

This chapter addresses the implications of recent changes in the nature of conflict for military operations and for the demands placed on armed forces, in particular for reserve forces. The chapter looks, first, at the traditional roles of reserve forces in both all-volunteer armed forces and in armed forces built on the conscript system. The problems created for reserve force generation by changes in the international security situation are examined, with special attention to the challenges facing Central and East European armed forces. The chapter concludes with ideas and recommendations for how to develop reserve forces so that they can make an effective contribution to current and future military operations.

The New Security and Defense Environment

The current changes in the security and defense environment amount to a revolution in the nature of conflict. Success in conflict will increasingly depend on flexibility in accommodating to change and to new threats; the ability to identify what should be retained from the past and what should be discarded; and the ability to identify, prioritize, and invest in the new elements that will be needed to cope with future security threats.

If, as Napoleon said, in war the "moral is to the material as three is to one," then—important though technology is in the new conflict, be it battle, peacekeeping, national reconstruction work, counter-insurgency operations, or internal security duties—people are even more important to victory or defeat. The most competent of our enemies can get access to the most advanced of technologies and deploy them asymmetrically, forcing us to spend a thousand dollars when they spend only a few. Al Qaeda, for example, displays an excellent example of network-centric warfare. Success in the future, therefore, depends not so much on technology as on cleverness in using it. Thus personnel are the key element in military capability of the future: how people are organized and trained to use the equipment they have, and how well they are motivated to conduct the conflict; to what extent they have the support of their own government and populations; and how well they can compete with the opposition for the hearts and minds of the peoples amongst whom the conflict is played out.[1] This is the first factor that

---

1. See, for example, General Sir Rupert Smith, *The Utility of Force: The Art of*

makes the job of a reservist more complex in today's conflicts than in past wars.

The second such factor is that future operations will be joint and must be integrated. As a matter of course, a country's armed forces will need to interact at the tactical level with forces and entities from other ministries and agencies, with non-governmental bodies, with public organizations, and with commercial companies. Future defense and security operations, even for the United States, are unlikely to be stand-alone but instead undertaken as part of a coalition. The structure and nature of such coalitions are unpredictable and likely to be highly variable. The reservist, therefore, will need the flexibility and breadth of training and education to cope with this, just as will a regular.

Furthermore, future defense and security operations may well be in areas of the world where the forces involved have little or no recent experience, and there is no existing coalition or alliance infrastructure to support operations. As expert knowledge of all likely deployment areas overseas cannot be assumed, reserve officers, just as regulars, will need to be able at short notice to learn about the special conditions of the host region or theater of operations. All members of a nation's armed forces will increasingly have to deal at the tactical level with the cultural and behavioral aspects of the opponent, taking into account their societal norms.

Recent experience in Iraq has shown that the information environment is of paramount importance in modern operations. Officers at the tactical level will have to ensure that their tactics support higher strategic and political objectives. They will need to understand that what may appear to be a military success at the tactical level could be a disaster at the strategic level. Future conflicts will require new intelligence systems, and intelligence will play an ever more important role, with significant implications for command and control. Officers at the tactical level may well have a better grasp of strategically significant information than their higher military commanders or political leaders. The news media will be an all-encompassing but uncontrollable environment, and mass-media considerations will become a significant factor in political and military appreciations. These issues have a fundamental impact on traditional military hierarchies and chains of command. News media will bring technical in-

---

War in the Modern World (London: Penguin Allen Lane, 2005).

cidents involving privates and corporals to the public's attention in real time, and out of context, provoking perhaps a political reaction, possibly providing material for an adversary's propaganda machine, all having disproportionate impact, and all beyond the immediate control of the local commander. The burden this places on the soldier in contact with the enemy is formidable, and will require a degree of training and education that may be beyond what a reservist can be expected to achieve.

Overall, the main characteristics of future conflict are likely to be its unpredictability; its breadth and depth; its variety; and the short notice at which it occurs. These characteristics raise issues of training and education as part of the development of personnel policies. I distinguish training from education. The essence of training is to identify best practices from past experience and to use them as a basis or model for planning future operations. The assumption is that all future problems will be new iterations of past problems, and that experience is the best asset in solving such problems. This may be true in a period of stability in the international security system. However, the scope and breadth that future military operations are likely to cover are now so great that it is simply not possible to train service personnel to be ready to tackle every problem that they may face. The pace of change is so rapid that it has become impossible to predict likely forms of future conflict or even its geographical locations. Consequently, training alone is no longer a reliable basis even for junior-officer professional development.

Instead, more time must be spent on education: to teach an understanding of basic principles, imparting not only technical knowledge, but also a deep understanding of a wide variety of essential military, social, and political factors. It requires the cultivation of an ability to apply mature consideration and judgment and to include a great many unforeseeable variables into decision-making. Officers must be practiced in applying their knowledge, expertise, analytical capability, and judgment to become competent at using the intellectual tools with which the teaching process has provided them. Education, of course, is altogether more demanding for armies than training. It has serious implications for the traditional practices of command, and for the whole structure of the officer career-development process. This is a crucial issue for building military capabilities to meet future threats. It poses a particular challenge when developing modern reserve forces with adequate flexibility and competence to be able to make an effective contribution, because part-time reservists, as they are currently organized in countries such as the United States and the UK, simply do not have enough time to absorb all the necessary training and education needed.

Traditional Roles of Reserve Forces

Because it respects the sovereignty of its member nations, NATO has created an interface by which its members can develop interoperability, but it has never dictated the shape or size of its members' forces. There is no standard NATO model for force structure or reserves: every nation has chosen its own model. There are, as a consequence, several radically different models of reserves within NATO. Any plans or ideas for future reserve structuring must take this factor into account.

RESERVES AS AN ELEMENT OF A REGULAR FORCE STRUCTURE: THE U.S., UK, AND CANADIAN MODELS

In NATO's early years, all of its members had similar force-generation structures as part of the legacy of World War II. However, the common practice of long-period national service—with a large reserve army for territorial defense and a professional cadre for training, mobilization, and readiness—gradually became differentiated under the influence of geography, history, and postwar experience. The UK, Canada, and later the United States, for example, abandoned conscription and national mobilization altogether and went to a fully professional ready force. In the British case this was a return to a pre-1916 historical tradition. The UK abandoned its "reserve army" or "shadow army" structure with a large mobilization base years ago, in favor of a small army, navy, and air force, using a small mobilization reserve primarily to "top up" the regular forces with specialists. The United States retained, in addition to an armed forces reserve, its traditional state-controlled militia, the National Guard. This is not just an internal security force but a balanced military force which has been raised to a level of combat efficiency more or less equivalent to that of U.S. regular forces and capable of integration with them for major operations. This is most evident in the Air National Guard. Canada's all-volunteer force has a large reserve component more akin to the UK system than to that of the United States.

In addition to their primary function, in all three countries the reserves also came to play the particularly important role of maintaining a close relationship between the armed forces and civilian society. In the UK, and even more so in Canada, these reserves preserve the regimental regional affiliations traditional to the army systems of these countries, even as force reductions and the operational necessity of combined-arms units have somewhat eroded this tradition in the active-duty forces.

The geography of these three countries means that any military deployment is an expeditionary operation. Consequently, their adoption of, or reversion to, an all-volunteer force structure meant that, when the Cold War ended, their force structures suited the kinds of operations that new security threats demanded.

RESERVES IN A FULLY CONSCRIPT SYSTEM

At the other end of the organizational and conceptual scale, the Scandinavian countries opted in the postwar period for a total national territorial-defense model relying almost entirely on conscription.[2] This model was "total" in that it enabled the mobilization of the entire population and its material assets for defense against invasion of the national territory. The Soviet system was a variant of this; West Germany and the former Warsaw Pact countries of Central Europe had a less extreme version of this model. The armed forces of the Central European countries were given specific roles as subordinate components of a Soviet theatre (offensive) operation, rather than having a primary duty to protect national sovereignty. They were therefore standardized on Soviet lines, and never developed truly national systems.[3]

Under such a total defense model, the prime role of the regular cadre, principally officers, is to train personnel for the reserves. The true strength of the armed forces should therefore be measured in its mobilizable numbers rather than, as in the case of the United States and the UK, in its regular ready strength. During the Cold War, this often led British or U.S. analysts to underestimate the real strength of conscript systems which depended for their employment on mobilized reserves. The principal advantage of such a model is that its personnel and support costs are lower and it permits even small countries to field very large forces quickly by mobilizing.

The disadvantage is that the system is not flexible; its forces may be ill suited to the needs of modern operations in response to new threats. In an

---

2. See Chapter 7 in this volume by Hannu Herranen.
3. See chapters in this volume on Romania (Matei, Chapter 14), the Baltic states (Urbelis, Chapter 4), and Slovakia (Švec, Chapter 18).

early example of this, the Soviet Army's careful, even obsessive, preparation for World War III left it unable to adapt to conflict in Afghanistan in the 1980s. In the case of the Scandinavian countries and West Germany, integrating military systems and societal functions was important to the process of national reconstruction in the 1950s and 1960s, but as a result, changing the system now is very difficult. Central European armies were seen by much of the population as foreign impositions, representing the rulers and not the people. This shaped national attitudes to armed forces which today complicate reform, making it difficult to generate the popular support necessary to sustain volunteer forces. In Lithuania, for example, popular support for the armed forces had to be improved by a determined program over several years to change the ethos of service, and in particular to do away with the ill-treatment of conscripts that was typical of the Soviet armed forces in the 1980s.

Elsewhere in NATO, France, Spain, Belgium, and the Netherlands, each having some degree of historic experience in colonial expeditionary warfare, moved in the 1990s from a conscript base to fully professional forces. In contrast, both Greece and Turkey, having for a long time engaged in military confrontation, have maintained a traditional World War II model of conscription and ready forces at a high level of defense expenditure.

This, then, is the starting point for the process of building a strong reserve. Each nation approaches the issue of force generation—including the use of reserves—on the basis of its historical experience, traditions, and strategic location. As a result, NATO has not resolved the problem of force generation, nor come to terms with the question of how to maintain an effective reserve. Most European countries today can be said to waste defense funds because the force structures they sustain, typically on 1.5–2 percent of GDP, produce very little in the way of deliverable military capability against any likely threat. There is in many countries inadequate political will to change these circumstances.

The Interdependency of Defense Reform and Societal Reform

One of the challenges for defense reform is the impossibility of detaching defense reform from societal reform. The changing security equation has demanded a fundamental change in the relationship between armed forces and their societies. Recruitment, funding, management and leadership, civil-military relations, and democratic control have had to change completely. Attempts at reform, even failed ones, have improved understanding of the relationship between the military and society. Countries such as Germany cannot institute such radical military reform as they perceive they need without a correspondingly great reform of their social systems. If, for example, Germany were to abandon conscription in favor of professional regular forces, the national healthcare system would be in danger of collapse, so much does it rely on the virtually free labor provided by young men who opt for civilian service as an alternative to military conscription. Germany, therefore, has retained conscription. But the time available for the training of these conscripts is not adequate to train and educate them to a level sufficient for deployment in today's complex operations.

THE REDEFINITION OF THE CONCEPT OF "SECURITY"

A second practical difficulty is reflected by changes in the meaning of the term "security." National security used to be synonymous with "defense." Reserves were forces to be mobilized for defense, and their role was unambiguously that of war-fighting and, in certain specific cases such as the U.S. National Guard, internal security as well. But now it is recognized that defense is only one element of security, although there is no agreed boundary on what the term "security" should encompass. Equally, the meaning of the term "deterrence" now needs re-definition. In the Cold War, deterrence was achieved by conventional forces, frequently territorial reserves, backed up by nuclear weapons. This was true both for NATO and the Warsaw Pact. Today there is no agreement as to what constitutes deterrence against the new security threats. Where the military does have a deterrent role, this today may be expressed by pre-emption or by a guarantee of drastic retribution. These are radically different functions for armed forces to perform in addition to traditional territorial defense, and they demand very different kinds of military and societal organization (not to mention equipment and training). Armies are now as likely to find themselves assisting with the delivery of aid in a foreign country as they are to find themselves fighting. Peacekeeping forces may have to fight to create peace. Having destroyed a country's resistance, a military force is likely to have to contribute to rebuilding its infrastructure and institutions, working with non-governmental organizations (NGOs) to do so. Many post-combat tasks require policemen, customs officials, and other civil administrators, but countries generally do not keep large available reserves of non-military security organizations. All of these changes have placed new and taxing demands on Europe's armed forces, expanding the capabilities required of all troops, reserves included. In these roles, reservists whose limited training could have restricted their utility in today's more complex combat, could actually be more effective than regulars because they can bring expertise from civilian professions to bear on the problems of post-conflict reconstruction. Here, perhaps, is an indicator of how reserve units might be configured in the future.

Obstacles to Defense Reform in Europe

Many European countries, both East and West, have been unwilling or unable to pursue defense reform as far or as fast as logic or U.S. or NATO pressure would prefer, and this has significant implications for reserve forces. In the face of the new security threats acknowledged by most European nations today, it would make sense for most countries to move away from armies based on territorial defense towards armies—and to some extent also policing forces, intelligence services, and the like—that are able to go to where the threat is to be found and neutralize it there. This requires armed forces and other security agencies capable of being deployed abroad and employed in fighting as well as other difficult tasks such as post-conflict reconstruction. They must also be sustained, which requires rotation of troops, supply lines, popular support at home, defense infrastructure systems, and the like. Many countries have concluded that this requires a regular professional force instead of a conscript one. This fundamentally affects the issue of reserve forces. Conscript systems generate their own reserves on a large scale, in that ex-conscripts form a large pool from which reserves can be drawn. The pool of ex-servicemembers created by all-volunteer forces is tiny by comparison and the relatively small training base structure of an all-volunteer force makes reservist training more of a problem. Maintaining a reserve alongside an all-volunteer force, therefore, tends to be more costly, and as all-volunteer forces are expensive and defense budgets everywhere are tight, it is reserve forces that usually bear the brunt of cuts.

RESERVE FORCES UNDER PRESSURE

The net result of all these complex problems has been to put the whole concept of sustaining a strong reserve under pressure. This is manifest in different ways depending on national and military attitudes and traditions, and tackling the issue therefore needs very careful and precise differentiation of the various national models.

The first argument that must be made is that it is indeed important to have a strong reserve. Reserves are crucial because they can offer a "low-cost low-readiness" territorial defense structure, freeing up resources for employable ready forces to deal with new threats. However, it cannot be taken for granted that their importance is accepted. Military leaders understand their importance. But several things combine to weigh against this in practice, especially amongst personnel of regular armed forces such as those of the UK and the United States. Regular forces personnel in peacetime tend to be rather scornful of reservists. Postings of regular officers as staff or instructors to UK reserve units are usually considered second or third-rate appointments, even though it is accepted that the regular army needs to be "topped up" with reservists for combat operations. Although in the United States, the National Guard has its own complete rank structure and may therefore be less prone to this attitude, there is still a degree of tension and unhealthy rivalry among the Guard, the reserves, and regular forces. When regular armed forces come under financial pressure, the tendency can be for the armed forces leadership to propose reductions in the reserve forces budget so as to preserve as much as possible of the regular structure. This need not, however, necessarily be the case. Where there is strong democratic control of armed forces, in which the civilian leadership understands military issues and has a vested interested in maintaining local military structures, reserve forces can maintain their strength and roles.[4]

Forces of countries that do not face a threat to their national sovereignty or territorial integrity traditionally invest in structure and equip-

---

4. During its post–Cold War downsizing, the United States actually preserved more reserve structure than regular structure. While the personnel strength of U.S. active forces dropped by 33 percent between 1990 and 2003, Selected Reserve personnel strength declined by just 23.5 percent. This was largely because of very strong political support for the National Guard from governors and in Congress. During the mid-1990s, the government failed to reduce Guard combat divisions, despite a decision to do so made by the Defense Department during the 1993 Bottom-Up Review, and despite repeated expert military advice, including that of the Roles and Missions Commission of the mid-1990s.

ment rather than capability. By this, I mean that such forces invest a very high proportion of their budget into weaponry and into creating a force structure which provides the maximum opportunity for rank and command in a military system when reward and authority are allocated on the basis of how much equipment or how many sub-unit elements one is in charge of.

By contrast, countries in imminent danger of critical conflict, in which the future of the state or nation is at risk, tend to invest less in front-line structure and weaponry and more in reserves of all kinds: reserves of ammunition, people, and training to produce real capability to fight. This is because the real enemy for them is their combat opponent, rather than a domestic politician intent on reducing defense expenditure. In such circumstances, armed forces have no difficulty at all understanding the value of investing heavily in reserves because these are so essential to conducting the conflict and are a cheaper means of generating combat power.

However, the new security threats do not persuade most countries of NATO that they are fighting for national survival, even though the threat has elicited a primarily military response as in Iraq or Afghanistan. Consequently, despite the extent to which, for example, UK forces have been overstretched by current operations, there has been no serious effort to review the policy on reserves or to develop a better national capacity for generating reliable reserves for future operations in the war on terror. Furthermore, U.S. and UK advice to Central European countries in the throes of transition has tended to push them in the direction of small and fully professional forces rather than maintaining reserves. This has the benefit of ensuring that these countries can provide at least some effective troops for a coalition operation. But it often fails to take account of local considerations, such as those pertaining to Central and Eastern European countries discussed below.

THE PARTICULAR PROBLEM OF THE CENTRAL AND EASTERN EUROPEAN MILITARY LEGACY

Because the Soviet military legacy stressed the importance of mobilizing the Warsaw Pact nations for World War III, there was a long-standing residual belief amongst the military elites of the successor-states, and much of the population, that this was the only way to organize a military system. This commitment to a national mobilization system with a small regular cadre was reinforced by vested interests in maintaining a skeleton force structure and a large reserve because this brings rank, command, and status (and, perhaps, opportunities for financial profit for unscrupulous senior officers). Maintaining such large "World War III" force mobilization structures is, however, a waste of national assets when there is no likelihood of a general war in Europe. This is even more true if reduced budgets have caused cuts in training and manning. These nations are paying for an illusion of military power. Russia is the most obvious victim of this type of policy but it is also true in Nordic countries. It is no wonder, therefore, that within NATO, the UK and the United States exhort countries to abandon such old practices in favor of an efficient "modern" solution, that is, a regular professional force.

But there is another factor at play. For countries that not only have a lifelong tradition of conscript and reserve force structures, but also share land borders with bigger and potentially or historically threatening neighbors, the reserve may be seen as the ultimate protection against territorial aggression. It is unrealistic in such cases to expect either military leaders or the population to be willing to abandon national mobilization or give up the reserve. It is just not politically or humanly reasonable at this stage in their development to ask countries such as Poland to trust in NATO and to accept that the danger of a traditional threat has vanished.

However, if countries that still fear a historic threat, such as those bordering on a large powerful neighbor, try to support both a regular deployable force and a traditional reserve mobilization system, they will achieve neither effectively. The model of reserves practiced by the UK and the United States will not help them in their current circumstances. Both the United States and the UK, because of their geography, face no popular concern about military invasion or domination by a large neighbor. Both are rich countries able to afford relatively expensive solutions, and both have exceedingly stable political systems.

Cost, expertise, and social custom represent the most formidable obstacles to military reform in small countries. Without useful traditions or adequate knowledge of how to construct and sustain regular forces, it will take them a long time to get real value for money from new structures. Small countries face the problem that the professional armed forces they can afford will be so small that they cannot be balanced, and thus will be inadequate for national defense. Yet neither NATO nor the EU yet have mechanisms to ensure reliable role-sharing.

Designing Reserve Structures for the Future

Finding a new concept for reserve forces is today the most important single organizational issue for all countries and armed forces in order to develop their capability to deal effectively with new security threats. Between the extremes of fully professional forces on the one hand and an expensive national mobilization system principally tailored for World War III on the other, new concepts of reserves need to be developed. These should enable countries with a tradition of mobilization, a belief in the importance of military service for nation-building, a historical fear of a larger neighbor, or a cultural aversion to or fear of a fully professional armed forces to establish a "low-cost low-readiness" territorial defense structure which would not use up so much of the national defense budget, leaving the country without adequate resources to develop serious employable ready forces to deal with new threats.

If this is a priority challenge for security planners, then the second and closely linked challenge is to evolve ideas and mechanisms to facilitate prioritization and sharing of roles within and among allied armed forces. This will almost certainly require that supra-national organizations such as NATO and the EU manage such a system. NATO must face this fact in the very near future or suffer a serious loss of credibility if, for example, it cannot persuade or enable members to provide adequate forces in Afghanistan. Thus a new and effective reserve system could be of real help if it allowed for an armed force to maintain "niche capabilities" for specific and limited military functions in order to contribute to a multi-national force. This is the essence of the third challenge: to devise ways to improve the quality and utility of reserves to supplement regular forces in those countries that have already made the transition from conscription to fully professional armies. This will require not only more conceptual effort and resources to develop procedures for recruitment, retention, training, and equipping reserves. It will also need new initiatives in civil society, by both employers and government, to enable recruits to be mobilized without too severe a financial or career penalty. It will also require armed forces to give new priority and status to reserves so that they are no longer viewed as the "poor relation" within the overall force structure.

WHERE DO WE GO FROM HERE?

Building and sustaining a strong reserve must be an integral element in an overall policy for developing new levels of military and security capability to meet new threats. The initial task is to subject the issue to study: sorting out the different forms of reserve, differentiating among them, and establishing the conditions for which they were developed. It will be necessary to evaluate the potential utility of reserves, assessing the various combat or support roles that they might play in each of the main kinds of operation that modern armed forces may be called upon to perform: high-intensity expeditionary warfare, peace support operations, or homeland defense and internal security duties.

Next, the cost of various types of reserve forces must be compared to that of regular forces. This will require evaluating to what extent regular forces can be deemed to be genuinely professional, especially given the very high level of turnover amongst junior ranks.[5] The results of this study may not be as advantageous to professional forces as expected, if they are compared to efficient and well established conscript forces with a two-year conscription period. A similar evaluation of the professional level of standing reserves (such as those in the UK, United States, or Canada) might also find a disappointing result, as these too are subject to high levels of personnel turnover. But without a clear evaluation of these facts, it is difficult to begin the process of improving the effectiveness of reserves.

Not all countries accept automatically that new security tasks can be accomplished more cost-effectively by regular forces. Finland is making a very strong case for the use of conscripts (see Chapter 7 by Hannu Herranen in this volume). Thus, the third phase of work needs to be an assessment of the effectiveness of different models of conscript-mobilization forces, their limitations, and their advantages, taking into account especially the different lengths of conscript service (which has a significant impact on conscripts' skill levels and therefore their capabilities if called upon for reserve service) and intangibles such as popular support, morale, and motivation. This evidence base can then be used to

---

5.   See, for example, Chapters 13, 14, and 15 in this volume by Lopez Diaz, Matei, and Villani, indicating that Spain, Romania, and Italy, are establishing very short periods for initial volunteer enlistments.

develop more flexible ways of creating reserves with higher levels of capability, training, and availability.

A most important model would be that of a low-cost low-readiness reserve system that could provide a credible territorial defense capability, satisfy national or cultural needs to link armed forces with society, and reassure the population of a country living with a historical fear of a larger neighbor. Two tasks are necessary for this phase. First is the issue of creating reserves of non-military security forces such as police, customs and immigration officials, and the like. They will need to be ready to work with armies across traditional boundaries, breaking down the barriers and stovepipes that still characterize the security sector.

Secondly, plans must be made and doctrine, procedures, safeguards, and practices reshaped to integrate non-military forces into future operations, along with the private commercial organizations that are rapidly coming to play such a prominent role by taking on tasks in combat or post-combat zones which were previously the monopoly of uniformed soldiers. Perhaps taking the place of contractors is a new role for reserves, or perhaps a new quasi-military status should be developed for civilian organizations.

Whatever steps are taken, reserves will be an absolutely essential element of the solution.

Chapter 17

Transformation of the Reserve Components of the U.S. Armed Forces

John D. Winkler, Robert J. St. Onge, Jr.,
Karen I. McKenney, and
Jennifer C. Buck

The United States, along with many of its allies and friends, is in the midst of a transformation of its armed forces to ensure that they can meet the challenges of the twenty-first-century security environment. These are challenges dominated by a global war on terrorism and also by the rapid development and availability of advanced technology, asymmetric tactics and operational concepts devised and used by adversaries, and dangers associated with weapons of mass destruction. Transformation to meet these challenges involves acquiring new and upgraded weapon systems; developing new military tactics, techniques, and procedures; and organizational change. It also involves revolutionary changes in the use and management of military personnel.

This chapter examines one aspect of the transformation in military manpower and personnel management: the transformation of the U.S. reserve components. The chapter begins with an overview of the structure of the reserve components and how they are currently being used to support U.S. military operations.[1] It then turns to two aspects of today's transformation: arguing for rebalancing the mix of active and reserve forces,

The authors would like to acknowledge the contributions and assistance of Dan Kohner; Lieutenant Colonel Greg Bennett, USMCR; Colonel Chuck Barham, USA; and Barbara Bicksler in preparing this chapter.

1. In this chapter, references to the "reserve components" and "reserve forces" include both the Reserve and National Guard, unless otherwise stated.

and presenting a new approach to managing active and reserve forces. The chapter concludes with some observations about reserve forces that we believe have wider applicability outside the United States.

Structure of the U.S. Reserve Components

The U.S. reserve components comprise about 1.1 million service-members—approximately 44 percent of the nation's total military manpower—as of December 31, 2005. There are seven reserve components. Six are part of the three military departments: the Army Reserve, the Army National Guard, the Air Force Reserve, the Air National Guard, the Navy Reserve, and the Marine Corps Reserve. The Army and Air National Guard differ from the others in that each has both federal and state missions: they comprise the organized militias and can be used to enforce state laws, but they also can be called on by the president or Congress to serve as federal assets during national emergencies. The seventh and smallest reserve component, the Coast Guard Reserve, belongs organizationally to the Department of Homeland Security, but works closely with the Department of Defense.[2] The federal reserve components provide the regular active-duty forces with critical augmentation, unit and individual, for capabilities that are not routinely needed on active duty in peacetime.

KEY FEATURES

The reserve components are located in nearly 5,000 cities across the United States. While they are integrated into the total military force, these servicemembers are part-time personnel. The typical reserve unit trains for two days per month and an additional 14 days per year. The units are made up of citizen-soldiers who play dual roles both as professional military personnel and as citizens of their communities. The existence of the reserve components follows a long-standing U.S. tradition of citizen-soldiers. From the very beginning of the nation, distrust of large standing armies resulted in a tradition of reliance on citizen-soldiers who would answer the call to arms in emergencies and then return to their civilian

---

2. During times of war or when directed by the president, the U.S. Coast Guard comes under the operational command of the U.S. Department of the Navy.

occupations when the crisis passed. These local and state formations and organized militias predate the U.S. Constitution, which explicitly recognizes their place in the U.S. military structure.

Today's increased reliance on the reserve components is a product, in part, of several key features in the evolution of the reserves, in particular the Abrams Doctrine and an evolving "Total Force" policy. In the aftermath of the Vietnam War, then Chief of Staff of the Army General Creighton Abrams asserted his belief that the nation must never go to war again without calling up "the spirit of the American people," which meant calling up the National Guard and reserves. By involving the guard and reserves from communities and families across America, the will of the people is brought to the fight. This philosophy has become known as the Abrams Doctrine.[3]

During the same period, the Total Force concept emerged through a series of policy memoranda, the first of which was signed in 1970 by then Secretary of Defense Melvin Laird. The Total Force policy emphasized increased reliance on the reserves, initially for war fighting, and later for the full spectrum of military requirements including missions such as peacekeeping and, more recently, homeland security. The initial Total Force doctrine directed the military departments to consider both active and reserve components together in all force planning, programming, budgeting, and employment. Influenced by the Abrams Doctrine, the Total Force—comprising both active and reserve components—was designed in such a way that mobilization of the reserves would be necessary to conduct an extended conflict.

Thus, reserve-component missions and structures complement those of active-duty forces, and the active and reserve components share complementary designs. The federal government provides the resources for equipping and training reserve forces. Like the active force, the reserve components are an all-volunteer force; they are composed of personnel with and without prior military experience. The reserve components have traditionally been a way to maintain military capabilities not often

3. For further discussion of the Abrams Doctrine, see Lieutenant General Thomas J. Plewes, "Reserve Duty Changed Forever," *American Forces Press Service* (Washington, D.C.), January 22, 2002; and *The Annual Report of the Reserve Forces Policy Board: Manpower, Personnel and Force Structure* (Washington, D.C.: Office of the Secretary of Defense, May 2001), Chapter 3.

Table 17.1. Organization of U.S. Reserve Manpower

Individual Ready Reserve		281,902
Selected Reserve		825,427
Units	798,130	
Individual Mobilization Augmentees	27,097	
Total Ready Reserve		**1,117,329**

Source: Office of the Assistant Secretary of Defense for Reserve Affairs. Data as of December 31, 2005.

Note: The National Guard, including the Army National Guard's 333,438 members and the Air National Guard's 105,846 members, constitutes about 53 percent of the selected reserve force.

used in peacetime but needed for wartime operations, with lower sustaining costs. As the Total Force concept has evolved, it has emphasized the use of the reserve components to support a wider range of operational requirements and has sought to reduce barriers to the integration of the active and reserve components. As a result, guard and reserve forces are a primary source for augmenting active-component forces in emergencies when rapid and substantial expansion of the active force is required. For example, reserve forces typically provide the airlift and refueling capabilities required in the early stages of most operations.

ORGANIZATION AND MIX

Most individuals in the reserve components, including the National Guard, are members of either the "selected reserve" or the "individual ready reserve" (which together comprise the ready reserve) as shown in Table 17.1. The selected reserve force, of approximately 825,000 reservists, consists of units and individuals designated as essential to contingency or wartime missions. They are so-called "drilling reservists": paid members who train a minimum of 38 days per year, either as part of a unit or as individual augmentees. The selected reserve, which constitutes roughly 75 percent of reserve manpower, can be called for use by the president. The National Guard, including both the Army and Air National Guard, constitutes about half of the selected reserve force.

The other 25 percent of the ready reserve manpower are members of the individual ready reserve (IRR), which includes approximately 282,000 individuals. Most of these reservists have a remaining military service obligation, are subject to recall, and in general are seen as individuals who are drawing their military service to a close. A few are selected reservists

Table 17.2. Comparison of Active and Selected Reserve Manpower

Service	Total Strength	Active Component	Reserve Component	
			Reserve	National Guard
Army	1,005,481	48% 484,069	19% 187,974	33% 333,438
Navy	428,267	83% 353,635	17% 74,632	N/A
Marine Corps	218,397	82% 178,577	18% 39,820	N/A
Air Force	528,764	66% 347,398	14% 75,520	20% 105,846
Coast Guard	47,709	83% 39,512	17% 8,197	N/A
All Services	2,228,618	63% 1,403,191	17% 386,143	20% 439,284

Data as of December 31, 2005.

Note: Reserve-component data reflect selected reserve only; they do not include members of the individual ready reserve.

who are between assignments. Members of the individual ready reserve do not perform, or receive pay for, regularly scheduled training.

Overall, the selected reserve force represents about 37 percent of the total force—44 percent if the individual ready reserve is included. However, as Table 17.2 shows, the size of the reserve components as a percentage of total available military manpower varies considerably by service. The Navy and Marine Corps Reserves are fairly small compared to their active-duty counterparts. The Army, on the other hand, draws more than half of its capability from the guard and reserve. These differences drive the mobilization requirements of the individual services. This relationship between the active and reserve components has remained relatively stable.

The size of the ready reserve (the selected reserve plus individual ready reserve) reflects a 32 percent reduction since 1989, when the United States began a significant reduction in the size of its total force, including both active and reserve components. (In the same period, the active forces have declined by a similar amount, or about 34 percent.) The pressures associated with this downsizing are another factor that has spurred greater reliance on the reserve components. Today the guard and reserve have been integrated into the planning and execution of all military operations and have been an essential element to their success.

Use of Reserve-component Forces

Each reserve component contributes to the total force in different ways, spanning the spectrum from dedicated peacetime roles, such as domestic emergency response and natural-disaster relief, to wartime support alongside their active-duty counterparts. Downsizing of the U.S. armed forces, reduced defense budgets, and increasing operational tempo have all contributed to increased use of the reserve components. Furthermore, the reserve components are a repository for many military capabilities traditionally used in the later phases of a major theater war, such as military police, civil affairs, and reconstruction. These capabilities have become unexpectedly crucial in the military operations of recent years. Thus, today's strategic environment requires a reexamination of how the active and reserve capabilities are organized and used.

CONTRIBUTIONS IN PEACETIME AND RECENT CONTINGENCIES

Reserve personnel are involved in many ongoing contingencies including those in Bosnia, Kosovo, Southwest Asia (including Iraq and Afghanistan), and the Sinai. The contribution of the reserves to military operations has increased dramatically, from an annual rate of approximately 1 million duty-days of mission support before the Berlin Wall came down in 1989 to nearly 13 million duty-days per year during the later part of the 1990s, as Figure 17.1 illustrates. Reserve contributions include operational support to combatant commands, such as individual staff augmentation, airlift, or refueling missions; support to exercises; mobilizations to military operations worldwide, most recently to Afghanistan and Iraq; response to domestic emergencies such as Guard support to state governors in the event of forest fires, hurricanes, and floods; and counter-drug operations.

The increase in the number of reserve deployments has had a significant impact on the use of the reserves in the past decade and a half, as the two spikes in Figure 17.1 depict. The first spike, primarily in fiscal year 1991, reflects support to Operations Desert Shield and Desert Storm. The second spike in reserve contributions, from fiscal years 2002–2005, shows the impact of the global war on terrorism, reflecting operations both at home and abroad. It appears that for the foreseeable future, reserve contributions will remain at a level higher than the steady-state period of the mid-to-late 1990s. At what level a new steady state might be reached will depend on the requirements for guard and

Figure 17.1. Reserve Component Support to Total Force Missions

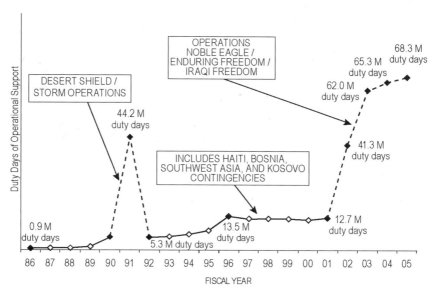

Note: Dotted lines indicate periods where partial mobilizations were in effect: Operation Desert Storm in fiscal year 1991 and Operations Noble Eagle, Enduring Freedom, and Iraqi Freedom beginning in fiscal year 2001.

reserve personnel in ongoing operations in the global war on terrorism as well as the demands of future contingencies.

MOBILIZATION OF RESERVE COMPONENTS SINCE SEPTEMBER 11, 2001

The number of reserve-component members that have been called to active duty since September 11, 2001—that is, those reservists mobilized to support the global war on terrorism—provides another view of the degree of reserve-component involvement in ongoing military operations. Figure 17.2 illustrates the tremendous increase in the number of reservists on active duty since late 2001, beginning with the initial buildup immediately after the attacks on the World Trade Center and the Pentagon as reserve-component members began to provide support to homeland security operations.

The initial call-up of the reserves after September 11, 2001, was followed immediately by a buildup to support major combat operations in Afghanistan; about 40,000 reserve-component members were involved at the peak of operations there. After the end of major combat operations in Afghanistan in late 2002, the number of reservists on active duty fell to around 33,000. In early 2003, the number of reservists on active

Figure 17.2. Reserve Component Members on Active Duty, September 11, 2001–December 31, 2005

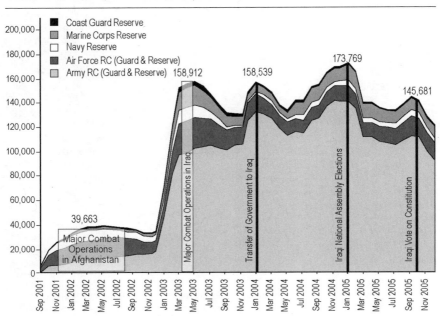

duty surged again in the buildup for combat operations in Iraq. At the peak of combat operations in Iraq, in May 2003, about 159,000 reservists were mobilized. Subsequently, the number of reserve-component members mobilized has fluctuated based on requirements to support significant events such as the transfer of government to Iraq, the Iraqi national assembly elections, and the Iraqis' vote on their constitution.

The peak number of reserve-component members mobilized at any one time, slightly less than 175,000 reservists, was in January 2005, corresponding to the Iraqi national elections. That number decreased dramatically to about 122,000 as more security responsibilities were turned over to Iraqi forces. Overall, the percentage of U.S. reserve forces in Iraq decreased from about 40 percent in mid-2004 to about 20 percent as of December 31, 2005.

In contrast to Figure 17.2, which shows the number of reserve-component members on active duty at particular points in time, Table 17.3 shows the total number of reservists mobilized since September 11, 2001. To meet mobilization requirements, about 475,000 selected reserve mem-

Table 17.3. Total Number of Reserve-component Members Mobilized, September 11, 2001–December 31, 2005

	Number of Members	Number Mobilized	Percent Mobilized
Army National Guard, Army Reserve	817,882	310,300	37.9
Air National Guard, Air Force Reserve	216,775	95,433	44.0
Navy Reserve	109,245	28,424	26.0
Marine Corps Reserve	60,603	33,838	55.8
Coast Guard Reserve	11,136	6,827	61.3
Total Selected Reserve Force	1,215,641	474,822	39.1

Note: Does not include 10,473 individual ready reserve members mobilized between September 11, 2001, and December 31, 2005.

bers had been called to active duty between September 11, 2001, and December 31, 2005.[4] This is about 39 percent of the total number of members (1.2 million) who served in the selected reserve during this period of just over four years. In other words, over half of all reservists who have been in the selected reserve since September 11, 2001, have not been mobilized.

At first glance, these data might suggest that the reserve components have not been significantly over-burdened as a result of current U.S. operations and the dramatic increase in the number of mobilizations. Yet in certain specialties, where demand outpaces the inventory of available personnel, problems exist. Given the pace of U.S. involvement in military operations since the end of the Cold War, and given that many of the operational capabilities to support these missions are concentrated in the reserve components, demand for reserve support is likely to remain high.

STRESS ON THE FORCE

The U.S. Department of Defense, the U.S. Congress, and the American public are concerned about overuse of the reserve components. Three primary factors determine stress on the force: frequency, duration, and percentage of reserve personnel used.

---

4.   This number does not include the approximately 10,000 members of the individual ready reserve who have also served during this period.

Frequency refers to how often individual reserve-component members are called up to participate in military operations. Since 1996, about 16,000 reserve members have served in both current military operations in Afghanistan and Iraq, and also in at least one other previous operation in Bosnia, Kosovo, or Southwest Asia. Additionally, another 83,000 members have been called up more than once to support the operations in Afghanistan and Iraq—almost all of them volunteers. Over the ten years between 1996 and 2006, however, of the approximately 2.1 million members who have been in the selected reserve during that time, about 8.5 percent, most of them volunteers, served in military operations more than once. Although there are concerns about frequent call-ups for certain high-demand specialties, overall, the frequency of multiple call-ups for most reservists does not appear to be unusually demanding for the total reserve force.

However, the duration of these call-ups—the amount of time for which a reserve-component member is mobilized—has increased. For example, during Operations Desert Shield and Desert Storm, the length of the average tour by a reservist was 156 days. In regional contingencies such as Kosovo, Southwest Asia, and Bosnia, most tours between 1996 and 2003 were about 200 days. In recent operations in Afghanistan and Iraq, the average tour length has been 346 days, counting those who had completed their activations as of December 31, 2005.

Furthermore, the military services have called on significant portions of some skill categories such as security, motor vehicle operators, intelligence, air crews, and civil affairs. Data on actual usage rates suggest that some functional areas are being used at rates that cannot be sustained for long durations. At this point, more than four years into the current mobilization, a usage rate of 60 percent or more for any skill category raises concerns, and there are areas where this has occurred, as depicted in Figure 17.3.

Rebalancing the Mix of Active and Reserve Forces

Given these concerns, recent and projected utilization rates suggest the need to rebalance the size of certain skill inventories within and between active and reserve forces to add more people to high-use specialties. Further innovative management approaches can also help to reduce stress on the force.

Figure 17.3. Selected Higher-Use Career Specialties within Occupational Categories (as of December 31, 2005)

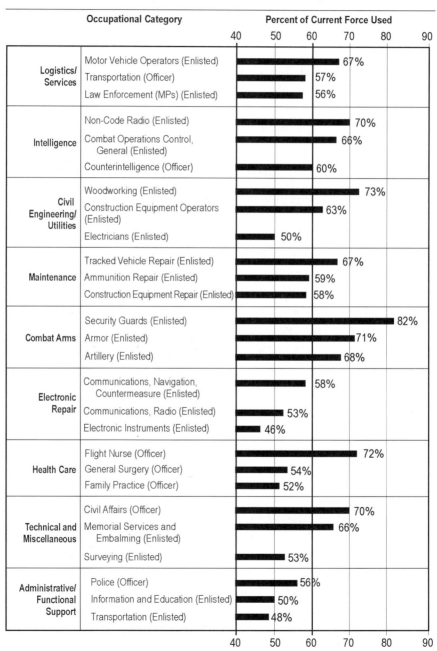

Note: Each occupational category has low-use specialties as well.

Plans to rebalance the U.S. armed forces are based on a number of assumptions. Principal among these assumptions is the expectation that the global war on terrorism will be a protracted one. The level of operational tempo in the future is likely to remain substantially higher than the levels prior to September 11, 2001. It will include continuing operations in the continental United States, Afghanistan, Iraq, and other overseas areas. Emerging contingencies requiring rapid-response operations are also likely, causing troop levels to spike. Some spikes may be of relatively small size and duration, but others might require forces up to the level of major combat operations, as in Iraq.

A steady-state commitment of reserve forces over the next three to five years may require about 100,000 to 150,000 troops, or between 36 and 54 million duty-days per year—a level slightly lower than that of the past few years. All reserve components will contribute, but this requirement will be filled primarily by Army National Guard and Army Reserve forces. The Department of Defense is working to mitigate the stress that has been experienced by sustained use of some reserve components. For example, the Department is employing and training personnel from all services for assistance in the more highly stressed specialties in the Army such as civil affairs, security forces, intelligence, medical, transportation, explosive ordnance disposal, and facility engineer teams. Although mobilization periods will vary among the services, reserve-component members can be expected to be mobilized for periods from 12 to 18 months. It is expected that the early conflict phase of any future operations will be met by designated response forces from both the active and reserve components.

NEAR-TERM INITIATIVES

The Department of Defense and the military services have identified changes that will be needed to meet three force management goals: enhance early responsiveness, resolve stressed career fields, and employ better management practices.

To meet the requirements for rapid-response forces early in a contingency, the services are structuring their active and reserve forces to reduce the need for involuntary mobilization. The services are positioning themselves to rely more on active-duty forces, volunteers from the reserve component, and enhanced readiness—that is, fully manned, trained, and equipped units—to meet early-response requirements. In order for reserve-component forces to be able to respond quickly, perhaps with a very short warning period, the military services plan to rely more on volunteerism for selecting early-deploying forces, rather than involuntarily mobilizing many reservists. That is, individuals will volunteer in advance of a conflict to be part of an early response force and will train for this mission.

Each of the services has identified a number of measures to enhance readiness for rapid-response requirements. For example, over the next several years the Army is converting many lower-priority active-duty positions to higher-priority specialties and training more people for chemical-weapons response, military police, engineering, medical, transportation, and quartermaster (e.g., fuel and water supply) duties. Similarly, the Navy has increased the number of positions for ship and port security in order to meet the requirements for elevated force protection levels without involuntarily mobilizing reserve forces.

To help resolve stressed career fields, the Army and the Navy have identified areas where the mix of forces between active and reserves could be rebalanced, have programmed initial efforts to do so, and have accomplished about half of the projected changes. The Marine Corps and Air Force have also initiated efforts but to a lesser degree. Table 17.4 shows what has been achieved through September 30, 2005, and plans for future rebalancing initiatives. In total, the services rebalanced about 70,000 positions in fiscal years 2003 through 2005. For example, the Army converted 3,000 active-component field artillery positions and 9,000 reserve-component positions in field artillery, air-defense artillery, and combat engineer specialties to supply increased military police, special forces, and intelligence capabilities.

The Navy has converted 1,000 active-component positions to security forces. The Marine Corps converted 2,000 active-component positions to security forces and is activating more air-naval gunfire liaison companies. The Marines are also converting 1,000 reserve-component positions to intelligence and security specialties. The Air Force is adding 4,000 personnel to its active-duty security forces by adjusting accessions and converting certain active-component positions. Looking to the future, the services plan to rebalance another 55,000 positions during fiscal years 2006 through 2010. The result of these changes will be improved early-responsiveness capabilities and reduced stress on high-demand specialties.

Table 17.4. Rebalancing Initiatives

Service	Spaces Rebalanced FY03–FY05	Spaces to be Rebalanced FY06–FY10	Career Fields to be Augmented
Army	24,000	21,000	Quartermaster; Medical; Engineer; Military Police; Special Operations Forces; Intelligence
Navy	33,000	29,000	Security Forces
Marine Corps	6,000	4,000	Air Naval Gunfire Liaison Companies; Security Forces; Intelligence
Air Force	7,000	1,000	Security Forces; Aircrews; Maintenance
Total	70,000	55,000	

Note: For total number of military spaces rebalanced FY 2003 to 2005, data as of September 30, 2005.
Source: Office of the Assistant Secretary of Defense for Reserve Affairs.

In addition to adding more personnel to high-demand specialties, the military services are also turning to improved personnel management practices to relieve stress on the force. The services seek to achieve greater flexibility in utilizing the total force, while reducing the stress on critical career fields and the need for involuntary mobilization. Each service has unique needs, but there are a range of approaches that can help ensure that the services have access to individuals with the skills and capabilities required for both emergent operations and sustained, day-to-day activities. Some of the concepts under consideration provide additional opportunities for reserves to volunteer for active duty or to serve for more frequent or longer periods of time, provide better predictability regarding future activations, capitalize locally on reserve talents, and improve the mobilization process. Some of these practices are explained in more detail later in this chapter.

Meeting Emerging Missions and Requirements

Over the longer term, emerging missions and new requirements will lead to further changes in how reservists in the U.S. armed forces are structured and organized. The United States faces a range of emerging missions associated with homeland security and the global war on terrorism that present tremendous challenges to the Department of Defense. Changes to unit organization and methods of employment and more flexible accession options are keys to meeting the requirements of new and emerging missions. Some of these potential changes are discussed here.

BLENDED OR MIXED UNITS

Reserves will always play a role in augmenting active forces, particularly where "surge capability" is needed in high-demand specialties. New organizations might blend or mix active and reserve personnel together in the same unit to provide important enhancements. By using reserve personnel to augment active-component units and the systems they operate, the military services could increase the firepower or productivity of a fixed number of systems, even operating systems around-the-clock if such a capability is needed. Mixed units provide a way to leverage the strength of each component to meet military requirements.

There are already some examples of such units. For example, the Air Force has made extensive use of mixed units in its strategic airlift and medical evacuation forces. By sharing flying and maintenance responsibilities, these units offer the benefits of "force multiplication" and a high level of integration. Because the active and reserve members of the unit train together, wartime tasks can be tailored to the capabilities and limitations of each individual in the unit. Moreover, the augmenting personnel can deploy rapidly to the theater because the equipment for both components deploys with the active unit. More such units could be created.

RESERVE CONTRIBUTIONS TO HOMELAND DEFENSE

One of the most visible emerging missions is homeland defense. While defense of the homeland has always been a priority mission area for the Department of Defense, this mission has received renewed focus since September 11, 2001. Homeland defense is a total-force mission, and there is clearly a role for reserve components in meeting its myriad of requirements. The department has examined how the reserve components might be factored into the homeland defense missions. It will be up to the U.S. Joint Forces Command, which is the force provider, in conjunction with U.S. Northern Command, which is the lead combatant commander, to determine exactly how and when the reserve components will be used in future homeland defense scenarios. Elements of the homeland defense mission to which the reserve components could contribute include air defense of the continental United States, ballistic missile defense, and port and maritime security.

REACHBACK OPERATIONS

The information and technology revolutions have made the battlefield an increasingly high-technology arena, a situation that will continue in the future. To stay ahead, the U.S. military must continue to master new and emerging technologies and incorporate these advances into its weapon systems and concepts of operation. A consequence of this high-technology arena is an increase in the type and numbers of functions that can be conducted at sites far away from the physical battlefield: this is called "reachback."

Reachback refers to the ability of forces in the theater to be connected electronically to sites in the continental United States or other locations to accomplish essential tasks and missions. By employing reachback operations, the in-theater force can be smaller and more agile; corresponding combat support and physical security requirements are also reduced. Reachback can provide additional capabilities to combatant commanders without requiring additional mobilizations. Thus, it is an effective and efficient way to tap reservists' civilian skills. By using computer connectivity, reserve units and individuals can provide mission support during drill periods and on short-duration active-duty tours. This concept could add tremendous value to operational missions.

Examples of functions that can be conducted through reachback include telemedicine; expert technical assistance in areas such as chemical and biological warfare matters; comprehensive command and control via satellite communications and web-based information technology; and provision of intelligence and other information to the war fighter by units and assets in remote "nondeployed" positions and by unmanned aerial vehicles controlled by satellite link to ground stations in the continental United States.

ROTATIONAL OVERSEAS PRESENCE

The military services are placing high priority on ensuring that reserve-component members are provided with adequate notice of deployments, with the goal of a minimum of 30 days notification prior to activation. The services aim to develop models for troop rotation that provide reservists with even longer notification timelines and less frequent deployments. Such models, along with improvements in the mobilization process, will give force providers more and better information on the reserve forces being activated—including the range of skills available and the frequency and duration of deployments. By using reservists in certain mission areas, the ability of the services to provide predictable periods of service is enhanced.

The predictability and long lead time associated with overseas-presence missions allows for substantial planning and preparation of units, individual servicemembers, their families, and their employers. Thus, this would be a particularly appropriate mission in which to use reserve-component units. Use of reservists for rotational oversees presence leaves active-component units free to support rapid-response requirements that may arise. The services are thus better able to manage the operational tempo of the total force. In addition, they are better able to plan for and utilize reserve training periods, leading to an increase in individual and unit readiness.

FLEXIBLE ACCESSION OPTIONS

The Department of Defense must create more flexible ways for the military to obtain the services of civilians who have the skills that can meet military requirements, but who do not have the traditional career orientation generally required by the services. Some of the skills that are useful to the uniformed military are difficult to acquire through traditional accession policies, require extended periods of training, or have requirements of urgent but limited duration. Examples include advanced technical skills such as those possessed by engineers, scientists, or information-technology professionals. Moreover, technology is changing so rapidly that the active-duty military can no longer train people fast enough or retain them long enough to stay on the cutting edge of new technology. The challenge is most visible in such key areas as information technology and biometrics, areas where the military finds it hard to provide compensation and working conditions that would attract and retain specialists for an entire career. Without tapping into this talent, technological advantage is lost to the military. Thus there is a need for innovative partnership programs with the private sector that could allow the Department of Defense to make use, when needed, of individuals who have acquired such skills outside the military.

Transforming Personnel Management

The services will need to adopt multiple approaches to resolve force imbalances, reduce the number and frequency of involuntary mobilizations, meet emerging requirements, and support new operational demands. Yet the personnel management structure in place today does not reflect the realities of how the total force is being used, nor support optimal employment of the force, much less provide a structure within which the services can take advantage of the types of innovative concepts described in this chapter. To acquire and maintain capabilities that will meet a wide-ranging and uncertain set of demands, and to support surges in activity, methods used to access and manage personnel must have greater flexibility to permit a wider range of opportunities for reserve service. A new personnel management paradigm is needed.

We have, therefore, developed a new approach to personnel management that acknowledges the changes that have occurred in how military service is performed and that would provide individual servicemembers greater flexibility in supporting the missions of the Department of Defense. This new paradigm, which we refer to as the "continuum of service," aims to create flexibility in providing needed capabilities and to ensure a more seamless and cost-effective management of military forces. It prescribes both organizational and systemic change so that the U.S. Department of Defense can manage individuals more effectively throughout their military careers, while meeting the full spectrum of military requirements in peacetime and wartime with greater efficiency and economy of resources.

Historically, the Department of Defense has managed its personnel in two separate groups: "full-time" active-duty personnel who serve 365 days per year and "part-time" reserve personnel who typically train a required minimum of 38 days per year. Within each of these two groups, the department has rigid structures for managing people. To move from one category to the other, a servicemember must be discharged and then reenter military service.

The concept behind a continuum of service abandons this distinction between active and reserve components and instead establishes a range of service options, from full-time duty to intermittent availability in the event of crisis or mobilization. Between these extremes of full-time or intermittent participation is a pool of individuals who can be involved at varying levels of participation, and who may move one way or the other along the continuum as circumstances in their lives and the needs of the department change. Movement along the continuum should be transparent, seamless, and supported by a continuum of benefits commensurate with service-member contributions. Compensation must be structured and set at appropriate levels to attract the high-quality personnel needed to meet the requirements of new and emerging missions.

What the continuum of service offers is a system of management and resource allocation that supports, accommodates, and enhances varying levels of reserve-component participation. The continuum of service can also take better advantage of the spirit of volunteerism by providing more ways in which military service can be performed to support Department of Defense missions. These two important characteristics of the continuum of service are examined in detail.

OPPORTUNITIES FOR EXTENDED SERVICE

The continuum of service envisions that individuals should be able to select among and move between varying lengths of military service and to perform military service in new, nontraditional ways. The Department's experience since September 11, 2001, shows that some members of the reserve component are willing to be part of units where they are required to serve more than the traditional 38 days per year, yet less than full time. According to statistics maintained by the U.S. Department of Defense, members of the selected reserve have performed a per-capita average of approximately 122 duty-days annually for the past three fiscal years, a significant increase since the beginning of the global war on terrorism. Reserve components have had little difficulty finding volunteers for temporary assignments, which indicates the existence of a labor market that is responsive to expanded part-time participation opportunities. This market can be drawn upon more for selected skills.

In some segments of the reserve community, participation by reservists already occurs at levels greater than standard part-time 38 days per year, but less than permanent full time. However, to accommodate how the reserves are actually being used, the military services have had to work around the current system in assigning duty status, allocating resources, fulfilling accountability standards, and managing forces. Recent legislation has provided for a structured mechanism that will help efficiently expand the roles and responsibilities of reserve-component members. This legislation eliminated regulations that restricted the duration of voluntary duty that a reservist could perform. Now, reserve members can serve voluntarily for up to three years without counting against the active-component personnel limits.

The concept of "variable participation of reserves" is another option for managing personnel who may offer their services on a continuous part-time basis or for extended but intermittent periods of active duty. This tool would represent an expansion of existing methods for employing reserves. The pool of participants would consist of a small group of individuals and units who are no longer limited to the traditional 38 days per year of reserve training. These personnel could be asked to commit voluntarily to continuous or intermittent extended duty through formal agreements when their services are needed to meet warfighting and other operational requirements. The length of the annual participation requirement would vary by individual or unit and would be specified in volunteer agreements with a military service.

Variable participation of reserves would be most useful in the segments of the force where reserve volunteers serve in sizable numbers today, including Air Force maintenance crews and air crews, Navy and Marine Corps command staffs, and Army exercise command-and-control elements. It could also support emerging missions such as those related to space, information operations, intelligence, medicine, and other high-technology areas. Participants could compose volunteer units and detachments prepared to meet unanticipated or rapidly developing operational and support needs. Such a program could focus on specialized capabilities including those needed early in an operation, such as cargo handling or transportation.

The ability to enter into formal agreements with individuals and units would provide commanders and the military services with greater flexibility to satisfy mission requirements as they evolve. If volunteers can be used in selected functional areas, requirements that are not in effect 365 days per year can nevertheless be met on a timely basis. While the traditional 38-day training program might well remain the mainstay of reserve participation, variable participation would provide the option of a more robust structure for contribution of part-time service. Those reservists in the civilian labor market who frequently change jobs, or who are accustomed to working flexible schedules, part-time, or in a virtual setting (such as through telecommuting) might find this reserve option more attractive than current options.

ENHANCED VOLUNTEERISM

Another aspect of the continuum-of-service proposal focuses on individuals who are not currently serving in the military. These are people with a needed civilian high-technology skill who would agree to serve on a stand-by basis to provide service as needed. This service could be performed in uniform or as a civilian volunteer. One group of particular interest is military retirees. Following the terrorist attacks on the World Trade Center and the Pentagon, many military retirees, both active and reserve, expressed a strong desire to serve in some capacity. Retirees represent a large source of trained and experienced manpower often left untapped. In some situations, retirees may serve most effectively through a return to active duty, while in others they could provide useful services to military agencies as civilian volunteers. To take advantage of this valuable source of manpower, the department needs structured mechanisms to track and utilize retiree volunteers.

The continuum of service could also accommodate mission augmentation, to be performed by civilian volunteers who are trained to service standards. Existing volunteer auxiliaries such as the Coast Guard auxiliary could be expanded to attract individuals from all age groups who wish to volunteer their talents. Auxiliaries offer a way to manage and employ those military-retiree volunteers who are not required on active duty. Under the Coast Guard auxiliary model, for example, civilians regularly deploy on cutters and Coast Guard aircraft as augmentees, just like their active-duty and reserve counterparts. The Civil Air Patrol provides the Air Force with similar operating capabilities. Such models could be extended and adopted more broadly.

By developing its partnerships with communities, corporations, and academia, the department could also acquire certain skills and individuals to meet military requirements that cannot be fully met through traditional contracts. For example, the department currently has a program that matches experienced civilian engineers who have expertise in wireless communications with a military need for spectrum managers, who are in short supply in both the active and reserve components. Another example might be a partnership with colleges and universities to take advantage of the skills of university faculty, staff, and students in areas such as supercomputing, biotechnology, communications technology, disaster management, acoustics, or defense against terrorism.

The department might develop a special affiliation program to call upon such individuals as needed.

DoD partnerships with corporations might involve supportive relations: the department might have access to certain skilled individuals for a period of time and, in exchange, the department would provide them with training and leadership skills, and perhaps employee benefits, saving the company money. In return, the company might provide advanced training and might guarantee access to its employees who would volunteer for this program when their skills are need for particular projects.

To develop successful partnerships with businesses, academia, or community organizations, the military will have to provide flexible participation options (such as participation from a civilian location rather than a military facility) that accommodate individuals' civilian obligations along with the military duties for which they have volunteered. It will also require a desire on the part of civilian organizations and individuals to partner with the Department of Defense.

Overall, the continuum-of-service proposal aims to provide more flexibility in creating needed capabilities and to ensure more seamless and cost-effective management of military forces. It seeks to capitalize on changes in the U.S. labor market, in which increasing numbers of people are able and willing to arrange time off from school or job to provide specialized skills that the Department of Defense may need from time to time, either as part of an expanded, part-time military career or on an episodic, voluntary basis. In essence, the continuum of service would establish a labor market that would allow varied forms and levels of military participation, encourage such participation through appropriate incentives, and eliminate barriers to voluntary participation. Altogether, the continuum-of-service paradigm can create a military force that is both operationally integrated and administratively seamless. As such, it would represent an important step forward for the all-volunteer force.

Final Observations

The reserve components will continue to make a significant contribution to America's defense and to play a critical role in the success of the all-volunteer force. The reserves provide an important means to increase the return on the Defense Department's investment in its manpower, and particularly on its training investments and the experience that comes with longevity in service. To ensure such longevity, the military services and the Department of Defense must create an environment in which it is desirable to serve. As the total force transforms to meet today's challenges and those of the future, it is essential that the reserve components be part of that transformation, with attention to both individuals and families, because "soldiers enlist, but families re-enlist."

The initiatives described in this chapter reflect a strategy to ease the stress on the reserve forces and manage these forces to offer the Department of Defense greater flexibility and efficiency. Flexible service options across active and reserve forces can increase volunteerism and simplify DoD access to needed skills and capabilities. Innovative approaches can also reduce manpower costs in high technology and other civilian-acquired skill areas. By enlisting employers, universities, associations, and others in developing new affiliation and participation programs, the reserve forces system can work more effectively, with benefits for all parties including the employer, the Department, and the individual.

The concepts in this chapter are proposed as solutions to security challenges facing the United States, but we offer these ideas for consideration by other nations as well. While each country is unique, with its own resources, constraints, traditions, demographics, threats, and challenges that shape its security forces and their reserve formations, all can learn from the experiences of others. Some of the factors that today shape the U.S. active and reserve forces were learned or borrowed from the experiences of others over the past decades as allies worked together for a common purpose. It is our desire that, as we continue to cooperate, to share lessons learned, and to seek interoperability, the ideas presented here and those that will emerge in the future will be helpful to those nations wishing to transform their own forces, especially their reserve components.

Transformation requires innovation and creativity. It requires breaking old paradigms for military service and overcoming cultural traditions. Success in transforming the reserve components—through rebalancing the force and through new approaches to personnel management—will enhance the capabilities of the total force and strengthen the all-volunteer force.

Chapter 18

Strategic Trends for Reserves in Small European Countries

The Example of Slovakia

Peter Švec

For most of the twentieth century, modern powers maintained large armed forces comprising a core of well-prepared professional soldiers, surrounded by a large pool of reserves—men and women called out of civilian life through compulsory service and trained for a relatively brief period of time. Huge reserves were a significant component of many such armies. At the time it gained its independence, Slovakia inherited one-third of the Army of the former Czech and Slovak Federal Republic with all its Warsaw Pact–era legacies, including an unhealthy military culture and, on paper at least, huge untrained reserves. Although with independence, Slovakia was in a good position to rebuild a modern armed force, this opportunity was not fully explored.

By the turn of the century, dramatic changes in the global security environment made the concept of large standing armies supplemented with reserve forces less appropriate. Today, new challenges and missions require high-quality forces that are ready for new and very demanding approaches to waging wars: indirect, non-linear, and asymmetric. Many NATO countries have concluded that small, elite, professional armies, using advanced military technology, will most effectively deal with these emerging threats and missions.

Yet circumstances in some countries—such as outdated military infrastructures and budgetary constraints—have made it difficult to transition to the high-cost and high-quality militaries necessary to succeed in the new security environment. Instead countries such as Poland, Hungary, and Austria rely on a small core of high-quality professionals supplemented with reserve forces. While reserve forces may be cheaper in peacetime than active-duty personnel, they are often not as well prepared to operate and maintain high-technology equipment as their active-duty counterparts. Nor are they typically trained for the challenges of twenty-first century combat.

What role, then, can reserve forces play in the new strategic landscape? The primary role of the military is warfighting, and twenty-first-century combat challenges will test even well-trained active-duty troops. It is unlikely, therefore, that traditional reservists would have the skills or expertise required for modern warfare. If we are willing to redefine its role and responsibilities, however, a reconfigured and modernized reserve force can remain an important component of a nation's military structure and contribute to its security priorities and international obligations. Instead of serving as a less expensive and less effective substitute for active-duty troops, reserve forces could be used for a wide range of specific types of operations such as peacekeeping. Reserves could become a separate, essentially paramilitary corps within the national security structure ("paramilitary" in that they lack capability for full-scale war missions). Reserve forces of most countries are fully capable of performing less demanding missions such as peacekeeping or policing. However, their ability to contribute fully to peace-enforcement or peacemaking missions is very questionable. Such a division of labor would require less training and expertise of reservists. It also would free up the active-duty personnel currently assigned to these support missions to focus instead on combat preparedness.

As part of its overall military modernization effort, Slovakia is making substantial changes to its reserve force. Using the Slovakian experience as a guide, this chapter explores changing perceptions about reserve forces, and discusses how smaller countries could restructure their reserves so that they remain useful in today's radically changing strategic environment. Among the issues addressed are the functions and size of reserve forces and their overall preparedness and affordability. I also discuss how refocusing reserves on essentially paramilitary functions such as medical support, protection, or policing may make the best use of reserve resources and also help countries better prepare their active-duty forces for future security challenges. While the focus here is on reserve forces in smaller countries, some aspects of this discussion may be relevant to larger countries as well.

Recent Developments in Slovakia

In 1993, when Slovakia gained its independence from the Czech Republic, each new nation took a share of the Army of the Czech and Slovak Federal Republic that was proportional to its population. These forces were based on the Warsaw Pact model of mass mobilization and heavy mechanized formations. They were subject to the limitations of the Conventional Forces in Europe (CFE) Treaty, whose obligations were assumed by Slovakia and the Czech Republic.

From the very beginning, any efforts at military reform faced obstacles presented by the inherited institutional and military culture. This legacy military culture was anti-innovation and anti-learning. It lacked vision, decisiveness, or an acceptance of personal responsibility, and instead was fixated upon reaching decision by committee, then clinging rigidly to those decisions already reached. A culture based on distrust spent excessive effort on inspecting people; a mentality of zero tolerance for defects led to a culture of risk avoidance. This legacy culture focused, not on enabling things to be done, but rather on preventing things from happening. In a culture that did not make any effort to develop military leadership, many of the leaders shaped by this legacy culture had little understanding of strategic priorities. Without an integrated approach to military planning, there was no coherence in leadership, doctrines, tactics, procedures, or technologies. The inherited culture was characterized not by strategic and conceptual thinking, nor by networking, but by technical and tactical issues, short-term thinking, and isolationism. Obsessed by security and secrecy, it might be described as a "guided tour" culture that refused to acknowledge and plan for a future for which there may be no map. It was rigid, whereas the modern battlefield requires adaptivity and flexibility.

In such an environment, even full-time professional soldiers could not be expected to cope well with the challenges of the modern battlefield. Given this history, Slovakia was ready for radical changes in order to take advantage of its potentially very high-quality personnel.

In January 2001, therefore, Slovakia launched a major military modernization plan called "SR Force 2010." A critical part of the modernization effort was the preparation of the first military strategy document in

Slovakia's history.[1] This document articulated a framework for addressing security threats and international commitments in today's changing security environment.

Actual results from the SR Force 2010 reforms have been mixed. The proposed Officer Education and Training Program, Noncommissioned Officer Program, Unit Readiness Reporting Program, and Unit Training Management Program all showed good progress in their early stages, although they later showed signs of faltering a bit. More troubling, however, was the fact that the majority of crucial reforms, such as personnel reform, training reforms, air force reform, and overall reform of military culture, to cite just a few examples, never really got off the ground.

Some of the problems in achieving the promised reforms resulted from flaws in the underlying plan and a failure to anticipate all of the factors that could affect results. Defense budget cuts also took a toll, as did unanticipated costly deployments, to Afghanistan for example. High rates of turnover among senior military leaders and civilian managers led to confusion about the direction of the reform process. In addition, the Slovakian defense establishment, like those in other former Warsaw Pact countries, continued to suffer from the anti-reform military culture described above. Too many leaders at all levels in Slovakia's military and its broader defense establishment continue to resist reform, slowing or watering down the plans. As a result, despite a promising beginning in some areas, the reform process stalled.

Despite significant implementation challenges, the strategic documents of SR Force 2010 informed the planning process in several ways.[2] First, they clarified that the threat of major armed conflict—if any—would offer a very long warning time and therefore a considerably longer preparation time than had been available during the Cold War era. Second, the new military strategy introduced, for the first time in any of the region's mili-

---

1. See "Military Strategy of the Slovak Republic," approved by the National Council of the Slovak Republic on October 25, 2001, issued by Ministry of Defense of the Slovak Republic in December 2001, p. 10.
2. Apart from the ground-breaking "Military Strategy of the Slovak Republic," the SR Force 2010 strategy was set down in a series of documents, but many of them reflected old thinking; they included "Long Term Plan for the Structure of the Armed Forces of the Slovak Republic," "Military Personnel Management System," "Training Management System," and "Concept of Slovak Air Forces Transformation."

Table 18.1. Risk Assessment in Slovakia's Military Strategy

Threat	Likelihood	Warning and Preparation Time	Impact on Vital Interest	Risk Accepted
Major Armed Conflict	Low Probability	Reasonably Long	High	High
Regional Armed Conflict	Moderate Probability	Relatively Short	Moderate	Moderate
General Non-Military Threats	High Probability	Relatively Short	Moderate to Low	Minimal
Natural Disasters	Unpredictable	Very Short to None	Low to Moderate	Minimal

Source: "Military Strategy of the Slovak Republic," approved by the National Council of the Slovak Republic on October 25, 2001, issued by Ministry of Defense of the Slovak Republic in December 2001, p. 10.

taries, the concept of risk assessment in force planning. This concept helped military planners make sound decisions about what level of risk the nation was willing to accept, based on the likelihood that specific threats would occur or on the impact they would have upon the country's vital interests. Based on these two elements, the strategy called upon Slovakia to build an affordable and practical armed force. Table 18.1 details the concepts developed in the strategy document.

The new strategy allowed military planners to take a revolutionary new approach to force planning. SR Force 2010 included many bold recommendations—such as massive cuts in the number of heavy equipment weapons platforms—which were initially rejected out of hand by many in the military establishment. Yet Slovakia could not ignore reality: the costs of these systems were skyrocketing, and Slovakia had limited resources to purchase, operate, and maintain them. So by April 2001, it was clear that the number of main battle tanks would have to be reduced from 272 down to perhaps a single battalion of no more than 50. Reductions in the number of combat aircraft would also be significant, to no more than one squadron of 18 aircraft and, according to the analysis in the new Air Forces Concept, even this relatively small number is far in excess of what Slovakia can afford. Some planners, therefore, even discussed the possibility of eliminating combat aircraft altogether due to their high costs.[3]

The plan also called for dramatic reductions in the active-duty force. These reductions would coincide with Slovakia's move, as planned in SR Force 2010, from a conscription-based military to an all-volunteer professional force by 2006. This has already been accomplished, despite considerable opposition. (See Table 18.2.) Active-duty forces are to be cut by more than 50 percent under SR Force 2010, dropping from more than 58,000 in 1993 to less than 24,000 in 2006, as Slovakia completes the transition to an all-volunteer force. SR Force 2010 also reduces the number of civilians in the Slovak military, from over 20,000 in 1993 to just 4,500 by 2006.[4]

Table 18.2 shows the gradual downsizing of major components of the Slovak Armed Forces from 1993 through 2001, as well as reductions proposed in 2001 under SR Force 2010. The strategic document also called upon military planners to review and revise the size, structure, and mission of Slovakia's reserve forces which, on paper at least, included several hundred thousand reservists who were responsible for huge stocks of military equipment.[5] The review concluded that the reserve system was obsolete and inconsistent with the concepts laid out in the new military strategy. The reserve training plan, for example, did not include updated analyses of mobilization requirements or reflect new assumptions about warning and preparation times; in fact these new assumptions were rejected by many. In practice, reserve training was practically nonexistent: there was almost none between 1993 and 1997, and fewer than 1,000 reservists received refresher training between 1997 and 2001. Mobilization drills had not been practiced since the mid-1980s.

---

3.   Others, including myself, favor exploring ways, including perhaps unconventional solutions, to maintain some of these capabilities within existing budgetary constraints.

4.   These civilians take on roles in logistics, infrastructure, medical, and intelligence, as well as other responsibilities.

5.   During the Cold War, the Warsaw Pact countries typically maintained reserve components five to eight times larger than their active-duty forces. Although Slovakia's current reserve figures are not yet publicly disclosable, it is important to note that the majority of Slovakia's reserve units existed only on paper, and did not reflect actual force strength.

Table 18.2. Major Components of the Slovak Armed Forces (selected years)

	CFE limits set for 1995[a]	1993	1995	1997	1999	2001	SR Force 2010 Goal
Manpower[b]	46,667	58,346	52,015	45,483	39,072	30,800	23,737
Main Battle Tanks	478	995	644	478	272	272	52
Armored Personnel Carriers	683	1,370	749	683	683	667	164
Artillery	383	1,058	632	383	383	316	96
Combat Aircraft	100[c]	146	116	113	72	56	18
Combat Helicopters	40[c]	19	19	19	19	19	18

a. Maximum numbers permitted under the Treaty on Conventional Forces in Europe (CFE Treaty) as of 1989, adjusted in 1992 to apply one-third of the limit for the Czecho-Slovak Federal Republic to Slovakia. The CFE Treaty established four concentric zones in which there are limits on the number of tanks, armored combat vehicles, and artillery. Slovakia is part of the innermost zone with the smallest limits, along with Belgium, Luxembourg, the Netherlands, Germany, Poland, Hungary, and the Czech Republic.

b. Manpower data in this table include active-duty uniformed troops only. The figures for reserve forces are not available, but it is clear that the reserves will drop from a level several times that of the active forces, to just a fraction of active forces.

c. As of 1995 adjustment requested by Slovakia.

To address these problems, Slovakia has developed new concepts of mobilization and reserve-force operations that incorporate current assumptions about threat warning and preparation times.[6] Under the old system, mainly those reserve units required to provide security for strategic sites would be mobilized. The composition, equipment, and training of these units effectively limited their roles to land-force operations. Special forces and air forces were largely made up of active-duty troops; they utilized reserves only for a few support activities, such as logistics or construction engineering.

---

6. "Military Strategy of the Slovak Republic"; "Long Term Plan for the Structure of the Armed Forces of the Slovak Republic."

Under the new mobilization system, the number of reservists will drop dramatically. It is estimated that Slovakia's reserve force will be reduced from several hundred thousand (on paper) to less than 10,000. These cutbacks will also make the reserves a much smaller component of the total force: they will go from being more than five times larger than the active-duty force to just about one-third the size of the active-duty force proposed under SR Force 2010.

The new system of reserves has three components: active reserves, inactive reserves, and registered citizens. The intention is to use all three to augment the armed forces during deployment or war. Active reserves will be made up of reservists who have completed their compulsory military service or, after 2006, their professional military service, and who volunteer for three- to five-year terms of additional active reserve service. They will participate in several weeks of training annually. Inactive reservists would also be volunteers, mostly drawn from among former military officers. They would not participate in regular refresher training, but if called up, they would receive training during the long preparation time envisioned prior to mobilization. For the third category, Slovakia intends to begin national registration of all males of a certain age group after conscription is discontinued in 2006.[7] Assuming sufficient lead time for preparation, the government could call up these registered civilians in the event of a large-scale emergency. Any registered citizens called up for extraordinary service would undergo comprehensive training, starting (as originally proposed) with one month in the National Defense Academy.

While this new reserve program is a substantial improvement over Slovakia's former Warsaw Pact–style mass-mobilization system, it is not good enough. It is essentially the old western-type reserve-force system, developed to operate during the Cold War, which relies on reservists to supplement active-duty forces in combat operations. Even with the new training regimen for active reserves and the anticipated lead time to prepare inactive reserves, it is unlikely that reserve forces would have the skills or equipment needed to operate effectively in a twenty-first-century combat environment. Moreover, stepped-up training of re-

---

7. Slovakia also intends to compile an inventory of its stockpiled material resources, including ammunition and major equipment, that would be used in the event of war or national emergency.

serves during an emergency would drain scarce resources away from active-duty troops just when they must shoulder primary combat responsibilities.

Implications of the New Security Environment for the Overall Force

The changes to Slovakia's reserve system are part of the broader reform of its overall armed force, an effort designed to transform Slovakia's Cold War–era military into a force capable of operating in the twenty-first-century security environment. Yet even the substantial reforms proposed in SR Force 2010 (or its less ambitious revision, SR Force 2015, issued in 2005) will not keep pace with today's continually changing military challenges.

A crucial problem facing military planners today is the high cost of fielding an armed force capable of meeting the challenges of modern warfare. As the nature of war changes, it requires high-quality, well-trained, and appropriately compensated troops as well as expensive, technologically advanced weapons and the highly skilled personnel to operate them. Slovakia and other small countries may aspire to such forces, but they do not have sufficient resources to upgrade their current forces, which are simply too large.

Based on recent developments in NATO's 2004 force planning process, it is clear that Slovakia's future active-duty armed forces will have to be reduced even more than the levels stated in SR Force 2010 in order to free up enough resources to fund investments in deployability and force versatility. Slovakia's estimated active-duty force for 2006 is 24,000 troops, about the size of a single U.S. Army division, but this is substantially more than the country can afford if it hopes to field a top-quality armed force.

As members of NATO, countries must be able to safeguard their own sovereignty and also contribute militarily to the alliance. The most important indicators of these abilities involve defense expenditures and whether the armed force is appropriately sized and trained. In 2001, Slovakia's defense expenditures totaled $376 million, or 1.9 percent of GDP.[8] This level of spending translates into $70 per capita. Defense

---

8. The Slovakian government has committed to maintain defense spending at a minimum of 1.9 percent of GDP until 2006. Thereafter it is supposed to

spending for 2005 totaled about $873 million, with most of this increase due to a substantial change in the currency exchange rate in favor of the Slovak Koruna. This spending level translates into approximately $165 per capita, but this is still significantly below per-capita defense expenditures in well-developed NATO countries. (For example, Belgium spends $470 per capita annually, and the Netherlands $650.)

Comparing annual total defense expenditures per servicemember can create a rough picture of the relative technological sophistication of various countries' militaries. A low per-troop expenditure, as in Slovakia, suggests an overlarge force that may be insufficiently trained. In 2001, Slovakia spent approximately $11,750 per troop annually, well below the NATO "floor" of about $60,000 and far below the top-performing countries such as the Netherlands, which spent roughly $121,550 per troop.[9] By 2005, Slovakia's expenditures per troop had nearly tripled to $36,000, still well below the NATO floor, while the Netherlands spent more than $200,000. While part of the increase resulted from changes in the exchange rate, substantial reductions in numbers of troops also contributed to Slovakia's higher per-troop expenditures.

If Slovakia is to develop a superior-quality armed force, it must continue to reduce force size so that it has more resources available to invest in equipping and training each member. In order to bring expenditures per troop more in line with the top NATO countries, the Slovakian armed forces should total no more than 12,000 troops, just half the SR Force 2010 target.[10] This would set per-troop expenditures at $72,750 even with no budget increase. Such reductions are necessary if

---

increase up to 2 percent of GDP. It must be understood that, given social and economical realities, this level is quite unrealistic, and lowering defense spending is the most probable course of action.

9.   Figures are calculated from official NATO figures; <www.nato.int>.

10. My own analysis suggests that with defense expenditures at 2 percent of GDP, Slovakia will not be able to afford more than 12,000 active-duty troops. Thus, Slovakia might ultimately think along the lines of two lighter brigade-size formations. One-third of the combat units might be specialized for mountain and urban operations, with some lighter supporting units and a small air force. The already downsized reserve force must be reduced as well, from the target level of 10,000 stated in SR Force 2010 to no more than one-fifth the size of the active-duty force.

Slovakia is to modernize its shrinking inventory of major equipment and provide high-quality training. Even if these force reductions are implemented, some military capabilities—such as combat aircraft (discussed below)—will remain unaffordable for Slovakia and many other small NATO countries.

In the new and rapidly changing security environment in which Slovakia's downsized and better trained military will operate, success in war will depend as much on sensors and information systems as on the traditional platforms of conventional warfare, such as tanks, ships, and airplanes. Across Europe and North America, militaries are working to capitalize on the power of information technology by moving toward network-centric operations, in which all the elements of a force have the capability to collect, share, and access information and to collaborate. The information advantage achieved in such an environment is expected to lead to more capable fighting forces.[11] Slovakia's ability to contribute militarily will depend on how well it meets the challenge of bringing its forces into the information age. This will be expensive. Moreover, the challenges and opportunities of this new security environment are demanding even for well-trained active-duty forces, and thus it is unlikely that traditional reservists will have the training or capacity to contribute in these demanding circumstances.

In addition to moving toward network-centric operations, Slovakia and other former Warsaw Pact countries must adapt their military organizations so that they can conduct expeditionary operations. All nations—from the traditional great powers to small countries like Slovakia—will face adversaries whose aim is simply "not to lose," rather than to win, and who may be non-state actors. Nations will face different forms of warfare, such as terrorism, special operations, information warfare, urban warfare, and ecological warfare. What is most important in this new combat environment is a shift in emphasis from weapons and targets to the effects of a military operation.

In network-centric operations, weapons, including platforms and munitions, are only part of the network. The most sophisticated weapons platforms will be useless without information about suitable targets. If Slovakia is not able, for example, to operate sensors to acquire infor-

---

11. "Network Centric Warfare," U.S. Department of Defense Report to Con-

mation, nor to integrate sensors with tanks, ships, or aircraft through NATO's networks, there is no reason to acquire or operate the most advanced fighter aircraft or to employ precision-guided munitions. Small countries like Slovakia should not invest in precision-guided munitions if they would be unable to acquire information about suitable targets.

These new information and network capabilities can be costly; such assets have become unaffordable even for some large and wealthy nations. Affordability has become the most important issue for military planners, and small nations with limited defense resources must decide what capabilities to abandon in order to pay for new technological advancements. Can small nations afford a modern combat aircraft, or combat helicopters? How many tanks or state-of-the-art self-propelled howitzers, if any, can they afford? Can they afford the ammunition necessary for training, or the support technology for network-centric operations? Are sophisticated surface-to-air missiles realistically affordable for these countries?

As small countries restructure their militaries to respond to new security challenges, traditional capabilities will compete for scarce budgetary resources against emerging capabilities designed to modernize the force. Limited defense budgets in all of the former Warsaw Pact countries will force military planners to prioritize among these new capabilities. Only what is necessary will be funded, and only small deployable forces of well prepared, fully professional troops can be justified. The challenge for small armed forces which are pursuing technologically-based capabilities is how to redesign their force architecture to take full advantage of improving—but still limited—capabilities in some traditional areas.

The skyrocketing costs of combat aircraft illustrate the dilemma facing military planners in small countries. The average unit cost of a P-51 Mustang fighter-bomber in 1945 was about $52,000.[12] In 1965, one F-4 Phantom cost around $1 million.[13] By the mid-1980s, an average fighter aircraft cost around $25 million. Today, the newest fighter in the U.S.

---

gress, July 31, 2001, <www.defenselink.mil/nii/NCW/>.

12. "The U.S. Army Air Forces at War: A Statistical Portrait of USAAF in World War II," *Air Force Magazine*, June 1995, p. 34.

13. Martin Van Creveld, *Command in War* (Cambridge, Mass.: Harvard University Press, 1985), p. 314.

arsenal, the stealth F-22 Raptor, costs some $150 million per airplane,[14] while a modern "Stealth" bomber costs up to $500 million each.[15]

Not surprisingly, these sharp cost increases in air-delivered capabilities, which are currently the most technology-intensive systems available, have resulted in much smaller inventories worldwide. In 1944, the U.S. Army Air Forces alone had more than 37,000 combat aircraft,[16] and during World War II the United States produced nearly 100,000 aircraft in a single year.[17] By 1997, however, there were only about 34,000 combat-capable aircraft operating worldwide.[18]

Because of the way air force capabilities are deployed, this shrinking inventory could have serious repercussions, especially for smaller countries. Traditionally, the main mission of any air force is deterrence. Advocates say that if air power is to be used to win a war, then it has to be shocking, sudden, and overwhelming. It has to cause substantial damage to strategic and operational "centers of gravity": the facilities and equipment that are most important to the adversary's continued conduct of the war. Given these realities, a small nation simply cannot afford to expand the operational capabilities of its air force in the hope of becoming a powerful regional force. A credible deterrent capability is reached only if the air force can achieve a very high operational tempo over a sustained period of time. For smaller countries, money spent modernizing or acquiring new combat aircraft would drain scarce resources away from other reform priorities, and would still probably be insufficient to fund a truly effective air combat force. Even if the money were available to purchase such assets, poorly trained reservists would be ill-equipped to operate them effectively.

In the countries of Central and Eastern Europe, reform efforts are constrained by limited funding and outdated Warsaw Pact force struc-

14. All cost figures are in current dollars.

15. Martin Van Creveld, *On Future War* (London: Brassey's, 1991), p. 208.

16. "The U.S. Army Air Forces at War: A Statistical Portrait of USAAF in World War II," p. 30.

17. Paul Kennedy, *The Rise and Fall of the Great Powers: Economic Change and Military Conflict from 1500 to 2000* (New York: Random House, 1987), p. 354.

18. Author's calculations based on International Institute of Strategic Studies (IISS), *The Military Balance* (various years) (Cambridge, U.K.: IISS, var. dates).

tures.[19] Small countries still face traditional security problems: how to command respect, how to deter aggression, and how to maintain military capacity without draining the civilian economy. These problems now present themselves in a new and different security environment in which poorly trained conscript and reserve-based militaries are not of much use. The armed forces of NATO countries must be able to defend their borders and contribute to the full range of NATO missions. Fulfilling these responsibilities will require small countries such as Slovakia to strike a balance between force quality and quantity. If a force is oversized—even if its absolute numbers are small—quality will suffer. Relying on inadequately trained and equipped reserves can bloat an armed force, degrading its quality and operational capability.

Coping with Smallness

As we enter the twenty-first century, there are several distinct categories of armed forces—in terms of quality and ability—that can respond to contemporary challenges. The top category is the unique dominion of the U.S. armed forces, which today enjoy a command of the global commons: the air above 5,000 meters, the open ocean, space, and cyberspace.[20] It would take at least ten to fifteen years for any other force to approach the level of supremacy of the U.S. active-duty force, and even the U.S. reserve force would likely outperform any potential adversary in conventional combat.

The second category includes several major or regional powers, mainly western, that can match the United States in certain key tactical capabilities, but not in all strategic areas. Some nations in this category, such as Singapore, Israel, or the major European powers, maintain fairly large reserves that are capable of participating effectively in some full-scale war operations.

---

19. See Chris Donnelly, "Reshaping European Armed Forces for the 21st Century," NATO on-line library, <www.nato.int/docu/articles/2000/a000 913a.htm>.

20. The concept is similar to British "command of the sea" in an earlier era. See Barry R. Posen, "Command of the Commons: The Military Foundation of U.S. Hegemony," *International Security*, Vol. 28, No. 1 (Summer 2003), pp. 5–46.

The third category includes many traditional NATO and European Union countries that have only limited abilities to respond to contemporary strategic challenges unless they pool their military resources with other nations. Their reserve forces, which are essentially paramilitary units, could probably participate in small peacekeeping operations, but they are not sufficiently trained or equipped to fight in a full-scale war.

The fourth category includes a wide range of countries, from small to former superpower, located all over the globe. These nations—including every former Warsaw Pact country—are stuck somewhere between World War I and World War II in terms of their military culture, doctrinal approaches, and military thinking. These countries cannot afford sizeable reserve forces; they face more than enough challenges simply trying to reform their active-duty units. At best, they may be able to train and field a few select essentially paramilitary reservists for noncombat duties such as peacekeeping operations.

The fifth and final category includes numerous obsolete militaries, such as those in some Asian, Latin American, and African countries, that are incapable of waging any full-scale war operations. These paramilitary forces would be unable to respond to the challenges arising out of the new security environment.

Three options may be considered by fourth- or fifth-category countries, including many former Warsaw Pact and Central or Eastern European countries that wish to remain militarily effective: pooling units, sharing capabilities, and specialization. The first, pooling technology-based resources, is usually not a viable option, since even the combined resources of small countries may not amount to a substantial array of assets. Pooling the operation of, for example, several types of single-role old-fashioned aircraft would not enhance or integrate potentially incompatible resources.

The second option is to share cost-intensive capabilities such as combat aircraft; strategic airlift; intelligence, surveillance, target acquisition, and reconnaissance (ISTAR); electronic warfare; and possibly even heavier ground-strike capabilities. Sharing capabilities might ultimately result in two distinct kinds of armed forces. The first would be supranational or genuinely federal combined armed forces made up of all the costly technology-based capabilities of a multi-national force, such as combat aircraft, heavy air transport, electronic warfare units, and similar capabilities.

Another kind of force that could result from sharing capabilities would be a national defense force for each country, possibly similar to a national guard. Although designed to handle challenges to a state's own security, these national forces might also be able to help meet international obligations. These might require considerable updating of forces: the militaries of Slovakia and many of its neighbors, for example, currently use the traditional heavier mechanized formations that were favored by the Soviets during the Warsaw Pact period, but such formations are ill-suited even for the mountainous terrain of Slovakia, not to mention many contemporary battlefields. A shift towards lighter mountain forces could better meet national and regional security challenges. If these units were properly equipped, adequately funded, and sufficiently trained, they could be well suited for force pooling and perhaps some role specialization. Developing a combination of supranational armed forces and national defense forces would require very difficult political discussions, both within and among nations. But as difficult as this course may be, the alternative is worse: the armed forces of small countries could become irrelevant. Given the high costs of military technology and equipment, small countries simply cannot afford to maintain fully professional, deployable, top-quality, traditional active-duty armed forces that are trained and ready for full-scale, high-intensity combat operations.

The reserve forces of most smaller countries are not sufficiently trained or equipped to operate effectively on today's battlefields. Nor, arguably, should countries spend scarce defense resources trying to train reserves for true combat functions. Fourth- and fifth-category countries do not have sufficient defense resources to bring their reserve forces up to combat-ready levels. Instead, military planners must direct their limited financial resources to the active-duty personnel who will carry out combat operations.

The third option—role specialization—offers an opportunity to utilize the specific skills and strengths of reserve forces for focused missions. Many peacekeeping missions may be ideally suited for essentially paramilitary reserve forces, preserving valuable active-duty assets for more demanding operations.

Peacekeeping operations from the mid-1980s to the mid-1990s suggest that reserves organized for single purposes—such as civil affairs, engineering, transportation, or military police activities—have been effective. Such specialization could give countries a way to utilize the training of retired military personnel and the skills of civilian specialists. It would also allow reserve units committed to peacekeeping missions to hone their particular skills much better than they could during routine or general reserve training. Properly trained reserve forces might meet the demands of peacekeeping missions more effectively than combat units that lack specialized training in the kinds of activities required for peacekeeping operations.

Specialization could also have positive effects on the active-duty force. Turning over responsibility for peacekeeping and other essentially paramilitary operations to reserve forces would free up active-duty forces to concentrate on combat operations and on sharpening their war-fighting skills. Having reservists specialize in less demanding or nonmilitary roles would also reduce their training costs, and make more resources available for active-duty troops and traditional defense functions.

Other paramilitary activities traditionally performed by armed forces might be described as protection functions, such as homeland or civil protection, policing, guarding facilities, and mine-sweeping. While many of these functions may be important national priorities, they are not defense functions, and they need not be supported by defense personnel, equipment, or financial resources. In recent years many such protection functions have fallen to active-duty forces, but it is not necessary to assign such tasks to a society's most expensive and highest-trained military assets.

A wide range of paramilitary roles could be tasked to reserve forces, including installation guarding; security; border protection; military police and provost activities; civil-military cooperation (CIMIC); postal and courier delivery; field ambulance and field hospital units and medical specialists; veterinary or animal support; airfield damage repair or construction; engineering; de-mining; transport; movement control; railway control or repair; equipment support; chaplains and psychological support; financial and legal support; and nuclear, biological, and chemical protection.

Many of these functions, although paramilitary in nature, support high-priority security efforts, such as counter-terrorism, anti-terrorism, or assisting in recovery operations following a terrorist attack. They could also support critical law-enforcement operations such as the fight against organized crime and similar activities.

Specialization of reserve forces offers small countries the chance to meet international requirements and to use some of the valuable resources resident in their reserves. In contrast, specialization may not be a good choice for active-duty forces if it diverts them from their combat focus to noncombat activities. Using active-duty units for peacekeeping missions, for example, could degrade readiness, since it would divert units from combat training and maintenance of equipment. While major powers can afford to train and allocate some active units for noncombat missions, smaller nations do not have sufficient troop depth to do so.

Even if it is limited to reserves, the specialization model only works if the reserves get the proper individual and unit training necessary to meet mission requirements. Otherwise their use and effectiveness will be limited, and there is a risk of the reserves turning into what a British defense analyst has described as "an undervalued, generally poorly resourced part-time military job."

If they are properly focused and trained, reserve forces can help meet a country's international and domestic obligations, particularly if they specialize in paramilitary operations such as peacekeeping. It also makes sense to have a reserve mobilization system in place. But given the demanding nature of warfighting on today's battlefields, it seems unreasonable to expect reserves to take on combat responsibilities.

Conclusions and Recommendations

It is especially appropriate for small countries to reevaluate the concept of reserves. If small countries must rely on some mobilization reserves to hold and protect territory, those forces must be adequately manned, trained, and maintained. However, the primary role of the military is warfighting, and traditional reserves in small countries cannot maintain the level of competency required for modern warfighting.

The principal question concerning future reserves of smaller NATO countries is not how large a reserve force should be, but for what purpose it should be maintained and at what quality. Depending on the answers to these questions, a strong reserve system may well be appropriate for specific and focused purposes such as civil defense duties, peacekeeping operations, humanitarian relief, and disaster relief operations. Many support functions that have traditionally been handled by active-duty military units could also be turned over to the reserves. Slovakia is likely to have an ample supply of reservists willing to take on these paramilitary activities; its experience suggests that the salaries associated with international operations provide a strong incentive for reservists to participate, even when these activities involve long-term deployments outside of the country.

For Slovakia and other small countries, properly trained and focused reserves offer a potential opportunity for cash-strapped militaries whose active-duty personnel would otherwise be diverted from combat training. Active-duty forces should be reserved for high-intensity combat operations, to fight alongside other top-quality armed forces and gain valuable field experience that they would not otherwise acquire. New ways of defining active and reserve force roles could reduce costs, save lives, increase efficiency, focus training better, and give military planners the flexibility to use scarce defense resources for defense functions and roles.

There are still many unanswered questions about the appropriate role for reserves in the new security environment. Do reserves need to be network-centric, capable of performing multiple roles, or trained for full-scale operations? Should small countries such as Slovakia train their armed forces for less intensive or smaller-scale operations? If so, would they be prepared for real combat functions? Is peacekeeping a military or a paramilitary activity, and who should be responsible for such missions, reserves or active-duty forces? These and other issues will require further exploration as Slovakia and other small countries continue efforts to reform their armed services and determine the most appropriate roles for their active and reserve forces.

Conclusion

Chapter 19

The Way Ahead

Transformation of Personnel Policies

Curtis L. Gilroy and Cindy Williams

Across Europe and North America, nations are transforming the way they fill their military ranks to meet the challenges and opportunities of the future. For some countries, the transformation entails shifting from compulsory service to an all-volunteer force. For others, it means reallocating duties and realigning roles and missions to bring out the best in a mixed force of conscripts, reservists, and volunteers. For all, it includes reviewing and reforming the complex web of policies and structures designed to attract able and qualified men and women to serve.

Each nation makes its own decisions related to military personnel policies, and does so for its own mix of reasons: military, societal, demographic, economic, and political. In the countries of Europe and North America, some such policies are rooted in a shared heritage while others reflect solutions to problems that all modern militaries face.

The fundamental proposition of this book is that countries and militaries can learn from each other's experiences with military personnel policies. The authors of this volume offer numerous ideas and lessons from the transformations ongoing in their countries. Although policies that work well in one country may not translate directly to other countries for a variety of reasons, including cultural differences or historical precedent, the policies and reform efforts in one country can suggest creative policies and solutions in another. They may provide evidence for how much changed policies might cost and how they might work in practice, offer ideas for designing workable implementation plans, and help others avoid disruptive and costly mistakes. This volume is meant as a vehicle for such learning.

In this concluding chapter, we draw on the rest of the book for insights and lessons from the personnel policy transformations already undertaken or that are underway in Europe and North America. We find that:

- the transformation of military personnel policies is vital to the fundamental overhaul of military affairs;

- an all-volunteer force (AVF) model can offer important economic advantages for nations seeking to transform their military capabilities to deal with new threats and missions while capitalizing on modern technologies;

- AVFs are not well suited to every set of circumstances, and a mixed model that includes both conscripts and volunteers is still a sound choice for some countries;

- the transition to an AVF can be challenging and more costly than anticipated;

- to be successful in attracting, retaining, and motivating qualified people, and getting the right people into the right jobs, all-volunteer forces must be competitive employers and effective human resource managers;

- transformation of reserve forces to complement shrinking active-duty forces and meet the security needs of the future presents the nations of Europe and North America with important decisions and challenges;

- these countries are developing creative solutions to the challenges of filling their ranks with the right people.

The remainder of this chapter develops each of these conclusions more fully.

The Transformation of Military Personnel Policies is Vital

Having the right men and women in uniform in the right jobs—trained, ready, and committed to contributing to their nations' military operations, and creative in solving military problems—will make the difference between the aspirations and the reality of transformation. Much more than in the past, the people of tomorrow's militaries must be trained to anticipate and deal with surprise. They must be readily deployable, technically savvy, and trained in foreign cultures and foreign languages. Even relatively junior people must be capable of making tough decisions quickly in difficult situations.

Well-crafted military personnel policies are central to bringing the right people in, developing their talents, getting them into appropriate jobs, motivating them to do what is required, and keeping them in the force for as long as their nation needs them. Many of the military personnel policies that served nations well enough during the Cold War are no longer relevant or effective, but stand in the way of progress and improvement. Updating them will be a crucial aspect of the military transformations underway today.

For the newer members of NATO, vast changes in their domestic political, social, and economic environments are key drivers of personnel policy transformation, as are the demands of integrating into a new alliance. The nations of Central and Eastern Europe and the Baltic States, like other countries, need skilled people who can contribute capably alongside alliance and coalition partners in international operations. Like many of their alliance partners, they are reducing the number of people in uniform and looking to replace quantity with quality. They are shedding legacies of the communist past, when too many officers were promoted for political reasons, and when non-military work such as agricultural labor was often a key mission. They are also building up professional cadres of non-commissioned officers.

Bringing the right people into the militaries of Europe and North America will be complicated by challenges on the supply side. Rickard Sandell describes how youth populations will probably shrink dramatically across most of Europe. The resulting competition for human capital will pose challenges for recruitment and retention in all-volunteer forces. Supply problems may cause difficulties even for militaries that keep conscription, since those militaries typically rely heavily on career volunteers, and to some extent on people who "volunteer" to be conscripted, as Vaidotas Urbelis notes. The situation will be made more difficult if fewer eligible youth are inclined toward military service, as seems to be the case in the United States.

The authors of this book describe a wide array of changes underway in the militaries of Europe and North America that will transform military personnel policies to keep up with transformation in other aspects of military capability. Most widely heralded are the decisions by some dozen European countries to shift from a mixed force of conscripts and volunteers to an all-volunteer military.

As the following section describes, AVFs are expected to offer important advantages for many countries. Whether in a mixed force or an all-volunteer context, however, other reforms will be just as important to ensure that militaries can compete effectively as employers, put the right people into the right jobs, and motivate them to work hard, fight with courage, and endure the travails of military life.

An AVF Model Can Offer Important Economic Advantages

An AVF model can offer significant economic advantages that, together with other factors, can affect a country's decision to make a transition to a volunteer military. One reason is that a volunteer military is a more motivated force: people tend to perform better if they volunteer for a job than if they are coerced into it. John Warner and Sebastian Negrusa report that in the United States, a volunteer force resulted in a higher quality force as measured by aptitude levels. A high-aptitude force is more easily trained, performs better, and presents fewer disciplinary problems. Jolyon Howorth also points out both the need for and the trend toward more educated and higher-aptitude forces in Europe. Empirical evidence in the chapter by Bernard Rostker and Curtis Gilroy shows that a high quality and highly motivated force is also more productive. The formidable and rapidly changing security challenges facing today's armed forces, as well as the advanced technologies of modern warfare, make fielding high-quality and well trained troops more important than ever.

At first glance, a volunteer force might seem more expensive in budgetary terms, because entry-level volunteers must typically be paid more than draftees. From an economic point of view, however, a volunteer force is actually less expensive. The most obvious reason is that volunteers typically stay in service longer than draftees, and the longer periods of service produce savings in areas such as training and reenlistment costs. With a conscripted force, in contrast, shorter enlistment terms and higher personnel turnover result in substantial costs, as Warner and Negrusa report. High turnover means more recruits; more recruits mean more training; and more training means more trainers. Draftees who are assigned jobs requiring complex skills need longer training times, which reduces the time they are available to perform in operational units. Thus in a conscript military, a higher proportion of military resources would be diverted from core readiness missions into support for military training.

Experience in the United States shows that draftees are also less likely than volunteers to re-enlist. Because draftees typically serve only one short term, a conscripted force needs to be considerably larger than a volunteer force in order to accommodate the more rapid turnover. Further, because reenlistments are relatively low, a draft force tends to be younger and less experienced, which can have an adverse effect on job performance and personnel readiness and which also increases costs, especially when militaries require a high degree of technical skill and experience.

A conscript force imposes other types of costs as well. Draftees are commonly paid less than the going wage in the private sector. According to Keith Hartley, when a lower military entry wage is paid to draftees, labor tends to be undervalued, giving militaries an incentive to "hire" or enlist too many individuals instead of relying on more productive alternatives such as the use of more career personnel or new capital equipment. Such an increase creates a cost to society in general, because that labor supply could be more productively employed elsewhere. Hartley argues that conscription, especially in the UK, has been an inefficient method of procuring military personnel.

Finally, in a conscripted force, it is often hard to field a high-quality and effective non-commissioned officer (NCO) corps. The AVF model, on the other hand, can more easily create a quality NCO corps by emphasizing longer periods of service and fostering training. The NCO corps becomes the backbone of both technical and troop leadership within the enlisted force and also plays a vital role in the readiness of an armed force. Rostker and Gilroy argue that the high quality of the U.S. NCO corps is due in part to emphasizing personnel quality during recruiting, ensuring competitive pay, and providing meaningful training and rewarding career paths.

AVFs are Not Suited to Every Set of Circumstances

An all-volunteer force is not suited to every circumstance. While in the long run a volunteer military is usually cheaper than a conscripted force in terms of its real cost to society, Warner and Negrusa cite studies showing that, under some circumstances, conscription can have a lower social cost than an equally capable volunteer force.

Warner and Negrusa note that the economic advantages associated with an AVF may not accrue to a country whose armed forces are large relative to the size of its population. This can be true in times of all-out war, as it was for most of Europe and North America during World War II, or for countries such as Finland for which territorial defense remains a primary role of the military (as Hannu Herranen explains). Further, for countries with smaller youth cohorts relative to the size of the overall population, recruiting sufficient volunteer personnel can be difficult. As Sandell points out, the military-age population in many NATO countries will decline considerably over the next forty years, and as a result NATO nations will face difficulty recruiting during this period; some countries transitioning to a volunteer military could face a crisis in recruiting. Even those nations maintaining conscription may find it difficult to fill out their forces. When the force size is large relative to the size of the youth cohort, therefore, a conscripted force may actually be more attractive.

Cost and population size are not the only considerations. Some countries prefer a conscripted force because they consider it important for all citizens to serve. In the chapter describing the experience of the Baltic States, Vaidotas Urbelis cites Estonia as one country in which the majority of the population feels that all men should fulfill a military obligation. In other countries, such an obligation to serve is less of a factor. In Lithuania, for example, public support for conscription is waning, and in Latvia, only 22 percent of the population now wishes to retain conscription.

Some countries, including Estonia, Denmark, and Germany, see conscription as an effective way to recruit volunteers. In Europe and North America, conscription has typically been associated with short terms of enlistment. After World War II and until conscription ended in 1973, U.S. conscripts typically served for two years. Since the end of the Cold War, most European countries have shortened the period of service to a year or less. Yet during the period of compulsory service, some conscripts find that they have a taste for military life, and choose to reenlist or even take up full careers in the military. Bertel Heurlin describes how Denmark will maintain a mixed model because it values both the fact that conscription contributes a source of new recruits for homeland defense and that it makes the military more representative of society, even as the rest of Denmark's force is made up of deployable volunteers. Gerhard Kümmel reports that Germany will retain conscription, but as part of a model that relies increasingly on volunteers. About half of Germany's career soldiers are recruited from the pool of conscripts. In response to economic analyses that find a German volunteer force of about 200,000 to be cheaper than a conscripted force, however, Germany has reduced the duration of conscription to nine months, and will cut the proportion of draftees in the force from a Cold-War level of 45 percent to 12 percent by 2010.

Some countries that plan to keep conscription see it as a way of fostering broad citizen support for the military, particularly in the reserve forces. Both conscription and sizeable reserve forces are credited with involving the public in support of the national defense and reinforcing national pride. Chris Donnelly's chapter on sustaining a strong reserve stresses the point that, in all countries, the reserves are the most sensitive link between the armed forces and society. Hannu Herranen discusses the importance of a conscripted force for Finland, and describes the reliance on a large reserve force in its national military strategy for territorial defense.

The Transition to an AVF can be Challenging

Although an all-volunteer force can offer distinct advantages over the long term, the transition from a mixed force of conscripts and volunteers to one that relies entirely on volunteers can be challenging. Attracting the right people to join and stay in the force is typically more difficult and more costly than anticipated.

Six chapters of this volume relate the experiences of a diverse collection of countries during their transitions to all-volunteer forces. All of them describe initial challenges in keeping the ranks filled with the right people.

As Rostker and Gilroy note, what looked like success in staffing the U.S. AVF during its first few years may have lulled leaders into a false sense of security. By 1979, however, six years after conscription ended, the Army fell short of its recruiting goals by 17 percent, and far too many recruits did not meet the services' standards for quality. Retention rates for troops in their first term of service (typically under contract for four years) were also substantially lower than anticipated. The resulting high turnover rates strained a training establishment that was already overburdened by having to deal with significant numbers of low-quality troops.

The UK, too, experienced problems in filling its ranks in the decade following its transition to an AVF. As Keith Hartley points out, troop totals rarely exceeded 90 percent of their targets between 1963, the first full year of the UK's AVF, and 1975. According to Sylvain Daffix, Vincent Medina, and Cyr-Denis Nidier, France also experienced recruitment difficulties during its more recent transition to a volunteer force, especially in attracting people with skills in health care and information technologies, which are in great demand in the private sector.

Juan Lopez Diaz points out that Spain made a deliberate choice to emphasize quality in its recruits even if that meant falling short of its numerical targets. The U.S. experience with low-quality recruits during the late 1970s suggests that Spain made the right decision for the long term, but its near-term force totals suffered as a result: the size of Spain's active-duty force was less than 90 percent of its goal in 2003.

Romania is making the shift to an AVF, with the end of conscription scheduled for 2007. Mihaela Matei anticipates that attractive pay levels for volunteers will avert problems in keeping most of Romania's military occupations filled with the right people, but she fears that retention will be a problem for people with aviation, information technology, and other skills that are highly valued in the private sector.

Italy ended conscription in January 2005. As Domenico Villani details, even before the last conscript was called up, the Italian forces fell so far short of their goals for recruitment of the important new category of three-year volunteers that military leaders feared a crisis in the future force. Italy's leaders hope that the situation will improve as a result of recent changes designed to expand the pool of one-year volunteers and to improve career prospects and pay for those who commit to longer terms of service.

Rising budgetary costs can also be a problem during the transition to an all-volunteer force, as several authors note. To put an end to recruitment, retention, and quality problems in the late 1970s, the United States was compelled to offer double-digit military pay raises for two years in a row. The UK and France both anticipated that downsizing and adopting AVFs would save substantial sums of money; instead their spending for personnel rose considerably, despite sizeable reductions in the number of people in uniform.

AVFs Must be Competitive Employers and Effective Human Resource Managers

To be successful in recruiting, retaining, and motivating the right people, countries moving to an all-volunteer force must be competitive employers. The same is generally true even for countries with a mixed force of volunteers and conscripts, and for the professional core in a military that is otherwise made up largely of conscripts.

One way to become more competitive is to set military pay comparable to what servicemembers could earn in the private sector or in other public-sector jobs. Pay is not, by itself, sufficient to guarantee the success of a volunteer military. But offering a compensation package that individuals perceive as equitable can be a first step toward success. The extensive experience of the United Kingdom, Canada, and the United States with a volunteer force shows the importance of maintaining military-civilian pay comparability. Military pay in the UK and the United States is explicitly linked to private-sector pay, and the UK and United States conduct periodic reviews of military-civilian pay comparability. Most NATO countries, in contrast, tie their military pay scales to public-sector pay. The chapter by Warner and Negrusa considers the effect of compensation on volunteer forces in general; Hartley's chapter addresses the importance of pay comparability in the UK; and Rostker and Gilroy discuss its role in the United States. All three chapters conclude that tying military pay to private-sector rather than public-sector payrolls is critical, since the military must compete with the private sector for its manpower. Among countries transitioning to AVFs today, as Domenico Villani and Vaidotas Urbelis point out, Italy and Latvia are also recognizing that pay comparability will be crucial. Other European nations may also soon find it prudent to tie military pay more closely to earnings in the private sector.

Variations in pay by occupation or duty are also significant. Pay differentials play a role not just in expanding the manpower pool, but more importantly (as the chapters by Hartley and by Rostker and Gilroy both describe), they channel military personnel into hard-to-fill occupations that require special skills, or compensate them for special-duty assignments and potentially hazardous deployments. All countries offer these differentials, but they must be large enough to be effective and meaningful to servicemembers. They are cost-effective, since they are targeted to particular groups and need not be paid to every member.

Non-cash benefits to members and their families can also be important motivators. The United States found early in its AVF that while militaries "enlist soldiers," they "retain families." For members of the U.S. military, housing, health care, pensions, military stores, child care, and recreational facilities can be highly valued non-pay benefits.

In her chapter, Deborah Clay-Mendez advises countries moving to a volunteer military to pay attention to the mix of cash, deferred, and in-kind compensation. Based on the U.S. experience, she suggests that countries should proceed cautiously when introducing new benefits (such as family housing or on-base child-care facilities) that the beneficiaries might begin to view as entitlements. Once such programs are in place, they are often difficult to modify or reduce, particularly if they benefit a broad constituency, such as all military members with children.

She also urges countries to consider making all military compensation costs visible within their defense budgets' personnel accounts, rather than scattering them through the facilities or upkeep accounts, offering them as tax breaks, or shifting them to nonmilitary budget accounts—all of which the United States does today. By including all compensation costs for service men and women in the military personnel account, countries can ensure that the true costs of manpower are transparent to decision-makers and not underestimated. Clay-Mendez argues that benefits that are provided in-kind are generally less efficient than cash payments, costing governments more than their value to the recipients. Deferred benefits can also be less efficient if members have a strong preference for benefits today rather than benefits later.

Nations considering a move to a volunteer force must also remember that career considerations are very important to those who volunteer to join, whether they anticipate a career in the military or expect to move on, after a short term, to jobs in the private or public sector. For those who want a military career, the armed forces must offer challenging and fulfilling career paths: useful and meaningful training, in-service education, and rewarding assignments. Members must believe that the promotion system is fair and they can advance on merit and performance.

For those who are interested in only a short term of service, mechanisms that help with the transition to civilian life can also be attractive incentives to serve. The United States makes college scholarships of varying amounts available to nearly all servicemembers after they leave the military. It also emphasizes the military's role in training servicemembers in skills that will make them valuable to outside employers. Some countries offer additional skills training for servicemembers re-entering the private-sector workforce. Counseling and job placement can also be important tools. Juan Lopez Diaz describes agreements of the Spanish Ministry of Defense with private firms and government agencies. Domenico Villani's chapter discusses the Italian program to provide jobs in government departments to short-term volunteers once they leave the military. The promise of a civilian job can be an effective incentive for prospective volunteers for military service.

Volunteer militaries must not only be competitive as employers; they must also practice sound human resource management. Leadership at the highest levels of government, from both civilian and uniformed leaders, is critical in garnering support for a nation's transition to an all-volunteer force. Once the commitment has been made to a volunteer military, skill will be needed to manage this new force. In describing the situation in Romania, Mihaela Matei describes the crucial role of sound personnel management both during the transition phase and once the professional volunteer model has been fully implemented. Rostker and Gilroy discuss the management issues faced by the United States during the AVF's challenging early years, including recruiting, pay and benefits, personnel selection, and promotion and career development, and also the mistakes it made, sometimes more than once.

Leaders and managers must be adaptive and open to new ideas, and must whenever possible formulate manpower and personnel policies on the basis of empirical research rather than on what might be politically expedient. Management is a difficult task, and a volunteer military requires constant vigilance.

Nations Face Challenges in Transforming their Reserve Forces

The nations of Europe and North America also face important challenges as they transform reserve forces to complement shrinking active-duty forces and to meet the security needs of the future. As we have seen in many of the chapters, strategies for training and integrating reserves depend in large part on what a country asks its reserve forces to do and on how reserves relate to their active-duty counterparts. As Donnelly explains, reserve systems across North America and Europe vary considerably, influenced by differences in geography, relationships with neighboring countries, historical experience, and defense resources.

Some central and eastern European countries, for example, maintain large reserve mobilization structures, vestiges of a Cold-War strategy for defending their borders against invasion. The threat of such invasions, however, virtually disappeared with the end of the Cold War, and new security realities argue for smaller, highly trained professional forces. Longstanding historical concerns about aggressive neighbors may make it difficult for some countries to give up their mobilization forces, but as Donnelly argues, smaller countries generally cannot afford to develop high-quality deployable forces while still retaining their Cold War–era mobilization systems.

Some countries have accepted this premise, and have begun to replace obsolete reserve structures with professional armed forces designed to meet twenty-first-century security needs. Denmark is transforming its large mobilization structure, as Bertel Heurlin explains, into a minimally trained reserve force whose role would be limited to homeland security activities. Unlike reservists from the Cold War era, who were expected to take up arms in case of war, Denmark's new generation of homeland defense reservists are, as Heurlin says, "not trained to fight in a regular war" and are "hardly soldiers at all." Defense resources that previously supported the reserve system will instead support a small, highly trained, and well equipped professional force that will give Denmark a more prominent role in the international security arena.

Examining reserve forces in small countries, Peter Švec offers a proposal that echoes Denmark's strategy for a smaller, separate, and less militarized reserve force. Švec argues that small countries like Slovakia must use their defense resources to support lean, highly skilled, and well-armed professional forces. He suggests that poorly trained and poorly equipped reserves in these countries would not have the capacity to participate in modern-day combat operations. Instead, he proposes, reservists should be assigned to paramilitary activities such as peacekeeping, thereby allowing countries to focus scarce defense resources on professional warriors to do the actual fighting.

But as Donnelly points out, societal, historical, and economic factors have led some countries to resist wholesale abandonment of their Cold War mobilization structures. Hannu Herranen explains the prominent role that reserves still play in Finland's conscript military. Finnish reservists actually receive more training than their active-duty counter-parts, and therefore they are normally the troops who represent Finland in international peacekeeping and crisis-management operations. Her-ranen notes that Finnish reserves hold their own among other national forces in these operations, and that their low personnel costs enable Finland to focus more of its defense resources on procurement. It is un-clear, however, whether infrequently trained reservists would be able to meet the evolving challenges of today's security environment. Herranen acknowledges that the rigorous training necessary to prepare troops for twenty-first-century security operations cannot be acquired through the sporadic refresher courses typical of reserve training.

Larger and more affluent countries such as the United States and the United Kingdom face different challenges regarding their reserve sys-tems. While some smaller countries are defining separate and less com-bat-oriented roles for their reserve forces, reserves remain an integrated, critical, and sizable component of the U.S. armed forces. As John Winkler, Robert St. Onge, Jr., Karen McKenney, and Jennifer Buck ex-plain in their chapter, the challenge for U.S. military planners is to maximize reservist contributions without overusing or destabilizing the reserve force.

Over the past several years, increases in operational tempo, reduc-tions in spending, and cutbacks in active-duty forces have increased the utilization of U.S. reserve forces. As Winkler and his co-authors note, fighting the global war on terror has put additional stress on the force. In recent deployments in Iraq and Afghanistan, the average duration of deployments has been double what it was during the first Gulf War, and mobilization of reservists with certain high-priority skills is well above sustainable levels. Mobilization may occur with little or no lead time for reservists, their families, or their employers.

All of this affects the morale of reservists and their families. The longer, more dangerous, and more frequent deployments posed chal-lenges for recruiting and retention during 2005. Uncertainty over the timing and length of deployments may also threaten the longstanding support of civilian employers, whose cooperation is critical to the con-tinued success of the U.S. reserve system.

With the United States committed to pursuing the global war on ter-rorism, the operational tempo is likely to remain elevated for the fore-seeable future. If the military plans to continue its reliance on reserves to help fight terrorism, it must develop strategies that reduce stress on reservists while still preserving their substantial contributions to military operations. Reforms advocated by Winkler and his co-authors include rebalancing the force mix to increase the number of people with skills that are called upon repeatedly; encouraging broader participation by offering Guard and Reserve members greater choice about how much time they will commit to active service and how frequently they will be called upon; and implementing strategies to increase the predictability of timing and frequency of reserve deployments.

As they transform their militaries, a key issue for the countries of Europe and North America will be how to utilize their reserve forces most effectively. The size, capabilities, and responsibilities of reserve forces will vary from country to country. Properly structured and managed, reserve forces can enhance a nation's ability to operate effectively in the new security environment.

Countries are Developing Creative Solutions

Countries on both sides of the Atlantic thus face similar challenges in keeping their armed forces filled with the right people and motivating them to do what is needed of them. Nations are rising to such challenges with creative solutions, some of which we highlight here.

EXPANDING THE RECRUITING POOL

Given the declining size of the youth cohort in Europe, one of the most important reforms a country can adopt is to expand the pool from which potential servicemembers are drawn by seeking recruits from nontraditional or underrepresented sources, including women, immigrants, ethnic minorities, and even foreigners. Keith Hartley and Juan Lopez Diaz note that the UK and Spain are both working to recruit women, and Spain has opened all of its military posts to women. Spain has also undertaken recruiting programs aimed at immigrants and has raised the ceiling for immigrant participation in the military.

ADVERTISING CAMPAIGNS

As the United States learned during its transition to an all-volunteer force, mass media advertising can be a cost-effective way to reach out to young people, both to create an awareness of military service and to provide information about specific opportunities in the armed forces. France, Spain, and Romania have expanded advertising and other public information efforts to improve the public image of the military and attract recruits, as described by Sylvain Daffix, Vincent Medina, and Cyr-Denis Nidier; Juan Lopez Diaz; and Mihaela Matei, respectively.

IMPROVING MILITARY PAY

Making military pay more competitive with what members would earn in the private sector can be crucial to helping the armed services compete with other employers. Adjusting pay for specific occupations can help a military attract qualified people to stay in hard-to-fill positions, without greatly overpaying those with less valuable skills. In their chapters, Sylvain Daffix, Vincent Medina, and Cyr-Denis Nidier; Mihaela Matei; and Domenico Villani respectively note that France, Romania, and Italy have made significant investments in military pay increases in conjunction with the adoption of all-volunteer forces. Keith Hartley describes a recent fundamental reform of the UK's military pay system that ties pay more directly to performance and allows the services to offer targeted bonuses in specific occupations to ensure an appropriate distribution of qualified people across occupations and ranks.

IMPROVING MILITARY CAREER PATHS

Many countries are developing more varied and challenging career paths, which are important incentives for both all-volunteer and conscript forces. For example, as Gerhard Kümmel mentions, Germany's conscripts are now offered the opportunity to serve for 23 months as "extended volunteer-service conscripts." They are paid better than conscripts and keep the same re-employment rights in the civilian sector as conscripts, but unlike conscripts they can be deployed to military operations outside Germany. This is a major advantage for a military that contributes substantially to expeditionary operations but prohibits its shorter-term conscripts from being deployed. Bertel Heurlin describes a recent major "two-pillar" reform of military service in Denmark that will reduce the period of conscription to four months and shift conscripts entirely to a homeland security role, while improving careers and opportunities for professional servicemembers and those on temporary contracts.

IMPROVING POST-SERVICE CAREER OPPORTUNITIES

Improving the post-service employment prospects of servicemembers through training, civilian qualification programs, and job placement can be crucial to recruitment and retention, especially in economies where labor is relatively immobile or employment opportunities are limited. Keith Hartley, Gerhard Kümmel, Juan Lopez Diaz, Mihaela Matei, and Domenico Villani all discuss important measures their countries are undertaking in this area, such as Spain's decision to reserve 10 percent of national police posts annually for eligible separating servicemembers.

QUALITY-OF-LIFE INITIATIVES

Whether in an AVF or a mixed force, good family benefits and a satisfactory quality of life can make the difference when volunteer servicemembers decide whether to sign a second contract or to make a career of the military. Even in a conscript force, young people have some control over whether and how enthusiastically they serve. Several chapters make note of improvements in this area, including new or updated single living quarters and family housing, new child-care centers on or near military posts, reimbursement of child-care expenses, programs to help families cope with the strains of deployment and other aspects of military life, travel discounts for servicemembers and their families, and scholarships for children whose education would otherwise be disrupted by frequent moves.

ROLE REALIGNMENT

An obvious but sometimes overlooked way to alleviate a military's personnel problems is to free active-duty members from work that might more appropriately be done by others, thus enabling them to focus on core military competencies while reducing the number of military positions that would be expensive or difficult to fill with people in uniform. As the chapter by Winkler and his co-authors note, the United States is working to realign roles and people across its total force of active-duty, reserve, and government civilian workers as well as private-sector contractors. Kümmel notes that Germany has created new public-private partnerships for activities such as transportation and vehicle management that could be handled well by private-sector firms. Romania is beginning to look to the private sector for some activities that require high-technology skills.

Maintaining the Momentum

The plans for transforming military personnel policies in Europe and North America are ambitious. In some cases, planned measures have already been instituted, and reverting to the old ways seems unlikely. For example, France is well down the road with its all-volunteer force. In other countries, however, the plans for transformation have yet to be matched by the reality of implementation. As Peter Švec suggests in his chapter, even the best-laid reform plans can be slowed, watered down, or reversed when budgets are cut or leaders fail to press them forward. Maintaining the momentum of reform—and paying for it—will be crucial if plans are to be turned into actions that make a genuine difference for the individuals who serve their countries and for the armed forces as institutions that serve their nations.

About the Authors

Jennifer C. Buck has been the U.S. Deputy Assistant Secretary of Defense for Reserve Affairs for Resources since July 1994. She has served in various budget and resource management positions in the Office of the Secretary of Defense, the Defense Contract Audit Agency, the U.S. Navy, and Army National Guard. Ms. Buck holds a degree from the University of Virginia and has done graduate work at the George Washington University and George Mason University.

Deborah Clay-Mendez is the former Deputy Assistant Director for manpower, logistics, and support programs of the National Security Division of the U.S. Congressional Budget Office (CBO). She previously served as a senior analyst at CBO, where she authored studies on a wide range of defense issues, including DoD retail activities at military bases, public and private roles in the depot-level maintenance of military equipment, aggregate trends in military readiness, and DoD's role in providing family housing. Dr. Clay-Mendez has also served as an economist and military operations research analyst on the staffs of the Assistant Secretary of Defense for Program Analysis and Evaluation, the Joint Economic Committee of the U.S. Congress, and the Center for Naval Analyses. She received her doctorate in economics from Harvard University.

Sylvain Daffix is a researcher at France's Economic Observatory of Defense (Observatoire économique de la Défense) of the Ministry of Defense, a research department devoted to defense economics. His doctorate is in economics and his research focuses particularly on France's defense industrial base.

Chris Donnelly is a Senior Fellow in the UK's Defence Academy. He has also taught at the Royal Military Academy, Sandhurst, where he was subsequently head of the Soviet Studies Research Centre. He served four NATO Secretaries General as a Special Adviser, and has also been an officer in the Territorial Army (Intelligence Corps). His current area of interest is new security threats and responses, particularly in Central and Eastern Europe. Mr. Donnelly has written two books and many articles on Russian and Eastern European defense issues.

Curtis L. Gilroy is Director of Accession Policy in the Office of the U.S. Secretary of Defense, where he has oversight of all active-duty military recruiting for the United States. Holding a doctorate in economics, he has twenty-five years of experience in applying economic analysis and policy research to military manpower issues to include recruiting, retention, compensation, and force management. Before joining the Office of the Secretary, he was the senior economist with the Department of the Army. He has an additional ten years of experience in studies of the civilian labor market, and has taught economics at the university level. He is an author and editor of numerous books and scholarly articles, most recently, *The All-Volunteer Force: Thirty Years of Service* (co-edited with Barbara A. Bicksler and John T. Warner).

Keith Hartley is Director of the Centre for Defence Economics at the University of York in the UK. He serves as Managing Editor of the journal *Defence and Peace Economics*, and has been consultant to the United Nations, the European Commission, the UK Ministry of Defense, and the House of Commons Defense Committee. His most recent publications include *Economics of Conflict* (co-edited with Todd Sandler).

Hannu Herranen began serving as the Chief of Personnel of the Finnish Defense Forces in January 2006. Lieutenant General Herranen was previously the Deputy Chief of Personnel and head of the National Defense Policy Unit at Finland's Ministry of Defense. He attended the Finnish Military Academy and holds a Master of Science degree from the U.S. Industrial College of the Armed Forces.

Bertel Heurlin is Jean Monnet Professor of European Security and Integration in the Department of Political Science at the University of Copenhagen in Denmark and member of several national advisory committees on defense and security policy. He is chairman of the new Danish Institute for Military Studies at the Royal Danish Defense College. He has been a member and chairman of several NATO scientific committees, including the NATO Fellowship Program and the NATO Advisory Panel on Security-Related Civil Science and Technology. He is the author or editor of numerous books and scholarly articles, most recently, *Missile Defence: Global, Regional and National Implications*.

Jolyon Howorth is Jean Monnet Professor of European Politics at the University of Bath, UK. Since 2002, he has been Visiting Professor of Political Science at Yale University. He has also taught at the University of Paris III and the University of Wisconsin, and has held Visiting Professorships at Harvard University, the Institut d'Etudes Politiques (Paris), the University of Washington, Columbia University, and New York University. He has been a Senior Research Fellow at the European Union's Institute for Security Studies. His recent publications include *Defending Europe: The EU, NATO and the Quest for European Autonomy* (co-edited with John T.S. Keeler).

Gerhard Kümmel is a Senior Researcher at the Bundeswehr Institute of Social Research (SOWI), Strausberg, Germany. He also serves as president of the German Working Group on the Armed Forces and the Social Sciences (AMS), and as Vice President of Research Committee 01: "Armed Forces and Conflict Resolution" of the International Sociological Association. His current research focuses on the integration of women into the Bundeswehr. Among his recent publications is *Military Missions and their Implications Reconsidered: The Aftermath of September 11th* (co-edited with Giuseppe Caforio).

Juan Lopez Diaz is a colonel in Spain's Marines and presently serves as Spain's military attaché in Pretoria, South Africa. He has commanded platoons, companies, and a battalion; and has served as a Military Observer with the UN Protection Force (UNPROFOR) in the former Yugoslavia, and in the Spanish Ministry of Defense in the Teaching and Recruitment Branch. He has participated in numerous combined amphibious operations with NATO and European forces. He attended Spain's Naval Warfare Course and completed the NATO Defense College Course in Rome.

Mihaela Matei is advisor to Romania's deputy minister of defense. She holds degrees in political science from Bucharest University and has published many studies on defense planning and democratic civilian oversight of the armed forces in Romania. From 2003 to 2005, she was Head of the Strategic Affairs Directorate in Romania's Ministry of Defense; in this capacity, she worked extensively on Romania's accession to NATO. Her recent publications include "Bridging the Gap in Civil-Military Relations in Southeastern Europe: Romania's Defense-Planning Case," with George Cristian Maior in *Mediterranean Quarterly.*

Karen I. McKenney has served in the U.S. Department of Defense as the Acting Deputy Assistant Secretary of Defense, as Principal Director for Reserve Affairs for Readiness, Mobilization, and Training, and as Principal Director for Reserve Affairs for Material and Facilities. She has also served in acquisition, construction, and financial management positions in the U.S. Army. She is a graduate of the Industrial College of the Armed Forces and holds a masters degree in public administration from the George Washington University.

Vincent Medina, formerly a researcher at France's Economic Observatory of Defense (Observatoire économique de la Défense), has a post-graduate degree in economics. He is co-author with Cyr-Denis Nidier of "Pricing War within a Real Option Framework," *Defence and Peace Economics.*

Sebastian Negrusa is a PhD candidate in economics at Clemson University. His primary fields of interest are labor economics and applied econometrics. He specializes in defense economics, and his PhD dissertation focuses on the estimation of a structural dynamic retention model for the U.S. military. His most recent publications include "Evasion Costs and the Theory of Conscription" (with John T. Warner) in *Defence and Peace Economics.*

Cyr-Denis Nidier heads France's Economic Observatory of Defense (Observatoire économique de la Défense). A graduate of France's naval academy and of its defense engineering school (ENSTA), Commander Nidier holds a graduate degree in mathematical economics from Panthéon-Sorbonne University. Commander Nidier is co-author with Vincent Medina of "Pricing War within a Real Option Framework," in *Defence and Peace Economics.*

Bernard D. Rostker is a Senior Fellow at RAND. He has served as the Under Secretary of Defense for Personnel and Readiness, Under Secretary of the Army, and Assistant Secretary of the Navy for Manpower and Reserve Affairs, as well as Special Assistant for Gulf War illnesses to the deputy secretary of defense. He has also been Principal Deputy Assistant Secretary of the Navy for Manpower and Reserve Affairs, and Director of the U.S. Selective Service System. At RAND, he directed its Defense Manpower Research Center and helped establish the Arroyo Center, where he directed the Force Development and Employment Program and was the Center's Associate Director. He has also worked at the Center for Naval Analyses, the Systems Research and Applications Corporation, and the Office of the Assistant Secretary of Defense for Systems Analysis. He holds a doctorate in economics from Syracuse University and is a fellow of the National Academy of Public Administration. Among his many publications is, recently, "Changing the Officer Personnel System" in Cindy Williams, ed., *Filling the Ranks: Transforming the U.S. Military Personnel System.*

Rickard Sandell is a Senior Analyst at the Elcano Royal Institute in Madrid, where he is head of research in demography, population, and international immigration. He holds a PhD in Sociology from Stockholm University. Dr. Sandell has directed and participated in a number of research projects sponsored by the Tercentenary Foundation of the Bank of Sweden and the Swedish Council for Research in the Humanities and Social Sciences. His work has been published in leading academic journals including the *American Journal of Sociology*, the *American Sociological Review*, and the *European Sociological Review.*

Robert J. St. Onge, Jr., works with MPRI, a defense contracting firm that provides training, simulation, and other services related to national security worldwide. He has also served as the U.S. Deputy Assistant Secretary of Defense for Reserve Affairs for Readiness, Mobilization, and Training. Prior to his retirement from the U.S. Army as Major General, he served in a variety of staff and command assignments in the United States, the Republic of Vietnam, and Europe. A graduate of the U.S. Military Academy, he also holds advanced degrees from Purdue University, the Army's Command and General Staff College, and the U.S. Army War College.

Peter Švec retired as a General Staff Colonel from Slovakia's Air Force, having begun his career with the former Czecho-Slovak Air Force. He left the military briefly to become a member of the last Federal Parliament of the Czech and Slovak Federative Republic, then served the Slovak military as a flight instructor, transport aircraft flight commander, Chief of Mission Planning and Air Space Management, Chief of Air Intelligence and Early Warning Administration, and Chief of Special Operations. In a variety of two and three-star posts with the General Staff of the Army of the Slovak Republic, including Deputy Chief of the General Staff for Operations, he took the lead in many military reform efforts and authored many doctrinal documents. He is a graduate of the Army Command and Staff Course, Camberley, UK, and the Royal College of Defence Studies in London. He has been editor-in-chief of the ministerial periodical *Military Horizons*, and has published widely on defense and management topics. After his retirement from the military, Colonel Švec became the Flight Operations Manager for the commercial airline SkyEurope.

Vaidotas Urbelis is a researcher at the Institute of International Relations and Political Science at Vilnius University in Lithuania. He is the author of numerous publications on the Baltic states' security policies, civil-military relations, and strategic studies. Dr. Urbelis graduated from the Institute of International Relations and Political Science at Vilnius University. His most recent publication is *U.S. Grand Strategy and its Implications for Lithuania*.

Domenico Villani has held both command and staff positions in Italy's Army and in its Military Academy. Lieutenant-General Villani was Commander of the multi-national BRIGADE WEST in Kosovo. In posts with the Army General Staff in Rome, he was responsible for recruitment and personnel issues, and he has served as Chief of the Personnel Department of the Italian Defense General Staff as well as president of the advisory board on female personnel military service. He holds degrees in strategic sciences and diplomatic and international sciences.

John T. Warner is Professor of Economics at Clemson University. He has also taught at the University of North Carolina at Chapel Hill and served as a member of the professional staff of the Center for Naval Analyses. Professor Warner has been a Visiting Professor at the U.S. Naval Academy and a visiting scholar in the Office of the Under Secretary of Defense for Personnel and Readiness. He received his PhD from North Carolina State University. He has conducted numerous studies of military enlistment, retention, and compensation policy for the Department of Defense. He is the North American editor of *Defence and Peace Economics*. He recently co-edited *The All-Volunteer Force: Thirty Years of Service* (with Barbara A. Bicksler and Curtis L. Gilroy).

Cindy Williams is a Principal Research Scientist in the Security Studies Program at the Massachusetts Institute of Technology. She formerly served as Assistant Director for National Security at the Congressional Budget Office (CBO). She has served as a director and in other capacities at the MITRE Corporation; as a member of the Senior Executive Service in the Pentagon's Directorate of Program Analysis and Evaluation; and as a mathematician at RAND. Her areas of specialization include the U.S. defense and security budget, command and control of military forces, and military personnel and pay policies. Dr. Williams holds a PhD in mathematics from the University of California, Irvine. She is an elected fellow of the National Academy of Public Administration, and is a member of the U.S. Naval Studies Board, the Council on Foreign Relations, the International Institute for Strategic Studies, the advisory board of Women in International Security, and the editorial board of *International Security*. Her recent publications include *Filling the Ranks: Transforming the U.S. Military Personnel System* and *Holding the Line: U.S. Defense Alternatives for the Early 21st Century*.

John D. Winkler has been the U.S. Deputy Assistant Secretary of Defense for Reserve Affairs for Manpower and Personnel since 2001. Previously a Senior Behavioral Scientist at RAND and Associate Director of the Manpower and Training Program at RAND's Arroyo Center, he holds a doctorate in social psychology from Harvard University.

Index

BCSIA Studies in International Security

Published by The MIT Press

Sean M. Lynn-Jones and Steven E. Miller, series editors
Karen Motley, executive editor
Belfer Center for Science and International Affairs (BCSIA)
John F. Kennedy School of Government, Harvard University

Agha, Hussein, Shai Feldman, Ahmad Khalidi, and Zeev Schiff, *Track-II Diplomacy: Lessons from the Middle East* (2003)

Allison, Graham T., Owen R. Coté, Jr., Richard A. Falkenrath, and Steven E. Miller, *Avoiding Nuclear Anarchy: Containing the Threat of Loose Russian Nuclear Weapons and Fissile Material* (1996)

Allison, Graham T., and Kalypso Nicolaïdis, eds., *The Greek Paradox: Promise vs. Performance* (1996)

Arbatov, Alexei, Abram Chayes, Antonia Handler Chayes, and Lara Olson, eds., *Managing Conflict in the Former Soviet Union: Russian and American Perspectives* (1997)

Bennett, Andrew, *Condemned to Repetition? The Rise, Fall, and Reprise of - Soviet-Russian Military Interventionism, 1973–1996* (1999)

Blackwill, Robert D., and Michael Stürmer, eds., *Allies Divided: Transatlantic Policies for the Greater Middle East* (1997)

Blackwill, Robert D., and Paul Dibb, eds., *America's Asian Alliances* (2000)

Brom, Shlomo, and Yiftah Shapir, eds., *The Middle East Military Balance, 1999–2000* (1999)

Brom, Shlomo, and Yiftah Shapir, eds., *The Middle East Military Balance, 2001–2002* (2002)

Brown, Michael E., ed., *The International Dimensions of Internal Conflict* (1996)

Brown, Michael E., and Šumit Ganguly, eds., *Government Policies and - Ethnic Relations in Asia and the Pacific* (1997)

Brown, Michael E., and Šumit Ganguly, eds., *Fighting Words: Language Policy and Ethnic Relations in Asia* (2003)

Carter, Ashton B., and John P. White, eds., *Keeping the Edge: Managing - Defense for the Future* (2001)

de Nevers, Renée, *Comrades No More: The Seeds of Political Change in Eastern Europe* (2003)

Elman, Colin, and Miriam Fendius Elman, eds., *Bridges and Boundaries: Historians, Political Scientists, and the Study of International Relations* (2001)

Elman, Colin, and Miriam Fendius Elman, eds., *Progress in International Relations Theory: Appraising the Field* (2003)

Elman, Miriam Fendius, ed., *Paths to Peace: Is Democracy the Answer?* (1997)

Falkenrath, Richard A., *Shaping Europe's Military Order: The Origins and Consequences of the CFE Treaty* (1994)

Falkenrath, Richard A., Robert D. Newman, and Bradley A. Thayer, *America's Achilles' Heel: Nuclear, Biological, and Chemical Terrorism and - Covert Attack* (1998)

Feaver, Peter D., and Richard H. Kohn, eds., *Soldiers and Civilians: The Civil-Military Gap and American National Security* (2001)

Feldman, Shai, *Nuclear Weapons and Arms Control in the Middle East* (1996)

Feldman, Shai, and Yiftah Shapir, eds., *The Middle East Military Balance 2000–2001* (2001)

Forsberg, Randall, ed., *The Arms Production Dilemma: Contraction and - Restraint in the World Combat Aircraft Industry* (1994)

George, Alexander L., and Andrew Bennett, *Case Studies and Theory Development in the Social Sciences* (2005)

Gilroy, Curtis L., and Cindy Williams, eds., *Service to Country: Personnel Policy and the Transformation of Western Militaries* (2006)

Hagerty, Devin T., *The Consequences of Nuclear Proliferation: Lessons from South Asia* (1998)

Heymann, Philip B., *Terrorism and America: A Commonsense Strategy for a Democratic Society* (1998)

Heymann, Philip B., *Terrorism, Freedom, and Security: Winning without War* (2003)

Heymann, Philip B., and Juliette N. Kayyem, *Protecting Liberty in an Age of Terror* (2005)

Howitt, Arnold M., and Robyn L. Pangi, eds., *Countering Terrorism: - Dimensions of Preparedness* (2003)

Hudson, Valerie M., and Andrea M. den Boer, *Bare Branches: The Security Implications of Asia's Surplus Male Population* (2004)

Kayyem, Juliette N., and Robyn L. Pangi, eds., *First to Arrive: State and - Local Responses to Terrorism* (2003)

Kokoshin, Andrei A., *Soviet Strategic Thought, 1917–91* (1998)

Lederberg, Joshua, ed., *Biological Weapons: Limiting the Threat* (1999)

Mansfield, Edward D., and Jack Snyder, *Electing to Fight: Why Emerging Democracies Go to War* (2005)

Martin, Lenore G., and Dimitris Keridis, eds., *The Future of Turkish Foreign Policy* (2004)

May, Ernest R., and Philip D. Zelikow, eds., with Kirsten Lundberg and Robert D. Johnson, *Dilemmas of U.S. Diplomacy and Intelligence Analysis, 1945–1990* (2006)

Shaffer, Brenda, *Borders and Brethren: Iran and the Challenge of Azerbaijani Identity* (2002)

Shaffer, Brenda, ed., *The Limits of Culture: Islam and Foreign Policy* (2006)

Shields, John M., and William C. Potter, eds., *Dismantling the Cold War: U.S. and NIS Perspectives on the Nunn-Lugar Cooperative Threat Reduction Program* (1997)

Tucker, Jonathan B., ed., *Toxic Terror: Assessing Terrorist Use of Chemical and Biological Weapons* (2000)

Utgoff, Victor A., ed., *The Coming Crisis: Nuclear Proliferation, U.S. Interests, and World Order* (2000)

Williams, Cindy, ed., *Holding the Line: U.S. Defense Alternatives for the Early 21st Century* (2001)

Williams, Cindy, ed., *Filling the Ranks: Transforming the U.S. Military - Personnel System* (2004)

The Robert and Renée Belfer Center for Science and International Affairs

Graham Allison, Director
John F. Kennedy School of Government
Harvard University
79 JFK Street, Cambridge MA 02138
Tel: (617) 495–1400; Fax: (617) 495–8963
http://www.ksg.harvard.edu/bcsia   bcsia_ksg@harvard.edu

The Belfer Center for Science and International Affairs (BCSIA) is the hub of research, teaching and training in international security affairs, environmental and resource issues, science and technology policy, human rights, and conflict studies at Harvard's John F. Kennedy School of Government. The Center's mission is to provide leadership in advancing policy-relevant knowledge about the most important challenges of international security and other critical issues where science, technology and international affairs intersect.

BCSIA's leadership begins with the recognition of science and technology as driving forces transforming international affairs. The Center integrates insights of social scientists, natural scientists, technologists, and practitioners with experience in government, diplomacy, the military, and business to address these challenges. The Center pursues its mission in four complementary research programs:

- The **International Security Program** (ISP) addresses the most pressing threats to U.S. national interests and international security.

- The **Environment and Natural Resources Program** (ENRP) is the locus of Harvard's interdisciplinary research on resource and environmental problems and policy responses.

- The **Science, Technology, and Public Policy Program** (STPP) analyzes ways in which science and technology policy influence international security, resources, environment, and development, and such cross-cutting issues as technological innovation and information infrastructure.

- The **Program on Intrastate Conflict** analyzes the causes of ethnic, religious, and other conflicts, and seeks to identify practical ways to prevent and limit such conflicts.

The heart of the Center is its resident research community of more than 140 scholars: Harvard faculty, analysts, practitioners, and each year a new, interdisciplinary group of research fellows. BCSIA sponsors frequent seminars, workshops and conferences, maintains a substantial specialized library, and publishes books, monographs, and discussion papers.

The Center's International Security Program, directed by Steven E. Miller, publishes the BCSIA Studies in International Security, and sponsors and edits the quarterly journal *International Security*.

The Center is supported by an endowment established with funds from Robert and Renée Belfer, the Ford Foundation and Harvard University, by foundation grants, by individual gifts, and by occasional government contracts.